THE BANALITY OF GOOD

THE BANALITY OF GOOD

The UN's Global Fight against
Human Trafficking   *Lieba Faier*

Duke University Press   *Durham and London*   2024

Project Editor: Brian Ostrander
Typeset in Garamond Premier Pro by Westchester Publishing Services

Library of Congress Cataloging-in-Publication Data
Names: Faier, Lieba, author.
Title: The banality of good : the UN's global fight against
human trafficking / Lieba Faier.
Description: Durham : Duke University Press, 2024. |
Includes bibliographical references and index.
Identifiers: LCCN 2023047387 (print)
LCCN 2023047388 (ebook)
ISBN 9781478030560 (paperback)
ISBN 9781478026297 (hardcover)
ISBN 9781478059523 (ebook)
ISBN 9781478094074 (ebook other)
Subjects: LCSH: United Nations Convention Against Transnational
Organized Crime (2000) Protocols, etc. (2000 December 12) | United
Nations Convention Against Transnational Organized Crime (2000
November 15) | Human trafficking—Japan. | Human trafficking
victims—Japan. | Human trafficking—Prevention—Government policy—
Japan. | Human trafficking—Prevention—International cooperation. |
Human trafficking (International law) | BISAC: SOCIAL SCIENCE /
Anthropology / Cultural & Social | SOCIAL SCIENCE / Gender Studies
Classification: LCC K5297.A42003 F35 2024 (print) | LC K5297.A42003
(ebook) | DDC 345.52/02551—dc23/eng/20240317
LC record available at https://lccn.loc.gov/2023047387
LC ebook record available at https://lccn.loc.gov/2023047388

Cover art: UN General Assembly Hall, New York, NY.
Courtesy Directphoto Collection/Alamy.

This book is freely available in an open access edition thanks to TOME
(Toward an Open Monograph Ecosystem)—a collaboration of the
Association of American Universities, the Association of University
Presses, and the Association of Research Libraries—and the generous
support of Arcadia, a charitable fund of Lisbet Rausing and Peter Baldwin,
and the UCLA Library. Learn more at the TOME website, available at:
openmonographs.org.

For Ruben, who has taught me that other worlds are possible,
and Hirshl, who makes me want to help build them

Contents

Abbreviations

AI	Amnesty International
AIC	Australian Institute of Criminology
AWA	Asian Women's Association
AWL	*Asian Women's Liberation* (*Ajia to josei kaihō*) journal
BAN	Basel Action Network
CATW	Coalition against Trafficking in Women
CATW-AP	Coalition against Trafficking in Women–Asia Pacific
GAATW	Global Alliance against Traffic in Women
ICAT	The Inter-agency Coordination Group against Trafficking in Persons
ICCPR	International Covenant on Civil and Political Rights
ICESCR	International Covenant on Economic, Social and Cultural Rights
ILO	International Labour Organization
IOM	International Organization for Migration
JICA	Japan International Cooperation Agency
JNATIP	Japan Network against Trafficking in Persons
KCWU	Korean Church Women United
MOFA	Ministry of Foreign Affairs

MOJ	Ministry of Justice
NGO	nongovernmental organization
NPA	National Police Agency
ODA	Official Development Assistance
OTIT	Organization for Technical Intern Training
RRATVJ	Return and Reintegration Assistance for Trafficked Victims in Japan
TIP	Trafficking in Persons
TITP	Technical Intern Training Program
TVPA	Trafficking Victims Protection Act
UN	United Nations
UNHCR	UN High Commissioner for Refugees; UN Refugee Agency
UNICEF	United Nations International Children's Emergency Fund
UNICRI	United Nations Interregional Crime and Justice Research Institute
UNODC	United Nations Office on Drugs and Crime
UNTFHS	United Nations Trust Fund for Human Security
UNVTF	United Nations Voluntary Trust Fund for Victims of Trafficking in Persons, Especially Women and Children
WCO	Women's Consultation Office (Fujin Sōdan Sentā; Fujin Sōdanjo)
WEP	Women Empowerment Program
WHO	World Health Organization

Preface

The fight against human trafficking is often assumed to be a straightforward matter of good versus evil. It is one of the few issues that regularly receive bipartisan support in a searingly divided US Congress. The commonly accepted strategy has been to criminalize those practices labeled as human trafficking, arrest those who engage in such activities, and help victims return to their pre-trafficked lives. Not only has this approach been endorsed by the US government, but it has brought together 180 countries, thus far, as parties to the UN Protocol to Prevent, Suppress and Punish Trafficking in Persons, Especially Women and Children (Trafficking Protocol), as well as active participants in the UN-sponsored global counter–human trafficking campaign.

This book argues for a different approach.

I first learned about the Japanese government's participation in the UN's global counter–human trafficking campaign from caseworkers I knew through my work with grassroots migrants' rights organizations in Japan during the 1990s. During a phone conversation early in the summer of 2005, a friend working with one such organization in Chiba suggested that I focus my next research project on the Japanese government's efforts to counter human trafficking. "It's what everyone is talking about," he told me. After the UN General Assembly's adoption of the Trafficking Protocol in 2000, the Japanese government faced increasing pressure from the US State Department to undertake a counter–human trafficking campaign focused on the exploitation and abuse of foreign migrant women working in the sex industry—especially those from the Philippines, which the US government identified as one of the largest groups of trafficking victims in the world. The Japanese government began sponsoring workshops, symposia, and meetings with international organizations and NGO (nongovernmental organization) staff to develop a formal plan of action centered on international guidelines.[1]

Initially, NGO caseworkers in Japan and the Philippines were cautiously optimistic about the possibilities of this project, and when I set out to study Japan's counter–human trafficking campaign in the mid-aughts, I planned to examine how national governments, international organizations, and grassroots NGOs were engaging in unprecedented collaborations to fight human trafficking into the country. However, in the years that followed, as I volunteered at assistance organizations and spoke with NGO caseworkers, international organization staff, and government officials, I increasingly observed that the global approach to this issue was sidelining, if not displacing, the expertise and guidance of the experienced NGO caseworkers whose labor was so central to it. Even more troubling to them, the protocol seemed *by design* to turn a blind eye to the political-economic realities of labor migrants' lives. As I listened again and again to the disappointment and frustration of these NGO caseworkers, my research shifted to examining how, why, and to what ends their vision for these efforts was being ignored.

Some feminist scholars have argued against the very premise of counter–human trafficking programs, maintaining that the category of "trafficking victims" deprives migrant workers of agency and is simply based in the conviction that all prostitution should be legally abolished.[2] These scholars have also critiqued the carceral framework that structures these efforts and have highlighted their anti-migrant foundations.[3] Although I agree with many of the specific charges of these arguments, I also worry that a wholesale dismissal of this movement risks ignoring the abuse and violence that I witnessed in my years working with migrants' rights groups in Japan and the Philippines.

Despite their reservations about the current global counter–human trafficking campaign, many NGO caseworkers whom I greatly respect and admire remain invested and active participants in this work. As I explain in this book, in their view, the fight against human trafficking marks an insistence that something must change in the lives and treatment of migrant workers. For them, this fight is not new but part of a much longer and broader tradition of grassroots activism in Asia centered on political-economic justice and anticolonial, antiracist, and antisexist politics. They do not see a contradiction in simultaneously viewing their clients as victims of violence *and* insisting on their clients' agency and personhood. Indeed, for them the two are inextricable. They understand that in a legal sphere, victimhood is not a non-agentive, objectified status so much as an entitlement by a rights-bearing subject to restitution and a hearing on account of experiences of violation. When these NGO caseworkers recognize their clients as victims of human trafficking, they do so to foreground the structural violence that makes labor migrants unacceptably vulnerable to violations of their human rights.

These NGO caseworkers are sometimes themselves former labor migrants, and they work for grassroots shelters and support groups that have long mobilized against the abuse and exploitation that many migrant laborers face. Such organizations differ from many of the newer, expressly anti-human-trafficking organizations that formed in response to the international attention garnered by the UN Trafficking Protocol. In Japan, these latter organizations tend to be headed mostly by Japanese professionals (academics, journalists, attorneys) that primarily engage with governments and international bodies on a public stage, such as at conferences and meetings, to draft more effective legal strategies. Although older migrants' rights groups can be included in, and sometimes work together with, these newer organizations, caseworkers from these long-established groups have worked directly and intimately with foreign workers over many years. For them, fighting human trafficking means going beyond legal strategies to arrest traffickers; it means supporting vulnerable migrants and working for real political-economic change to prevent their abuse in the first place. These NGO caseworkers contend that even if the UN Trafficking Protocol may claim to guarantee migrants' civil and political rights, such as the right to bare life and to due process and a fair trial, we still need to work to protect migrants' economic and social human rights, such as the right to fair and safe work and to a decent standard of living with adequate food, clothing, and housing.[4] In other words, when these NGO caseworkers appeal to migrants' human rights, they do so in recognition of the inherent limits of dominant liberal rights frameworks centered on individual civil and political rights and as a strategy for advocating for a jurisgenerative reworking and expansion of what protecting these rights can mean.[5]

Particularly in the case of the Philippines, with its recent history of authoritarian regimes, NGO caseworkers' calls for migrants' human rights puts them at odds with the government. Consider that in the 1970s and 1980s, Ferdinand Marcos Sr. legitimated his dictatorship by claiming that liberalism was an inappropriate political model for the Philippines because a totalitarian regime could better promote the social and economic human rights that were preconditions for liberal freedom.[6] Consequently, some grassroots activist groups in the Philippines today invoke liberalistic notions of human rights both to safeguard against government overreach and as a means for challenging the Philippine state's social and economic policies, calling for redistributive justice and affirmative action for vulnerable groups.[7] These activists understand that just as legal codification legitimizes centralized states as liberal, it provides an enjoined transparency that opens these states up to critique.[8] For these activists, claims to liberal subjectivity and human rights are not statements of global absolutes but strategic assertions of entitlements in the present; demanding them does not preclude hoping for broader and more far-reaching changes in the future.⁹

With the UN-sponsored project to fight human trafficking, these grassroots NGO workers found themselves between a rock and a hard place: committed to helping labor migrants as best as they were able and stymied by the formal procedures for doing so. Some years into these efforts, one confided about his work assisting women who would ultimately be repatriated, "Sometimes I don't feel good about the work that I'm doing. These migrants have nothing back home." Yet he also could not bring himself to leave the movement, steadfast in his commitment to migrants' rights and worried that abandoning the project would only make things worse. Under the UN Trafficking Protocol, these NGO caseworkers found themselves weighing whether it was worse to watch labor migrants remain in deeply exploitative or abusive situations in Japan or to push for their formal recognition as victims of human trafficking so that they could return to economically desperate situations back home with few resources at their disposal. This choice was not one that they wanted—or should have had—to make.

My conversations with NGO caseworkers suggest that rather than arguing over the legitimacy of the concept of human trafficking, we need to be asking how and why these local experts' more culturally, geographically, and political-economically informed understandings of the violence glossed by this term— and their educated strategies for addressing it—have been evacuated by the prevailing global counter–human trafficking campaign.

This book undertakes this task. The following chapters historically and ethnographically explore how the globalized institutional approach of the UN-sponsored counter–human trafficking project uncouples the suffering of trafficked persons from everyday relationships of political domination and economic inequality that render labor migrants vulnerable. It considers how the bureaucratic protocols of this project not only ignore these links but also evacuate the perspectives of those intent on making these connections. It argues against models of global governance that propose single universal solutions on a global scale, asking instead how we can begin to think differently about the forms of violence now identified as human trafficking to make real change in labor migrants' lives.

Acknowledgments

Beginning a book with a statement about the inadequacy of words feels paradoxical. Yet I struggle to find language sufficient for expressing the deep appreciation and gratitude that I feel for all who enabled and supported my research and writing.

First, I am deeply indebted to the NGO workers who shared their thoughts, feelings, and experiences with me, and especially those working with the organizations where I volunteered in Japan, the Philippines, and the United States. I refrain from naming you here to protect your privacy; however, you have taught me so much about how to think about and care for others. Government officials and international organization staff also generously gave of their time. I truly appreciate your willingness to talk with me and your openness about your work and personal commitments.

I would not have been able to complete this project without the friendship and intellectual generosity of Kamari Clarke, Hannah Landecker, and Purnima Mankekar. Thank you not only for your brilliant insights but also for always being there personally and professionally. I only hope that I can reciprocate and pass on all that you have shared with me.

Kathy Chetkovitch is hands-down the world's best developmental editor. Thank you, Kathy, for making time for me and, above all, for your sharp eye, brilliance, and wit.

I am grateful to the Social Science Research Council, the American Council of Learned Societies (ACLS), and the Japan Foundation for the Abe Fellowship that funded my initial fieldwork for this book. Grants from the UCLA Terasaki Center enabled me to conduct follow-up research in Japan. Many thanks to Noel Shimizu for coordinating those grants. My writing was generously funded by an ACLS Fellowship and a Howard Fellowship from the George A. and Eliza Gardner Howard Foundation at Brown University. The Center for the Study of Women at UCLA provided funding for a book workshop that dramatically improved my writing and analysis. I am especially appreciative of the close readings and sharp insights of Lisa Rofel, Hannah Landecker, Kamari Clarke, Purnima Mankekar, and Akiko Takeyama, who participated in that workshop. I also thank Grace Hong, Rosa Chung, Kristina Magpayo Nyden, and Kasi McMurrary for making it logistically possible.

As an Abe Fellow, I could not have asked for a more wonderful sponsor at Tokyo University than Shinji Yamashita. Thank you, Shinji, for your amazing guidance and kindness. I also owe much appreciation to the Department of Anthropology for graciously arranging my affiliation. Staff at the National Women's Education Center in Saitama, and especially Miho Watanabe, went out of their way to be welcoming and helpful. Through the Abe program, I met David Leheny and Katya Burns, who were excellent guides in Tokyo as I began to navigate the world of global governance. David's scholarship has consistently offered a model for mine. Dada Dacot has been a colleague and friend since we first wandered through the streets of Tokyo together. Legal scholars Daniel H. Foote, Yasuzo Kitamura, Miho Omi, and Lawrence Repeta provided invaluable insight and shared stories and articles. I also thank Mika Miyoshi for friendship and support as I began this project.

I could not ask for more collegial and inspiring colleagues than those in the Department of Geography at UCLA. I thank especially John Agnew, Juan Herrera, Helga Leitner, Adam Moore, Shaina Potts, and Eric Sheppard for reading and discussing drafts of chapters. I am particularly indebted to Adam for suggesting that I look at the WikiLeaks Public Library of US Diplomacy, which proved invaluable for my research. Kasi McMurray deserves special recognition for managing our department so adeptly and thoughtfully.

At UCLA School of Law, Aslı Bâli, Stephen Gardbaum, and Patrick Goodman graciously permitted me to audit their courses. I am especially grateful to the awe-inspring Aslı Bâli, who patiently answered my questions about international law and the United Nations. Other legal scholars on campus—Hiroshi Motomura, Kal Raustiala, and Lara Stemple—offered resources, assistance, and insight. Lara, in particular, provided much-needed advice for approaching legal studies. I thank the Departments of Anthropology and Sociology and the Center for the Study of Women at UCLA for inviting me to present my work. At UCLA, Akhil Gupta, Sherry Ortner, Mariko Tamanoi, Chris Kelty, Roger Waldinger, Gail Kligman, Susan Slyomovics, Kyeyoung Park, Ruben Hernandez-Leon, and Michael Salman offered helpful feedback and suggestions. Kirstie McClure allowed me to sit in on her graduate seminar on Hannah Arendt and was always willing to answer questions in the Playa Room.

Former writing group members Jessica Cattelino, Hannah Landecker, Rachel Lee, Purnima Mankekar, Abby Saguy, and Juliet Williams created a warm and productive intellectual space and engaged so thoughtfully with my work.

This book project grew out of conversations with Hirokazu Miyazaki, Annelise Riles, and Amy Villarejo while I was a postdoc at Cornell University. Early portions of this book were presented at the Triangle East Asia Colloquium, San Diego State University, Seoul National University, the University of Kansas, Pomona College, UC Santa Cruz, and Chuo University. I thank especially David Ambaras, Yasuzo Kitamura, Soo-Jung Lee, Sungsook Lim, Pardis Mahdavi, Akiko Takeyama, Lisa Rofel, Heath Cabot, and Andrew Mathews for their invitations to give talks and their thoughtful engagements with my work. In Los Angeles, Jennifer and Jane Courtney were wonderful sounding boards, helping me formulate my ideas. Suzy Lee offered incredibly detailed feedback on an early chapter and much intellectual and personal inspiration. When I conducted research in Washington, D.C., Jordan Sand, Denise Brennan, and Janie Chuang provided excellent advice and warm companionship.

Over the years that I worked on this project, I also benefited from amazing research assistance. Kaoru Kuwayama helped me arrange and conduct interviews in Tokyo. I am grateful for both her knowledge of grassroots activism and her skill as an ethnographer. In Los Angeles, Naoko Watanabe did first-rate legal research for me. Ryoko Nishijima did careful surveys of pre–World War II Japanese newspapers. Stephanie Santos helped with interview transcription in Tagalog. Emi Foulk and Mari Izumikawa assisted with correspondence and interview transcriptions in English and Japanese. Alexa Boesel provided much-appreciated editorial assistance as I was finishing up my manuscript.

I could not have dreamed of a better editor than Gisela Fosado at Duke University Press. I feel lucky to have worked with her and her assistant, Alejandra Mejia, who graciously answered my many questions. I am also grateful to two anonymous Duke University Press reviewers whose insightful and spot-on feedback made this book immeasurably better.

Good friends and wonderful family keep me sane and remind me to laugh during the ups and downs of research and writing. Many thanks and much love go to Rachel Luft, the Aaronson-Murphy clan, Kamari Clarke, Purnima Mankekar, Michael Ross and Tina Williams, Hannah Landecker and Chris Kelty, Jennifer Golub and Ray Marcus, Beth and Steve Callaghan, and Jennifer Courtney and Guy Stevenson for so many meals, conversations, and good times. I look forward to having more with you.

My late mother, Daveen Faier, never got to see this book completed, but I can imagine the look of pride on her face.

Sandra Luft first introduced me to Arendt's work, and my understanding of the banality of good took shape during conversations at her dinner table. I thank her for teaching me to associate discussing political philosophy with eating delicious food and for being both an inspiring scholar and my loving Aunty Sunny.

Finally, every single day Ruben and Hirshl Hickman help me find joy and possibility in life. Without question, they are for what I am most grateful.

Introduction

The trafficking of persons, particularly women and children, for forced and exploitative labor, including for sexual exploitation, is one of the most egregious violations of human rights which the United Nations now confronts. . . . Criminal groups have wasted no time in embracing today's globalized economy and the sophisticated technology that goes with it. But our efforts to combat them have remained up to now very fragmented and our weapons almost obsolete. The Palermo Convention gives us a new tool to address the scourge of crime as global problem.

—SECRETARY-GENERAL KOFI ANNAN, "Address at the Opening of the
Signing Conference for the United Nations Convention against
Transnational Organized Crime"

Global governance is characterized by a dramatic discrepancy between commitments on paper and actual improvements in conditions.

—THOMAS WEISS AND RAMESH THAKUR, *Global Governance
and the UN: An Unfinished Journey*

During the summer of 2005, I traveled to Tokyo to visit a dear friend, Cherie, who was a caseworker at Tahanan, a grassroots migrant women's shelter that had recently been contracted by the Japanese government to house and assist women officially identified as victims of human trafficking.[1] At the time, the Japanese government was beginning to take active steps toward ratifying the United Nations' Protocol to Prevent, Suppress and Punish Trafficking in Persons, Especially Women and Children (Trafficking Protocol), which had been adopted in 2000 and came into force in 2003. As soon as I arrived at the apartment that Cherie shared with her young Japanese Filipina daughters, she began talking about a site in her suburban Tokyo neighborhood where the police had planned a "rescue" of Filipina women who had reportedly been "sex trafficked." She ushered me into her Toyota station wagon and drove us to a nearby 7-Eleven, which was across the street from the site where the women were allegedly being held.

In addition to working at Tahanan, Cherie answered phones at a grassroots helpline in Tokyo that provided counseling to Filipina migrants who faced problems ranging from unpaid wages to exploitative labor conditions to sexual assault, including some cases in which women were indentured, forced into prostitution, confined, abused, threatened with violence, and sold as chattel. We had met nearly ten years earlier when I was volunteering with this helpline. I had always known Cherie to be equanimous, even when she was assisting migrants who had suffered extreme abuse, so I was surprised that she was shaking as we entered the convenience store. She whispered with urgency that I should take a magazine from the rack by the store's front window and pretend to read it. She then nervously directed my attention out the store window to the apartment building across the street.

The building looked like any small residential development in the city. It was two stories tall, covered with brown tile, and composed of what appeared to be ten single apartments—five on each floor—off an open-air corridor, with a small empty parking lot beside it. I noted that the shades were drawn on all the windows. Cherie explained that the police had collected evidence about the building so that they could bust the operation as part of what had been, until recently, an unprecedented government crackdown on sex industry establishments employing foreign women. She then added in a strained whisper, "The police said that women were locked in the apartments. Men stood as lookouts and wouldn't let the women leave." I asked Cherie how the police knew this. Cherie explained that they had learned about the apartment complex from a woman staying at Tahanan. The police had begun conducting surveillance on the site, and they had observed men coming in and out of the apartments at all hours of the day and night. Cherie added that a national news station had done a story on the case. Suddenly, she jabbed me in the arm with her elbow and gave me a pleading look. "Don't stare," she insisted. "We don't want anyone to see us." Cherie trembled as she ushered me out of the convenience store.

When we had made it back to Cherie's car, I asked how she felt about the Japanese government's new counter–human trafficking program. Cherie conveyed ambivalence. On the one hand, she had long been part of grassroots activist networks that had lobbied both the UN and the Japanese government to address the mistreatment of migrant workers in Japan, including but not limited to foreign women in the sex industry. She, along with many with whom she worked, had felt vindicated the previous year when the Japanese government had responded to international pressure to comply with the Trafficking Protocol by adopting the Action Plan of Measures to Combat Trafficking in Persons (hereafter the Action Plan).

On the other hand, Cherie was starting to question how the Japanese government's efforts were unfolding on the ground. The Trafficking Protocol officially fell under the United Nations Convention against Transnational Organized Crime. Although official statements, like the one in Annan's address, stressed that the protocol promotes human rights, official efforts were overwhelmingly focused on criminal justice measures.[2] The Japanese government had been working with NGOs to develop formal protection and assistance procedures for migrants identified by Japanese police or immigration officials as victims of trafficking; however, justice officials were recognizing only a small select group of foreign women working in the sex industry as being entitled to this assistance, and once identified, these women were swiftly being repatriated. Moreover, those foreign women caught up in rescue operations but not afforded such status were being deported on criminal charges of visa overstay (*fuhō taizai*, "illegal presence").

Cherie had begun to wonder if these counter-trafficking efforts were truly helping migrants or if they were leaving them in more dire situations. In the early 1990s, Cherie had come to Japan from Davao City as a migrant worker to support her mother and younger siblings after her father died and her family lost its small coconut farm. She knew that most Filipina labor migrants in Japan were similarly desperate to support their families, had likely incurred large debts to travel abroad, and had few means for earning money at home. Simply repatriating them with limited resources hardly seemed like a solution. At the same time, Cherie had time and again worked with migrant women at Tahanan who had faced grave exploitation and abuses in Japan. Leaving them to remain in such abusive situations felt unconscionable. Cherie was beginning to doubt that the official counter-trafficking program could resolve this predicament. Recalling her first trip to observe the apartment building with shelter staff, Cherie began to cry, "There were men going in and out. It was very emotional—the helplessness, the feeling of dread. Part of you thinks that maybe the women inside just want to make some money and then go back home. But what if there is someone there who isn't willing and just can't get out, and you don't know because they are inside the building?"

In this book, I take the ambivalence of NGO caseworkers like Cherie toward official protocols for assisting victims of human trafficking as a point of departure for understanding how a UN-sponsored global counter–human trafficking campaign has been playing out on the ground. I explore the incongruities between the official procedures of this globalized project and the needs of those whom the Trafficking Protocol aims to assist. An international legal instrument, the Trafficking Protocol established a formal definition of human trafficking to serve as a model for state, regional, and local legislation on the issue.[3] Parties to the protocol agree to a counter–human trafficking framework centered on "the 3Ps": prosecution, protection, and prevention.[4] As of this writing, 180 state parties have ratified the Trafficking Protocol, and numerous legal initiatives have been developed on international, regional, and national levels, creating a "transnational legal order" centered on the issue.[5] Over the past two decades, hundreds of millions of dollars have been spent on counter–human trafficking efforts worldwide.[6]

However, a protocol is more than an international treaty. It is also a program of rules and procedures. Along with providing an influential template for domestic legislation, the Trafficking Protocol set the stage for the development of a new globally scalable regime of norms and guidelines for how national governments, NGOs, and international organizations should actively work together in this fight. It has inspired data collection and formal knowledge-sharing on a global scale centered around commensurable, quantifiable measures of those practices defined as human trafficking.[7] It has prompted international organizations to produce a wide range of guidelines, handbooks, and collections of what they identify as "best practices" and "recommended principles" aimed at providing global models for both undertaking and evaluating human trafficking countermeasures.[8] It has also provided a basis for these organizations to provide "technical cooperation" by sponsoring trainings, workshops, and symposia for government officials and domestic NGOs across the globe.[9] The result, in legal scholar Hila Shamir's words, is "a remarkably uniform" collection of protocols for fighting human trafficking.[10]

This book takes this collection of protocols as the object of its analysis, ethnographically examining their everyday enactment in Japan's official counter–human trafficking campaign. It examines what happens when an intent to "do good" and address human suffering meets the bureaucratic forms and everyday procedures of global governance. At first glance, Japan appears to be a success story of these efforts. Japan has generally been recognized as a destination country for human trafficking. In other words, it has been identified as a country to which migrant workers are coercively, if not forcibly, brought and kept under conditions of sexual and labor exploitation, often by members of what the US State Department has identified as "Japanese organized crime syndicates (the Yakuza)."[11] The primary groups initially identified as trafficking victims were migrant women working in the sex industry from the Philippines, Thailand, Colombia, South Korea, and eastern Europe, with Filipina entertainers initially highlighted as the largest group.[12] In more recent years, a limited amount of attention has also been paid to labor migrants from China and other Asian countries who have come to Japan as part of the Technical Intern Training Program (TITP, Ginō Jisshū Seido).[13] However, the overwhelming focus of the counter–human trafficking campaign in Japan has remained on women in the sex industry, and particularly, in recent years, on Japanese women and girls (see the conclusion for a more detailed discussion).

In the decades before the Trafficking Protocol's adoption, grassroots activists in both Japan and migrant-sending countries had lobbied the Japanese government to address the abuse of migrant workers in Japan. However, they made little headway.[14] Even in-depth reporting about the exploitation and abuse of Southeast Asian migrants in Japan's sex industry by the International Labour Organization (ILO), the International Organization for Migration (IOM), Human Rights Watch, and the United Nations Global Programme against Trafficking in Human Beings did little to prompt the Japanese government to take action.[15] Things only changed when the US State Department ranked Japan on the newly created Tier 2 Watch List of its 2004 *Trafficking in Persons Report* (*TIP Report*). This report puts the diplomatic weight of the United States behind the protocol by evaluating and ranking countries in regard to their official counter-trafficking efforts.[16] Concerned about its reputation in a global arena, the Japanese government immediately switched its official position and announced that it would "seize leadership in Asia on this issue."[17]

Soon the Japanese government formally adopted its Action Plan and created an Inter-Ministerial Liaison Committee and Task Force on Trafficking in its cabinet to oversee the plan's implementation.[18] The 2004 *TIP Report* had identified Filipina women entering Japan on "entertainer visas" as one of the largest groups of "trafficking victims" in the world, and in 2005 the Japanese government promptly tightened requirements for this visa.[19] The Japanese police also began raids of establishments like the one in Cherie's suburb. Within two years, the number of Filipina women entering Japan on entertainer visas dropped by nearly 90 percent, declining from 82,741 in 2004 to 8,607 in 2006—a shift enthusiastically noted in US State Department cables and reports.[20] Around the same time, the Japanese government also began adopting assistance guidelines published by international organizations, holding conferences and symposia on human trafficking, sponsoring international agencies' counter–human trafficking initiatives, and convening police trainings with US officials and international organization staff. By 2017, Japan had ratified the UN Trafficking Protocol, and in 2018 and 2019, it received the *TIP Report*'s highest-tier ranking.[21]

However, as official counter–human trafficking protocols have been adopted in Japan, NGO caseworkers directly working with migrant workers have expressed reservations about the banal outcomes of these efforts. They point to the persistent abuse of migrant workers despite the government's formal steps to comply with international standards. They argue that despite the focus on assisting foreign women in the sex industry, these women have in reality become more vulnerable, as procuring a visa has become more challenging and police raids have pushed the sex trade further underground, where it is harder to track.[22] They point to how official efforts have had little impact on the exploitation and abuse of migrants in many industries that hire foreign workers through the legal TITP, such as agriculture and manufacturing. They assert that the minimal support provided to repatriated trafficking survivors leaves them vulnerable to re-trafficking. International organizations themselves acknowledge that despite their considerable expenditure of money and effort, the problem of human trafficking is only growing on a global scale.[23]

How can such a high-profile campaign, on which so many committed people have worked so diligently, fall so short of its stated objectives? The following chapters explore this question in depth. In the remainder of this introduction, I first offer some background on the labor migration of Filipina women into the Japanese sex industry. (This group comprises a plurality of those foreign nationals who initially received assistance through the Japanese government's official counter–human trafficking program.)[24] I then turn to a brief discussion of the emergence and limitations of a global solution to address the abuse and exploitation that migrants experience, and the attendant banality of good that has stymied and gravely compromises the UN's approach.

The Structural Vulnerability of Filipina Migrants in Japan

Studies of Filipina migration to Japan have repeatedly argued that political economic and geopolitical inequities lie behind this migration trend.[25] The Philippines' nearly four hundred years of colonial occupation—initially by

Spain (1565–1898) and then by the United States (1898–1942 and 1945–46) and Japan (1942–45)—entrenched practices of foreign resource extraction on the archipelago and established deeply rooted inequalities both within Philippine society and between the Philippines and countries in the Global North. Both the United States and Japan continue to have imposing economic presences in the country. Both have been key and influential sources of bilateral aid and direct investment, and corporations based in both countries rely on resources and labor from the Philippines to produce profit back home; indeed, Japan and the United States have often worked in tandem to support each other's interests at the Philippines' expense.[26] Trade agreements between the countries have overwhelmingly served Japanese and US-based corporations and consumers at the expense of those in the Philippines.[27] The governments of, and corporations based in, both countries have also left behind significant environmental damage, whether from abandoned military bases, unsustainable resource extraction, or waste disposal agreements.[28] For instance, Peter Dauvergne has described the devastating consequences of Japanese logging on the Philippines, which began in the mid-1960s and by 1997 resulted in only 20 percent of the country retaining significant forest cover.[29] Meanwhile, the export of timber from the Philippines enabled Japan to retain its forests while building homes in urban areas for a growing middle class.[30] Today, Japan imports raw materials from the Philippines, while also relying on the country for labor and as a market for finished products. Despite the promise of development support, the Philippines has consistently run trade deficits with Japan. In addition, the 2006 Japan-Philippines Economic Partnership Agreement removed tariffs on the import of forms of Japanese waste into the Philippines, including manufacturing residues, chemical and industrial waste, used batteries, and waste pharmaceuticals, by defining them as "goods."[31] As elites in the Philippines have partnered with, and benefited from, relations with US and Japanese governments and corporations, the majority of Philippine nationals have suffered. The cumulative result of these relationships in the Philippines has been widespread environmental destruction, the displacement of rural populations left without subsistence means, and low wages and negative health consequences for workers in the limited jobs created through development plans—for instance, in tourism and export processing zones.[32]

Most Filipina labor migrants go to Japan to manage the income insecurity and insufficient work prospects created by this history.[33] Their migration is part of a broader trend of overseas labor migration that began during the Marcos regime, with support from the International Monetary Fund and the World Bank, to inject foreign currency into the struggling Philippine economy. Over the past half century, this trend has only intensified as the national economy has become increasingly dependent on migrant remittances.[34] Meanwhile, although agriculture could offer livelihood possibilities in the Philippines, land reform in the country has repeatedly failed.[35] The unemployment rate remains high. The cost of medical care is unaffordable to all but the most privileged, in part because foreign corporations, such as US-based pharmaceutical companies, insist on maximizing profits at the expense of health and lives. Most Filipina migrants working in the Japanese sex industry come from the most economically desperate communities in the Philippines. These communities are up against a political system both intergenerationally locked by a coterie of elite families with ties to powerful states and burdened by the failures of development policies endorsed by international funding agencies, multinational industry, and powerful centralized state investors.

Scholars agree that Filipina women's decision to migrate for work abroad is an expression of their agency; most Filipina overseas labor migrants self-identify as mothers, daughters, and sisters, and they, like Cherie, are motivated by feelings of both duty and love to endure even extreme exploitation abroad to support their families and find a better life.[36] Yet migration paths for these women are limited, particularly for the majority who lack postsecondary educations or other specialized skills. Consequently, they often find themselves facing a dark dilemma: continue living economically impoverished lives at home or risk abuse and exploitation working abroad.[37] This risk inheres in part because accessing jobs abroad is so difficult. For instance, the Japanese government does not issue visas for work that it deems unskilled. Consequently, Filipina women have had to rely on middlemen and incur heavy debt to find jobs in Japan, where, subject to strict immigration laws and the always-present threat of deportation, they are all the more vulnerable to exploitation and abuse.[38] A significant number of these women have experienced labor demands far exceeding job recruitment descriptions; substandard or unpaid wages; substandard food and housing, which employers are required to provide; insufficient time off from work; indenture; forced labor, including coerced or forced sex work; constant surveillance; restrictions on their movement; and, in some cases, physical and sexual abuse, assault, and enslavement.[39] In Japan, like the United States, industries employing migrant workers—not only in the sex industry but also in agriculture and factory work—have been minimally regulated.[40] Few tax dollars are allocated to protect the rights of noncitizens, and particularly those of irregular migrants. Meanwhile, the Philippine national economy's dependence on foreign remittances has made its government reluctant to intervene in the abuse and exploitation of its overseas workers.[41]

The mistreatment of Filipina migrants in Japan has emerged in the context of these braided histories of colonialism, neoliberal policy, economic exploitation, corruption, state failure, sexism, racism (including intra-Asian racism), and cultures of greed and domination, which have shaped relationships between people in Japan, the Philippines, and the United States for over a century.[42] One might thus expect that an effort to address the extreme forms of abuse and exploitation faced by these migrants would take these structural vulnerabilities into account and focus on transforming the political economic realities of their lives. In fact, the Trafficking Protocol states that in the interest of preventing human trafficking, "State Parties shall take or strengthen measures, including through bilateral or multilateral cooperation, to alleviate the factors that make persons, especially women and children, vulnerable to trafficking, such as poverty, underdevelopment and lack of equal opportunity."[43] The preface to the 2020 *Global Report on Trafficking in Persons* reiterates this point, arguing the need to "tackle the structural inequalities that leave women as well as children and marginalized groups vulnerable to human trafficking."[44] However, in practice, almost no attention has been paid to this issue.

Instead, the enactment of the Trafficking Protocol has prioritized a single modular institutional protocol for prosecuting traffickers and repatriating victims. The current website of the United Nations Office on Drugs and Crime (UNODC) describes its "response" as follows: "*help* countries to draft, develop and review the laws, policies, and action plans they need to effectively combat human trafficking"; "*train* and *mentor* the people who use these instruments to apprehend, prosecute and convict traffickers and protect and support the victims"; "*supply* studies, toolkits and models for training, research and policy reform purposes"; and "*form* partnerships with international, governmental and non-governmental organizations and support joint investigations into trafficking crimes."[45] All of these strategies focus on working with established agencies to disseminate a global, bureaucratic protocol; none of them address the need, cited in the UNODC's own 2020 *Global Report*, to "tackle the structural inequalities" shaping migrants' lives.[46] How and to what ends has this modular globalizable bureaucratic strategy come to seem the most appropriate and desirable way for the UN to eradicate the wide-ranging forms of violence and abuse that are now glossed as human trafficking—not only forced prostitution and sex trafficking but also extreme labor exploitation in a broad swath of industries as well as the sale of human organs?[47]

The modular globalized approach of the UN-sponsored counter-trafficking campaign is not unique to efforts to fight human trafficking. Rather, the campaign's methods follow from broader strategies of global governance that gained traction after the end of the Cold War, when international relations were no longer constrained by a bipolar dynamic.[48] These strategies rest on a notion of globality in which the earth is viewed as a singular object to be managed on the whole by a shared humanity.[49] This notion of globality was first articulated by the environmental movements of the 1960s, which were focused on threats of planetary nuclear annihilation and poignantly reinforced by the Apollo missions' delicately beautiful images of a singular, shared "blue planet."[50] During the 1970s, this new singular conception of globality led to the emergence of what historian Mark Philip Bradley has called a "new global affect toward power and territoriality" in which the global became a novel scale for political participation.[51] A growing number of newly formed NGOs began to take up issues such as human rights, economic inequality, and gender inequality as global problems. Technological innovations, such as the growth of the civil aviation industry and new modes of electronic communication, also contributed to the emergence of a new form of civil society that, by the 1990s, could imagine itself as global in a singular, universalizable sense.[52]

By the 1990s, many contemporary problems, like human trafficking, came to be viewed as warranting a global response. Transnational collaborations among governmental and nongovernmental entities came to be seen as crucial to facilitating the technical cooperation and spread of international norms central to global governance.[53] The UN became a clearinghouse for promulgating such norms by attaining the consent of member states and creating collaborations among international organizations, NGOs, and state bodies.[54]

This commitment to technical cooperation through transnational collaborations figures importantly in the UN's global approach to combating human trafficking. A key justification for the Trafficking Protocol has been the "urgent need to increase technical cooperation activities in order to assist countries . . . with their efforts in translating United Nations policy guidelines into practice."[55] Former UN secretary-general Ban Ki-moon emphasized the importance of these collaborations in an official press release for the 2010 UN Global Plan of Action to Combat Trafficking in Persons—one of a number of expansions of the UN's counter–human trafficking project since the adoption of the Trafficking Protocol: "The only way to end human trafficking is by working together, between States and within regions, among United Nations entities and in public-private partnerships."[56]

Yet coordinating diversely positioned stakeholders for a single global agenda is not a simple matter. Creating a uniform global project requires strategies that can be scaled up and disseminated. It requires identifying a lowest common denominator that applies across different cases in different geographical sites, necessitating the "disentanglement" of the specificities of history, place, and political economy that create friction and gaps among disparately located and invested groups.[57] It demands consistency of practice and a common language that can link institutional bodies with different visions and approaches in a single technical practice.

Bureaucratic strategies have facilitated this governance at scale. Bureaucratization enables the uniform management of large populations by rationalizing administrative tasks through the standardization of rules and procedures.[58] It authoritatively promotes the legitimacy of a single legal order through pretensions of neutrality that standardize forms of audit and review.[59] In line with such an approach, the past few decades have witnessed the efflorescence of what Peter Larsen calls an "international guidance culture" that enables interinstitutional collaborations for norm compliance by standardizing everyday bureaucratic protocols across cultural, geographical, and institutional divides.[60] Such guidelines also enable an institutional division of labor that breaks down complex problems into manageable bites for different institutional bodies to oversee. Meanwhile, they erase history, political-economic inequality, and cultural and geographical differences in the interest of establishing a standardized institutional practice—a protocol—to link and coordinate among national governments, international organizations, and NGOs on a global scale. They also offer measurable standards for regulating national governments and evaluating compliance with international norms, guiding the critiques of NGO caseworkers who are involved in the protocol's day-to-day enactment into formalized, bureaucratic channels where these critiques are both contained and managed.

The Banality of Good

As this book explores how the bureaucratic logic of global governance plays out in the Trafficking Protocol's everyday enactment, it argues for attention to the *banality of good* that laces this endeavor. I use this expression to refer to the perils of this campaign's globalized institutional approach, which ultimately privileges technical prescription and bureaucratic compliance over the needs and perspectives of those it means to assist. I borrow the term *banality* from Hannah Arendt, for whom the word refers to a rote thoughtlessness in political life.[61] In her reporting on the Jerusalem trial, Arendt famously wrote of the "banality of evil" when reflecting on German Nazi Adolf Eichmann's testimony.[62] To her horror, Eichmann appeared a strikingly ordinary bureaucrat, "terrifyingly normal" in his disengagement from and "inability to think" about the consequences of his actions.[63] For Arendt, thinking required a measure of humility. She identified it with a Socratic practice in which the end was not reaching a solitary or fixed solution but the ability to engage in a "soundless solitary dialogue"—to engage in an ongoing practice of questioning oneself as one endeavored to see the world from another's perspective.[64]

Arendt was troubled by the logics of bureaucratic organization that had developed with the introduction of totalitarianism into the world; she believed that these logics had turned bureaucracy into an instrument of evil insofar as they were designed to maintain the status quo by precluding individuals' responses to contingency and difference.[65] She drew attention to Eichmann's thoughtlessness to illustrate how people can be ensnared in a machinery of harm not on account of an innate evil nature or of merely being a cog in the wheel of bureaucracy but specifically through a conditioned neglect to consider how one's actions impact others.[66] She refused to see evil behavior as reflective of an individual's immutable sinfulness, corruption, or depravity, and she also rejected the notion that it was a simple result of submitting to institutional hierarchy. Rather, she aimed to hold individuals accountable for their injurious behavior, asking how such actions were facilitated, and thus could be interrupted, by both human thought and practice.[67]

Arendt's notion of banality teaches us that the tolerance of even extreme forms of violence is not necessarily the consequence of exceptional or aberrant belief or action.[68] Rather, it can result from a banal self-deception encouraged by bureaucratic organization: the neglect to question taken-for-granted assumptions in the face of formal, accepted practice. This understanding of banality shows that one can perpetuate injury on account of not only what one does but also what one thoughtlessly fails to do or avoids doing. It resonates with the concept of banality put forward by Achille Mbembe, who also connects broader patterns of political-economic violence to the mundane and thoughtless actions of individual actors who are simply following the rules, mean well, and are enjoying their lives.[69]

Building on Arendt and Mbembe, this book explores how the structures and logics of modern institutional life encourage a kind of unthinking, so that the rote adherence to an institutional protocol comes to stand in for necessary structural change. Focusing on the everyday enactment of counter–human trafficking efforts in Japan, it considers how practical adherence to the global counter–human trafficking protocol, in the face of its obvious and acknowledged inadequacies, allows those behind the project to unthinkingly hold that it is accomplishing "good" even though it is actually doing little to address the root causes of the violence it claims to fight. From this view, the harms of the Trafficking Protocol's banal good are not a consequence of the sinful nature or bad intentions of those involved in its institutional enactment; to the contrary, many government officials and international agency staff mean to do well in supporting this campaign. Rather, this book explores how globalized political projects aimed at doing good—such as those intended to fight, in Annan's words, "the most egregious violations of human rights"—both enable and provide cover for an injurious rote thoughtlessness as their bureaucratic structure neglects, and thereby sidelines, critical consideration of structural inequality.

My examination of the banality of good that laces the global counter–human trafficking project extends a long tradition of scholarship that explores how socially and legally sanctioned forms of violence inhere within those practices commonly understood as *progress, justice,* and *right.* These studies have examined forms of violence that elude attention or are hidden, disavowed, and unrecognized, such as structural violence, legal violence, and bureaucratic violence.[70] Sociologist Randall Collins and anthropologist Michael Herzfeld, in particular, have focused on bureaucratic systematization and indifference as ways that bureaucracies depersonalize violence and thereby eliminate any individual sense of moral responsibility for it.[71] For instance, Herzfeld argues that bureaucratic indifference is a strategy by which modern nation-states deflect responsibility for those outside their imagined community, thereby justifying and normalizing practices of exclusion.[72]

However, being thoughtless is not the same as being indifferent. Whereas indifference reflects a logic of disregard, thoughtlessness rests on a practice of self-deception. Consider that the global counter–human trafficking protocol is fully premised on caring about victims of human trafficking. International agency staff and government bureaucrats assert their humanitarian concern about trafficking victims and their determination to address their suffering. Ethical commitments to equality, justice, and human rights vest their work. In the face of these commitments, the banality of good does not reflect a bureaucratic apathy to suffering so much as a deflection from considering, or an unwillingness to delve into, its inconvenient causes and forms. Bureaucracies are technologies for government administration in modern societies; they were established to provide consistency and continuity in the management of large populations.[73] They channel political action into formal procedures that are convenient and manageable for stable governance at scale. Anything inconvenient to such frameworks of action is rendered irrelevant. This approach is anything but compatible with nuanced or comprehensive social change. Rather, it creates ways of seeing that are also ways of not seeing.[74] It offers institutional practices of care that are careless.

THE CONSEQUENCES FOR NGO CASEWORKERS

Committed NGO caseworkers, like Cherie, struggle to reconcile the mismatch between their clients' needs and the Trafficking Protocol's modular, globalized approach as they work on a day-to-day basis to provide assistance to migrants who need it. The predicament faced by these caseworkers is at the heart of this study. The on-the-ground enactment of Japan's official victim assistance and protection process is structured by a standardized protocol for interinstitutional collaboration in which national governments manage the arrest and prosecution of human traffickers, the IOM repatriates identified "trafficking victims," and both rely on established NGOs in destination and sending countries to shelter, counsel, and reintegrate victims.[75]

Yet the word *collaboration* carries the double meaning of working toward a common goal and cooperating with an adversary, and this ambivalence is palpable in relations among NGOs, centralized state governments, and international organizations executing the protocol. The international legal system that developed in the years following World War II relies on the willingness of nation-states to cooperate with international institutions and adopt global norms.[76] Because Article 2 of the UN Charter protects the "sovereign equality" of all members, the UN system has few direct means at its disposal to impose compliance.[77] International legal instruments are binding only insofar as member states consent to be bound by them.[78] Moreover, since the UN's establishment, political-economic inequalities among these states have shaped how the organization is run.[79] These inequalities are masked by a myth of territorial sovereignty: the notion that all nation-states are uniformly sovereign (i.e., they all have territories that they rule as sovereign) and thus can be treated as interchangeable parts.[80] However, at the same time, NGOs and international organizations involved in UN projects (including UN agencies) are dependent on funding from member states, which contribute unequally; moreover, some members states (e.g., permanent members of the Security Council) have more political pull than others. Consequently, the pressure to comply with global norms applies unequally to different national governments, with some dominating others, and unequal political economic relations within the UN shape relationships among international organizations, member states, and NGOs participating in UN projects in ways that perpetuate the status quo.[81]

Ethnographic studies have demonstrated the gaps between the stated objectives of international policy and its everyday practice.[82] These studies have taught us much about the establishment of hegemonic international regimes and the manufacture of consent to them.[83] They have also demonstrated how these projects are inconsistently vernacularized, and have examined outward forms of resistance to them.[84] However, we know less about the ways that efforts at global governance have systematically sidelined and evacuated the perspectives of those, like grassroots NGO workers, who find themselves ambivalently incorporated into their day-to-day enactment of these projects as both invested and troubled participants. We have limited understanding of how the modular, globalized design of these efforts contributes to a neglect of the ethical impasses and dark dilemmas that NGO caseworkers like Cherie face.

For both political legitimacy and logistical support, the global counter-trafficking campaign in Japan and the Philippines actively depends on the work of grassroots NGO caseworkers. Many of these caseworkers had worked with migrant laborers for years, if not decades, before the Trafficking Protocol was adopted. In Japan, these caseworkers are often themselves immigrants who share cultural and linguistic backgrounds with their clients; if they are Japanese or come from a different background, they have characteristically spent extended periods of time in migrants' home countries and speak their native tongues. All the grassroots NGO caseworkers that I met were deeply committed to their work, most laboring part-time at low wages and without benefits, if they were not volunteers. Many of these caseworkers recognized the dilemma that migrants in Japan faced when channeled into official assistance programs for trafficked persons, which almost without exception resulted in their repatriation. In working with clients, NGO caseworkers took into account the complex calculations that many vulnerable migrants must make, weighing their experiences of hardship and abuse abroad against both their determination to financially assist their families and their resources for economic survival at home. As Vicente, a caseworker at a migrant shelter in Japan, put it, "They don't have anywhere to go. For many, their life of extreme poverty in the home country is much worse than what they have now."

Consequently, these NGO caseworkers often emotionally and ethically struggled with their work in official counter–human trafficking campaigns. As

I explain in chapter 1, some NGOs in Japan had become involved in these efforts after years of bearing witness to the extreme forms of abuse and violence that some foreign women in the sex industry suffer at the hands of private citizens (i.e., employers, recruiters, and clients). These NGO staff were frustrated that their clients had for years been criminalized, rather than assisted, by the Japanese government. They were also personally troubled that some of their clients seemed to believe that they deserved their exploitation and abuse (further discussed in chapter 8). Hoping that official attention to the issue might usher in real change, these NGO staff members encouraged their clients to identify as trafficking victims both so that their clients would not blame themselves for their abuse and to stress their clients' entitlement to legal and economic rights.[85] They also relied on this framing to argue against their clients' criminalization under Japanese law and to fight for their clients' legal right to restitution and a hearing on account of their experiences.

However, as Japan's counter–human trafficking project increasingly took shape on the ground, these same NGO caseworkers began to have concerns about the effectiveness of these efforts. Some tried to express their concerns through official channels, moving their critiques beyond the category of "hidden transcripts."[86] Yet they found their input systematically repressed, ignored, or evacuated through institutional hierarchies in which national governments retain final say.[87] Despite their problems with the global counter-trafficking project, they worried that the situation would be even worse if they did not continue to do what they could. "Someone has to do this. At least if it is me, I know that I will be seriously considering the women's needs," Cherie once commented with resignation. Facing women in grave, sometimes life-threatening situations, these NGO caseworkers opted to participate so as to at least do triage.

In the face of a global protocol, these caseworkers found themselves forced to choose between compromising their commitments and working to support migrants under the protocol's constraints or losing the resources and access to assist them at all. Lacking other alternatives, they found themselves holding a poisoned chalice of collaboration in a global counter-trafficking campaign. Throughout this book, I reflect on NGO caseworkers' experiences with the banal everyday practices of the global counter-trafficking regime. I pay special attention to how they *thought* about these issues, including questioning their own roles in the assistance chain. I also consider how their frustration sometimes manifests not as an overt form of resistance or dissent but in the ambivalence, restlessness, and discontent that ultimately pushes some NGO caseworkers to leave, taking their insight, expertise, and experience with them.

While grassroots NGO caseworkers' experiences and perspectives are at the heart of this study, they were by no means the only people with whom I discussed the counter–human trafficking protocol. I interviewed a diverse cross-section of people involved in these efforts—government bureaucrats, some of whom felt passionately about fighting human trafficking and some of whom were simply doing their jobs; committed, disillusioned, and occasionally confused international agency staff; and feminist activists, both those who had been involved with the issue for decades and those who had been spurred to action by the Trafficking Protocol. I also conducted participant observation at NGO offices in Japan, the Philippines, and the United States, and I augmented my interviews and fieldwork with legal studies, detailed excavation of policy documents, and historical research on global feminist activism and grassroots women's movements in Asia. Different chapters are built around variously sourced material, moving between the establishment and text of guidelines and protocols and the experiences and perspectives of those who execute them.

I draw on these mixed methods to produce a necessarily multi-sited ethnography of global governance. My ethnographic approach to the topic differs from most studies of international law, which usually focus on the drafting and adoption of multilateral agreements, the cultivation of international norms, and the politics of government compliance with them. This work speaks to formal political processes, but it teaches us little about how and to what ends international agreements are enacted on a day-to-day basis. Ethnographers are committed to understanding social and political life through its quotidian enactment. The global fight against human trafficking is enacted through a shifting network of institutional activities: the drafting and citing of guidelines; the circulation of documents; the completion of forms; the setting of funding expectations and conditions; the commissioning of state, international organization, and NGO labor; and the standardization of practices for identifying victims, assisting them, and moving them within and across national borders. These activities span geographically and institutionally diverse sites, including UN headquarters, national and local government offices, and grassroots NGO shelters. I bring an ethnographic eye to these practices in the interest of identifying how sets of shared affects and cultural logics work to link them together. At the same time, I pay attention to how those enacting the protocol are unequally positioned within it and to the discrepancies of resources allocated to them.

My ethnographic approach to global governance builds on the work of anthropologists who have pioneered strategies for studying the politics embedded in the everyday practice of nation-states, international law, and NGOs—three political agencies linked through the UN Trafficking Protocol's global governance model. First, Aradhana Sharma and Akhil Gupta have demonstrated that the seemingly technical, routine, repetitive, and, in their words, "banal" practices of modern bureaucracies are central to both the ways that nation-states produce themselves as political bodies and the micropolitics of centralized state governance in their citizens' lives.[88] I contribute to their insights into the injurious effects of state proceduralism by considering how such effects can also be produced on a transnational scale through the proceduralism of global governance. Second, I build on work by Annelise Riles, who has explored how the international system is constituted through technocratic and aesthetic practices as much as through government strategy.[89] Riles analyzes the textual production and ratification of the UN Platform for Action and the Beijing Declaration to highlight how technocratic and aesthetic logics shape the drafting of international law. I expand her insights to consider how such technocratic and aesthetic logics also shape the *enactment* of international agreements once they have been adopted. Finally, I build on ethnographic studies of NGOs by Erica Bornstein, Julie Hemment, China Scherz, and others that explore how cultural and moral logics inform the ways that NGO staff negotiate the investments of governments and international funding agencies.[90] I augment their analyses by considering how the experiences of NGO staff are shaped by the very technocratic practice of global governance as it structures NGO collaborations with government agencies and international organizations. My approach also responds to a call by cultural and political geographers for more ethnographic attention to how geographical processes relate to everyday institutional practice.[91] Contributing to this project, I look to how a global-scale campaign is performatively articulated through local enactments of shared bureaucratic routines, which link distinct political bodies and noncontiguous spaces into a single program of governance. In other words, I explore how a global protocol "comes to matter" as international law through the day-to-day practice of its proceduralism, which involves the establishment and enactment of a modular, standardized practice across nation-states and local sites.[92]

A NOTE ON RESEARCH METHODS

Because the Trafficking Protocol is being enacted in some capacity in nearly every country across the globe, and its practice is constantly evolving, a single ethnographer could never expect to capture it in its entirety. Most ethnographers today acknowledge that our research is partial and situated; we do not aspire to holism or comprehensiveness so much as offer positioned insight into the structures and logics of the contemporary world. I began ethnographic fieldwork for this book in 2004, when Japan's official counter–human trafficking campaign was just beginning, and I conducted focused research until 2007, returning to Japan in 2010 and 2014 and maintaining ongoing contact with activists in the country, some of whom visited me in the United States. In the meantime, I audited courses at UCLA School of Law in international, human rights, and comparative law (2013–14), and I conducted documentary research through to the present. This book offers a window into the UN global trafficking project based on the specific path my research took.

Because my project at once involved "studying up" and learning about efforts to assist a vulnerable population, I recognized early on that some information would be inaccessible.[93] Although many government officials were forthcoming, some seemed evasive or even hostile, and all were constrained in what they were willing or able to share. In most cases in Japan and the United States, government offices expected me to submit my interview questions beforehand for approval. In the United States, I was sometimes referred to public relations officers in US agencies. In one memorable interview at a government ministry in Japan, a civil servant responded to my submitted questions by reading responses off published ministry brochures. Another Japanese civil servant requested that our interview be held away from the office and visibly sweated and shook throughout our meeting, clearly nervous about the implications of anything that was said even though I assured the person that anything included in my writing would be unattributable.

In some cases, people offered additional information "off the record." In a handful of revealing cases, former government officials were willing to speak more freely about their government experiences. In one case, a government official privately contacted me and shared personal impressions of their work at length over the course of several years. I have taken some liberties and shifted inconsequential details about people's identities to ensure that they will not be identified. Doing multi-sited research involving multiple organizations in three different countries over many years had advantages insofar as I sometimes heard part of a story in one organization or country and the rest of the story in others. In part because, as I explain in chapter 6, communication among organizations assisting trafficked persons is restricted, I often found myself patching together information gathered from people in different agencies or countries. Some preliminary conclusions were confirmed and embellished by US embassy cables in the Public Library of US Diplomacy, created by WikiLeaks. Available cables overlap with the years of my primary research when Japan's TIP program took shape and buttressed my findings.

When I began my project, the UN Trafficking Protocol had already been adopted, and most official UN activities related to my research are well documented and widely available online. I thus opted against conducting fieldwork at UN events. My focus is not on the UN as an organization that executes a global plan so much as on how a UN-sponsored global project is articulated through unequal everyday interactions between government officials, international organization staff, and grassroots NGOs in different local sites. For insight regarding everyday workings of the UN, I rely on work by Michael Barnett, Sylvanna Falcón, Sally Engle Merry, and Annelise Riles, as well as analyses by historians, international relations scholars, and political figures, including Mark Bradley, Judith Kelley, Margaret Keck and Kathryn Sikkink, Mark Mazower, Samuel Moyn, Jan Eckel, and Madeleine Rees.[94]

My research with grassroots NGOs in Japan, the Philippines, and the United States was facilitated by my earlier involvement with organizations assisting Filipinx migrants in Japan, including previous research with Filipina migrants working in hostess bars. My access to these organizations was granted on the condition that I not write about their clients' cases or risk retraumatizing their clients by asking about their experiences. Survivors of violence are often reluctant to talk about their experiences. When trafficking survivors' voices do appear in this book (chapter 8), it is primarily regarding their experiences of assistance and empowerment programs.

The Chapters

This book is organized into two sections. The first three chapters of the book explore how the good of contemporary efforts to fight human trafficking came to be imagined and institutionalized as a global project, first in the UN and then in Japan. The following five chapters ethnographically examine the banalities of the Japanese government's official victim assistance and protection process as it has played out on the ground. Overseen by the IOM, the process is organized through a division of labor in which staff at different organizations perform discrete, specialized roles that are coordinated through a standardized protocol. These chapters highlight the work and perspectives of grassroots NGO caseworkers providing direct assistance to migrant workers in this assistance chain alongside the impasses that they confront.

I begin by considering how human trafficking came to be recognized as a global problem during the last decades of the twentieth century. Mobilizations to address many forms of exploitation and abuse currently identified as human trafficking began in the early 1970s among grassroots women's groups in Asia.

These groups developed anti-capitalist and anticolonial strategies to address the sexual and labor exploitation of women in the region by Japanese tourists and US military personnel. Chapter 1, "A Global Solution," explores how feminists in the United States sidelined and encapsulated these efforts during the 1980s to frame human trafficking as a uniform global issue that warranted a single global response. The US-based feminist movement then adopted an institutional model to lobby national governments and international organizations to develop a global solution. As they did so, they evacuated many of the essential critiques and much of the promise of the earlier Asia-centered movement. Key contemporary migrants' rights NGOs in Japan trace their roots to this earlier movement, and one objective of this book is to refocus attention on both their extension of it and its yet-unfulfilled promise.

Chapter 2, "The Protocol's Compromises," considers how US-based globalist feminists found their own visions sidelined as national governments and international organizations prioritized fighting transnational organized crime over protecting women's rights when developing the UN Trafficking Protocol. Why did feminist activists continue to support the Trafficking Protocol's adoption despite this reorientation of focus? This chapter considers the compromises that lay at the heart of the protocol for both UN member-state governments and differently positioned feminist supporters in the United States, Japan, and the Philippines.

The third chapter, "The Institutional Life of Suffering," turns to how and why Japanese government officials came to support global counter–human trafficking efforts after doing little for decades to address even extreme abuse and exploitation of foreign labor migrants within the country's borders. I focus on how caseworkers at grassroots NGOs and a foreign embassy in Japan circulated narratives of foreign migrants' experiences of abuse and exploitation in the hopes of moving Japanese government officials to act. However, although the circulation of these accounts did affect government officials, it did not do so in the ways and to the ends that NGO caseworkers had hoped. This chapter shows how the institutional circulation of stories of suffering at once holds together a global counter–human trafficking project and creates rents and gaps within it.

The following five chapters turn to the everyday banalities of the victim assistance pipeline adopted in Japan, considering its basis in international guidelines promoted by the US State Department. Chapter 4, "'To Promote the Universal Values of Human Dignity,' a Roadmap," examines the victim identification protocols presented to the Japanese government by the US government as part of what was identified as a "Roadmap to Tier 1" for meeting *TIP Report* standards. Drawn from an IOM handbook on trafficking victim assistance, these victim identification guidelines are one example of the guidance culture that has come to define the global counter–human trafficking protocol. Focusing on the explicitly acknowledged inconsistencies and contradictions of these recommended guidelines, I illustrate how the global guidance culture that developed around the Trafficking Protocol has turned procedural conformity into cover for recognized procedural inadequacies.

Chapters 5 and 6 consider how strict adherence to official victim assistance and protection protocols results in the failure to protect migrants who have suffered extreme forms of abuse and exploitation. Chapter 5, "Banal Justice," considers the unprotection of migrants who have suffered indenture, confinement, malnourishment, and sexual abuse but who do not receive official recognition, and thus protection, under Japan's Action Plan on account of procedural technicalities. Chapter 6, "The Need to Know," turns to how the official protocol compromises the ability of NGO caseworkers to assist migrants who qualify as trafficked persons. It focuses on the "need to know" protocols that govern information management among different agencies involved in the official assistance process, illustrating how they impair caseworkers' ability to monitor and assist their clients.

Chapters 7 and 8 shift to the Philippines to examine reintegration projects for repatriated trafficking survivors from Japan. Trafficking survivors often return home to more precarious circumstances than those they initially left. In the interest of preventing retrafficking, the Japanese government has both directly and indirectly funded reintegration projects for repatriated survivors. "Funding Frustration," chapter 7, explores the ambivalence and frustration of grassroots NGOs with the funding priorities of these efforts. Frustrated with their treatment as subcontractors by international organizations and national governments, some of these NGO caseworkers eventually quit, taking their insights, expertise, and experience with them. Finally, chapter 8, "Cruel Empowerment," explores an official project aimed at empowering trafficking survivors that was funded by the Japanese government–sponsored UN Trust Fund for Human Security (UNTFHS) and administered by the ILO. I contrast this project's strategies with those of the Women Empowerment Program (WEP), independently pioneered by a grassroots NGO in the Philippines that was also subcontracted by the UNTFHS-ILO program. The juxtaposition reveals the cruelty of the approach to empowerment taken by the UNTFHS-ILO Empowerment Project, which thoughtlessly ignored the structural vulnerabilities of migrants' lives and thereby created "a relation of attachment to compromised conditions of possibility."[95] I demonstrate that whereas the UNTFHS-ILO unthinkingly celebrated individual empowerment as an end unto itself, the WEP self-consciously incorporated the limits of its personal empowerment project into a broader vision of political activism and community building ultimately aimed at necessary social transformation and structural change.

My interactions and conversations with NGO caseworkers drew my attention to the unthinking cruelty of the UN-sponsored counter–human trafficking project. They taught me the importance to their work not only of conviction and selfless commitment but also of self-critical reflection. Inspired by Foucault, scholars in the social sciences and humanities have paid much critical attention over the past several decades to how the politics of knowledge shape social and political life. Yet less attention has been paid to the roles of other human faculties, like thinking, in creating sustainable social change. For Arendt, thinking and knowing are very different activities.[96] Knowing is a "world-building" activity through which knowledge bearers construct rules and edifices; it is cumulative, instrumental, and practical.[97] Thinking, in contrast, does not produce "moral propositions or commandments," nor does it result in a final code of conduct or definition of good and evil.[98] Rather, it is a humbling experience of being caught up in a moment of perplexity, an ethical struggle that works to "unfreeze" what has been rigidified by previously taken-for-granted definitions, doctrines, and concepts.[99] It involves weighing in the moment the contingencies at hand to interrupt the flow of programmatic action, take measure of it, and look after what has been left behind.[100]

I learned about this kind of thinking from grassroots NGO caseworkers who strained against the rigidity of counter-trafficking protocols as they thought about how to best assist their clients. These caseworkers wrestled with the contingencies of their clients' everyday lives as they struggled to do good by them. They often found themselves in an ethical quandary, weighing whether it was better to encourage migrants to submit to Japan's Action Plan or to stay in grossly abusive work situations. This book explores how the technocratic protocols of the global counter–human trafficking project produce such ethical impasses for NGO caseworkers. It highlights how its globalized institutional practice forecloses possibilities for case-sensitive political action and sidelines locally grounded and culturally relevant approaches. It asks how we can begin to understand differently the violence now identified as human trafficking so that we can more responsibly address it. It pushes us to consider what banal programmatic action we need to interrupt to truly confront these "egregious violations of human rights."[101] Only by understanding these dynamics can we begin to develop strategies for promoting human rights that allow us to *think*.

I

A GLOBAL SOLUTION

———

Over the past decade, the singularly most effective work against sex tourism and mail-order bride traffic has been launched by Asian feminists, particularly the Asian Women's Association in Japan and the Third World Movement Against the Exploitation of Women in the Philippines. . . . By the early 1980s their actions caused a significant reduction of sex tours between Japan and the Philippines, for example. It was then that we began to see these agencies appearing in the United States.

It was for this purpose that an International Feminist Network Against Female Sexual Slavery was organized in 1980 and launched its first meeting in Rotterdam in 1983.

—KATHLEEN BARRY, *Female Sexual Slavery*

Migrant women who are sent to Japan in the form of human trafficking, the number of which has risen dramatically to 70 or 80,000 per year, are suffering sexual exploitation and human rights violations as workers in the sex industry's lowest rungs. On top of sexism, women from Asia face racial discrimination as Asians; moreover, because they are undocumented and working illegally, many are simply deported without any means to recover from their human rights violations. . . . We must take on the long-term challenge of transforming the unjust economic structure between countries like Japan, which have become economically powerful, and Asian countries, which are being sacrificed to them, and change how we [in Japan] live our lives.

—ASIAN WOMEN'S ASSOCIATION, "Let's Protect the Human Rights of Asian Migrant Women!"

Field Reflections, Tokyo, Summer 2006

At Tahanan, women migrants who are officially identified as victims of human trafficking share space with those who are escaping domestic violence or, for one reason or another, need assistance and have nowhere else to go. Like other grass-roots NGOs in Japan that support migrant women, the organization survives on a shoestring budget, relying on donations for funding and on committed volunteers and part-time staff for day-to-day operations.[1] The shelter head is allowing me to volunteer as part of my research in part because I am willing to come in on weekends to give regular staff a break.

The shelter space is modest. Clients sleep on futons in shared tatami-floored bedrooms; they cook meals together in a small communal kitchen; and they eat, chat, and watch movies on an old television in a narrow living room crowded with stacks of floor cushions, a low folding table, a few plastic chairs, and wall cabinets full of paperwork, secondhand clothes, and toys for accompanying children. Often women of different nationalities stay at the shelter at the same time. Residents sometimes enjoy talking and laughing with each other; they sometimes simply co-exist; and occasionally tensions, and even fights, break out among them.

Women staying in the shelter seem to have a range of different feelings about being there—including both relief and profound frustration—and these emotions seem sometimes to overlap or fluctuate over time. Residents must surrender their cell phones when they enter Tahanan. This procedure is standard in many women's shelters that house domestic violence survivors. Shelter staff are concerned that women fleeing abusive situations could otherwise be contacted by their abusers, who could then convince the women to reveal the location of the shelter, putting not only the women but also staff and other residents at risk. Residents only leave the shelter with chaperones, a practice viewed as a matter of not only protection but also practicality. Most residents are unfamiliar with the baroque tangle of streets and alleyways surrounding the shelter, and many do not speak enough Japanese to ask for assistance if they get lost.

I let the women in the shelter initiate and guide my interactions with them. As a white, US-born woman who communicates in a variable mixture of English, Japanese, and Tagalog, I am a curiosity to some. Others are shy or reluctant to talk with me; and still others seem flatly uninterested in my presence. I have been providing English and Japanese lessons at women's requests. I answer questions about the US and myself; I listen when women want to talk about their lives and experiences in Japan or at home; and sometimes I simply play with children to give exhausted moms a break. I also assist the women with meal preparation and cleanup (they seem to appreciate my endless willingness to wash dishes), and, on occasion, I have escorted *residents on trips to a local supermarket. The women plan group meals and create a shared shopping list, and I carry the money provided by the shelter, using it to pay for the groceries and leaving the women to make decisions about what to eliminate when desired items exceed available funds. I am self-conscious on these trips that my presence seems parental; I wonder how much the women mind. I sense that they view the fact that they are required a supermarket escort as both symptomatic and the least of their concerns: many of the women already seem to be struggling with cabin fever, confined to the small shelter while their cases are processed, and they all appear anxious to return to work and earn for their families back home.*

Shelter staff recognize the women's frustration with the constraints of shelter life. Some staff are themselves former migrant workers who identify in a range of ways with residents' predicaments; others are Japanese nationals who are in relationships with foreign labor migrants or who grew up or spent extended periods of time abroad. Shelter staff work long hours at minimal wages. Many have long identified as committed activists, opposing the Japanese government's restrictive policies toward migrant workers, and many are also familiar with the cultural and political-economic issues that the women face at home. They see themselves as trying to support residents to the best of their capacities. At the same time, despite their concerns about residents' circumstances at home, many staff seem resigned to the fact that they can do little to change them. They recognize that any assistance provided at the shelter will be temporary and do little to address broader structural inequalities shaping these women's lives.

I open with this ethnographic anecdote to give a sense of the migrant women's shelter in Japan where I volunteered; I include the epigraphs to offer some historical context for this shelter's emergence. The story of the global fight against human trafficking does not ordinarily begin with grassroots activism in Asia. The launching of a global project to counter human trafficking is usually attributed to the work of Kathleen Barry, Charlotte Bunch, and Shirley Castley, who sponsored the 1983 Global Feminist Workshop to Organize against Traffic in Women in Rotterdam, the Netherlands.[2] The workshop was inspired by Barry's 1979 book, *Female Sexual Slavery*, and it provided the occasion for establishing the Coalition against Trafficking in Women (CATW), which became the powerful public face of a global counter–human trafficking effort in the late 1980s and early 1990s.[3]

However, elided by this more widely told origin story is the earlier movement of grassroots women's groups in Asia, and specifically in Korea, Japan, and the Philippines, that both informed Barry's writing and inspired the development of grassroots NGOs like Tahanan.[4] As detailed in this chapter, beginning in the early 1970s, women's groups in Asia built a regional coalition to respond to a burgeoning Japanese sex tourism industry in the region, describing how Japanese sex tourists were turning women into "sex slaves" (*sei no dorei*).[5] This earlier Asia-centered movement took anticolonial, antiracist, and anti-capitalist positions, stressing attention to how race, class, citizenship, and geography differently and unequally shaped women's lives.[6] It did not aspire to unite all women on the planet into a single group opposing global patriarchy, as Barry and Bunch did. Rather, it advocated for a model in which those in more economically privileged countries, such as Japan and the United States, took national and personal responsibility for the ways that they benefited from colonial legacies and the ongoing economic exploitation of women abroad and actively worked to challenge these dynamics and build more just and equitable relations for all. We cannot understand the frustration of caseworkers at NGOs like Tahanan with current globalized efforts to fight human trafficking without paying attention to this history. Moreover, to imagine other possibilities for the counter–human trafficking movement, we need to shift how we understand its emergence.

In this chapter, I trace an alternative genealogy for the emergence of the current global campaign to counter human trafficking by rerouting it through the efforts and visions of women's groups in Asia, particularly in Japan, Korea, and the Philippines. I explore how the subsequent activism of US-based globalist feminists like Barry and Bunch sidelined and evacuated their perspectives and strategies, and I ask how and to what ends women's groups in Asia participated in globalist feminists' efforts. I argue that the globalized vision adopted by US-based feminists neglected and obscured the structural factors foregrounded in the earlier activism of women's groups in Asia even when US-based feminists believed that they were being inclusive.[7] I show how US-based feminists encapsulated that earlier movement by supplanting it with one focused on lobbying international organizations and on legal, as opposed to political-economic, change.[8]

I focus on the displacement of the earlier Asia-centered movement for two reasons. First, I do so because, as previously mentioned, the roots of current grassroots organizations in Japan and the Philippines, like Tahanan, lie within it. Tahanan was established in the early 1990s by grassroots activists in Japan who recognized that the abuse and exploitation experienced by foreign migrant women was based in culturally specific forms of sexism, intra-Asian racism, and political-economic inequalities.[9] These activists aimed not only to provide direct assistance to foreign women in need but also to change the cultural attitudes and economic practices in Japan that affected them. By disentangling these activists' visions from the dominant narrative of the contemporary global counter–human trafficking campaign, we can see how a seemingly inclusive global model has been built through feminist denials and exclusions.[10]

Second, I trace this alternative genealogy to illustrate the banalities that can accompany the rescaling of local and regional political projects as global ones. The political strategies we identify to fight forms of violence rest on our understandings of their nature and scale.[11] The focus of US-based feminists on human trafficking as a singular global phenomenon enabled them to embrace a modular institutional approach. This global frame of action also paradoxically narrowed the focus on structural issues to one centered on individualized incidences of criminal violence. The result has been a hyperopic global project centered on protecting bare human life from criminal individuals—an approach that blots out the specific histories, geographies, political-economic relations, and bigotries that shape peoples' motives and experiences.[12]

In what follows, I explore how grassroots women's groups in Asia first conceptualized a regional movement to fight many of the forms of violence currently included under the umbrella of human trafficking. I then consider how feminists based in the United States drew on these efforts as they built a global movement. Their unselfconscious endeavor to craft a global feminist movement by working through international institutions—an instance of what Janet Halley has called "governance feminism"—effectively sidelined other more politically, culturally, and geographically grounded (and conceivably more effective) grassroots movements aimed at structural change.[13] Later chapters will show how the visions of this earlier Asia-centered movement persist within the global counter–human trafficking campaign through the work of grassroots activists in Japan and the Philippines. In these activists' work, we can see alternative possibilities for addressing the forms of violence now identified as human trafficking.

The 1960s and 1970s: Grassroots Women's Groups in Asia Organize

In the early 1970s, when grassroots women's groups in Asia began mobilizing against Japanese sex tourism in the region, few in both the United States and the United Nations were paying attention to forms of exploitation and abuse that have come to be readily identified today as human trafficking under US and international law.[14] Although in 1949 the UN General Assembly had approved the Convention for the Suppression of the Traffic in Persons and of the Exploitation of the Prostitution of Others, the treaty received limited support and attention. During the 1960s, the topic of contemporary slavery became the subject of scattered Anglophone publications by men; however, the issue was often met with public apathy.[15] For instance, in the early 1960s, the feature-length documentary *Slave Trade in the World Today*, which was based on one of these publications, received a lukewarm response at best.[16] A *New York Times* film review quipped that the movie "focuses on a horrendous evil that does not appear to affect its victims too horribly," going on to describe the "slaves" represented in the film as "apathetic to their reported plight" and claiming they do "not seem unhappy," while characterizing their slavery as "a condition that they do not seem to abhor."[17]

Second-wave feminist movements in the United States during the 1960s and 1970s also showed little interest in these issues. Mobilization focused primarily on domestic matters, particularly those important to white, middle-class women, such as gender discrimination and the right to work and equal pay.[18] Few considered the impact of US imperialism or the sexual and labor exploitation of women of color in either the United States or abroad.

Moreover, the issue was also regularly dismissed within the UN. By 1979, only 49 countries had ratified the 1949 UN Convention for the Suppression of the Traffic in Persons and of the Exploitation of the Prostitution of Others. The prohibition of slavery was accepted as a *jus cogens* norm, a fundamental overriding principle of international law. However, the practices that today fall under the UN's definition of human trafficking were often considered legally distinct from those of slavery, and they were often set aside for political and bureaucratic reasons.[19] In 1974, when a Working Group on Slavery was created within the United Nations Commission on Human Rights, the chief of research for the commission recognized that there was little official interest in reopening the issue of sexual slavery because delegates simply denied that the problem existed in their countries.[20]

In contrast, women's groups in Korea and Japan were actively mobilizing during this time to oppose the exploitation of women in the then-growing Japanese sex tourism industry in Korea. The Japanese economy had recently experienced a decade of what the Japanese government called "income doubling"; national GDP numbers were steadily rising, and the value of the yen was climbing.[21] A new class of consumers had emerged in Japan, and growing discrepancies between the yen and other currencies in Asia meant that international travel was increasingly affordable to them. Korea, a quick and inexpensive flight away and a former colony where Japanese was still spoken, had become an appealing destination for Japanese men. Many of these male tourists arrived in groups for sex tours with licensed *kisaeng* (courtesans) working in government-regulated districts and hotels.[22] The authoritarian Korean government headed by Park Chung-hee, who had trained in imperial Japanese military academies, was encouraging the sex tours as a means to bring foreign currency into the country and rebuild and develop the Korean economy according to an export-oriented model.[23] The industry was heavily regulated by the Korean government, following the model of the government-regulated commercial sex industry that served US military personnel, and overwhelmingly controlled by men.[24] Sex-tour *kisaeng*, who worked under exploitative and physically demanding conditions, were encouraged to understand their participation in the sex industry as a form of national self-sacrifice.[25] They were required to be government certified and were regularly monitored, receiving mandatory health tests and lectures about how they were contributing to national growth.[26] While some Korean women knowingly entered the industry, others, migrating to Seoul from economically ravaged rural areas, were forcibly recruited through coercion, abduction, and debt bondage.[27] Women college students and progressive Christian women's groups in Korea began mobilizing to oppose the government-endorsed treatment of sex-tour *kisaeng*. They viewed the sex tours as a contemporary economic manifestation of Japanese colonial invasion, and the treatment of *kisaeng* as consistent with other forms of government-sponsored violence against Korean women, including their abduction and organized rape by Japanese troops during the colonial occupation of Korea and the sexual assault and rapes perpetrated by US troops in the country. These women's groups began protesting and reaching out to Japanese women to join their cause.[28]

A group of Japanese activists soon began to collaborate with these Korean activists.[29] In 1973, the Korea-Japan National Council of Christian Churches held a conference in Seoul to raise Japanese support for the Korean democracy movement.[30] The Korean Church Women United (KCWU), a core organization of progressive Christian women in Korea, put *kisaeng* tourism on the conference agenda.[31] In a newsletter circulating at the conference, Kim Yoon-ok, a member of the KCWU, published an appeal to the Japanese delegates in attendance, writing, "We wish to call your attention to the shameful fact that many Japanese tourists, whose numbers have been ceaselessly swelling, are making Korean women into 'sex slaves'" (*sei no dorei*).[32] Arguing that the circumstances of *kisaeng* parallels those of the Korean women who were forced to sexually serve Japanese occupying forces during the colonial period, the article implored Japanese delegates to join them in mobilizing against Japanese tourists' sexual exploitation of Korean women.

Kim's article caught the attention of Matsui Yayori, a foreign correspondent at the *Asahi Shimbun*, one of Japan's oldest and largest national newspapers, who attended the conference and was then involved in the budding *ribu* (short for *ūman ribu*, or "women's lib") movement in Japan.[33] In her speeches and writings, Matsui repeatedly describes her deep shame and horror upon reading Kim's appeal.[34] She had heard about the organized rape of Korean women by Japanese soldiers from her father, a progressive Christian minister who had been stationed in Manchuria during the Japanese occupation.[35] However, she had situated Japanese exploitation of Korean women in the past, associating it with historical wartime atrocities. Confronted with the ongoing nature of Japanese imperialism in Korea, Matsui began to see the *kisaeng* tours as an economic extension of Japan's treatment of Korean women during its colonial occupation of the country and as epitomizing "the ugly relationship between economic and sexual exploitation."[36]

When Matsui returned to Tokyo, she began to collaborate with other Japanese women to organize a movement to oppose Japanese men's sex tourism in Korea, helping coordinate twenty-two women's organizations into a network, the Women's Group Opposing *Kisaeng* Tourism.[37] In 1973, Ewha Womans University students had demonstrated against *kisaeng* tourism on campus and at Kimpo International Airport in Seoul, connecting the industry with the Park dictatorship's brutal regime.[38] In 1974, members of Matsui's network followed the Korean students' lead, distributing leaflets and organizing protests at Haneda Airport in Tokyo.[39] The leaflets accused Japanese men of being "arrogant" and part of an "assault force," and they urged them to engage in "sincere inner reflection of the past" and to "find a new way to live together with Asians."[40] The women also petitioned travel agents, corporations, and the Japanese government to put an end to these tours. Their efforts met with some success: in the following years, the numbers of Japanese men traveling to Korea dropped dramatically.[41] However, rather than tapering off, Japanese men's sex tourism shifted to other parts of Asia that had also formerly been occupied by Japan, such as the Philippines and Taiwan. Matsui soon began to support similar protests in these countries, collaborating with women's groups there.[42]

Matsui saw a "fundamental difference" between Japanese sex tours in Asia and "the usual type of relationship established between Japanese men and the prostitutes whose services they purchase[d] in Rome, New York, or in their own country."[43] For Matsui, this difference "could not be discussed in psychological or moral terms alone."[44] Rather, she insisted on the political-economically "exploitative structure of sex tourism."[45] Japanese tourists bought package tours through Japanese travel agencies, traveled on Japanese airlines, stayed at Japanese hotels, and patronized Japanese-owned businesses when abroad. This structure benefited the Japanese economy at the expense of workers in Asia. Matsui was also angered that women in Asia were bearing the brunt of such neo-imperialist endeavors and that the Japanese and Korean governments were complicit in the channeling of Japanese capital into nation-building projects in Korea that benefited first and foremost national elites. She began to reflect on her responsibility as a Japanese national for Japan's ongoing political-economic exploitation in the region, particularly of Korean women. She was determined to work with Korean women for change.

From that point, Matsui focused much of her professional life as both a journalist and an activist on reaching out to grassroots organizations in Asia, trying to learn from them about the violent legacies of Japanese imperialism and the contemporary effects of Japanese economic investment and tourism in the region. She endeavored to bring that knowledge back to Japan in order to change Japanese government and corporate policies and consumer practices.[46] Much of her work centered on personal and national accountability, including trying to understand how the lives of people in Japan were connected to those of people in other parts of Asia and how people in Asia saw Japan. Through her writing and organizing, she stressed Japanese women's personal and national responsibility toward women in Asia, and she encouraged critical self-reflection. Matsui wanted all Japanese citizens, including Japanese women, to recognize their complicity in this violence and work for structural change. Her self-questioning with a focus on change, and her encouraging of others to do the same, became a hallmark of her activism.[47]

Matsui's critical perspective grew in part out of personal reflections on her own life of marginality and privilege. Matsui's father, who grew up in imperial Japan, had been disowned from his family for converting to Christianity. He and Matsui's mother had both worked as ministers, and they had struggled to make ends meet for their family of eight, experiencing much discrimination on account of their religion. Matsui had also been bedridden with tuberculosis for years as a teenager, and thus grew up feeling isolated and separate from her peers. Despite not graduating from high school, Matsui passed the entrance exam for the Tokyo University of Foreign Studies. During college, she traveled to the United States and Europe, where she was revulsed by the flagrant racism that she both witnessed against African Americans and experienced as a Japanese woman. She later traveled through Asia, where she became increasingly aware of Japan's colonial legacies and economic presence in the region. She was deeply affected by the disparities of wealth that she witnessed across Asia, Japan, the United States, and western Europe.[48] She came to see Japan as replacing western Europe and the United States as colonial occupiers in Asia. She wrote of her travels through Asia: "I recognized my own ignorance of, and indifference to, our Asian neighbors. That Japan's economic development had been achieved through the sacrifice of other Asians was a fact of which I had been unaware, and it shamed me."[49]

In response, Matsui worked to build a regional, anticolonial and anticapitalist movement sensitive to racial, socioeconomic, national, and geographical inequalities among women.[50] In 1977, building on the momentum of the anti-sex-tourism movement, Matsui began working with Tomiyama Taeko and Goto Masako to establish the Asian Women's Association (AWA), a feminist organization focused on Japan's economic and political presence in Asia.[51] Matsui also worked to communicate the experiences of women in Asia to Anglophone audiences and to represent them in international circles; one of the AWA's objectives was to make the writings of Japanese activists accessible to a wider audience by translating them into English. In 1974, Matsui published an essay titled "Watashi wa naze kīsen kankō ni hantai suru no ka: Keizai shinryaku to sei shinryaku no kōzō o abaku" (Why do I oppose kisaeng tourism? Exposing the structure of sexual and economic aggression) in *Onna Erosu* (Woman Eros), a new Japanese feminist journal.[52] Femintern Press, which published *Onna Erosu*, also circulated an English translation of the essay as part of a broader effort to disseminate the work of Japanese feminists and thereby correct asymmetries of knowledge created by the dominance of English and Euro-American feminisms.[53]

These efforts proved fateful. Matsui's writing, along with the efforts of grassroots groups in Asia, began to attract the attention of feminists in Europe and the United States, including Kathleen Barry and Charlotte Bunch, who had also been receiving copies of the AWA's English-language newsletter *Asian Women's Liberation*.[54] Matsui was invited to present portions of her essay at the 1976 International Tribunal on Crimes against Women in Brussels, at which Barry was a speaker.[55] It was at this event that feminists in the United States and Europe began reframing the forms of abuse and exploitation that women's groups in Asia had understood as gendered and racialized manifestations of colonial and neocolonial economic policies as simply "man-made forms of women's oppression" and "crimes against women."[56] Ultimately, this shift in framing enabled feminists like Barry and Bunch to reduce the complex issues highlighted by Matsui and the AWA to singular matters of global patriarchy and violence against women.

The 1980s I: A Globalist Feminist Movement Encapsulates the Groundbreaking Approach of Women's Groups in Asia

As the first epigraph illustrates, Barry was impressed by the mobilizations of women's groups in Asia against *kisaeng* tourism. She cited Matsui's work as "ground-breaking."[57] However, even as Barry drew on these efforts, she ignored their nuanced focus, stripping out considerations of colonial, historical, and political-economic exploitation and instead characterizing the issues as a single fight against "female sexual slavery."[58]

In 1977, the recently established US-academic feminist journal *Frontiers: A Journal of Women's Studies* published an abridged and adapted English translation of Matsui's *Onna Erosu* essay under the title "Sexual Slavery in Korea." Interestingly, Matsui had not used the expression "sexual slavery" (e.g., *seiteki doreisei*) in her original 1974 essay. Rather, she twice used the phrase "*sei no dorei*" (sex slaves) to refer to *kisaeng*, echoing its use by women's groups in Korea.[59] Although the semantic shift is slight, it marked a significant one for feminist organizing on the issue. For Matsui and the Korean activists whom she cited, the term "*sei no dorei*" referred to a specific group of women in Korea who shared an experience akin to enslavement on account of colonial legacies and ongoing political-economic relations between Japan and Korea. However, for Barry, the expression "sexual slavery" denoted a singular worldwide system of violence that called for unified feminist organizing on a global basis.[60] In other words, by shifting attention away from Japanese men's treatment of Korean women as "*sei no dorei*" to focus on a system of "sexual slavery," Barry stripped out the cultural, national, and historical specificity of Matsui's argument to articulate a singular, abstract, deterritorialized global practice.[61]

This shift served Barry's conviction that all forms of prostitution were inherently degrading to women and that any woman doing such work was the victim of a universal form of cultural sadism that normalized all sexual exploitation of women.[62] With a global campaign in mind, she worked with feminists in the United States to try to get the issue on the agenda for the 1980 World Conference of the United Nations Decade for Women in Copenhagen. Although these efforts were initially resisted within the UN, Barry was able to put sufficient pressure on the NGO Forum planning committee to have a workshop scheduled at the last minute.[63] Barry then joined Charlotte Bunch, Shirley Castley, and others to organize the Global Feminist Workshop to Organize against Traffic in Women, Rotterdam, the Netherlands (Rotterdam Workshop), which was held on April 6–15, 1983. Bunch and Castley shared Barry's position that prostitution qua female sexual slavery was an incidence of "women's oppression in the world."[64] They understood the cause of this violence to be "patriarchal nationalism" on a global scale.[65] They viewed the workshop as an opportunity for establishing an international network that would focus on fighting what they viewed as a global form of oppression.[66]

Twenty-six women attended the meeting, including activists, religious figures, social service providers, academics, and lawyers from grassroots women's organizations in Africa, Australia, western Europe, the Middle East, Latin America, the United States, and Asia.[67] The proceedings of the workshop included the writings of many of these representatives, including an excerpted translation of Matsui's 1974 article.[68] As Bunch and Castley explained, "When we call for an international network, we are recognizing the need for a global perspective and for global cooperation because the problems we address cannot be solved in one country alone."[69]

Focused on building a movement based in shared experiences of women across the globe, the workshop overlooked racial, national, and class inequalities among women, including the call put forward by grassroots activists in Asia like Matsui for critical self-reflection and accountability by women in the Global North. The sidelining of these issues was not happenstance. Barry's prostitution-abolitionist position, which viewed prostitution as rooted in the global oppression of women, informed the erasure of class, geography, citizenship, and race in her analysis. These erasures in turn created tensions between women from the Global North and the Global South at the NGO Forum, which ran parallel to the 1980 UN conference in Copenhagen; feminists from the Global South had been insisting on attention being paid to political-economic differences and inequalities among women.[70]

In the face of these tensions, Barry and Bunch recognized that to organize women in different parts of the world into a single globally scaled movement, they needed a framework that bypassed these inequalities and differences. Bunch had noticed during the NGO Forum that, as she later relayed to feminist political scientists Margaret Keck and Kathryn Sikkink, "the workshops on issues related to violence against women were the most successful . . . they were the workshops where women did not divide along north-south lines, that women felt a sense of commonality and energy in the room, that there was a sense that we could do something to help each other."[71] "Violence against women" had not been part of the agenda for the first UN Decade for Women (1975–85); rather, it focused on "Equality, Development, and Peace."[72] However, after the Copenhagen conference, Bunch adopted this framework as a strategy for building a globally scaled international women's movement. Bunch recognized the need for feminists in the United States to learn from women in other countries and respond to their commitments and concerns.[73] However, her focus on building a single global movement overtook her commitment to doing so. Instead, Bunch pressed for the development of a "global consciousness."[74] She prioritized the need for a single global approach, writing, "We must understand and recognize the commonality of patriarchal oppression experienced by all women if we are to devise a common strategy to eradicate female sexual slavery."[75]

The novel framework of "violence against women" provided globalist feminists a platform to lobby national governments and international organizations for a single globalized solution for geographically, culturally, and political-economically disparate issues. However, the inclusion of prostitution in this new category should not be taken for granted. Sex work had not been understood in such terms when Barry was writing her book. For instance, at the 1976 International Tribunal on Crimes against Women, discussions of prostitution were placed alongside pornography as "sexual objectification of women" and separate from the category of "violence against women," which included discussion of "women battering," "forced incarceration in mental hospital and marriage," "castration of females: clitoridectomy, excision and infibulation," "violent repression of nonconforming girls," "torture of women for political ends," and "brutal treatment of women in prison."[76] Moreover, none of the three speakers that presented on prostitution at the event framed sex work as a form of violence in and of itself. Rather, Margo St. James, the founder of the sex workers' rights group COYOTE, began her testimony identifying as a "whore" and spoke about the oppression of streetwalkers by the police, the courts, and the "traditional sexist legal system."[77] In addition, Matsui Yayori spoke about Japanese men's sex tourism in Korea, tying it to imperialism and political-economic exploitation, and another Japanese feminist argued that Japanese women working in legal "Turkish baths" were not fairly compensated for their "physical labor," including intimate massages and other sexual services.[78] In both cases, prostitution was presented as a "deliberate" and "conscious choice" even if it involved forms of labor exploitation on account of "a lack of alternative job opportunities or extremely poorly paid ones."[79]

When Barry and Bunch adopted the category of "violence against women" and included prostitution in it, they shifted how sex work should be understood in relation to a wide set of geographically and culturally diverse practices. The category "violence against women" became a frame for linking a range of issues—sex work, discrimination against lesbian women, forced prostitution, wife battering, military rape, and prison sexual abuse, among others—and attributing all to a single root cause: "patriarchy."[80] As Bunch stated, "We understand that there exists ONE universal patriarchal oppression of women which takes different forms in different cultures and different regions."[81] The overarching "violence against women" framework then justified the call for a single global solution to address these multifarious practices, offering a "common advocacy position" for feminists across the globe.[82] Finally, by presenting "violence against women" as a violation of women's human rights, Barry and Bunch linked the globalist feminist movement to the then-growing international human rights movement. This framework ultimately shifted the focus of feminist organizing from a grassroots model to an institutional one.

By 1980, human rights had become a popular political cause with growing international cache and political pull among international organizations and national governments.[83] This new movement espoused an understanding of human rights based in a novel form of Anglo-American "liberal internationalism," which had begun to take shape during the middle of the twentieth century in the United States and western Europe.[84] During this time, a narrative of liberalism centered on Locke came to be seen as the West's constitutive ideology in ways that it had never before.[85] The new liberal internationalist ideal took as its central tenet the minimalist, institutionally manageable, and fatalist goals of securing individual freedoms and criminalizing atrocity, setting aside the welfarist focus on quality of life that informed earlier state-bound liberal traditions.[86] It foregrounded rights claims focused on individual freedom and criminal violation at the expense of entitlements to quality of life, including health, work, and shelter.

One organization at the forefront of this new movement was Amnesty International (AI). Founded in the UK in 1961 as a grassroots letter-writing campaign, AI had grown by the end of the 1970s into an international organization that boasted a membership of half a million people. The organization had found that it could exert influence in national and international arenas by gathering and distributing information about certain kinds of human rights abuses.[87] Over the course of the 1980s, AI pioneered a new form of institutionalized, expert-led political activism that modeled bureaucratic strategies for working across NGOs, governments, and international institutions to push for political and civil human rights.[88] As both journalists and politicians turned to AI for information on human rights abuses, it shifted from grassroots mobilization to a professionalized model that relied on experts who produced reports for national governments and international organizations.[89] Centered on influencing media, policy elites, and wealthy donors, this new form of information activism focused on processing information gathered through fact-finding and cultivating well-informed experts who could gain access to corridors of power, setting out to foster a reputation—and political capital—as the source of credible, high-quality research.[90]

Feminist groups around the world witnessed the increasing prominence of AI's campaigns. They started to view a human rights framework as a means for amplifying issues affecting women and extending the scope of human rights to better include women's experiences.[91] Bunch explained, "Promotion of human rights is a widely accepted goal and thus provides a useful framework for seeking redress of gender abuse."[92] Globalist feminists in the United States also began turning to institutional strategies pioneered by international human rights organizations such as AI—engaging in fundraising, producing reports, and lobbying governments and international organizations—as a model for building their global movement.[93] They had previously been mistrustful of what an organization like the UN could accomplish, criticizing the male domination of the institution and believing that the existing system was "patriarchal."[94] However, they recognized that a human rights framework would enable them to cultivate both domestic and international forms of institutional power for building a transnational feminist movement. In 1989, Bunch established the Center for Women's Global Leadership at Rutgers University. During the 1990s, the center would become the base from which Bunch would organize the Global Campaign for Women's Human Rights. Stopping violence against women, with human trafficking as a key instance of this violence, became a centerpiece of Bunch's fight to "change the world," and she turned her focus to UN events as venues for pressuring the agency and national governments on the issues.[95]

The 1980s II: Women's Groups in Asia Embrace an Alternative Understanding of Human Rights

The differences between US-based globalist feminists' approach and those of grassroots activists in other parts of the world became more pronounced as globalist feminists began formally lobbying international institutions. As feminists like Barry and Bunch shifted to an institutional human rights model to fight global patriarchy, activists in Asia, like Matsui, were expanding the focus of their work to address diverse forms of Japanese exploitation in Asia, including Japanese deforestation in the region, the displacement of Indigenous people on account of Japanese development, and economic exploitation by Japanese corporations. All were forms of Japanese political-economic domination in Asia that reflected a disregard for people's well-being in the region.[96]

In the 1980s, the AWA expanded its focus to include the struggles of Asian migrant women in Japan.[97] A growing number of migrant women from Asia, and especially the Philippines, Thailand, and Korea, had been coming to Japan to work in the sex industry. Other women from these and other countries had arranged marriages with Japanese men. An increasing number of these women needed assistance for issues ranging from domestic violence and labor exploitation to sexual abuse.[98] Recognizing the absence of resources in Japan to support foreign women who were exploited or abused, grassroots women's groups began establishing helplines and women's shelters, like Tahanan, to assist them.[99]

Many of these groups had also been influenced by calls for women's human rights. For instance, in 1986, after hearing discussions of women's human rights at the UN's 1985 Nairobi conference, the Japan Women's Christian Temperance Union established the HELP (House of Emergency of Love and Peace) Asian Women's Shelter, a *kakekomidera* (women's refuge center) to house both Japanese women fleeing from situations of domestic violence and Asian migrant women in distress.[100] Women's groups in Japan and the Philippines also participated in transnational organizing around the issue. Publications by Japanese women's groups included discussions of international women's rights meetings, and these activists also framed their work as a fight for women's human rights.[101] In 1988, GABRIELA, a large and active grassroots Filipina feminist coalition, launched the "Women's Rights Are Human Rights" campaign in the Philippines.[102]

Significantly, as suggested in the preface, women's groups in Asia invoked human rights in different ways and to different ends than did US-based globalist feminists. For instance, even when grassroots activists in Japan took up the call for women's human rights in the context of stopping human trafficking, they were not focused on fighting a universal global patriarchy so much as on developing more just ways for people in Japan to "liv(e) together with our Asian neighbors."[103] These activists were focused on addressing colonial legacies and racial discrimination and expanding the economic and social human rights of women in the region, such as the guarantee of fair wages and work conditions, adequate housing, and medical care. They posited that political-economic inequities between Japan and other parts of Asia, such as wage differentials, had motivated large numbers of women in the region to come to Japan.[104] Moreover, they understood the abuse and exploitation of these migrant women as manifestations of social *and* political-economic violence: products of specific forms of sexism and racism in Japan in the context of colonial legacies and contemporary political-economic inequalities.[105] When these activists adopted the framing of "human trafficking" to refer to the abuse and exploitation of women in the sex industry in Asia, they highlighted the structural violence that made the women vulnerable to abuse, including colonialism and neoliberal capitalism, which had enriched countries like Japan and the United States at the expense of women in the region.[106] For instance, as cited in the epigraph, the AWA's October 1989 issue of *Asian Women's Liberation* attributed the *jinshin baibai* (human trafficking) of migrant women from Asia in the Japanese sex industry to these women's location at the bottom of racial, sexual, and economic hierarchies in Japan; Japanese and American exploitation in Asia; and the complicity of Asian governments in sacrificing these women to national economic development.[107] In response, the AWA called for people in Japan to change their lives and thereby the unequal economic relations between Japan and Asia that made these migrant workers vulnerable to abuse.

In our interview, one longtime Japanese feminist who had been involved in the counter–human trafficking movement in Japan and Southeast Asia since the 1980s explained that for her, human rights meant working "to reduce the social inequality between the rich and the poor." She contrasted how she used the expression with how she saw it used in the West, explaining, "When I think of human rights in relation to crime prevention, that feels Western—the notion that bad things or people should be penalized, that one must protect the weak and the innocent." Instead, she took a position against capital accumulation by the few at the expense of the many, including acting responsibly to support coexistence not only among human beings but also with animals, plants, and other beings. She believed that efforts should not just focus on women and human trafficking per se but also include men and other migrant workers who were being exploited and abused—all were marginalized by current social and political-economic relations. Like Matsui, she also called for those privileged by current social and political-economic relations to consider their role in perpetuating this violence. She explained, "It is my belief that the people who are oppressed shouldn't be the ones that have to fight. It should be those who are oppressing others that need to change. Empowering oppressed individuals won't solve the problem. People who are oppressing must change to solve the issue."

Even in cases in which feminists in the Philippines argued against the notion that Filipina women in the sex industry "chose" this work, these feminists did so based on political-economic rationales. For instance, Aurora De Dios, a founding member of CATW–Asia Pacific (CATW-AP) in the Philippines, foregrounded the roles of "grinding poverty" and trade regimes established under the World Trade Organization (WTO) and the General Agreement on Tariffs and Trade in constraining possibilities for women in the Philippines, arguing that "where poverty is the major problem, there really is no choice."[108] De Dios was referring to the fact that the Philippines' accession to the WTO in December 1994 left many Filipina women with few viable options to support themselves and their families.[109] The country was flooded with industrially produced agricultural imports, destroying the livelihoods of small, independent rice and corn farmers; meanwhile, land devoted to staple crops was turned over to export agribusiness plantations and real estate enclaves, destroying the country's food sovereignty.[110] Fifty percent of people in the Philippines depend for subsistence on agriculture, and these shifts benefited local elites, transnational corporations, and foreign investors at their expense, leaving them desperate for any income-generating activity.[111] Under such conditions, De Dios did not believe that one could say that Filipina women were "choosing" sex work. De Dios also rejected the "tendency to universalize" among the white Western feminists that she met through her work with CATW.[112] She instead stressed how "varying cultural, religious, and political contexts necessitate differences in approaches and priorities" among feminists.[113] She argued the need for a more "layered" analysis of women's conditions that took "into account the diversity of each social milieu."[114]

These positions contrast strikingly with those of Bunch and Barry, who argued against framing any forms of prostitution, including Japanese sex tourism in Asia, as being shaped by intra-Asian racism or economic inequalities even when they recognized that racism and economic inequalities shaped women's lives. Indeed, Barry openly dismissed the suggestion that women in other parts of the world who faced immediate subsistence needs might prioritize their economic security over what she viewed as globalizable feminist demands for childcare centers, free and legal abortion, or equal pay for equal work.[115] She also publicly rejected calls for attention to racism by some political activists in the United States as an intimidation tactic that trivialized feminist claims and pandered to "guilt politics" and "white, liberal guilt."[116] For her, the fight against patriarchy, as she defined it, subsumed all others. Laura Kang has argued that the articulation by feminists in the United States of human trafficking as a form of violence against women was based in long-standing racist and imperialist power/knowledge regimes that "disqualified, segregated, and demoted 'Asian women' from both humanity and women."[117] These logics made the insights and demands of activists in Asia seem incoherent and inconsequential to activists like Barry and Bunch even as those activists' ideas and labor were foundational to Barry and Bunch's global project.

The 1990s: A Globalist Feminist Project Becomes a UN-Centered Global Human Rights Project

In the 1980s, feminists in the United States and Europe had been highly mistrustful of UN-sponsored efforts toward women's issues. They organized the 1976 International Tribunal on Crimes against Women in Brussels precisely because they did not subscribe to the UN's International Women's Year goals.[118] Initially, Barry endeavored to create "a feminist revolution" within the UN.[119] She viewed the institution as a "patriarchal minefield" governed by "both national and international male interests."[120] However, Barry and Bunch ultimately turned to the institution to launch a formal international response to the problem of violence against women, pursuing consultative status for CATW with the United Nations Economic and Social Council, which it received in 1989. Meanwhile, Bunch's Global Campaign for Women's Human Rights had recruited a coalition of more than nine hundred organizations to work for women's human rights around the world.[121] Framing violence against women as a human rights abuse, Bunch identified the 1993 UN World Conference on Human Rights in Vienna as a "natural vehicle" to forward this agenda.[122] Bunch planned a Global Tribunal on Violations of Women's Human Rights (the Global Tribunal) as part of the NGO Forum accompanying the conference.

The Global Tribunal organizers knew that the event would not lead to binding legal resolutions or the direct provision of resources to women in need. Rather, they viewed it as a vehicle to give vivid, visceral expression to an international audience of what they believed were violations of women's human rights: "prostitution, trafficking in women, sex tourism, rape, sex mutilation, incest, battery, forced marriages, dowry and bride wealth, pornography, and the torture of political prisoners."[123] In 1992, Bunch's Center for Women's Global Leadership put out a call for women to testify about these different forms of violation. From its organization to its execution, the Global Tribunal was meant to represent women from all corners of the world as joined in a common cause.

Held in Vienna on June 15, 1993, in a six-hundred-seat auditorium equipped with simultaneous translation, a large screen, and video and audio equipment, the Global Tribunal included testimony by thirty-three women from twenty-five countries and was attended by more than one thousand women. The organizers worked hard to ensure a "diversity of issues and regions, as well as of race, ethnicity, socio-economic class, sexual orientation and physical ability" in their selection of themes and cases, with the ultimate goal of illustrating their common roots in global patriarchy.[124] Speakers described their human rights abuses in five interconnected thematic sessions: Human Rights Abuse in the Family, War Crimes against Women, Violations of Women's Bodily Integrity, Socio-Economic Violations of Women's Human Rights, and Gender-Based Political Persecution and Discrimination.[125] The issue of forced prostitution qua human trafficking opened the third segment on Violations of Women's Bodily Integrity. For this presentation, Lin Lap Chew, a founder and director of the Dutch Foundation against Trafficking in Women (STV, Stichting Tegen Vrouwenhandel), recounted the testimony of a client of the organization, a Polish woman who had been sex trafficked into Germany.[126]

By drawing attention to women as rights claimants and sexual harm as a form of violence, the Global Tribunal marked a turning point for a new kind of global feminist human rights project in which the fight against human trafficking figured centrally.[127] This framing made direct forms of violence by private individuals identifiable as human rights abuses and holding them accountable a conceivable strategy for human rights work. Until that point, human rights organizations had tended to restrict themselves to instances in which centralized states, as opposed to private individuals, were perpetrators of abuses.[128] However, during the 1980s, the Inter-American Court of Human Rights had found that national governments could also be held accountable for failure to prosecute systematic abuses of human rights if this failure was rooted in discrimination along prohibited lines (gender, race, religion, able-bodiedness).[129] The Global Tribunal argued that discrimination against women, as a protected group on the basis of gender, was the root cause of these abuses.

Following the Vienna conference, the UN General Assembly adopted a declaration on violence against women (UN Declaration on the Elimination of Violence against Women) and endorsed the universality of human rights, a notion that had long been contentious within the organization. This recognition of violence against women as a universal human rights issue transformed how human rights could be legislated on both international and domestic levels.[130] Until that point, human rights had been overwhelmingly recognized as a narrow matter of government violation of civil and political liberties.[131] Now any form of direct violence demonstrably rooted in prohibited discriminations could arguably be recognized as a human rights violation. In other words, violent actions taken by one private citizen against others, such as domestic violence or forced prostitution, could be shown to follow patterns based on prohibited forms of gender discrimination and thus found to violate the internationally guaranteed right to equal protection under the law.[132] Although at first glance this framework appears to broaden protected categories of people for the purposes of fighting human trafficking, in practice it shifts attention away from structural causes of violence beyond gender discrimination. Moreover, if the Global Tribunal made violence against women vivid and palpable as a human rights violation on a global scale, it did so by reducing disparate experiences diversely shaped by intersecting inequalities to representative instances of a singular form of gender discrimination. As Bunch and Reilly state, the Global Tribunal testimonies were meant to be "symbolic of the situation of many thousands of women who could not be there."[133] The focus was on identifying analogy and connection. As Bunch and Reilly explained, the testimonies would foreground "patterns of gender-based human rights violations" on a global scale.[134] A Polish woman's testimony about her experience being sex trafficked to Germany was presented as the same kind of violation as an

African woman's discussion of female circumcision, a Korean woman speaking about her experience with Japanese military rape during World War II, and state-sanctioned violence against feminists and lesbians. The Global Tribunal offered a public statement of the similarity and generalizability of all forms of "violence against women" that could then be addressed as analogous human rights violations at a global scale. Under this umbrella, a range of geographically, culturally, and historically distinctive forms of violence were framed as a single issue in need of a global solution.

Following the Vienna conference, gender violence as a human rights violation, and human trafficking as a paradigmatic example of it, became a centerpiece of women's rights movements worldwide.[135] Two years later, the Beijing Platform for Action was adopted at the Fourth World Conference on Women in Beijing, calling for international action against human trafficking as a form of violence against women. The issue was soon on the agenda of national governments and the UN. International agencies and human rights organizations such as the ILO, the IOM, and Human Rights Watch were publishing research on the issue, and as discussed in chapter 2, government representatives in the United States, Argentina, Poland, and elsewhere began to raise the issue domestically.

However, if the Beijing call was the culmination of a vision of shared feminist globality articulated at the Rotterdam Workshop in 1983, it also marked the cracks that had emerged within it. At Rotterdam, Barry had refused to share the stage with Margot St. James, foreshadowing the break that would emerge between "prostitution-abolitionist feminists"—those who argue that all forms of prostitution should be considered human trafficking and thus abolished—and feminists who support sex workers' rights, including those who oppose "forced" prostitution while recognizing sex work as a legitimate form of labor.[136] Moreover, Barry's position on prostitution was not universally embraced by other feminists committed to fighting sexual and labor exploitation. Just after the 1993 World Conference on Human Rights in Vienna, the Foundation for Women, a feminist organization in Thailand, became the host for the Global Alliance against Traffic in Women (GAATW). GAATW positioned itself in opposition to CATW's prostitution-abolitionist stance by recognizing sex work as a legitimate form of labor, advocating for policies that could better defend the rights of all migrants and women—not only those of sex workers—and defining human trafficking to include a range of purposes aside from work in sex industries.[137] (As we will see in chapter 2, the Trafficking Protocol would gain qualified support from members of both camps.)

Divides persisted not only between GAATW and CATW but also within these groups as ideals of gender justice were shaped by local ethical regimes and values. For instance, the Roman Catholic Church has a strong influence in the Philippines, and pro-sex workers' rights groups like GAATW do not openly exist there.[138] After the Vienna conference, feminists in the Philippines founded CATW–Asia Pacific and developed their own autonomous program and initiatives in South, East, and Southeast Asia.[139] However, whereas the US-based CATW refuses to differentiate between prostitution in different parts of the world, CATW-AP insists on also taking into account how "sex, class, race, and nationality all combine in the oppression of women."[140] Many who joined the group had long worked with grassroots organizations providing services for women in the sex industry, most of whom were poor, uneducated women from rural communities who faced cultural pressures to sacrifice themselves to support their families. They opposed dominant representations put forward by the police and the Catholic Church of women in the sex industry as, respectively, criminals or immoral.[141] Instead, they encouraged these women to see themselves as survivors and focused on them as potential activists and self-advocates who could empower themselves through forms of testimony and political engagement.[142]

These Filipina feminists supported a global movement against human trafficking as a means both for holding legally accountable those who exploit and sexually abuse Filipina women and for drawing attention to the political-economic conditions that made these women vulnerable in the first place.[143] For them, prostitution had to be understood first and foremost as "an attempt to survive."[144] These feminists were also concerned that military base prostitution, sex tourism, and Filipina labor in overseas sex industries—all industries where women faced poor working conditions and often exploitation, as well as violence—were unacknowledged components of government strategies for bringing foreign capital into the Philippine economy, to the overwhelming benefit of elite men.

After the Vienna conference, the UN created positions for a high commissioner for human rights and a special rapporteur on violence against women.[145] Radhika Coomaraswamy, a Sri Lankan lawyer, was the first to hold the latter position. She highlighted the divides in the counter-trafficking movement in the conclusion of her 1997 report "on violence against women, its causes and consequences."[146] She explained, "Unfortunately, the women's movement is deeply divided over [the human trafficking] debate, preventing a concerted international effort to bring about necessary and important changes with regard to international standards."[147] The prospect of consensus was difficult to imagine until UN member-state governments stepped in with their own agendas. As we will see in chapter 2, when national governments decided to act, they did not focus on human trafficking as a matter of violence against women. Rather, they reframed the issue once again, this time as a matter of transnational organized crime, and placed it under the auspices of the UNODC as opposed to a human rights unit.[148]

The response of women's groups outside the United States to growing UN involvement in the issue was mixed. Some women's groups in the Global South had resisted joining the global network against human trafficking established after Rotterdam.[149] They wanted to focus on their own regions, and they were (presciently) concerned that the organization would be located in "the West" and controlled by Western feminists.[150] They also realized that if they used international and regional human rights bodies and machinery to advance their cause, they would need to privilege lawyers and legal expertise over everyday questions of prevention and treatment.[151]

For others, the UN was the lesser of two evils. A prominent Filipina activist shared in an interview that the UN was a more credible party for grassroots groups because we "don't trust the government, particularly around issues of migration, because the government has too much of a stake in migrants' remittances." She explained that feminist NGOs in the Philippines strategically viewed the UN as a tool for pressuring the Philippine government to adopt human rights protections "even if the UN is not doing anything practical on the ground." Others, like Matsui, wrote of the marginality of Asian women's groups within the global feminist movement on account of the dominance of English, noticing that women from China, Korea, and Japan were excluded from preparatory meetings for international conferences because they did not feel confident with their English language skills.[152] Even after women's rights activists in the Global South joined these efforts, some came to regret their embrace of a human rights framework.[153] Similarly, Matsui's discomfort with the economic privilege of UN participants led her to question its potential for forwarding a human rights project. For instance, in a 1989 publication, she reflected on her attendance at the 1975 UN International Women's Year conference in Mexico City, "In the luxuriously appointed conference hall, one after another, beautifully dressed women representatives of various governments made speeches on women's inequality. Outside the hall I saw a poor Mexican-Indian mother holding her baby wrapped in a shawl, begging in the rain. I cannot forget that poverty-stricken mother and child, they seemed to be questioning my life in an affluent society."[154] For Matsui, speeches held in luxuriously appointed conference halls would never be enough to address the violence of colonial legacies and wealth inequality. For that, real structural change was needed.

Conclusion

This chapter has offered an alternative genealogy of how fighting human trafficking came to be framed as a singular global endeavor in the last decades of the twentieth century by focusing on the erasure of the visions and contributions of women's groups in Asia. In doing so, it has illuminated some of the banalities that lace this global project. Lost in US-based feminists' ambitions to fight global patriarchy were the commitments of grassroots women's groups in Asia to address the imperialist legacies and contemporary political-economic relations that shape inequalities among women and nation-states. While these grassroots groups focused on establishing small direct-assistance organizations and building domestic and regional networks, globalist feminists endeavored to scale up to an expertise-centered form of activism so that they could "change the world," which they conceptualized as singularly shaped by a global patriarchy.

What counted as globality was also at stake in this process. For globalist feminists like Barry and Bunch, the global was a bureaucratic field for action that one aspired to redirect and ultimately control with a singular feminist agenda. In contrast, for activists like Matsui, the global was not a homogeneous realm amenable to a bureaucratic program. Rather, it was a fraught arena crosscut by difference and inequalities to which those in more privileged nations needed to be accountable in their everyday lives. Matsui recognized that on account of language, nationality, and race, women's groups in Asia would never be recognized as full participants of this global so long as international institutions were dominated by US and western European interests.

Barry and Bunch's single-minded endeavor succeeded in articulating human trafficking as a global problem that called for a single global solution. Consequently, grassroots activists in Japan and the Philippines who came out of these earlier movements, like those at Tahanan, would find themselves both inside and outside a global counter-trafficking project. Yet this would not be the end of the story. Feminists in the United States and western Europe would soon find their own global feminist agenda sidelined by another—that of more powerful national governments and international organizations. The UN's involvement in developing a globalized institutional project to fight human trafficking reframed the issue once again. In chapter 2, I explore the fate of global feminist aspirations as they were taken up within the international institutions that these feminists courted, ultimately resulting in the adoption of the Trafficking Protocol. What US-based feminists had identified as violence against women would be reframed as a generalizable problem of criminal violation enacted by individual private citizens against other private citizens. The call by grassroots women's groups in Asia for a movement centered on matters of structural violence and historically and geographically accountable forms of collective responsibility would be swept up into a bureaucratic campaign focused on carceral justice.

2

THE PROTOCOL'S COMPROMISES

Those who have experience of multilateral conventions know that the negotiating process tends to be a long and difficult one. Governments inevitably bring to the negotiations basic differences in juridical concepts, in the unique features of their legal systems, not to mention the variety of political positions growing out of their domestic and foreign policy needs. This accumulated legal and political baggage has then to be painfully sorted through in the quest for compromise.

—LUIGI LAURIOLA, "Address on the Elaboration of a Convention against Transnational Organized Crime"

In 2007, Aimee, Girlie, and I interviewed an established Filipina feminist activist— I will call her Gloria Reyes—at her home in Bacoor. At the time, Aimee was a staffer at the anti-human-trafficking NGO in the United States where I had been volunteering. She is Filipina American, and out of both personal and professional interest, she wanted to accompany me to the Philippines to learn about the work of grassroots NGOs there. Girlie is a former client of the grassroots NGO where Aimee and I were volunteering and conducting research in Metro Manila; after receiving assistance from the organization, Girlie had become involved in its activism, and she accompanied us to the interview.

Gloria lived in a small complex of unpainted, two-story concrete buildings flanked by an unpaved parking lot. As we walked to her unit, we passed dogs and cocks tied up on leashes and small patios fully enclosed by metal grilles. The front door of Gloria's apartment was open behind its metal security door, and as we approached, she came to greet us wearing a loose blue duster. She welcomed us down a dim, narrow hallway to her kitchen, which doubled as her office and was full of dusty bookshelves and a few elderly desktop computers. We sat at the kitchen table under a single naked lightbulb. The windowless walls were brightly colored and hung with batiks, a contrast to the dusky space. A couple of portable fans circulated the hot, thick air. For hours, we discussed the extensive history of Gloria's grassroots organizing as her "research assistants," as she called the two women, came and went, busy working on her organization's latest grant-funded research.

Gloria shared story after story of her political activism, which spanned more than three decades and began with protests during the first Marcos regime for which she had been imprisoned. She discussed her work marching against the US military bases in the Philippines and, after they were closed, providing direct assistance to women who had worked in the red-light districts around them and were now struggling to make ends meet. The conversation then turned to her involvement with the UN's counter-trafficking project. Prostitution is illegal in the Philippines, and Gloria told us that women working in the sex industry were commonly arrested, sexually exploited, and prosecuted by police, while men who purchased these women's sexual labor, and sometimes also exploited or abused them, were treated with impunity. Gloria had fought for decades for both international and domestic legislation to decriminalize prostitutes and instead punish traffickers, syndicates, and abusive police and customers. She also had participated in the drafting of the Philippines' Anti-trafficking in Persons Act of 2003.

I asked Gloria about her experience with the drafting process. On the one hand, she was proud that the Philippines was the first country in Asia to adopt legislation in line with the UN Protocol, and that the legislation addresses specific issues in the Philippines. For instance, unlike counter–human trafficking legislation in other countries, the Anti-trafficking in Persons Act has a provision that explicitly prohibits sex tourism.[1] On the other hand, Gloria recognized the compromises that she and other feminist activists had to make in the achievement of this legislation. She shared her distaste for political haggling, "You see, in lobbying, there are issues that are compromised, and that's why lobbying is not my cup of tea. I mean, I will do that, necessarily. But if you could arrange other work for me, I would probably say 'No . . . um, excuse me, can I not do the lobbying and instead *get to organize or teach or do training?' Because you know how much compromise you have to make for the bill."*

The successful drafting of any international agreement rests on participating parties finding a basis for consensus. To reach that consensus, UN member-state representatives and other invested actors must negotiate their discrepant interests and concede to a shared objective. Compromise is considered par for the course. As is clear from the epigraph and the preceding anecdote, the drafting of the UN Trafficking Protocol was no different in this regard. To establish a counter–human trafficking program, both UN member-state governments and feminist activists had to compromise. Yet how they understood these compromises could differ significantly. The word *compromise* can carry different valences. To compromise can mean to settle mutually, with all sides making equitable concessions; however, it can also mean to settle for less than what is desirable or necessary and consequently handicap the outcome. An agreement can be rendered through a compromise with which all parties are satisfied; however, it can also be *compromised*, impaired and diminished on account of unsatisfactory concessions.

This chapter examines the politics of compromise that underpinned the adoption of the Trafficking Protocol. It asks how the protocol's enabling compromises rested on UN member states' sidelining of structural issues and thus the stakes of these compromises for feminist activists who were unequally involved—and variously invested—in its drafting. Tracing a constellation of perspectives on the protocol's compromises, I illustrate the ways that geographical and political positioning mattered to how, and to what degree and ends, the Trafficking Protocol's adoption could be viewed as an accomplishment by those invested in it.

I build on the work of Janet Halley, who identifies "compromise," alongside "collaboration" and "complicity," as central features of what she calls "governance feminism," feminist endeavors to wield institutional power.[2] Highlighting the contradictions lacing such a project, Halley argues that governance feminism benefits those with institutional power at the expense of others. Studies of governance feminism have built on Halley's conceptualization to explore the successes and failures of such strategies, primarily in the Global North. For instance, Elizabeth Bernstein has demonstrated that the successes of feminists in shaping anti-human-trafficking policy in the United States have rested upon their move away from models of redistributive justice and toward an embrace of carceral models.[3] Hila Shamir has similarly considered how neo-abolitionist feminists in Israel successfully collaborated with the Israeli government to eliminate human trafficking by establishing a rescue and rehabilitation infrastructure alongside a crackdown on undocumented migration, both of which did little to address the needs of women vulnerable to trafficking.[4] These arguments illustrate some of the political consequences of feminist collaboration with government entities, asking feminists to pay self-conscious attention to the stakes of their involvement. However, these studies tend to focus on the experiences of feminists in prominent institutional positions. Less attention has been paid to how and why feminists on the margins of institutional power in the Global South, like Gloria Reyes, must engage with strategies of institutional governance to have their work funded and included. Relationships among feminist NGOs, centralized state governments, and international organizations are shaped by competing strategies, objectives, and ethical regimes.[5] They are also shaped by differentials of power and unequal access to resources, which grassroots feminist NGOs in the Global South must negotiate in order to secure continued funding and any political say.

I argue that the global counter–human trafficking project's banal neglect of structural violence can be tracked in part through the compromises that grassroots activists in the Global South have been expected to make to support the Trafficking Protocol's vision. Specifically, I consider how grassroots feminists in the Philippines understood their participation in the adoption of human trafficking legislation in relation to their positioning vis-à-vis powerful institutional bodies. As a legal instrument authored by powerful national government representatives, the Trafficking Protocol was an accomplishment not only of institutional coordination and consensus but also of dismissal and silencing. Whereas compromise was celebrated by UN member-state governments and officials as a strategy for successful consensus, for grassroots feminists like Gloria, the protocol's compromises signified the limitations of their political pull and the deferral of necessary political economic change. How can we understand the good of these agreements when such a politics of compromise necessarily lies at their heart?

In what follows, I first explore why UN member states decided to adopt a protocol on human trafficking after years of not addressing the issue, considering how compromise figured in the framing of the project by the UN Ad Hoc Committee on the Elaboration of a Convention against Transnational Organized Crime. I then turn to how feminists with institutional ties in the Global North made sense of the Trafficking Protocol before returning to the views of grassroots feminists in the Philippines, like Gloria Reyes, on the compromises lacing their participation.

The UN's endorsement of a campaign to fight human trafficking completed the transformation into a globalized institutional project of what had begun in Asia as a regional grassroots movement centered on questions of collective responsibility. The inclusion of the Trafficking Protocol as part of the UN's fight against transnational organized crime at once provided grounds for national governments to build consensus on the issue and sidelined the visions of not only grassroots activists in Asia but also US-based globalist feminists. I begin with a brief history of how the UN project on transnational organized crime came to include a supplemental focus on human trafficking.

During the 1990s, as globalist feminists lobbied international agencies and state governments to fight human trafficking, they garnered support from powerful actors in the United States, Europe, and elsewhere. The issue resonated with many national governments, which had begun to feel threatened by new developments of globalization that were increasing the transnational movement of people, goods, and funds. These governments worried that such developments empowered transnational organized-crime syndicates, which had established international smuggling rings. National governments' ability to regulate their borders, and thus maintain state sovereignty, was at stake.[6] In 1992, in response to the brutal assassination of an Italian judge by the Mafia, the Italian government proposed to the UN General Assembly that a high-level meeting be organized to discuss transnational organized crime.[7] The World Ministerial Conference on Organized Transnational Crime was held in Naples in 1994, drawing more than two thousand delegates and participants from 142 states. Out of it came a proposal to develop a UN convention to address trafficking in arms and drugs.[8] By 1998, the UN Commission on Crime Prevention and Criminal Justice (CCPCJ) and the Economic and Social Council had recommended that the General Assembly adopt a resolution to form the basis for high-level diplomatic negotiations aimed at a "comprehensive international convention against transnational organized crime."[9]

Initially, addressing human trafficking was not part of the agenda. However, a proposal came forward during preparatory meetings to the convention for supplemental protocols that could provide a model for domestic criminal legislation regarding migration. Argentina was the first country to raise the issue of human trafficking. After the 1991 Ley de Convertibilidad de la Moneda had established parity between the Argentine peso and the US dollar, the country had become an attractive destination for foreign labor migrants. Large numbers of women from the Dominican Republic, followed by those from Paraguay and Brazil, began working in the sex industry, prompting concerns about sex trafficking.[10] In the late 1990s, as the Argentine economy fell into a deep decline, these concerns spread to include Argentine women being recruiting within and outside the country.[11] Alarmed by this prospect, the Argentine government officially proposed that a protocol on human trafficking be added to the Convention against Transnational Organized Crime. Italy, Austria, and the United States then joined Argentina, submitting two additional draft proposals in 1999 to serve as a basis for a supplementary protocol on human trafficking.[12]

The content and foci of the three draft proposals varied. Argentina's draft proposal focused overwhelmingly on sex trafficking. Referring exclusively to the "international trafficking in women and children," it explained that "these two categories of person are more vulnerable than men to the risk of being victims of certain types of illicit acts."[13] It advocated for criminalizing all forms of prostitution, "even with the consent of that person," as well as sex tourism and pornography.[14] Although the proposal's articles mentioned slavery, servitude, and forced and compulsory labor more broadly, the draft on the whole foregrounded sexual exploitation as human trafficking.

A second draft proposal titled "Draft Elements for an International Legal Instrument against Illegal Trafficking and Transport of Migrants" was submitted jointly by Italy and Austria. Demographic shifts within Europe during the 1990s had made western European governments concerned about sex trafficking. As Jennifer Suchland explains, the opening of borders of the former Eastern bloc and USSR had resulted in a growing number of women from eastern Europe coming to work in the sex industry in the region.[15] Until that point, women of color from Africa, Asia, and Latin America had primarily done such work, and the governments had not been moved to act.[16] However, western European governments shifted their position as a dramatic and noticeable increase of white eastern Europeans began working as prostitutes. International reports about eastern European women being forced into this work started circulating. In 1995, the IOM published an influential report arguing that the "trafficking in women from Central and Eastern European countries is increasing at an alarming rate."[17] The report offered a romantic view of white women trafficked from these countries, emphasizing the role that violent and well-organized criminal groups from eastern Europe played in this trend. In the report, post-Soviet women were represented as beautiful, smart but ill-informed, sexually naive, and vulnerable to exploitation; they were contrasted with criminally culpable "smuggled migrants" who required deportation. Human trafficking was framed as an aberrant criminal practice growing out of the failures of socialism rather than a result of the inequalities built into a global capitalist order. Such narratives came to dominate representations of human trafficking among policymakers in western Europe and inspired many to support drafting a UN protocol to address it.[18]

However, if eastern European women had been presented as innocent victims in official reports in western Europe, the draft proposal submitted by Italy and Austria did not propose strategies to address the harm experienced by these victims or any need to assist or protect them. Rather, it focused primarily on criminalizing those who facilitated the entry of undocumented migrants into the region. It targeted those who arranged, "in an organized manner, the illegal entry of a person into another State of which the latter person is not a national or not a permanent resident."[19] Although the draft was initially proposed as part of the development of a protocol on human trafficking, its focus was ultimately incorporated into the Migrant Smuggling Protocol.[20]

The third draft proposal came from the United States. During the 1990s, bipartisan consensus had been growing in the US Congress regarding human trafficking.[21] Then US first lady Hillary Clinton had taken an interest in the issue during her travels in Asia, where she had met with grassroots NGOs. She subsequently stressed the need for addressing human trafficking both at the Beijing conference and to her husband, then president Bill Clinton, whose administration laid the groundwork for the development of the Trafficking Victims Protection Act (TVPA) and US support of the Trafficking Protocol.[22] In 1995, on the eve of the Beijing conference, President Clinton established an Interagency Council on Women, appointing the First Lady honorary chair and placing human trafficking on the council's agenda. In the years that followed, US legislators began to prioritize the issue. Cases of migrants who had been tricked or coerced into grossly exploitative jobs, including prostitution, domestic servitude, and agricultural and garment sweatshop work, began to appear in US news reports. In 1997, a massage parlor near the US Capitol was exposed as having employed enslaved Russian and Ukrainian women, who were simply deported after a police raid. Occurring so close to the seat of federal government, the case caught the attention of legislators on both sides of the political aisle and gave momentum to the drafting of domestic legislation against human trafficking. In 1998, President Clinton asked the Council on Women, together with Attorney General Janet Reno, to address the issue. The result was the development of the 3Ps framework of preventing trafficking, protecting victims, and prosecuting traffickers, which has since figured prominently in both the TVPA and global efforts.[23]

At the time, as part of a broader strategy for abolishing prostitution in the United States, a coalition of evangelical Christians and prostitution-abolitionist feminist groups (such as CATW) had been lobbying government representatives to identify all forms of sex work as human trafficking.[24] However, the Clinton administration resisted criminalizing all forms of prostitution even while it declined to support legalizing it.[25] The administration also rejected arguments that counter–human trafficking efforts should focus primarily or exclusively on the sex trade, maintaining that other forms of exploitation, such as sweatshop labor and exploitative domestic servitude, should be included as violations in both the US TVPA and the UN Trafficking Protocol.[26]

In line with the administration's position, the US draft proposal expanded the class of potential trafficking victims entitled to protection.[27] For instance, whereas Argentina's draft referred only to women and children as potential victims, item (h) of the US draft preamble argued for an "international instrument against trafficking in *persons*, particularly women and children."[28] This phrasing suggested that men, not only women and children, could be trafficked and thus that trafficking might not be restricted to sexual exploitation but could include other forms of labor exploitation and abuse. Moreover, unlike the Argentine draft proposal, the US draft proposal pointedly resisted labeling all sex work as human trafficking. The US proposal also went further in advocating for victim assistance than did the Argentinian draft, which proposed simply "guaranteeing victims appropriate . . . assistance whenever State Parties deem it necessary" and promoting "the establishment of programmes . . . for temporary housing, psychological, medical and legal support and the safe return of the victims to their country of origin in cases where not arranged by that country."[29] Instead, the Clinton administration argued that human trafficking was a human rights violation and that victims were entitled to protection.[30] Correspondingly, the US draft proposal suggested providing victims compensation for damages, restitution from offenders, appropriate housing, and education and care for detained children.[31] It also advocated for immigration laws that permitted trafficking victims to remain in their destination country, either temporarily or permanently.[32]

After two years of negotiation among diplomatic teams in Vienna, incorporating recommendations of feminist organizations, input from sex workers' rights groups, and formal commentary by human and labor rights agencies, two migration-related supplementary protocols were drafted for the Convention against Transnational Organized Crime: one on migrant trafficking and the other on migrant smuggling.[33] As discussed in chapter 3, the Trafficking Protocol created a special category of migrants believed to be entitled to humanitarian assistance on account of the direct violence they had experienced as victims of human trafficking, while the Protocol against the Smuggling of Migrants by Land, Sea and Air (hereafter Migrant Smuggling Protocol) covered smuggled migrants, who would be criminalized alongside both smugglers and human traffickers. To maximize support, the definition of human trafficking adopted by the Trafficking Protocol (cited in the next section) endeavored to resolve differences among the different draft proposals, member-state governments, and interest groups. Following the US draft proposal, it maintained a broader class of potential victims, which included men and those who had been trafficked for all forms of labor exploitation, and it vaguely referred to the "exploitation of prostitution," opening the possibilities that one could engage in sex work without being a trafficking victim.[34] However, in line with the Argentine proposal, forms of victim protection and assistance were left to the discretion of national governments; the guarantees for victim assistance, compensation, and residency permission in the US draft proposal were ultimately not included in the Trafficking Protocol.

Together, the Trafficking and Migrant Smuggling Protocols garnered the support of UN member states by promising to deter unregulated migration and empower national governments in controlling their borders.[35] The notion that trafficking was a problem of transnational organized crime not only made law enforcement and prosecution a viable response but also supported the goal of developing a single global campaign to fight it. The adopted Trafficking Protocol also made consent immaterial to whether a person could be identified as trafficked, instead listing the effort to "achieve the consent of a person" through force or coercion as constitutive of the crime.[36]

In addition to providing the opportunity for the drafting of the Trafficking Protocol, the development of the Convention against Transnational Organized Crime provided the occasion for the UNODC to launch a three-year Global Programme against Trafficking in Human Beings, which aimed to create a "global inventory of best practices used in addressing organized criminal involvement in smuggling and trafficking."[37] Although one premise of the Trafficking Protocol was the protection of human rights, the understanding of human rights that it adopted was based in dominant liberal internationalist ideals, which limited rights protections to those of individual freedom and bare life against criminal violation.[38] The oversight of the UN's counter–human trafficking campaign by the UN Crime Program, as opposed to a unit focused on human rights or racism, helped shape this agenda.[39] Between the 1950s and the 1990s, the UN's Crime Program had gone from being expert led and focused on juvenile delinquency and correctional treatment to being government driven and centered on transnational crime and crime prevention.[40] This shift was in large part a response to newly independent countries, which joined the UN in increasing numbers in the 1950s and 1960s and pushed the General Assembly to take a more globalized approach that addressed the links between postcolonialism, underdevelopment, and crime.[41] During the 1980s and 1990s, as national governments began to see transnational crime as a national security issue, these newly independent states again pressed for a shift away from a soft-law approach in the Crime Program toward a more direct technical assistance and policy and action-oriented one.[42] Ultimately, the 1988 Drug Convention became a model for the program's shift toward hard law during the 1990s, when the Convention against Transnational Organized Crime and the Trafficking Protocol were being drafted under the oversight of the CCPCJ, which by then prioritized uniform criminal justice frameworks and technical models for globalizing them.[43]

Initiated in 1999, the UNODC's Global Programme against Trafficking in Human Beings focused on collecting data and establishing best practices with the ultimate goal of developing an international instrument that could facilitate forms of technical cooperation among governments, NGOs, and other international institutions and thereby create a global strategy for adoption by the international community.[44] Indeed, the stated goal for the three-year program was "a global strategy against human smuggling and trafficking" that would be "formulated in close consultation with relevant national and international organisations and experts, and presented for adoption by the international community at a global forum."[45] In November 1999, the program published its report, which stressed the need for "regional and/or international cooperation" among the international community to address the increase of "smuggling and trafficking of human beings" that had resulted from "the processes of globalisation."[46] Once the Trafficking Protocol was adopted the following year, the program set the stage for a global project centered around it, establishing the basis for the UN Trafficking Protocol to turn the good of fighting human trafficking into a mandate to develop a global institutional protocol for national governments to carry out.

The Accomplishment of Abstract and Technical Compromises

The United Nations Protocol to Prevent, Suppress and Punish Trafficking in Persons, Especially Women and Children, was formally adopted as a supplement to the UN Convention against Transnational Organized Crime at the 62nd Plenary Meeting of the 55th Session of the United Nations General Assembly, which was held at UN headquarters in New York City on the morning of November 15, 2000. Although the meeting occurred several years before I began my research for this book, an official video recording of the event is publicly viewable on UN Web TV, and a full transcript of the proceedings is also online.[47]

The online footage begins with a wide shot of the cavernous UN General Assembly Hall, which at nineteen thousand square feet has a seating capacity of eighteen hundred. The room is nearly vacant as the chair of the General Assembly, Harri Holkeri of Finland, calls the meeting to order. As he begins speaking, the camera catches a few people in professional attire filing across the forest-green carpet and taking seats in the rows of empty tables facing the large, two-tiered speakers' rostrum where Holkeri is perched on the top level. Wearing a navy-blue business suit, Holkeri is seated behind a wide wooden table flanked with green marble in front of a soaring gold wall panel featuring the UN logo. He reads his opening remarks in monotone English, reciting the day's topic—"Agenda Item 105: Crime Prevention and Criminal Justice"—and inventorying all the meetings and documents constituting its procedural background. Finally, without raising his eyes, he introduces Luigi Lauriola, Italy's UN ambassador and chairman of the Ad Hoc Committee on the Elaboration of a Convention against Transnational Organized Crime, who will present the Ad Hoc Committee's report.

Lauriola, who is wearing a black business suit, takes his position on the rostrum at a green marble podium below Holkeri's table. Glancing out into the still nearly empty meeting hall, he reads his prepared comments into two symmetrically placed microphones. He summarizes the history of the Ad Hoc Committee, mechanically listing the meetings and initiatives that preceded its 1998 formation. He acknowledges the number of countries that sent delegates to their meetings (125) and the participation of NGOs and other international organizations in the drafting process.

Lauriola then looks out into the hall, and his tone becomes impassioned. He first stresses the challenges that the multinational committee members faced in the "ongoing pursuit of consensus" that the protocol's drafting involved. He explains that "basic differences" in states' juridical concepts, legal systems, and domestic and foreign policy positions all had "to be painfully sorted through in the quest for compromise." He then credits the relatively quick and successful conclusion of the negotiating process to "an emerging political will, driven by newspaper headlines and public opinion . . . to search for a global response to organized crime on a global level." Finally, he concedes that although the "convention provides a framework and the tools for better international cooperation . . . what will be critical will be its implementation." He ends his speech urging, "Now it is up to you to develop and augment effective tools to give a global response to this global scourge."[48]

At first glance, the UN General Assembly Hall and Gloria Reyes's apartment seem worlds apart. However, the two are intimately—if asymmetrically—connected through the Trafficking Protocol. The fact that few were present to witness its formal adoption was immaterial to the protocol's enactment. What mattered, and what the protocol marked, was that states had successfully, if "painfully," come to a consensus regarding a multilateral treaty on human trafficking.

As Lauriola suggested, because an international legal agreement is an agreement among sovereign states, reaching this compromise required technical reconciliation among juridical differences and national policy interests. In other words, it meant identifying the lowest common denominator among centralized states' juridical concepts, legal systems, and domestic and foreign policy positions to appeal to the maximum number of potential signatories; the legal agreement is the compromise. As Lauriola explained, the consensus reached in the Trafficking Protocol was that a global response to human trafficking, as the protocol defined it, was necessary and that a set of legal norms for reaching this objective should be specified.

This compromise was reached in three interrelated ways. First, the specifics of how the agreement would be implemented were excluded from consideration. The good to which the protocol aspired was the adoption of a new legal instrument that declared *the intention* to fight a specified crime, protect victims of it, and prevent the crime from occurring again. However, what this enactment would entail on a day-to-day basis and how these practices would succeed remained unspecified and deferred. Moreover, the agreement not only deferred the everyday details of the protocol's enactment but also displaced onto others the responsibility for working them out. As Lauriola succinctly put it: "Now it is up to you." The actual work of putting the Trafficking Protocol into practice was beyond the scope of the Ad Hoc Committee and the protocol text. As we will see in later chapters, the implementation details would be spelled out in subsequent guidebooks and ultimately left to national governments' discretion. The Ad Hoc Committee's goal was *formal* consensus—that is, a consensus of convention and form on which to draft the text.[49] Both the means and the end of the Trafficking Protocol was establishing member-state consensus that *something* should be done on a global scale to stop human trafficking. Doing good per the protocol meant reaching consensus via compromise on a global scale. The very globality of the agreement defined its accomplishment.

Second, to encourage as many member states as possible to adopt and ratify the protocol, the definition of human trafficking included in the text was designed to be as flexible and as inclusive as possible.[50] This definition was spelled out in Article 3, paragraph (a):

The recruitment, transportation, transfer, harbouring or receipt of persons, by means of the threat or use of force or other forms of coercion, of abduction, of fraud, of deception, of the abuse of power or of a position of vulnerability or of the giving or receiving of payments or benefits to achieve the consent of a person having control over another person, for the purpose of exploitation. Exploitation shall include, at a minimum, the exploitation of the prostitution of others or other forms of sexual exploitation, forced labour or services, slavery or practices similar to slavery, servitude or the removal of organs.[51]

Following the US draft proposal, this definition of human trafficking expanded the categories of violence first identified by globalist feminists to include a range of practices that could affect people of all genders, implicitly rejecting the notion that human trafficking is exclusively a form of violence against women. Building on pressure from human rights activists, labor rights groups, and migrants rights NGOs, the Trafficking Protocol definition also broadened the prostitution-abolitionist focus on sexual slavery that had initially inspired globalist feminists by including the phrase "exploitation of the prostitution of others," thereby suggesting that prostitution did not in and of itself necessarily involve human trafficking. The exhaustive inclusion in the definition of so many forms of exploitation and violence gives an impression of both comprehensiveness and specificity. However, as will become clear in the chapters that follow, what reads as capacious enumeration in practice functions as ambiguous and abstract criteria, leaving the practice of victim identification to national government discretion. Under the UN protocol, what trafficked persons share is not gender, political economic vulnerability, or experiences of racial discrimination but circumscribed forms of criminal victimization. Forms of violation and abuse ranging from the exploitation of domestic workers in the Middle East to the indenture of agricultural laborers in the United States to forced prostitution in Japan are collapsed into a single type of criminal violence so that a single solution for addressing them—the Trafficking Protocol—can be claimed. The cultural, historical, geographical, and political economic contexts that allow for these different forms of exploitation and abuse fall outside the protocol's definition. Moreover, the vague terms for victim protection meant that national governments needed only to temporarily protect victims' bare life to comply with the protocol; as we will see, their quality of life or longer-term survival would remain unaddressed.

Even though the Trafficking Protocol did not take the shape envisioned by globalist feminists or women's groups in Asia—drafted under the auspices of fighting transnational organized crime, it was not even an official human rights instrument—many feminists found themselves rallying behind it. These feminists rationalized that even if activists and national governments could not agree among themselves on a definition of human trafficking, a single definition of the term in an international agreement would at the very least provide formal validation that certain forms of abuse and exploitation were human rights violations. This consensus regarding the utility of a single international definition led them to compromise and support it despite what that definition included. Their support, however, did not mean that they did not harbor reservations. In the remainder of this chapter, I consider why differently positioned feminists embraced the Trafficking Protocol and the different kinds of compromises that it demanded of them.

Practical Considerations for a Deeply Divided Movement

The desire for a single definition of human trafficking codified in international law ultimately led many prominent human rights and feminist activists in the Global North to support the Trafficking Protocol. Although, as we have seen, groups of these feminists disagreed fiercely among themselves as to how human trafficking should be defined and approached—for instance, whether sex trafficking included all forms of prostitution or only certain cases of what they variably defined as "forced prostitution"—many believed that the practical need for a single global definition of human trafficking overrode these concerns.[52] For these feminists, the Trafficking Protocol's accomplishment was twofold. First, it stood as public acknowledgment by the UN General Assembly that certain practices were forms of violence and should no longer be tolerated or condoned; a law on the books was evidence of progress, even if that law was compromised. Second, feminists who had supported a global solution for human trafficking believed that a formal definition would allow data to be collected and future programs to be developed on a global scale. Their support was premised on the fact that the specifics would be worked out later; they hoped to have a say in the forms these took.

Consider the support offered by Mary Robinson, who was then the UN high commissioner for human rights. As the first female president of Ireland, Robinson had been popular for her justice-oriented work on immigrants', women's, and lesbian and gay rights. She later expressed support for including intersectional feminist perspectives in the UN policy.[53] Robinson had been appointed by then secretary-general Kofi Annan as part of his efforts to reform the UN and more fully integrate human rights into the organization. On June 1, 1999,

Robinson distributed to the General Assembly an "Informal Note" of roughly five pages to be considered by the Ad Hoc Committee in their drafting of the Trafficking Protocol.[54] In the note, Robinson ultimately expressed support for the universal reach of the proposed document and the fact that it would establish a single definition of human trafficking to be applied across the globe. She explained, "There is as yet no universal instrument that addresses all aspects of trafficking in persons. In fact, 'trafficking' has never been precisely defined in international law and the most recent international instrument dealing with trafficking and related issues is now more than half a century old."[55] She shared that she was "greatly encouraged" by its development and the "potential significance" of a protocol on human trafficking.[56]

Robinson was not alone among feminists based in the United States and western Europe who supported the protocol's defining of human trafficking. I struggled to find direct commentary on the Trafficking Protocol from either Charlotte Bunch or Kathleen Barry, save for a brief mention by Bunch celebrating it as an example of how the UN has taken up women's rights issues.[57] Bunch mentioned the protocol in the context of arguing for the need to continue to pursue "women's equality" through international bodies and push for more representation of "women" within the UN.[58] However, the CATW and other feminists who have carried forward the prostitution-abolitionist agenda set out at the Rotterdam Workshop have celebrated their success in making "consent" irrelevant in the protocol's definition of human trafficking, leaving open the possibility that any sex worker could be identified as a trafficking victim.[59] On this basis, they have identified the Trafficking Protocol as a step forward while arguing that work remains to ensure that human trafficking is "interpreted correctly."[60] These feminists have criticized how sex workers' rights and human rights–centered groups worked to restrict the definition of sex trafficking in the protocol to "forced" prostitution.[61] They have argued for building on the protocol with a carceral, "perpetrator-focused approach" that targets and penalizes men who purchase sexual labor, looking to Sweden's laws against buying sexual services as a model and contrasting it with the Clinton administration's victim-centered approach.[62]

Meanwhile, Lin Chew, a founding member of both GAATW and the grass-roots Foundation against Trafficking in Women in the Netherlands (who, if you recall, had presented the testimony on human trafficking at the Global Tribunal in Vienna), stressed the importance of a single definition on the grounds that it would facilitate legislation: "The Trafficking Protocol is a big step forward in that it offers a comprehensive description of what constitutes the crime of trafficking, so that prosecution of the crime is facilitated, and states which have signed the protocol can use it as a basis to enact national legislation to combat trafficking."[63]

The year after the adoption of the UN Trafficking Protocol, Anne Gallagher, who served as adviser on trafficking to Mary Robinson and manager of OHCHR's Anti-trafficking Programme while the UN protocol was being drafted, concluded that "the development of agreed definitions of trafficking and migrant smuggling is a true breakthrough. . . . By incorporating a common understanding of trafficking and migrant smuggling into national legislation, state parties will be able to cooperate and collaborate more effectively than ever before."[64] Gallagher, like other feminists, hoped that the existence of a protocol would offer openings for their future say.[65]

Some feminists in the Global North also supported a single international definition of human trafficking because they believed that it would facilitate the institutional development of indicators and data collection on trafficking victims at a global scale. Gallagher noted as much in her piece, writing, "Common definitions will also assist in the much-needed development of indicators and uniform data collection processes."[66] By establishing a formal definition of human trafficking and then collecting data on it, the protocol promised to recognize human trafficking as a global phenomenon for states to measure and institutionally address.

However, if these feminists were ultimately supportive and hopeful that the UN Trafficking Protocol was formally recognizing human trafficking as a human rights violation, they also expressed some reservations about the ways that the protocol had been drafted. For instance, in a later essay, Gallagher prefaced her support of the UN protocol by acknowledging some of its shortcomings:

> The Trafficking Protocol makes an easy target for attack. Its origins lie in an attempt to control a particularly exploitative form of migration that was challenging the ability of States to control their own borders. Its parent instrument is a framework agreement to address transnational organised crime. While paying fleeting attention to the rights of trafficked persons, the Protocol, with its emphasis on criminalisation and border protection is nowhere near being a human rights treaty. On top of all that it does not even have a credible enforcement mechanism, allowing states parties wide latitude in interpreting and applying their obligations.[67]

Yet Gallagher saw these problems as temporary and manageable. The compromise for her was accepting a delay in realizing one's full objectives, which would eventually be reconciled. Gallagher had already explained that "these seemingly insurmountable flaws" did not stop the protocol from serving an important role insofar as it "provided the impetus and template for a series of legal and political developments that, over time, have served to ameliorate some of its greatest weaknesses, including the lack of human rights protections and of a credible oversight mechanism."[68]

Others had deeper concerns, including Mary Robinson, who expressed reservations that the Trafficking Protocol was compromising its support for human rights. In her "Informal Note," Robinson suggested that care be taken to ensure "that new international instruments do not conflict with or otherwise undermine international human rights law."[69] Her primary concern was that "the instruments under development are not human rights treaties but more in the nature of transnational cooperation agreements with a particular focus on organized crime."[70] She proposed the addition of specific references, provisions, and language affirming signatories' commitments to maintaining and protecting the human rights of not only those recognized as victims of trafficking but also, and more broadly, migrant workers and those seeking refugee status who might otherwise fall under the smuggling protocol. For instance, in section B, item 3, she writes, "Irregular or illegal migrants who are detained by the receiving State have a recognized right under international law to be treated with humanity and dignity—both before and after a determination is made concerning the lawfulness of their detention."[71] Robinson found the protocol draft inadequate in this regard. She advocated for a "direct and specific reference" in the protocols to this end.[72]

Robinson also suggested expanding the definition of trafficking to include broader understandings of forced labor. She noted, "While the draft definition does recognize that trafficking takes place for reasons beyond forced prostitution (reference to 'sexual exploitation'), it limits other purposes of trafficking to 'forced labour.' A preferable and more accurate description of purposes would include reference to forced labour and/or bonded labour and/or servitude."[73] Later in the document, Robinson argued for strengthening the "victim protection and assistance" provisions of the draft protocol.[74] She argued for including more precise provisions to obligate state parties to provide for the "physical, psychological and social recovery of victims of trafficking" and the possibilities of "obtaining remedies, including compensation."[75] She explained that to meet "basic international human rights standards" they needed to make specific reference to the provision of "adequate housing, appropriate health care and other necessary support facilities."[76] Robinson wanted more resources allocated for migrants who had suffered. As explained later in the book, Robinson eventually became disillusioned with the UN and left the organization; however, at the time, she limited her suggestions to a textual, institutional solution. She, like many others, supported the protocol, believing that it marked an accomplishment, even if that accomplishment was insufficiently robust and paid inadequate attention to human rights.[77]

Leveraging Compromised Legislation

Grassroots activists in the Philippines who worked on domestic anti-human-trafficking legislation in line with the Trafficking Protocol, like Gloria Reyes, similarly recognized the limitations of their political leverage and opted to compromise and accept proposed legislation with the hope that they could later make amendments to it and, in the meantime, better access resources for direct assistance and everyday overhead. As Gloria explained during our interview, she and other feminists in the Philippines engaged in compromises around legislation "because we always think that we can amend the bill at some point in time. It's a very practical consideration. . . . For as long as there is a bill, we can at least bring a case to court. Before there was nothing you could hold on to. So, these are flawed bills because they are not the originals that we drafted." Gloria's reasoning was eminently pragmatic. For her, the good of the protocol was that it cracked open a door. She was fully aware that she was not getting what she wanted—the passed legislation was "flawed"—but she had little choice but to accept what the government offered and use it as an in to push for more by bringing cases to court. The recognition that legislation is part of a broader political process, and thus presents the possibility for future refinement and change, was par for the course for grassroots activists like Gloria and part of how they rationalized their support of the protocol.

At the same time, support for the protocol and subsequent domestic legislation on human trafficking did not preclude Gloria's cynicism about its enactment. In our interview, she offered a jaded view: "Between the law and its implementation there is a lot to be said." As an illustration, she offered a somewhat different take than Gallagher's on the development of indicators and uniform data collection that the Trafficking Protocol enabled.

As we sat in Gloria's kitchen, she recalled how in the early years after the UN protocol was adopted, U.S. government officials would approach her and other Filipina activists at international conferences, requesting "baseline data" regarding the number of Philippine nationals being trafficked to the United States. The US government wanted the numbers for government publications and to calculate funding allowances for official budgets and grants, among other things.[78] Gloria recalled her utter shock that the US government would think to rely on financially strapped grassroots feminist groups in the Philippines for its statistics. "But that's your task!" she recalled thinking to herself. She was flabbergasted that such a well-funded and powerful bureaucracy was unable to come up with its own data.

Gloria recited some of the challenges involved in estimating numbers of trafficked persons. Because the forms of violence that are now identified as human trafficking involve a range of practices that are illicit, and thus carried out underground, estimates of their scale are notoriously difficult to calculate.[79] Moreover, as later chapters illustrate, because the UN definition is so vague and capacious, much ambiguity exists around who should and who should not be included in official counts.

Gloria shared some rumors that she heard—she could not say from where—about the statistics on human trafficking victims that some NGOs in the Philippines had provided to the US government. Apparently, some NGO staff, recognizing the looseness of their data but feeling pressure from a powerful entity to provide firm numbers, had decided that they had no choice but to "guesstimate" them. These NGO staff had later been stunned to find their speculative estimations cited in official US publications. After debriefing among themselves about how they had determined the now published numbers, these NGO staff had chuckled as they discovered the inconsistencies in their methods. However, once their guesstimates had been officially cited, they collectively understood, "We're kind of locked in." They had provided numbers, and now their "accuracy" needed to be maintained.[80]

I asked Gloria if she thought that it was important to have an accurate count of trafficked persons. Her response was again eminently pragmatic. She explained that the numbers are "convenient politically"; they are a tool for advocacy, "to go to Congress and prove that this trafficking is a real issue." But, she continued, "from a human rights perspective," having a precise number of trafficked persons on a national or global scale was irrelevant:

> *Ethnologically, it doesn't matter to me. Because at the end of the day, I know women are being "trafficked" anyway. If we have lower numbers, will it be less important? If we have bigger numbers, will it be more important? No. From a human rights perspective, it doesn't matter. No person should be commodified. If there were 100 women or 100,000 or 500,000 women trafficked; at the end of the day, it doesn't matter. Because if only 100 is the real number, there are 100 women who were victims—brutalized—who should not be. In other words, as long as there's a single person in that situation, it's a project that needs to be worked on.*

Gloria then contrasted the irrelevance of global estimates of human trafficking to the importance of collecting accurate statistics regarding the local number of women her NGO assisted. She explained, "For example, we plan to help 'X' women. We need the numbers to target, to organize, to analyze. We need to know, OK, there are probably now, in this month, maybe 500 women in the bars. We need that, for programming. But for advocacy, it's kind of a different thing."

Gloria saw her work in relation to two categories of action. The first was assisting women on an immediate, local level—a meaningful practice to which she was deeply committed and for which she was uncompromising about the need for accurate estimates to plan funding for resources and programming. The second was the uncomfortable but necessary work of engaging with governments and international institutions that made statistical requests that made little practical sense but that had to be accommodated to receive support for direct assistance.

Whereas the US government and the UN, including those working within it such as Robinson and Gallagher, wanted data to empirically attest to human trafficking on a global scale, Gloria believed that such numbers had little practical use. Her concern was resource allocation for those that her NGO aimed to assist on a local level. Gloria supported the UN and participated in international and government projects in part as a tool for enacting political change in the Philippines and in part as a means for supporting the grassroots organizations in which she was involved; however, she also shared her reservations about doing so.

One could be cynical and argue that activists like Gloria have sacrificed their integrity by passing off guesstimates in exchange for access to resources, power, and influence. These activists are self-conscious that they must compromise some aspects of their work to participate in these efforts. However, they do so only insofar as it enables them to maintain the integrity of those parts of their jobs that they find most meaningful: direct client assistance. As I discuss in chapter 7, during our conversation, Gloria described a project that her NGO had initiated during the 1990s for assisting women in the sex industry who had been struggling to support themselves and their children since the US base closed in Subic Bay. Gloria's NGO had raised funds to offer them financial assistance and interest-free loans in part by selflessly using money that international grants had allocated for their own staff salaries.

For them, the compromises enabling their support of the UN protocol were part and parcel of grassroots activism. Committed to assisting those in desperate situations, activists like Gloria Reyes, who have dedicated their lives to making a difference, regularly find themselves caught between their political investments and official expectations and protocols. Sometimes international organizations provide their only possibilities for funding and political influence. These activists' decisions to work within official systems of governance—in short, to engage in strategies of governance feminism—cannot be reduced to personal ambition or naivete; rather, they are motivated by a pragmatic weighing of their clients' needs and their options at hand.

Many grassroots human rights and antiracist feminist activists are ambivalent about working with the UN even when achieving visibility within it has become a strategic objective.[81] International organizations like the UN provide some of the few opportunities for networking and influencing discourses on human rights on an international scale as well as, as I discuss in chapter 7, access to much-needed funds.[82] The UN carries "moral authority" and offers a crucial space for negotiation.[83] Even when grassroots activists express disappointment with the organization or describe it as having lost its moral compass, their desires for visibility within it persist.[84] At the same time, the UN's colonial roots mean that institutional power rests primarily in the hands of a select group of national governments.[85] Grassroots feminists like Reyes are left with little choice but to play the only game in town. Those who do so wind up collaborating and compromising in ways that, some might argue, make them complicit.

However, given the reality on the ground, grassroots feminists in the Philippines were not necessarily deterred by the ambiguities and deferrals embedded in the Trafficking Protocol even if they were cynical about its effectiveness. The deferrals meant that there was still a possibility for accessing needed resources and possibly even shifting the protocol's direction and creating real change. Although too jaded to be optimistic, these grassroots activists held on to the hope that change could happen. Underfunded and often dismissed—and even politically targeted—by their own government, they were compelled to participate in global efforts even when they found them hollow. For these feminists, getting human trafficking defined in an international instrument offered a foot in the door for future strategizing and pressuring their government to act. Compromise was a strategic concession; it meant yielding to institutional power in the interest of gaining something "you could hold on to" in the interest of future change, even if that something was itself compromised.

Conclusion

Institutional deferrals and compromises both enabled the drafting of the UN Trafficking Protocol and shaped the good of the project it defined. The protocol offered what Christopher Kelty has called an "intermediary language," a common set of terms through which people and organizations who may not share the same objectives and who "may be unknown to each other can communicate precisely and efficiently."[86] However, the compromises necessary to develop this language did not equally position all involved. Consensus, compromise, and cooperation can be strategies for accomplishing shared agreements; however, they can also be strategies for taming and avoiding institutional change.[87]

Consequently, differently invested participants viewed the compromises underpinning the Trafficking Protocol in different ways based on whether they wielded institutional power or were trying to access and thereby change it. For UN officials and powerful member-state governments, the protocol's deferrals and compromises were deliberately structured into its architecture as capacious abstractions that enabled a textual agreement deferential to member-state sovereignty. These compromises ensured a vague and flexible treaty that would encourage a maximum number of signatories but defer and displace the parameters of the Trafficking Protocol's enactment to retain state power.

In contrast, prominent feminists in the Global North, like Mary Robinson and Anne Gallagher, found their political commitments compromised by the protocol, although not enough to derail their support of it at the onset. They found sufficient value in the establishment of a single official definition of human trafficking, and thereby the prospect of a global solution, to justify compromising other commitments—for example, to make it more of a human rights instrument—at least for the short term. Some of these feminists had played roles in shaping the text of the protocol, and its adoption would enable them to continue pushing forward with their agenda. Their compromises marked both the extent of their official access and the limitations of their power.

Grassroots feminists in the Philippines, like Gloria Reyes, were in a related but much more vulnerable position. For these activists, who depend for day-to-day operations on funding from international agencies and national governments, the need to compromise reflected the limits of their political power on an international stage and marked the limited resources at their disposal—they had no choice but to compromise if they wanted to have the funds and attention to continue their work. These activists were left to accept what UN member-state governments had conceded even if they felt that the resulting legislation was compromised. Whether or not they viewed the protocol's focus on a global solution as misguided, the train was leaving the station. They had no choice but to get on or be left behind. They could only hope that the vague language and deferrals structured into the protocol would allow them to continue their work while they mobilized for further, necessary change.

As later chapters will make clear, the single definition of human trafficking in the Trafficking Protocol settled very little. Despite the criteria it established for qualifying as a victim of human trafficking, national governments, feminist and migrants' rights NGOs, and local communities continue to dispute in practice who is entitled to this assistance. This tension persists not only in Japan but also in other parts of the world, where residents and governments disagree over whether established cultural practices are forms of exploitation and abuse.[88] Feminists also remain divided over the question of whether a woman could ever choose to do sex work or whether all prostitution is "forced."

As we will see, for grassroots activists in Japan and the Philippines, the formal consensus among UN member states celebrated by the Trafficking Protocol was tautological. The treaty marked its own textual achievement while deferring the question of how it ultimately would be put into practice. Ironically, this logic of deferral has encouraged feminists to support the protocol even as it foreclosed consideration of many of the issues that they hold dear. It left activists like Gloria Reyes at once inside and outside these efforts. They have found themselves stuck as their support of the formal consensus demonstrated by the protocol ultimately served the status quo interests of powerful national governments.

In chapter 3, I turn to how caseworkers in Japan tried to leverage the UN's adoption of the Trafficking Protocol to pressure the Japanese government to address their clients' mistreatment to their desired ends. We will see how the compromised premise of the protocol played out in these caseworkers' limited ability to do so.

3

THE INSTITUTIONAL LIFE OF SUFFERING

———

Gloria had a graduate degree in banking and finance but decided to try working in Japan because she had heard she could make more money, and would
be better able to support her four children. She gained accreditation as an entertainer and approached a promotion agency which was recommended by an
acquaintance. The agency told her she would have an initial debt of US$461 for
documentation plus US$1,000 for travel expenses.... She travelled from Ma-
nila to Tokyo with four other women and a promoter, entering with a genuine
passport and valid entertainment visa. After arriving in Tokyo, Gloria's passport
and other travel documents were taken from her. She was taken directly to a
club in Kinshi-cho, Tokyo.... At the club she met a top-ranking yakuza who
said he wanted her for himself. He negotiated with the promoter and paid her
entire debt plus "consolation money." She was then transferred to Nagoya to
become his forced "live-in girlfriend," or as Gloria described it, his "sex slave."

—ILO, *Human Trafficking for Sexual Exploitation in Japan*

Noi came from a poor community in rural Thailand. At 15, seeking to escape
rape and sexual abuse in her foster family, she found a foreign labor agent in
Bangkok who advertised well-paid waitress jobs in Japan. She flew to Japan and
later learned that she had entered Japan on a tourist visa under a false identity.
On her arrival in Japan, she was taken to a karaoke bar where the owner raped
her, subjected her to a blood test and then bought her. "I felt like a piece of flesh
being inspected," she recounted. The brothel madam told Noi that she had to
pay off a large debt for her travel expenses. She was warned that girls who tried

to escape were brought back by the Japanese mafia, severely beaten, and their debts doubled. The only way to pay off the debt was to see as many clients as quickly as possible. Some clients beat the girls with sticks, belts and chains until they bled. If the victims returned crying, they were beaten by the madam and told that they must have provoked the client. The prostitutes routinely used drugs before sex "so that we didn't feel so much pain." Most clients refused to use condoms. The victims were given pills to avoid pregnancy and pregnancies were terminated with home abortions. Victims who managed to pay off their debt and work independently were often arrested by the police before being deported. Noi finally managed to escape with the help of a Japanese NGO.

—US DEPARTMENT OF STATE, *Trafficking in Persons Report, June 2004*

In this and chapter 4, I consider how and why the Japanese government began to participate in the global fight against human trafficking. First, this chapter explores how and to what ends Japanese government officials were moved to support global counter–human trafficking efforts after hearing accounts of foreign migrants' suffering from NGO and embassy caseworkers. In chapter 4, I turn to how diplomatic pressure from the United States shaped Japan's victim assistance protocol.

To understand how and why countries like Japan sign on to multilateral agreements like the Trafficking Protocol, international relations scholars have focused on "the politics of compliance"—the domestic processes through which obligations codified in international treaties are interpreted and translated into domestic law by government bodies.[1] These scholars define compliance as "a state of conformity or identity between an actor's behavior and a specified rule."[2] They argue that centralized states comply with international norms, such as those articulated by the Trafficking Protocol, when government officials "internalize" these norms, coming to accept them as right and true.[3] Further, they suggest that domestic advocates, such as activists and NGO staff, can play an important role in this process by helping shift dominant discourses and values.[4] Yet these studies tell us little about how government officials as individuals come to accept certain normative values, such as humanitarianism, and how their acceptance of these values thereby shapes their attitudes and behaviors toward multilateral treaties when they act as government agents.

Although government work is structured by rote bureaucratic procedure, it is also infused with sentiment.[5] Officials craft senses of self, including forms of ethical personhood, through their jobs.[6] Moreover, over the past several decades, political action based on compassion has increasingly replaced a politics of entitlements and rights.[7] As victims have increasingly been expected to testify and bear witness to their suffering, suffering has been newly politicized as part of what Didier Fassin has called a "contemporary moral order" that drives government and international agency action on a global stage.[8] Since the Vienna conference, migrants' rights activists have called for national governments to address migrant abuse and exploitation as a matter of human rights. However, national governments have tended to interpret this call through a humanitarian lens of benevolent care that sidelines questions of political-economic justice. We thus need to understand how and why government officials are affected by humanitarian calls to action in such circumscribed ways.

I became attuned to the potential of accounts of migrants' suffering to move government bureaucrats, shaping their official decisions, during my interview with Mrs. Claudia Saito, a caseworker at a Latin American embassy in Tokyo. I conducted an interview at this embassy during the summer of 2006 after hearing from some NGO caseworkers that this embassy's staff worked particularly well with local NGOs. A few days after my conversation with these NGO caseworkers, I happened to meet Mr. Miguel Lopez, a representative from the Latin American embassy, at a US embassy event on human trafficking. After I shared my research interests with him, he readily invited me to his embassy for a visit.

Like most foreign embassies in the city, this one was located behind gates in a tony neighborhood near the city center. I arrived at the appointed time, and security buzzed me first into the embassy compound and then into an embassy building. Mr. Lopez met me at the reception desk and ushered me upstairs to a well air-conditioned room. He was wearing a dark suit and tie and invited me to take a seat on one of the padded black leather chairs that surrounded a large oval conference table. He then excused himself, returning ten minutes later with a casually dressed middle-aged woman carrying a stack of six black plastic binders. Mr. Lopez explained that Mrs. Saito was the embassy staff member who worked directly with trafficked persons; however, because she did not speak English, and I do not speak Spanish, he would remain to translate and contribute to the discussion. When I realized that Mrs. Saito also spoke Japanese, she and I used it some to communicate directly with each other.[9] Mr. Lopez did not seem to mind that he could not understand these exchanges; he clearly deferred to Mrs. Saito's firsthand experience.

I began by asking Mrs. Saito how she had gotten involved in efforts to fight human trafficking. She explained that she had moved to Japan in the 1990s after she had married a Japanese man who had been temporarily relocated to her home country for work. Finding herself with free time during the day when her husband was at his office job, she had begun volunteering at her embassy's library. She explained that she had wanted to do something "on the human side" to contribute to her home community in Japan, perhaps by offering cultural support and engaging in community building among immigrants like herself. However, while volunteering, she had unexpectedly witnessed many women from her home country coming to the embassy in distress—emotionally distraught and easily recognizable as having suffered physical and sexual violence. She was shocked and upset by what she learned of these women's experiences. She explained, "These women were brought from another country. They were kept in captivity, forced to work as prostitutes, and deceived by the people who brought them. In addition, there were debts and penalties imposed on them. And they were beaten and tortured." Despite this abuse, Mrs. Saito explained, "the police didn't accept that these women were victims of anything because they were in Japan illegally." She was angered that, after suffering so, these women did not receive any assistance. They were assumed to be criminals and deported by the Japanese government—with their embassy's help.[10] Mrs. Saito saw injustice in the women's treatment, and she became determined to help them. She stressed, as Mr. Lopez translated, "There was something *human* that should be done for these women, and the government should help them as *humans* of their country."[11] She spoke to a consul about what she had observed, and from that time on (1997), the embassy established a special section to assist female nationals who came to the embassy in "distressed conditions." Mrs. Saito became involved in this section as a caseworker, responsible for providing counseling to these women, documenting their grievances, and, after Japan's Action Plan was in place, helping them apply for formal recognition as victims of human trafficking.

Although I did not realize it until the end of our conversation, Mrs. Saito had brought documentation of her clients' grievances to our interview. Throughout our talk, the six black plastic binders that she had carried into the room had sat beside her on the conference table. Just as our time was running out, she explained that the binders were full of information about the women she had counseled: their names, addresses, the routes through which they had come to Japan, the agencies that they had gone through, and documentation of their exploitation, their suffering, and the torture on their bodies, including photographs.

Mrs. Saito did not offer to let me look through the binders, and I did not ask to do so, understanding that they contained confidential information. However, Mrs. Saito wanted to give me a sense of the extent of the violence to which they bore witness. At the end of our interview, she opened one of the binders in a dramatic demonstration, quickly fanning its pages. From my seat across the table, I could see that it was full of forms written in Spanish and protected in plastic covers. Mrs. Saito then explained that this was the "file of evidence" that she had initially used to lobby her consulate and the Japanese government for better treatment for these women; she now used it to support women's applications for status as trafficking victims.

This chapter considers how NGO and embassy caseworkers, like Mrs. Saito on the one hand, and US and Japanese government officials on the other, were variously affected by accounts of foreign workers' suffering in Japan to explore the uneven roles that these accounts played in shaping Japan's counter–human trafficking efforts. In recent years, feminist scholars have drawn attention to the role of affect in shaping political action. These scholars use this term to refer to those pre- and intersubjective intensities that are retroactively recognized as emotions, sentiments, or feelings and that move people to act by informing how they come to articulate themselves as subjects.[12] Carried through narratives and popular culture, these intensities circulate in what Sara Ahmed and Purnima Mankekar call "affective economies," and they assume force as what Kamari Clarke calls "affective regimes," which motivate involvement in political projects.[13] Mankekar and Clarke have productively focused on the connections produced through circulations of affect, such as the ways they inspire, respectively, nationalist projects or assemblages of international justice. However, less attention has been paid to how and why these circulations can also create gaps, tensions, and ruptures within communities or movements.

Just as people suffer in different ways and for diverse reasons, people are also disparately affected by others' pain.[14] Empathetic connection is not a straightforward, all-or-nothing process in which an individual comes to transparently and universally understand the perspectives, feelings, or experiences of another; rather, it is an uneven process of discerning aspects of another's experience in relation to one's own that can be tenuous, complex, and fleeting.[15] To understand the gaps between caseworkers' and Japanese government officials' visions for fighting human trafficking, we need to better understand how individuals involved in these efforts were disparately affected by accounts of migrant suffering and thus came to different conclusions regarding how to address it.

In this chapter, I ethnographically explore the *differential affects* of these accounts as they unevenly moved people to participate in global counter–human trafficking efforts. I build on Sara Ahmed, who argues that representations of suffering affect people not because they are inherently sentimental but because they are emotionally "sticky."[16] When they circulate, they stick with people in different ways as they articulate with other stories and ideas through which people craft their senses of self—stories and ideas that include those of modernity, humanity, gender, sexuality, race, and nationalism. Ahmed's argument helps us see how positionality matters to the affectivity of suffering in political life. It invites us to consider how different caseworkers' and government officials' personal experiences, orientations, and positionings within discourses of race, modernity, and nationalism shape the variegated responses that they deemed appropriate for fighting human trafficking, and thus the differential affects effected through the circulation of accounts of migrants' trauma and pain.

My focus on these accounts' differential affects helps resolve a tension between feminist scholars who have disagreed about the political potential of circulating accounts of suffering. One group of such scholars has questioned the potential of narratives of suffering to mobilize effective political change. For instance, Carole Vance describes documentaries on sex trafficking as "melomentaries" to highlight their melodramatic sensationalism and detachment from reality.[17] Erica Caple James focuses on the "political economy of trauma" through which humanitarian projects work in Haiti.[18] Tracking the ways that accounts of suffering move like currency within a global humanitarian economy, she argues that physicians, psychiatrists, lawyers, activists, clergy, and human rights observers instrumentally appropriate victims' experiences of suffering and transform these painful experiences into "trauma portfolios," which are analogous to stock portfolios in the sense that they go up and down in value as they are mobilized for self-interested ends.[19] In contrast, other feminist scholars, such as Rosa-Linda Fregoso and Shannon Speed, have more optimistically argued that personal accounts of suffering can be important tools for mobilizing political change.[20] These scholars illustrate the important role that ethnographic and artistic representations of suffering can play by capturing the impact of structural violence on individual bodies and connecting this violence to the broader social and political-economic relationships in which it takes place. For example, Speed relays stories of the suffering of Indigenous women incarcerated in detention centers at the US-Mexico border as a means of drawing attention to the forms of structural violence shaping their lives.[21] Similarly, Fregoso demonstrates that artistic representations of suffering can mobilize support for a decolonial human rights project precisely because they emotionally move people.[22]

Both sets of insights are relevant for understanding the different roles played by accounts of suffering in counter–human trafficking efforts. On the one hand, as James suggests, these accounts are regularly commodified and treated as fungible. Countless filmmakers, journalists, and writers have built careers by relaying trafficked persons' narratives of suffering. Feminist scholars have rightly criticized the media circulation of these stories, arguing that it sensationalizes the issue and objectifies those represented as victims.[23] The practice of linking these testimonies together in books, films, talks, and news media also contributes to the problematic notion that diverse forms of exploitation and abuse can be reduced to a single form of direct violence (i.e., human trafficking) and addressed through a single global solution. At the same time, these accounts of exploitation and abuse become fungible only because they circulate in moral and affective economies in which they compel political action. As personal suffering has assumed moral authority in an affect-driven politics, documented testimonials of it have increasingly come to serve as evidence of entitlement to humanitarian support.[24] Consequently, NGO and embassy caseworkers, like Mrs. Saito, have come to recognize that they must mobilize their clients' accounts of suffering to advocate for their clients, help their clients' access resources, and lobby for legal and political change.[25] For these caseworkers, circulating these accounts of suffering is not a means for acquiring currency so much as a tool for political ends.

In the remainder of this chapter, I consider how foreign migrants' accounts of suffering differentially affected government officials and NGO and embassy caseworkers, both as individuals and from their positions within the organizational structure of the project. I examine how personal positioning, occupational responsibilities, and political commitments intertwined to shape their corresponding responses to these accounts. I argue that at stake in these accounts' differential affects is the political potential that they can—and cannot—assume as they circulate. Attention to these differential affects, then, allows us to move beyond the notion that a global counter–human trafficking project rests upon a single moral geography of suffering or model of humanitarian reason, which can be resolved simply by fostering empathy among those in power. It helps us see the variegated roles that accounts of violence and abuse can play in the mobilization of political action. I begin by considering why these accounts stuck with NGO and embassy caseworkers, moving them to respond as both people and institutional actors, before turning to some of the ways they affected the government officials with whom I spoke.

Caseworkers Are Affected, Personally and Politically

Mrs. Saito was not alone in documenting the abuse and exploitation faced by her clients. Grassroots NGOs like Tahanan have included such accounting as part of their intake process since long before the Trafficking Protocol was adopted. My first assignment at a migrant support helpline in Tokyo in the mid-1990s was cataloging phone-log entries to identify and tally the numbers of calls received by the organization regarding unpaid wages, overwork, sexual abuse, rape, and domestic violence, among other issues. Back then, organization caseworkers were not documenting these violations as evidence of a single crime of human trafficking; rather, they were identifying the variety and extent of abuses experienced by migrant workers in Japan. The NGO then used the information for a range of purposes: to bear witness in public arenas to the scope of these abuses; to compare data and share information with other NGOs assisting foreign workers in Japan and other countries; and to report to donors and other members of their network as a means of being accountable for, and soliciting, resources for the different forms of assistance it provided.

At the time, Japanese media and government discourse widely represented foreign labor migrants as a social and political problem contributing to the deterioration of public safety. It rarely if ever acknowledged the contribution to the Japanese economy that these workers make by doing undesirable work at below domestic labor market wages—labor identified in Japan as "3K": *kitanai, kiken, kitsui* (respectively, "dirty," "dangerous," and "demanding"; also called "3D" in English). In 2000, the Japanese government enacted the first of a series of amendments to its Immigration Control and Refugee Recognition Act aimed at tightening residency requirements for foreign labor migrants, criminalizing undocumented entry, and expanding and streamlining deportation procedures.

By making "trafficking victim" a legal category for redress, the UN General Assembly's adoption of the Trafficking Protocol established a new set of international norms governing the treatment of some foreign migrants. The protocol rendered victims of human trafficking entitled to protection and resources on account of the circumstances of their suffering, which it identified as exceptional. After the 2004 US *Trafficking in Persons Report* (*TIP Report*) ranked Japan on the Tier 2 Watch List, the Japanese government began sponsoring workshops and meetings to discuss human trafficking to the country, and in a gesture of collaboration with local NGOs, caseworkers from some migrant-assistance organizations were invited to some of these events. These NGO caseworkers initially hoped such meetings would serve as long-awaited opportunities to advocate for their clients to government officials and international agency staff with real power to make a difference in migrants' lives.[26] Their records of their clients' experiences, such as those that informed the logs that I once tallied, assumed new political potential. Like Mrs. Saito, these caseworkers began reporting on their clients' abuse in meetings with Japanese and US embassy staff in hopes of changing the Japanese government's position toward foreign labor migrants, arguing that these workers deserved protection and assistance, not treatment as criminals.

For their part, these NGO caseworkers did not document their clients' suffering purely as an instrumental institutional tool. They were deeply affected on a personal level by what they heard, and they wanted others to be affected too. Relaying the details of their clients' experiences was a way of making these experiences palpable to those who had not heard them firsthand. Consider Mrs. Saito. Even though her class position and life in Japan differed in many ways from those of the women she assisted, her co-nationals' accounts of their suffering in Japan stuck with her. Indeed, she could not seem to let these accounts go, carrying them around in binders when she went to meetings with government officials and American researchers. These accounts moved Mrs. Saito to confront both her consul and the Japanese government. She wanted them to stick with others and thereby affect them too.

The affective stickiness of these accounts for Mrs. Saito was in part tied to her understanding of what it meant to be human. She believed that "as humans," her clients were entitled to certain consideration and rights; both their government and the Japanese government had a responsibility to them. ("The government should help them as humans.") These accounts also linked up with her understanding of herself as human—that is, as an ethical subject with a capacity for empathy ("something human . . . should be done for them"). In this regard, for Mrs. Saito, her clients' suffering rested on her notion of a shared humanity.

Yet a straightforward collapse of Mrs. Saito's understanding of a shared humanity into that which underpins liberal European traditions of human rights would miss a lot. Scholars have looked to the eighteenth century to find the roots of human rights and humanitarianism in the new emotional regimes of empathy and ethics that emerged in Europe and fostered the notion of a universal humanity composed of autonomous individual subjects.[27] However, later in our conversation, both Mrs. Saito and Mr. Lopez made clear that their response to their co-nationals' experiences was not simply based in a liberal humanism so much as an understanding of the larger structural inequalities that underlay the violence to which these women had been subjected, including the racism and sexism they experienced as foreign nationals in Japan. With Mrs. Saito in agreement, Mr. Lopez expressed concern that "to classify human trafficking as a human rights issue is too small—it minimizes the issue." He worried that within a human rights framework, "other human rights issues seem to take higher priority, such as weapons trafficking and drug trafficking." Instead, human trafficking needed to be dealt with, in his words, "on multiple levels, as cultural, gender, economic, political, and historical issues."[28] For both Mr. Lopez and Mrs. Saito, human rights were a matter less of a singular global humanity and more of the differences and inequalities that crosscut it.

Despite coming from more privileged class backgrounds, Mrs. Saito and Mr. Lopez had also experienced discrimination firsthand as Latin Americans in Japan. When they appealed to the Japanese government to recognize their co-nationals' humanity, they were also in some sense appealing for it to recognize their own. Mr. Lopez and Mrs. Saito also believed that stopping the abuse and exploitation of migrant workers in Japan required addressing the political-economic vulnerabilities faced by many of their co-nationals. Mr. Lopez shared concern that the UN protocol did not deal with the social and cultural problems of demand or of grassroots education about these issues. Mrs. Saito agreed, as I recorded in my notes: "There is almost zero sensitivity on the community level regarding the existence of this problem." They believed that stopping the abuse experienced by their co-nationals would require more education about difference and inequality, including political-economic inequities among nations. They were endorsing a vision of human rights that both included and exceeded that which informed the Trafficking Protocol.

Mrs. Saito was not alone among caseworkers in how she was affected by her clients' accounts of their abuse and exploitation. NGO caseworkers shared similar sentiments, expressing both political concerns and personal convictions about the labor exploitation, racism, and sexism that migrants experienced in Japan. As I've mentioned, many migrants' advocates were themselves immigrants or Japanese nationals who had lived abroad or had intimate partners who were migrants; a few NGO caseworkers had previously worked in the sex industry in Japan. Like Mrs. Saito and Mr. Lopez, these caseworkers sometimes connected their clients' mistreatment and abuse with their own experiences of social inequality in Japan. For them, their clients' accounts of suffering evoked feelings of identification and anger alongside senses of responsibility and political conviction. Their clients' accounts of suffering stuck with them for all these reasons. These caseworkers believed that their clients were due the same consideration that they would want if they found themselves in their clients' positions.

Like Mrs. Saito, many of these NGO caseworkers had been working with migrants since before the UN protocol or the TVPA were adopted. They worked with some of their clients over the course of many weeks, months, and even years. Because these caseworkers shared both multiple forms of identification and intimacies of care with their clients, their clients' accounts of suffering sometimes stuck with them on painful emotional levels. Cherie sometimes spoke of being overwhelmed by what she called "vicarious" and "secondhand trauma." Recall her shaking when we were in the convenience store. She told me that she had read somewhere that NGO caseworkers in the United States sometimes had to visit sites where their clients had been kept, in some cases under lock and key, to learn about their circumstances. Cherie found the thought of these experiences voyeuristic and emotionally overwhelming. "I wouldn't need to see it every time, Lieba," she said, looking out into the distance. Early on in my research, she recommended that I read clinical books on trauma and PTSD—for instance, Babette Rothschild's *The Body Remembers*—in order to understand the experiences of both her clients and NGO caseworkers, like herself, who work with them. Several NGO caseworkers in the United States who were themselves children of immigrants or had grown up in foster care told me that they similarly struggled to separate themselves from their work. One spoke of regularly being awakened by emergencies in the middle of the night in which clients were deeply distressed and even suicidal. She described how during these calls, she would try to coach her clients to self-soothe by instructing them to wear rubber bands on their wrists and to snap them whenever they felt the urge to injure themselves, a common experience for trafficking survivors, she reported. She struggled emotionally with her constant firsthand exposure to their pain, exhausted by being one more receptacle in a cascade of social and political-economic violence.

In addition to the political strategies they adopted to push for their clients' rights, these NGO caseworkers adopted strategies for personally coping with the violence to which they regularly bore witness. Some published essays about the systemic forms of violence that migrants experienced in Japan and the kinds of changes that they believed were needed. For one of many published examples, in 2010 Leny Tolentino—a cofounding director of Kalakasan, a support NGO for Filipina migrants in Japan—contributed an essay to the *NGO Report Regarding the Rights of Non-Japanese Japanese, Minorities of Foreign Origins, and Refugees in Japan*, compiled by the Solidarity Network with Migrants Japan. Kalakasan offers counseling, legal advice, and other forms of support to Filipina migrants and their children, some of whom have been identified as trafficked. In her essay, Tolentino argues that despite migrant women's decades-long presence in and contributions to Japanese society, they are still "treated as the 'other' and excluded from Japanese society and its safety nets."[29] She points to the "widespread discriminatory attitudes and prejudices" they face, "as well as feelings of indifference . . . among government officials and the populace."[30] Tolentino finds indifference to be codified in policies and legislation that provide minimal protection to migrant women, particularly those who are victims of domestic violence and trafficking. She identifies the sources of this violence in (1) the absence of a comprehensive policy that protects the social, economic, cultural, and human rights of migrants; (2) the existence of discriminatory policies, such as migrant registration programs, that disadvantage migrants;

(3) the indifference and discriminatory attitudes of public officials toward migrants; and (4) the lack of effort by the government to establish services to assist, educate, protect, and empower migrants.[31] Tolentino argues for changes to address these issues, including "gender- and multiculturalism-sensitive training programs for government staff and interpreters at all levels of the government to assume responsibility . . . so that victimization is not repeated."[32]

Other NGO caseworkers felt a need to put distance between their political commitments and their work. Cherie told me that she found herself at times taking a detached, pragmatic approach to her work responsibilities. She tried to step outside her personal anger regarding the violence and suffering her clients faced in order to focus on seeing the world through their eyes and understanding what they wanted. Doing this sometimes meant putting aside her critiques of consumer culture and gender relations in Japan to prioritize the immediacy of her clients' needs, including their medical, emotional, and psychological stability. For instance, she explained that some of her clients tell her that they want to remain in Japan because they are in relationships with Japanese men or are focused on acquiring trendy consumer items to bring home. Cherie shared that when she is in these situations, she tries to simply think about the person in front of her and not to let her broader political agenda inform how she responds. She believes that structural changes are necessary, but in the meantime, she does what she can to support women in distress, to try to be in the moment and put her clients' interests above her own beliefs. She explained, "When they tell me they want something, I ask, 'Is that really what you want?' And if it is, I have to help them in the way that they want to be helped." Cherie reflected, "Does that make me myopic, just seeing what is in front of me? Maybe my clients see that I don't have some underlying political agenda. I really just try to hear what they say. I think the only question to ask is, 'Will that work for her?'" On another occasion, Cherie recalled hearing someone say something publicly at a conference that had rung true for her as well. This person had pointedly ended her presentation by explaining, "Many people think it is dramatic or exotic to work on trafficking. Some people find drama in it. Sometimes it stops being about trafficking and it's just about the person's life." Cherie could not agree more.

Migrants' advocates like Mrs. Saito, Cherie, and Leny Tolentino bear witness to the abuse and exploitation that migrants face by translating their accounts into institutionally legible and relatable forms that they hope will stick with others. The history of the anti-human-trafficking movement in Japan is in part a history of some migrants' testimonies coming to be viewed as credible and legitimate when they had previously been dismissed. As Mrs. Saito explained, and Japanese officials affirmed, before anti-human-trafficking policies were adopted, undocumented migrant women were unilaterally treated as criminals and deported. Japanese government officials overwhelmingly assumed that women working in the sex industry had chosen to do so for reasons of convenience or immorality, and they resisted recognizing that such women could be exploited or abused. When Mrs. Saito and NGO caseworkers shared accounts of their clients' exploitation and abuse, they were asking Japanese bureaucrats to recognize their clients as people and address their suffering. These caseworkers documented the violence suffered by their clients so that it would be both translatable and undeniable for state and international bureaucracies. Documenting and circulating accounts of the violence that migrants experience has been one of the few available means for migrants' advocates to lobby for change. As Mrs. Saito explained of Japanese bureaucrats' responses to her presentation of her clients' experiences, "They can't refuse the file. There are many facts." She viewed her reports and forms as indelible material evidence of human rights violations that had to be addressed.

A "Stick" Approach to Enforcing International Norms

If Mrs. Saito and other NGO caseworkers were moved to share accounts of their clients' suffering for both personal and political reasons, these caseworkers could not control how those accounts would be received by government bureaucrats in Japan and the United States. They also lacked the institutional power to determine how violations of migrants' rights would be addressed or who or what would be held accountable by centralized state governments. As later chapters show, once their documentation of their clients' experiences became part of bureaucratic circuits, NGO caseworkers' calls for structural change were sidelined, banally reduced to the need to rectify appearances and follow proper procedures. Here I consider how government officials' affective responses to accounts of migrants' suffering shaped the endorsement of such banalities.

Consider the responses of some US State Department officials to NGOs' reports of their clients' experiences. The US embassy in Tokyo was tasked with gathering information about Japan's efforts to fight human trafficking for the Office to Monitor and Combat Trafficking in Persons in Washington, DC, to use in generating Japan's rankings and country reports in the *TIP Report*. As part of their data collection, US embassy officials invited caseworkers from local NGOs to discuss their cases.

US TIP ambassador John Miller explained to political scientist Judith Kelley his reaction to these meetings when preparing the fateful 2004 *TIP Report*, saying, "You couldn't listen to these NGOs without getting upset."[33]

NGO caseworkers' accounts moved Ambassador Miller to make the controversial decision of placing Japan on the Tier 2 Watch List. The US TIP Office, and by extension the State Department, hesitated before giving a close ally like Japan such a low ranking. In our interview, a staff member at the US State Department's TIP office explained in no uncertain terms that *TIP Report* country rankings often considered, if not prioritized, geopolitical factors. Ambassador Miller knew that the diplomatic burden of his decision would fall on the US embassy in Tokyo. Before finalizing the ranking, he traveled to Japan and invited Nancy Kassebaum, a former senator from Kansas who was then married to Howard Baker, the ambassador to Japan, to a meeting with local NGOs to convince the US embassy to support it. Apparently the NGOs' accounts of their clients' experiences stuck with Kassebaum as well. She proceeded to speak with her husband about what she had learned, and he agreed to go along with the ranking, which did indeed greatly upset the Japanese government.[34]

Mrs. Saito and other local NGO staff in Japan were pleased by Ambassador Miller's decision because they hoped that the ranking would put added pressure on the Japanese government to change its policies toward foreign migrants and enable migrants to be better accepted and find long-term stability in Japan. However, in our interviews, US embassy officials suggested that their concerns centered less directly on migrants' long-term socioeconomic well-being in Japan than on addressing immediate matters of labor law violations and incompetence among Japanese police and other foreign embassy staff. Although US ambassador Miller was moved by what he heard from caseworkers, the practical enactment of his decision focused on questions of policy and prosecution rather than on ensuring migrants' welfare in the long term.

This focus persisted despite the fact that some US embassy officials were troubled by the abuse faced by foreign workers in Japan, including those working in the sex industry, as labor violations based in discrimination. One such official explained:

> You understand that in the US there's this big debate about TIP in general ... whether it's right to consider prostitution as ... legitimate work. And frankly, I don't get into that aspect really. Because the practicality of the situation is—and this is how I often used to talk to Japanese colleagues, Japanese government colleagues—if you had a woman who came to Japan, or a Japanese woman who was working in Japan under similar work conditions, [it would be considered] totally unacceptable. So why do they allow this to happen to someone who is coming here just because they are working in an industry that may or may not be acceptable? ... I mean, if they're

going to make a pretense of having entertainer visas—and these people are entertainers—then they should be treated to the protections under that visa category. And, actually, the visa category carries a lot of protections. It regulates size of stage, hours to work, wages. It regulates dressing rooms.... I mean, the visa category is quite good. But those conditions were certainly not being regulated. Because, frankly, when Filipinos come here, they're first . . . well, number one, they're told they're going to come here as entertainers. Well, the only entertaining they do is, you know, running their hand up somebody's thigh. They're also told they have a work spot. With flying bookings—this is a situation where basically you're moved constantly from place to place—that's not part of the legal conditions for entertainers. So my approach really was, listen, put all the morals aside.... If we treat these people like workers, like they're supposed to be workers, they are not being treated fairly, and it is unconscionable. And, you know, this used to always get my goat at the ministries. I'd say, "OK, I got you in my room. I've invited you to come here and talk to me. I'm taking away your cellphone. I'm taking away your identification. I'm making you strip. You're going to have to do lewd acts for me. Now, is that acceptable?" And if it's not acceptable for you as a working person, it's certainly not acceptable for people who have come here under probably false pretenses. So that kind of gets people's attention.

Like NGO caseworkers with whom I spoke, this US embassy staffer described women on entertainer visas as legitimate workers entitled to having their labor rights protected, and this official recognized the specific vulnerability they faced as women and migrant workers. However, as a representative of the US embassy, this embassy staffer's strategies for addressing the women's abuse and exploitation were limited to arguing for more workplace regulation and increased labor law enforcement. The embassy's strategies did not extend to addressing the structural inequalities and gender and racial discrimination that caseworkers like Mrs. Saito and Cherie identified as making migrant women targets of abuse and exploitation in Japan in the first place. Rather, the US embassy's official solution was to push Japan to follow international norms and respond to US soft power. The embassy representative explained, "Other countries were starting to sign on [to the UN protocol]. There was a big movement to sign on to action plans and better laws and enforcement, and Japan was just kind of staying back where it was. And so that was a concern to all of us, really." The actionable problem, as this embassy official saw it, was that Japan was not following, as the official put it, "a big movement to sign on to action plans and better laws and enforcement" prompted by the adoption of the UN protocol.

Consequently, the US TIP Office believed it needed to step in more forcefully to ensure that they would. This official explained, "The TIP Report has this kind of 'stick' approach to dealing with trafficking and naming countries. It's a definite naming-shaming kind of philosophy."

Certainly, effective labor laws and their enforcement are important for reducing workplace exploitation and abuse; NGO caseworkers with whom I spoke also viewed the lack of workplace regulations and labor law enforcement as serious problems. However, what the embassy's solution neglected was why such mistreatment of migrants is tolerated (because, NGO caseworkers argued, migrant workers are viewed as racially inferior and disposable) and why migrants are so vulnerable to this abuse in the first place (because, NGO caseworkers argued, colonial histories and geopolitical inequalities have left many in the Philippines with few options to survive). Allocating tax dollars to fund workplace oversight necessary for protecting the rights of migrant workers, a good number of whom are undocumented, is important; however, even US government officials recognize that doing so currently garners little practical support in both Japan *and* the United States. In an interview with staff in the US Department of Labor's Wage and Hour Division—the federal office responsible for enforcing federal labor laws—I was told that, regretfully, the division was chronically underfunded and could not hire anywhere close to the number of staff necessary to undertake regular worksite inspections anywhere in the United States. Even when governments recognize that migrant workers' labor rights are being readily violated, little political will exists to fund the practices that would ensure their protection. Instead, encouraging formal compliance with international protocols banally stands in for taking active steps toward challenging discrimination toward migrants, recognizing their social and economic contributions, and dedicating sufficient resources to protecting their labor rights.

Matters of Law and Order and National Pride

If, like the US government, the Japanese government lacked the political will to fund sufficient monitoring of foreign migrants' worksites, it *was* shamed by Japan's ranking on the 2004 TIP Report's Tier 2 Watch List. As noted previously, under pressure from the US government, the Japanese government invited NGO and embassy staff to meetings with government officials to share their observations and relay their clients' experiences. Heartened by their sudden inclusion, NGO caseworkers prepared presentations based on years of work with labor migrants. Mrs. Saito brought her plastic binders. I know that she did because some Japanese bureaucrats mentioned both Mrs. Saito's notebooks

and these presentations, unsolicited, in our interviews. These officials suggested that the accounts of suffering relayed by caseworkers stuck with them,
although not quite in the ways that Mrs. Saito, Mr. Lopez, or NGO staff had
hoped. Rather, Japanese bureaucrats found these accounts emotionally sticky
for different reasons and to different ends.

For instance, while in Tokyo one summer, I interviewed Yoshida-san, a former
Japanese government official who had initially helped organize Japan's Action
Plan. We met in her large office at the university, where she was then employed
as a high-level administrator. We sat at a glass table under wide windows overlooking the suburban campus. When I asked her why she had gotten involved in
counter–human trafficking efforts, Yoshida-san recalled a meeting that she had
organized for Japanese government officials, foreign embassy staff, and NGOs.
She spoke specifically of the "eloquent" presentation at the event of a woman
from a Latin American embassy who was "very much an expert on that issue."
Yoshida-san could not remember Mrs. Saito's name, but she did "remember
her binders," which detailed the experiences of the women "who were victims."

I asked how Yoshida-san had felt when she heard Mrs. Saito discuss those
accounts. Yoshida-san first confirmed what Mrs. Saito and staff at other foreign
embassies and NGOs in Tokyo had told me regarding the Japanese government's
dismissal of the migrants' exploitation and abuse: "In those days, we in the government thought those women were just illegal immigrants." She said that she
knew that Filipina and other foreign women worked in bars in Japan, but she
had assumed that they came through undocumented channels to make money
and thus should be charged and deported as criminals. It had not crossed her
mind that they might be victims of human rights violations or a crime.

Yoshida-san explained that she was moved to change her views of the
women by the accounts of women's suffering that Mrs. Saito had shared. These
accounts had affected Yoshida-san, her heart going out to the women, and had
helped Yoshida-san see the women as subjects deserving of rights. However,
despite her recognition of the injustices that these women had faced as people,
Yoshida-san was not necessarily moved to address the widespread discrimination
against migrants described by Tolentino or the structural inequalities mentioned
by Mrs. Saito and Mr. Lopez. Mrs. Saito's clients' accounts were "unaffective"
in that regard because they were tied up with another concern that stuck with
Yoshida-san more deeply: her commitment to upholding Japan's standing in a
global arena. In light of this concern, these stories stuck to Yoshida-san like, one
might say, egg on her face. She explained that she had been "so embarrassed" when
a counselor from the US embassy showed her the US State Department's 2004
Trafficking in Persons Report, which included accounts from victims of human

trafficking and which criticized the Japanese government for its handling of such cases. Yoshida-san continued, "Most of the advanced countries are on the so-called Tier 1, but only Japan was ranked Tier 2. . . . If we do not do anything, the image of Japan will be damaged. So we must do something."

For Yoshida-san, these stories were affecting because they made Japan seem painfully behind the times on the international stage. They connected to her personal and institutional investment in Japan's standing as a modern, developed nation and, correspondingly, in maintaining Japan's place in the world alongside the, in her words, "advanced countries." Unlike Mrs. Saito, the affective pull of these accounts for Yoshida-san did not center on migrants' vulnerability as women, foreign nationals, or postcolonial subjects. These accounts also did not inspire her to work toward changing unequal political-economic relations between Japan and the women's home countries or to argue for better funding for worksite oversight or direct assistance for these women. Rather, she was moved to organize different governmental and nongovernmental officials—Japanese bureaucrats, foreign embassy staff, and NGO and international organization workers—to meet and develop a formal plan—Japan's Action Plan—which she hoped would, above all, resurrect Japan's standing in the eyes of the international community.

Yoshida-san was not the only government official who suggested that they had been personally affected by hearing stories of migrant workers' suffering. Kato-san's job involved coordinating the national offices enacting Japan's Action Plan. Formally appointed by the prime minister, he had been at his post for two years, having come from the National Police Agency (NPA). Before he would consent to meet me, he required that I send prospective interview questions.

I met Kato-san in a large conference room on the top floor of the Cabinet Office building in central Tokyo. He was gentle and personable, with kind eyes and trim but not austere salt-and-pepper hair. He wore a well-tailored business suit with a crisp blue-and-white-striped shirt and a Hermès silk tie. We greeted each other formally, bowing and exchanging business cards, and then we sat across from each other at an enormous conference table. Kato-san had a printout of my questions in front of him; he had marked x's next to the questions that he would not answer. I began by asking him how he had first learned about human trafficking. He explained that he had first heard of the situations of trafficked persons from "old friends who are journalists." He continued, "Many foreigners came to Japan in the latter half of the 90s. I heard about the cruel situations in which some were placed." He also told me that he had seen such cases while working in the Tokyo metropolitan police department—for instance, a case of a Filipina woman engaged in street prostitution whose passport had been taken by her pimp and who had been locked up. He explained, "Personally, I thought that this was wrong." I asked him how he felt when he learned about these situations. His voice rose and trembled with anger as he responded, "When you hear 'human trafficking,' it is difficult to understand that it actually exists today. This is not a time without law and order. I did not think it could occur so easily. I am very frustrated by it. . . . The methods of traffickers are ingenious. . . . Japanese police and immigration are unable to regulate all [of] this in Japan, and it is somewhat shocking."

Like Yoshida-san, Kato-san acknowledged that some migrants were victims of abuse and exploitation in Japan by those who eluded the law, and he expressed empathy toward them. He spoke of the cruelty in how some migrants were treated, and he viewed this treatment as wrong. However, also like Yoshida-san, these stories did not necessarily prompt Kato-san to address the structural injustices faced by migrant workers so much as they stuck with him as signs of a disturbing failure of Japan's national modernity. For Kato-san this modernity was not measured in terms of Japan's international standing, as it had been for Yoshida-san, but as a matter of maintaining national standards of law and order. ("This is not a time without law and order.") Consequently, and in line with the UN Trafficking Protocol, he viewed the problem of migrant suffering as a circumscribed criminal matter in which individual perpetrators needed to be checked by government bodies rather than as a broader issue that required addressing structural inequalities and discriminatory attitudes that made foreign migrants vulnerable to this cruelty in the first place. Kato-san did not recognize that current laws, such as immigration regulations, could in fact contribute to labor migrants' vulnerability.[35] His involvement in the issue, per his appointment, was tied to his commitment to public service as a law enforcement officer. As an employee of the NPA, he was invested in cracking down on traffickers and thereby arresting those who mistreat others as a means of upholding his commitment to an orderly and modern nation.

Conclusion

Since at least the Vienna conference in 1993, NGO caseworkers have publicly circulated accounts of their clients' suffering to draw attention to the exploitation and abuse that some migrant laborers face. These accounts are more than vehicles of representation and meaning; they are part of an affective economy that links different people, and thereby institutions, in a globalized movement against human trafficking. However, the affectivity of these accounts is inconsistent because they stick with people in different ways, making these accounts in some sense unaffective, and thus ineffective, in the ways that NGO caseworkers with whom I spoke had hoped that they would be. In this regard, these accounts not only hold counter–human trafficking efforts together but also reveal the rents, gaps, and snags within them.

We see these rents, gaps, and snags in the different ways that Japanese officials and NGO and embassy caseworkers are affected by migrants' accounts. Caseworkers that I interviewed were moved to respond to their clients' suffering on personal, professional, and political levels. These accounts emotionally stuck with them because of both their personal identification with their clients and their commitments to migrants' human rights. These caseworkers shared their clients' accounts to try to mobilize government agencies, which have more resources and political power. They hoped to mobilize government officials and international agency staff to recognize the structural vulnerability that their clients face and to take this structural violence into account in their approach to the issue. For these caseworkers, protecting human rights required attention to multiple social and political forms of inequality and difference, and their clients' accounts of their suffering called for both immediate intervention and care and broader political change.

However, US and Japanese government bureaucrats involved in shaping Japan's Action Plan were differently affected by these accounts. They may have been empathetically moved on a personal level by the cruelty and injustice that migrants experienced; however, their responses were also shaped by their sense of their professional responsibilities and, correspondingly, in the case of US officials, their investment in global norms and US global leadership, and in the case of Japanese bureaucrats, their self-conscious investment in Japan's national modernity and international standing. Caseworkers viewed advocating for broader social change as part of their jobs. However, government officials in positions to advocate for broader change were more inclined to approach the issues in terms that were familiar to and convenient for existing social and political relations. Their jobs involved maintaining diplomatic relations and upholding existing laws.

Some might argue that these government officials' responses simply reflected a lack of real empathy for migrant workers and that if these officials could truly empathize with foreign migrants, their responses might be different.[36] However, following Saidiya Hartman, I would suggest the opposite: These officials' responses reflected both their empathy for the migrants *and* empathy's inadequacy for mobilizing political change. As Hartman explains, empathy works as a form of substitution and thereby an erasure of another. It is, in her words, an "exercise in imagination" and a "fantasy" that "fails to expand the space of the other but merely places the self in its stead" on a conditional and temporary basis.[37] In other words, to empathize is to compartmentalize the suffering of another—a privilege of those who can safely detach themselves from it.

Consequently, the differential affects of these accounts of suffering, and the differential empathetic responses inspired by them, led government officials to different solutions for addressing migrants' suffering than they did NGO workers. Even if government officials empathized with migrants, the shared humanity that Japanese and US officials saw in migrants' accounts of suffering was a compartmentalized, stripped-down humanity: a civil and political subjectivity that guaranteed only bare life. Consequently, these officials felt a legal and bureaucratic obligation to affirm and enforce only those laws that protect the circumscribed human rights that guarantee such life. Migrants' powerful accounts of their suffering were not enough to override officials' professional and personal commitments and inspire them to push for significant change, at least not within the scope of their official positions.

We can see in the failure of migrants' stories to (thus far) compel meaningful action on the part of national governments both the contours of the structural violence faced by migrants and the erasure of this violence from institutional plans. We see that appeals to international human rights norms can be undercut even as they appear to be received, resulting in a banal institutional project. In other words, government officials do not need to be indifferent or callous to human suffering for their actions to have brutal consequences.[38] People care about others for different reasons and thus to various ends. One can be emotionally affected and still not *think*.

In contrast to empathizing, thinking in an Arendtian sense requires self-critically reflecting on one's difference from another even as one gives oneself over to trying to understand the other's pain; thinking does not stop at identifying with another's suffering so much as it pushes one to contemplate their direct and indirect relationships to it. In chapter 6, I return to how Vicente, Cherie, and other NGO caseworkers endeavored to think about the experiences of their clients to strategize around best serving their needs. First, though, I turn to the banalities embedded in the everyday practice of the global counter–human trafficking project's victim identification protocol, exploring how this protocol instrumentalizes human rights by turning rote compliance into a measure of its realization.

4

"TO PROMOTE THE UNIVERSAL VALUES
OF HUMAN DIGNITY," A ROADMAP

———————

2.1.2. PURPOSE OF SCREENING

It is important to properly screen persons referred as trafficking victims to service delivery organizations for assistance to ensure that they are in fact trafficking victims and not smuggled or other irregular migrants, or other individuals in an abusive or vulnerable situation who may be in need of assistance and/or protection. Furthermore, care should be taken to assess whether the presumed victim is in fact not a victim of trafficking or someone in need of assistance, but someone actually trying to infiltrate the service organization for other motives.

—IOM, *The IOM Handbook on Direct Assistance for Victims of Trafficking*

After the Japanese government enacted its Action Plan in 2005, Japan was removed from the US *TIP Report*'s Tier 2 Watch List. However, Japan's Tier 2 *TIP Report* ranking persisted in 2005 and 2006, to the Japanese government's chagrin. By 2007, when Japan was once again ranked at Tier 2, the Japanese government had had enough. Other countries considered highly industrialized—including Canada, all of western and northern Europe, Australia, New Zealand, and even South Korea, Hong Kong, and Malawi—were ranked at Tier 1.[1] The Japanese government firmly believed that it had met the minimum standards for a top tier ranking. It made its frustration clear to the US State Department, arguing that the *TIP Report* was "biased and unfair" and threatening to with-hold cooperation with the United States on future issues.[2]

The US State Department now faced another diplomatic bind. The researchers and grassroots organizations in Japan that debriefed the US embassy in Tokyo for the *TIP Report*'s Japan country narrative maintained that the Japanese government was not adequately recognizing victims of human trafficking and questioned its victim identification procedures.[3] They asserted that Japanese government statistics underestimated the actual number of trafficking victims in the country.[4] Yet the Japanese government resisted this assessment. It demanded that the US State Department's Office to Monitor and Combat Trafficking in Persons (hereafter the TIP Office) clearly explain its evaluation criteria and give assurances that meeting those criteria would result in a top tier ranking the following year.

The United States has long viewed Japan as a key ally with shared economic and security interests.[5] Strained US-Japan relations over *TIP Report* rankings was undesirable. To resolve the diplomatic tension, a meeting was quickly called between representatives from the Japanese government's Inter-Ministerial Task Force on Combating Trafficking and Mark Lagon, then the US TIP Office's director.[6] At the meeting, in a gesture of support and encouragement, Lagon provided a document—what later US embassy cables baldly referred to as the "Roadmap to Tier 1" (hereafter the Roadmap)—prescribing the steps the Japanese government needed to take to achieve a Tier 1 *TIP Report* ranking. Following the Japanese government's further request for more detailed instruction, the Roadmap was subsequently appended by a "clarification memo" that included explicit benchmarks against which Japan would be evaluated the next year and offered specific guidelines for victim identification protocols, in large part adopted from the recently published *IOM Handbook on Direct Assistance for Victims of Trafficking* (hereafter the *IOM Handbook*).[7] The TIP Office representatives explained to the Japanese government that by following the outlined procedures in the memo, as well as working toward ultimately ratifying the UN Trafficking Protocol, the Japanese government could come into compliance with US TVPA standards and receive a Tier 1 *TIP Report* ranking the following year.[8] According to a US embassy cable, when Lagon presented the Roadmap to the Japanese delegation, he explained that the *TIP Report* was written "in a spirit of partnership" and that the United States was committed to working closely with Japan, "not to export American morality, but to promote the universal values of human dignity."[9]

This chapter explores what official guidelines like the Roadmap, the clarification memo, and the *IOM Handbook* on which the two are based accomplish "to promote the universal values of human dignity." It asks how these guidelines enabled a banal neglect of the political-economic conditions of migrants' lives to be formally structured into a protocol ostensibly aimed at promoting human rights. As previously explained, because the UN lacks a means to directly enforce international treaties, and because Article 2 of the UN Charter protects the sovereignty of member states, international law is functionally normative, resting on nation-states' willingness to comply to benefit their diplomatic interests.[10] Japan's compliance with international human rights norms has been uneven since it joined the United Nations in 1956.[11] Generally speaking, the Japanese government, like many other UN member states, complies with international human rights treaties when doing so will advance its legitimacy and reputation in a global arena.[12]

Against this backdrop, the Japanese government's request for the Roadmap can be viewed as an example of how NGOs and activists in Japan have effectively leveraged what Keck and Sikkink call "boomerang" influence to pressure the Japanese government to act by strategically working through the US government.[13] It also marks the success of what political scientist Judith Kelley calls "scorecard diplomacy."[14] Kelley argues that because nation-states like Japan value their international reputation, pressuring them to conform to "prevailing standards and expectations" by publicly "grading" them, as the *TIP Report* does, is an effective means for influencing state behavior.[15] The US Government Accountability Office itself makes such a claim, which on the surface appears convincing.[16] Following the Lagon meeting, the Japanese government distributed a thousand copies of the *IOM Handbook* to "relevant ministries and agencies" and undertook a number of policy changes, which I discuss in the following pages.[17]

Yet while such arguments offer insight into how and why the Japanese government may be diplomatically pressured to formally comply with international treaties, they tell us little about how this compliance translates into everyday practice. Indeed, Kelley highlights Japan as a case in which geopolitical considerations interfere with the efficacy of grading strategies; as discussed in the conclusion, the United States resisted lowering Japan's rating and ultimately bumped it up to Tier 1 in 2018.[18] Kelley also points out that scorecard diplomacy solely impacts norms and policy outcomes; it does not necessarily reduce human trafficking.[19] She writes, "The use of grades, rating or rankings is a particularly potent way to elicit reputational concerns. Grades are powerful symbols that shape perceptions about the performance of the graded. Grades are far from neutral, however. They reduce a complex reality to a preferred interpretation and in so doing select what to call attention to and designate that as meaningful."[20] To understand how normative strategies like the *TIP Report* can appear diplomatically effective yet do little to change the situation on the ground, we need to consider not only the day-to-day practices to which they pressure centralized state actors like the Japanese government to conform but what stands to be achieved by this compliance in the first place.

Answering this question requires looking beyond international treaties like the Trafficking Protocol, which contains little in the way of practical, day-to-day prescription, to the guidelines issued by international organizations following the protocol's adoption. These guidelines work alongside the multilateral treaty to establish new international norms for fighting human trafficking on the ground. To give a partial sense of the scope of this overlapping and self-referencing collection, in 2002 the UN high commissioner for human rights issued *Recommended Principles and Guidelines on Human Rights and Human Trafficking*. In the years that followed came UNICEF's *Guidelines on the Protection of Child Victims of Trafficking*; the UNHCR's *Guidelines on International Protection, No. 7*; and the UNODC's *Toolkit to Combat Trafficking in Persons*. In addition, the ILO published both *Human Trafficking and Forced Labor Exploitation: Guidance for Legislation and Law Enforcement* and *Human Trafficking for Sexual Exploitation in Japan*. In 2009, the IOM also put out *Caring for Trafficked Persons: Guidance for Health Providers*, which, like the *IOM Handbook*, follows from the WHO *Ethical and Safety Recommendations for Interviewing Trafficked Women*.[21] Together, these guidebooks constitute what Peter Larsen calls a "guidance culture" surrounding the Trafficking Protocol.[22]

This chapter considers what such institutional guidelines accomplish for the global fight against human trafficking, and it examines whose interest these accomplishments serve. "Proceduralism," what Akhil Gupta and Aradhana Sharma call the following of routine, repetitive practices of governance, has been central to the imagining of the nation-state.[23] It enables a uniform, scalable model of governance that can be parsed into component parts for different agencies to manage. Global governance analogously aspires to consistent formal routines in the interest of articulating a singularly governable global polity. Virtually all fields of international action have witnessed a mushrooming of the production of guidelines and best practices in recent years.[24] What stands to be gained and what is banally neglected in addressing forms of violence like those currently recognized as human trafficking through this modular, globalized institutional practice?

Exploring this question, I turn a close eye on the victim identification protocol outlined in the *IOM Handbook* and recommended by the US TIP Office to the Japanese government, exploring its logics and the purposes that it serves. I make two interrelated arguments. First, I argue that the guidelines work on a pragmatic level to link an everyday protocol with the UN protocol, filling in the principles and procedures for undertaking a global counter–human trafficking campaign on the ground. Circulated locally, nationally, and transnationally, these texts serve as "interscalar vehicles" that synchronize the agendas of international agencies with those of government institutions, local NGOs, and individual lives by encouraging consistency of practice on a global scale.[25] They thereby effect, in the words of the *IOM Handbook*, a "generalized approach to human trafficking and the identification of victims" relevant "for all instances involving the referral of trafficking victims to service delivery organizations, irrespective of whether the organizations are located in countries of origin, transit or destination."[26] By producing uniformity across international and government agencies, the guidelines create the effect of a single, unified project. They also offer standards of practice for monitoring compliance in measurable ways, offering the architecture for a single "audit culture," exemplified here by the *TIP Report*.[27] Second, I argue that as these guidelines articulate the fight against human trafficking as a globally scalable everyday protocol, they also serve a logistical purpose by at once circumscribing who can in practice be assisted under the Trafficking Protocol and enabling compliance with established guidelines, such as the Roadmap, to banally stand in for measurable structural change.

Before proceeding, let me caution that those accustomed to the liveliness and color of ethnographic writing might be disoriented by the following discussion of bureaucratic texts. I have deliberately sustained the dry and monotonous tone and tenor of the documents that I analyze to bring readers inside my ethnographic experience. Returning home from Tokyo, Manila, and Washington, DC, my suitcases were stuffed full of papers: bundles of informational pamphlets about human trafficking; stacks of progress reports on current efforts; weighty packets of brochures enumerating government efforts; piles of guidebooks defining endorsed protocols; printout after printout of official PowerPoint presentations; folders bursting with conference and workshop proceedings; stacks of articles about these efforts by people involved in executing the protocol, some of whom I had met and interviewed. As I perused these materials in Los Angeles, my eyes glazed over at page upon page of summations, enumerations, explanations, clarifications, and justifications, the documents' contents blurring together, analogous executions of the same bureaucratic formula. Anyone who has worked in institutions will recognize this exhaustive and mind-numbing style as part and parcel of bureaucratic life. It is now also part of a global counter–human trafficking project intended to guarantee human rights. Ethnographers of such institutional processes must learn to read against the grain of bureaucratic documents to see the contradictions, aporias, and impasses embedded in them. Highlighting such textual contradictions, this chapter offers a strategy for understanding how a deep illogic structures some of the quotidian textual practices of global governance aimed at promoting human rights.

The Illogic of a Standardized Form

Both grassroots NGOs' appeals and US *TIP Report* assessments stress victim identification because it lies at the heart of the on-the-ground enactment of the Trafficking Protocol: one must first identify those who have been victimized to prosecute human traffickers and protect victims' human rights. Yet despite the celebration that the Trafficking Protocol includes a single definition of human trafficking, identifying trafficking victims in practice is rarely a straightforward process. According to both the *IOM Handbook* and US embassy cables, the most significant challenge is distinguishing those who qualify as trafficking victims from those who are considered "smuggled" or "other irregular" migrants. As the *IOM Handbook* spells out, "It is important to properly screen persons referred as trafficking victims to service delivery organizations for assistance to ensure that they are in fact trafficking victims and not smuggled or other irregular migrants."[28] This distinction is stressed because the UN Convention on Transnational Organized Crime draws a firm line between human trafficking and human smuggling, and the statuses of the subjects of its two corresponding supplementary protocols are very different. Trafficked migrants are identified as victims, entitled to assistance and the protection of their rights. In contrast, under the Migrant Smuggling Protocol, the assumed victim is the UN member state, whose laws have been violated both by migrant smugglers *and* the migrants who enlist them.[29] Thus, per this protocol, smuggled migrants are to be treated as criminals and deported. The US embassy reinforced this point in a cable: "Without formal victim identification procedures, Japan cannot guarantee that victims of human trafficking are not being deported as criminals."[30]

The UN protocol lists the kinds of experiences that constitute human trafficking and thus qualify for assistance. These qualifying criteria focus on a spatially and temporally circumscribed set of experiences: (1) being "recruit[ed], transport[ed], transfer[red], harbour[ed] or receiv[ed]" (2) by means of "the threat or use of force or other forms of coercion, abduction, fraud, deception, abuse of power or a position of vulnerability" or through "the giving or receiving of payments or benefits to achieve" one's "consent" of having another person control you (3) in order to be "exploit[ed]" for profit.[31] After a potential trafficking victim is brought to the Japanese government's attention by NGOs, shelters, or embassies where she has taken refuge, Japanese government officials must determine whether her experience meets these criteria.[32] Because the US State Department determined that the number of trafficking victims recognized by the Japanese government was too low, the clarification memo posited that insufficient training of law enforcement might be resulting in the mistaking of victims of trafficking for smuggled migrants. As a remedy, it suggested that police and immigration officers receive training in "formal trafficking victim identification procedures."[33] To this end, the Roadmap recommended that Japanese police and immigration officers "adopt standard procedures for identifying victims of trafficking in persons" and be trained in a "formal questioning strategy" aimed at eliciting information about "captivity, forced work, coerced sexual acts, and abuse by perpetrators."[34] This suggestion echoes the *IOM Handbook*, which proposes applying "a standardized system" to screen individuals who request assistance to determine whether their experiences meet Trafficking Protocol criteria.[35]

The *IOM Handbook*'s and Roadmap's proposed victim identification protocol involved a two-step process. First, screeners were to look for "indicators" to determine whether or not an individual might formally qualify as a "victim of human trafficking."[36] Both the *IOM Handbook* and the clarification memo include a list of indicators that "flag potential victims": age, sex, nationality, documentation status, location, any physical signs of abuse on the body, and any knowledge or assessment that the interviewee may qualify as relayed by the NGO that initially assisted the migrant and referred her to authorities.[37] If one or more indicators is present, the *IOM Handbook* recommends conducting a screening interview "consisting of a set of questions that focus on the recruitment, transportation, and exploitation phases of the trafficking experience."[38]

Per the guidelines, the interview should be guided by a "Screening Interview Form," which is included in the *IOM Handbook* (see figure 4.1).[39] This form was also appended to the US TIP Office's clarification memo as an "excellent example of victim identification procedures" and "an unofficial translation of the guidelines for victim identification used by U.S. law enforcement personnel, NGOs, and the general public."[40] A bureaucratic document, the form aims to standardize victim identification procedures, making the processes consistent and uniform (and thus scalable) across cases and countries.[41] However, it also embeds intractable contradictions into the screening process.

Some of these contradictions are tied to the Yes/No format of the interview form, which transforms the multilayered process of identifying and addressing injustice, endorsed by NGO caseworkers, into an instrumentalized procedure of completing forms by checking boxes. The form approaches human trafficking as involving two circumscribed phases: "the process: entry into trafficking"

Annex I **Screening Interview Form**

International Organization for Migration
IOM•OIM

Victim of Trafficking: Screening Interview Form

IOM Mission in _____   Confidential

INFORMED CONSENT

Has the individual been informed that IOM and/ or (name of partnering organization) reserves the right to share her/his individual case data for assistance purposes and only with IOM missions and partnering organizations involved in direct assistance?   (Yes/No)

Has the individual further been informed that IOM reserves the right to make a limited disclosure of non-personal data based on the information collected at the interview to law enforcement for the purpose of rescuing other victims that remain under the control of traffickers or preventing other potential victims from being trafficked?   (Yes/No)

Has the individual further been informed that IOM reserves the right to use (only anonymous, aggregate) data for research purposes?   (Yes/No)

Has the individual's full and informed consent been obtained to conduct the screening interview based on information given regarding the role of the organization, the voluntary nature of the interview and the use of the information provided by the individual as outlined above ?

Note: Informed consent is necessary for all services, such as medical examination and procedure, health assessments, assisted voluntary returns and reintegration assistance.   (Yes/No)

If the individual is a minor, has the consent of the parent(s)/ guardian(s) been obtained?   (Yes/No)

Signature of interviewer: _____   Date: _____

Registration Data   IOM Individual ID:

First name(s):   Country of birth:
Family name(s):   Place of birth:
Sex: (M/ F)   Last place of residence in country of origin:
Date of birth: Identity document (type, country, number and expiry date):
Is date of birth an estimate? (Yes/No)
Age (in number of years):
Citizenship:
Ethnicity:

Case and Interview Data

Type of referring organization/individual: (NGO/ International organization/ Law enforcement/ Immigration/ Government/ Embassy/ IOM Mission/ Hotline/ Self-referral-walk-in/ Family/ Friend/ Client/ Other/ NA/ NK)

Specify – Name:
 – Location:
Screening date: (dd-mm-yyyy)
Screening location:
First name and family name of interviewer:
Name of Organization/ Institution:
Contact Details of interviewer:

Address and telephone number of referring organization:

Interviewee's language:
Interpreter? (Yes/ No)
First name and surname of interpreter:
If Minor, first name and family name (s) address(es) and telephone number of parent(s) or guardian(s):

PROCESS: ENTRY INTO TRAFFICKING

1.0. How did the individual enter the process (Indicate multiple options if necessary)?
(Kidnapping/ Sold by member of family/ Sold by non-family member/ Adoption/ Educational opportunity/ Family visit/ Friend visit/ Labour migration/ Marriage/ Tourism/ Other/ NA/ NK)
  1.1. If OTHER, please specify:
2.0 Did entry into the process involve recruitment? (Yes/ No)
  2.1 If YES, how was contact initiated between the individual and her/his recruiter?
(Personal contact/ Employment agency/ Travel agency/ Internet advertisement/ Newspaper advertisement/ Radio advertisement/ Television advertisement/ Other/ NA/ NK)
    2.1.1. If OTHER, please specify:
3.0. If labour migration, what activity did the individual believe s/he was going to be engaged in following arrival at the final destination (indicate multiple options if necessary)?
(Agricultural work/ Begging/ Child care/ Construction/ Domestic work/ Factory work/ Fishing/ Low-level criminal activities/ Military service/ Mining/ Prostitution/ Restaurants and hotel work/ Study/ Small street commerce/ Trade/ Transport sector/ Other/ NA/ NK)

21/05/2009

FIGURE 4.1. "Annex I Screening Interview Form," from IOM, *IOM Handbook on Direct Assistance for Victims of Trafficking*, 50–52.

IOM Mission in   **Individual ID:**

3.1. If OTHER, please specify:
3.2. If FACTORY WORK, please specify manufacturing sector:
4.0. What was the individual told would be their benefits following arrival at final destination?
    4.1. Salary (Equivalent in USD per month)
    4.2. Other benefits:
5.0. In which month/year did the individual enter into the process?
6.0. Minor at time of entry into the process: (Yes/ No)
7.0. From which place/country did the individual enter into the process?
8.0. What place/country is the last (or intended) destination?
9.0. Did the individual travel alone? (Yes/ No)
    9.1. If NO, who did the individual travel with (indicate multiple options if necessary)?
    (Husband/ Wife/ Partner/ Relative/ Friend/ Recruiter/ Transporter/ Unknown persons/ Other/ NA/ NK)
        9.1.1. If OTHER, please specify:
10.0. Did the individual spend any time in transit place(s)/ country(ies)? (Yes/ No)
    10.1. If YES, please specify in chronological order:
    10.2. Did s/he engage in any activity in this place(s) country(ies)? (Yes/ No)
    10.3. If YES, which activity in first/only transit place/ country:
    (Agricultural work/ Begging/ Child care/ Construction/ Domestic work/ Factory work/ Fishing/ Low-level criminal activities/ Marriage/ Military
    service/ Mining/ Prostitution/ Restaurants and hotel work/ Study/ Small street commerce/ Trade/ Transport sector/ Unemployed/ Other/ NA/ NK)
        10.3.1. If OTHER, please specify:
        10.3.2. If FACTORY WORK, please specify manufacturing sector:
    10.4. If MORE PLACES/COUNTRIES in which individual engaged in activity, please add respective places/country(ies)/activity(ies)
    below:

11.0 Were any of the following means used to control the individual?

Physical abuse	(Yes/ No/ NA/ NK)	If YES, who by? (Recruiter/ Transporter/ Harbourer/ Receiver/ Other-specify)
Psychological abuse	(Yes/ No/ NA/ NK)	If YES, who by? (Recruiter/ Transporter/ Harbourer/ Receiver/ Other-specify)
Sexual abuse	(Yes/ No/ NA/ NK)	If YES, who by? (Recruiter/ Transporter/ Harbourer/ Receiver/ Other-specify)
Threats to individual	(Yes/ No/ NA/ NK)	If YES, who by? (Recruiter/ Transporter/ Harbourer/ Receiver/ Other-specify)
Threat of action by law enforcement	(Yes/ No/ NA/ NK)	If YES, who by? (Recruiter/ Transporter/ Harbourer/ Receiver/ Other-specify)
Threats to family	(Yes/ No/ NA/ NK)	If YES, who by? (Recruiter/ Transporter/ Harbourer/ Receiver/ Other-specify)
False promises/deception	(Yes/ No/ NA/ NK)	If YES, who by? (Recruiter/ Transporter/ Harbourer/ Receiver/ Other-specify)
Denied freedom of movement	(Yes/Partial/No/NA/NK)	If YES, who by? (Recruiter/ Transporter/ Harbourer/ Receiver/ Other-specify)
Giving of drugs	(Yes/ No/ NA/ NK)	If YES, who by? (Recruiter/ Transporter/ Harbourer/ Receiver/ Other-specify)
Giving of alcohol	(Yes/ No/ NA/ NK)	If YES, who by? (Recruiter/ Transporter/ Harbourer/ Receiver/ Other-specify)
Denied medical treatment	(Yes/ No/ NA/ NK)	If YES, who by? (Recruiter/ Transporter/ Harbourer/ Receiver/ Other-specify)
Denied food/drink	(Yes/ No/ NA/ NK)	If YES, who by? (Recruiter/ Transporter/ Harbourer/ Receiver/ Other-specify)
Withholding of wages	(Yes/Partial/No/NA/NK)	If YES, who by? (Recruiter/ Transporter/ Harbourer/ Receiver/ Other-specify)
Withholding of identity documents	(Yes/ No/ NA/ NK)	If YES, who by? (Recruiter/ Transporter/ Harbourer/ Receiver/ Other-specify)
Withholding of travel documents	(Yes/ No/ NA/ NK)	If YES, who by? (Recruiter/ Transporter/ Harbourer/ Receiver/ Other-specify)
Debt bondage	(Yes/ No/ NA/ NK)	If YES, who by? (Recruiter/ Transporter/ Harbourer/ Receiver/ Other-specify)
Excessive working hours	(Yes/ No/ NA/ NK)	If YES, who by? (Recruiter/ Transporter/ Harbourer/ Receiver/ Other-specify)
If OTHER means of control, specify:		

THE EXPLOITATION PHASE

12.0. What activity has the individual undertaken since her/his arrival in the last destination (indicate multiple answers if necessary)?
    (Agricultural work/ Begging/ Child care/ Construction/ Domestic work/ Factory work/ Fishing/ Low-level criminal activities/ Marriage/ Military
    service/ Mining/ Prostitution/ Restaurants and hotel work/ Study/ Small street commerce/ Trade/ Transport sector/ Unemployed/ Other/ NA/
    NK)
    12.1. If OTHER, please specify:
    12.2. If FACTORY WORK, please specify manufacturing sector:
13.0. How old was the individual when the activity began? (Age)
    13.1 How long did the only/ most significant activity occur? (Years/ Months/ Weeks/ Days and/or hours)
14.0. Were any of the following means used to control the individual during the activity?

Physical abuse	(Yes/ No/ NA/ NK)	If YES, who by? (Receiver/ Exploiter/ Clients/ Other- specify)
Psychological abuse	(Yes/ No/ NA/ NK)	If YES, who by? (Receiver/ Exploiter/ Clients/ Other- specify)
Sexual abuse	(Yes/ No/ NA/ NK)	If YES, who by? (Receiver/ Exploiter/ Clients/ Other- specify)
Threats to individual	(Yes/ No/ NA/ NK)	If YES, who by? (Receiver/ Exploiter/ Clients/ Other- specify)
Threat of action by law enforcement	(Yes/ No/ NA/ NK)	If YES, who by? (Receiver/ Exploiter/ Clients/ Other- specify)
Threats to family	(Yes/ No/ NA/ NK)	If YES, who by? (Receiver/ Exploiter/ Clients/ Other- specify)
False promises/deception	(Yes/ No/ NA/ NK)	If YES, who by? (Receiver/ Exploiter/ Clients/ Other- specify)
Denied freedom of movement	(Yes/ Partial/ No/ NA/ NK)	If YES, who by? (Receiver/ Exploiter/ Clients/ Other- specify)
Giving of drugs	(Yes/ No/ NA/ NK)	If YES, who by? (Receiver/ Exploiter/ Clients/ Other- specify)
Giving of alcohol	(Yes/ No/ NA/ NK)	If YES, who by? (Receiver/ Exploiter/ Clients/ Other- specify)

FIGURE 4.1. *Continued*

IOM Mission in		Individual ID:
Denied medical treatment	(Yes/ Regular/ Occasional/ Only in emergency cases/ No/ NA/NK)	If YES, who by? (Receiver/ Exploiter/ Clients/ Other- specify)
Denied food/drink	(Yes/ No/ NA/ NK)	If YES, who by? (Receiver/ Exploiter/ Clients/ Other- specify)
Withholding of wages	(Yes/ Partial /No/ NA/ NK)	If YES, who by? (Receiver/ Exploiter/ Clients/ Other- specify)
Withholding of identity documents	(Yes/ No/ NA/ NK)	If YES, who by? (Receiver/ Exploiter/ Clients/ Other- specify)
Withholding of travel documents	(Yes/ No/ NA/ NK)	If YES, who by? (Receiver/ Exploiter/ Clients/ Other- specify)
Debt bondage	(Yes/ No/ NA/ NK)	If YES, who by? (Receiver/ Exploiter/ Clients/ Other- specify)
Excessive working hours	(Yes/ No/ NA/ NK)	If YES, who by? (Receiver/ Exploiter/ Clients/ Other- specify)
If exploited for prostitution (sexual exploitation):		
Denial of freedom to refuse client	(Yes/ No/ NA/ NK)	If YES, who by? (Receiver/ Exploiter/ Clients/ Other- specify)
Denial of freedom to refuse certain acts	(Yes/ No/ NA/ NK)	If YES, who by? (Receiver/ Exploiter/ Clients/ Other- specify)
Denial of freedom to use a condom	(Yes/ Partial/ No/ NA/ NK)	If YES, who by? (Receiver/ Exploiter/ Clients/ Other- specify)
If OTHER means of control, specify:		

15.0. Did the individual experience exploitation? (If NO, proceed to 16.0) (Yes/ No/ NA/ NK)

16.0. If NO exploitation took place, was there any indication of a real and substantial threat of exploitation? (Yes/ No/ NA/ NK)
    16.1. If YES, what were the reasons that exploitation never took place? (Rescue/ Escape/ Other/ NA/ NK)
       16.1.1. If OTHER, please specify:

CORROBORATIVE MATERIALS

17.0. Additional corroborative materials

Police or other official reports	(Yes/ No/ NA/ NK)
Identity documents	(Yes/ No/ NA/ NK)
Travel documents	(Yes/ No/ NA/ NK)
Medical reports	(Yes/ No/ NA/ NK)
Copies of employment contract or recruitment offer	(Yes/ No/ NA/ NK)
Personal writings by the individual	(Yes/ No/ NA/ NK)
Hotline reports	(Yes/ No/ NA/ NK)
Other	(Yes/ No/ NA/ NK)

        If OTHER, please specify:

DECISION

18.0. Is the individual a VICTIM of TRAFFICKING? (Yes/ No)
    18.1. Please justify the decision made in 18.0:

19.0. Decision made by whom (Specify name(s)):

20.0. If the individual is a victim of trafficking, was the type of trafficking in-country or transnational? (In-country/ Transnational/ Both)

21.0. If the individual is a victim of trafficking, is s/he eligible for the IOM VoT assistance Programme? (Yes/ No)
    21.1. If NO, why? (Does not meet project criteria/ Has deportation order/ Suspected infiltrator/ Other)
       21.1.1. If OTHER, please specify:

22.0. If the individual is eligible for the IOM VoT assistance programme, is s/he willing and able to accept assistance? (Yes/ No)
    22.1. If NO, what are the reasons? (Please specify all that apply)
    (Does not trust IOM or partnering organization/ Is afraid/ Is self-sufficient/ Wants to apply for asylum/ Wants to stay in the country/ Other)
       22.1.1. If OTHER, please specify:

23.0. If the individual is NOT a victim of trafficking, is s/he in need of assistance? (Yes/ No)
    23.1. If YES, what is the individual's situation? (Please specify all that apply)
    (In need of emergency medical assistance/ Irregular status/ Victim of sexual or gender-based violence/ Other)
       23.1.1. If OTHER, please specify:
    If YES, please refer the individual to the appropriate service agency.

24.0. Additional Remarks:

FIGURE 4.1. *Continued*

phase and "the exploitation phase."[42] The section regarding the "entry into traf-ficking" phase begins by asking the interviewer to select among options how the individual entered "the process," such as "Kidnapping/ Sold by member of family/ Sold by non-family member/ Adoption/ Educational opportunity/ Family visit/ Friend visit/ Labour migration/ Marriage/ Tourism/ Other." The form then proceeds through questions about the details of the recruitment be-fore concluding with a series of Yes/No selections regarding the "means used to control the individual," including physical abuse, psychological abuse, sex-ual abuse, threats to individual, threat of action by law enforcement, threats to family, false promises/deception, denied freedom of movement, giving of drugs, giving of alcohol, denied medical treatment, denied food/drink, with-holding of wages, withholding of identity documents, withholding of travel documents, debt bondage, excessive working hours, and other means of con-trol to be specified. The next section focuses on "the exploitation phase." This section inquires into the activity "the individual has undertaken since her/his arrival in the last destination."[43] The selections for the means used to control the individual during this phase are the same as those in the recruitment sec-tion with the addition of a short section for those "exploited for prostitution (sexual exploitation)" that asks whether the individual was denied freedom to refuse clients, certain acts, or the use of a condom. The form then asks about the existence (YES/NO/NA/NK) of "corroborative materials," such as police or immigration reports, identity documents, travel documents, medical reports, copies of the employment contract or recruitment offer, personal writings by the individual, or hotline reports. A decision is then to be rendered as to whether the individual is a "VICTIM of TRAFFICKING? (Yes/No)."[44]

The exhaustive list of types of exploitation and how an individual was co-erced or forced into them seems comprehensive and makes the victim identi-fication process appear straightforward. However, the protocol embeds many contradictions, which are explicitly detailed in the *IOM Handbook* itself. First, the form explicitly frames human trafficking as a temporally and spatially bounded event limited to the processes through which a migrant has traveled abroad and the activities in which she was engaged while there. Clients' lives before the recruitment phase, including the historical and political contexts shaping their vulnerability to this recruitment, fall into its margins or off its pages, as do cultural beliefs and labor conventions in Japan. This approach dif-fers from the open-ended interviews conducted by NGO caseworkers as part of their intake process. The open format of these interviews allows the interviewee to share personal experiences that she finds relevant and provides context for her migration circumstances. For instance, migrants may share information about the family circumstances or local conditions of their hometown that left them vulnerable to exploitation. Such circumstances may involve events and relationships that predate migrants' travel to Japan but that may continue to impact their lives after they return home. In contrast, the protocol's form-driven interview is structured around Yes/No and multiple option questions that channel the interviewee's experience into established formal categories, stripping out contextual information to fit the established framework. The official form channels a migrant's personal history of abuse and exploitation into a recognizable pattern so that boxes can be checked and criteria can be met. This narrow logic follows from the Trafficking Protocol, which limits criteria for qualifying for assistance to direct forms of violence. The *IOM Handbook*, meanwhile, recognizes that the format is too constricting to be followed in an interview. It explicitly states that "the use of a questionnaire format is not likely to put the trafficking victim at ease and should therefore be best avoided wherever possible."[45] However, the US State Department presented the form to the Japanese government as recommended protocol for the screening interview, and any information gathered through a screening interview was to be fed into its established format.

Second, both US embassy cables and the *IOM Handbook* acknowledge the inadequacies of the interview process itself, particularly for distinguishing between "trafficking victims" and "smuggled or other irregular migrants," even while both endorse it.[46] First, the clarification memo cable explains that distinguishing trafficking victims from smuggled migrants is challenging because "victims rarely self-identify."[47] This statement is consistent with what both NGO caseworkers and former migrant workers reported to me: few migrants are familiar with the concept "human trafficking." One NGO caseworker relayed an experience assisting a Filipina woman who had escaped from a situation in which she had been confined against her will and forced to sexually service customers. During her intake interview, the caseworker had asked the woman if she had ever "heard of trafficking." The woman had looked at her blankly, responding, "What is trafficking? You mean like with cars?" The caseworker relayed that this Filipina woman's reaction was not uncommon among migrants whom she assisted. Second, and more concerning, NGO caseworkers reported that some migrants blamed themselves for their treatment or believed that it was legal or deserved. For instance, as described in chapter 8, former migrant workers to Japan with whom I spoke in the Philippines explained that it was only years later, after working with NGOs that educated them about their labor and human rights, that they realized that their experiences in Japan not only were against the law and violations of their human rights but also would have qualified as human trafficking; these women had held themselves responsible for how they had been treated. NGO caseworkers reported that few labor migrants knew that they were legally entitled to recourse for mistreatment, and some of these migrants even believed that their treatment was normal or deserved. Consequently, as the *IOM Handbook* explains, migrant workers who may have had experiences that would qualify them as victims of human trafficking based on the UN Trafficking Protocol may not realize this fact. Thus, they may not communicate relevant information about their experiences in their official screening interview, believing that their experiences were normal and permissible.

Third, the *IOM Handbook* explains that even if interviewees are aware that their treatment violates domestic or international laws, they may neglect to communicate relevant experiences to their interviewer because they do not feel comfortable sharing such experiences with another person, and especially with a stranger in a formal interview. The *IOM Handbook* lists a number of reasons why this may be the case, including shame, fear of reprisal, loyalty to one's trafficker, or general mistrust consequent to their experiences or prior run-ins with government officials in their home countries.[48] It explains, "Screening interviews are likely to be a challenging task" when one is interviewing "an individual who was able to survive and flee only by being very circumspect and suspicious of everybody and very careful with information."[49] It specifies that for reasons ranging from fear of retribution to severe memory loss on account of trauma, "the person may not feel able or be willing to be interviewed and answer questions that relate to traumatic and painful events."[50] The US embassy cable also recognizes this problem, explaining that victims may not remember "due to trauma or other causes (drug or alcohol use, for example)."[51] The *IOM Handbook* advises that this may be the case despite the screener's best efforts to be sensitive to the "condition of the victim."[52] It explains that "it is not uncommon for trafficked persons to react to the interviewer in a traumatized, hostile, suspicious, aggressive or defensive manner, or a combination of these."[53]

Because eliciting relevant information in a screening interview is so challenging, the *IOM Handbook* suggests as an alternative that an interviewer may be able to determine whether an individual had been trafficked based on the circumstances of their case, for instance if corroborating documentary evidence is available. In a section on "additional corroborative material," it states, "Additional supporting material may be used to corroborate the victim's account and help in the decision-making process. Documents or other supporting material may be available from the police or NGO partner, or be provided by the victims themselves."[54] The handbook offers a number of examples of potential forms of such evidence: "Police or immigration reports; any travel documents or travel tickets; immigration departure or landing cards; reports of any medical treatment provided for any injuries both prior to referral and treatment provided through the assistance process; copies of employment contracts or copies of the original advertisement; diary entries, letters written by the victim; witnesses' testimonies; photos on the situation of exploitation; medical or psychological analysis."[55] However, the US embassy in Tokyo also explicitly recognizes that getting the police to procure such evidence is challenging. A 2006 Tokyo embassy cable noted, "Embassy contacts in the Osaka Office of the National Police Agency report that the police do not like to investigate human trafficking cases; it takes too many officer-hours to close a case and is not career enhancing. In addition, restrictions on long-term undercover work and the nonexistence of plea-bargaining in Japan impose limitations on the ability of police to investigate TIP cases."[56] Thus, procuring supporting evidence for use in rendering a decision is challenging. Indeed, the country narrative on Japan in the 2006 and 2007 *TIP Reports* acknowledge "the difficulty of establishing the level of documentary evidence required for proving a trafficking crime."[57]

Just as the *IOM Handbook* recognizes that "additional corroborative material may not be available" to support an interviewee's claims, it puts limited faith in the reliability of the very interview protocol that it recommends as the best practice for victim identification.[58] It states that an interviewer may not be able "to obtain enough information to determine conclusively if the person is in fact a victim of trafficking."[59] The handbook explains that the interview protocol is a "model for identification under ideal conditions," qualifying that "field experience shows that ideal circumstances are rarely found."[60] Rather, the handbook explains that "depending on the national, regional or international context, contradictions and exceptions will exist in relation to many of the general points made," stressing that interviewers must "adapt and adjust the generalizations to their local conditions."[61] However, because the *IOM Handbook* can offer only generalized procedures, it provides little in the way of what local adaptations should be made. Instead, it acknowledges that the screening and identification of trafficking victims "will ultimately depend on the experience and judgement of local service delivery organization staff, based on their *cumulative assessment of all available information*."[62] However, as stated, the interview form treats NGO caseworkers' assessment as simply an indicator, and the final determination of a migrant's status rests with the government (see figure 4.1).

Further undercutting its own recommended victim identification protocol, the *IOM Handbook* cautions that individuals may try to falsely claim in an interview those experiences that would qualify them as victims of trafficking in order to access the benefits and assistance provided to such persons. As cited in the epigraph at the start of the chapter, it stresses the importance of ensuring that persons referred as potential trafficking victims "are in fact trafficking victims" and not others trying "to infiltrate the service organization for other motives," such as to access the protections and entitlements accompanying that status.[63]

Moreover, despite stressing the importance of properly identifying victims of human trafficking, and in particular distinguishing them from smuggled or other irregular migrants, both the US government and the *IOM Handbook* maintain that the distinction between "smuggling" and "trafficking" is itself unclear. As the chapter epigraph explains, the *IOM Handbook* recognizes that smuggled and irregular migrants are also often subject to exploitation and abuse. It additionally suggests that the line between these categories is not cut-and-dried. It states that "the victim of trafficking often starts out as a willing smuggled migrant" and that "smuggled migrants are often vulnerable to trafficking upon their entry into the destination country."[64] It also explains that the recommended screening process will not reliably distinguish between members of these groups: "The process is not and cannot be perfect and cannot guarantee against errors in the assessment of an alleged trafficking victim."[65]

Precisely because the line between the experiences of migrants who qualify as victims of human trafficking and those rendered smuggled or irregular is often blurry, the victim identification protocol recommended by the IOM and the US State Department rests on an illogical loop: One must screen referred individuals according to established protocols to determine that they are trafficking victims as opposed to smuggled or other irregular migrants. However, if one screens these individuals according to such protocols, victims of trafficking may be unwilling or unable to discuss the traumatic experiences that would qualify them as such, meaning that the screener may not be able to gather sufficient information to make a reliable or conclusive determination. Moreover, other individuals, such as smuggled or other irregular migrants, may try to falsely claim these experiences to access the benefits and assistance provided to victims of trafficking. Thus, one must follow established protocols for screening victims to determine whether an individual is in fact a victim of trafficking. This illogic prompts one to ask what purpose the standardized screening protocol really serves.

When Compliance Is What Counts

One purpose of victim identification protocols beyond identifying trafficking victims becomes clearer when one considers that just as the Trafficking Protocol defines a group of people who are eligible for humanitarian protection and assistance based on meeting formal criteria, it also excludes those who are not. For instance, as illustrated in chapter 5, undocumented migrants, including those whose work conditions were exploitative or abusive, are not entitled to the assistance provided by the Trafficking Protocol if official protocol is not followed. These migrants will instead be simply repatriated without assistance or held liable for criminal prosecution for illegal residence (*fuhō taizai*) in Japan in accordance with the Migrant Smuggling Protocol.

The stakes of identifying a migrant as a victim of human trafficking as opposed to a smuggled or other irregular migrant are thus quite high, both for individual migrants and for national governments. Migrants who are rendered "smuggled" can be held liable for criminal penalty in Japan, including fines and prison time. They forfeit lost pay, receive no protection upon returning home, and have little recourse if they were exploited or abused. In contrast, those recognized as victims of human trafficking under Japan's Action Plan receive protected status. They are issued a residency permit to remain in Japan so as not to leave the country with undocumented status, and the Japanese government arranges housing and protects them while they remain in the country. In addition, the Japanese government funds an international organization to arrange for their safe repatriation. Their medical care and psychological counseling in Japan can be financially covered. International organization staff in their home countries are paid to escort them home from the airport. Some limited reintegration assistance by NGOs in their home countries, including psychological counseling and job assistance, can be offered. Some identified as victims may be granted limited financial assistance from the Japanese government to complete school or vocational training back home. In other words, the Trafficking Protocol obligates migrant-receiving countries like Japan to provide financial and other resources to rescue, protect, assist, rehabilitate, and repatriate foreign migrants recognized as victims of human trafficking, including those who may have entered through illegal channels. Consequently, the compulsion to participate in a global counter–human trafficking project conflicts with national government investments in retaining domestic resources for citizens and legal residents. Governments of migrant-receiving countries thus have a disincentive to recognize large numbers of foreign labor migrants as trafficking victims even if they sign the Trafficking Protocol. This disincentive works against the pretense of the Trafficking Protocol as protective of universal human rights.

In practice, then, the official victim identification protocol establishes criteria not simply to recognize those migrants that qualify for assistance and protection but also to determine who can be *disqualified* from it. Those who can be legitimately disqualified because they do not fit Trafficking Protocol parameters include smuggled migrants "in an abusive or vulnerable situation who may be in need of assistance and/or protection."[66] In this light, we can see that victim identification protocols work alongside the definition of human trafficking in the Trafficking Protocol *to limit those eligible for assistance as trafficking victims to a select group who pass a screening interview.*

As legal scholars Sara Kendall and Sarah Nouwen tell us, "Millions if not billions of people have reason to consider themselves victims, individually or as part of a group. They are victimized by poverty, family abuse, hunger, floods, diseases, human-rights violations, financial crises, armed conflict, and inequality. If victimhood is conceptualized as a pyramid, this broad category of individuals who have suffered would form its base. However, victimhood as a legal category—juridified victimhood—is much narrower than that massive base. The legal process narrows the category of legally 'recognized' victims."[67] Protocols and guidelines, like those in the *IOM Handbook*, provide government bureaucracies a method for rationalizing their willingness to help some and their refusal to help others by delineating formal standards for claiming that some are not legally deserving of assistance.[68] The use of standardized bureaucratic procedures and forms to identify trafficking victims offers a cover of neutrality, transparency, and instrumentality to these processes.[69] By presenting a shared set of standards, guidelines work through prescription and articulation of normative practice. The guidelines' technical form suggests political neutrality; these are simply best practices. However, through them, procedural constraint becomes a means for legally justifying who is and who is not worthy of help.

At the same time, the guidance culture surrounding the UN Trafficking Protocol enables procedural conformity to become an auditable measure of progress for verifying compliance with international norms regardless of how many trafficking victims are identified or assisted. These bureaucratic expectations of auditable reporting foreclose reflection or dialogue by making visible demonstrations of procedural conformity an end to itself.[70] Indeed, a cable that followed the presentation of the Roadmap made clear that Japan would be first and foremost evaluated on the basis of its compliance to preferred formal protocols as opposed to concrete changes in migrant laborers' vulnerability and work conditions. The TIP Office explained that "Japan's efforts to complete Action 6 [of the clarification memo] will be evaluated in the 2008 TIP Report by whether proper victim identification procedures are being used by official personnel who have contact with foreign trainees and other laborers, NOT by whether these procedures have a 100% success rate."[71] In other words, the Roadmap and the *IOM Handbook* made the criteria for success in fighting human trafficking a matter of organizing trainings and adhering to prescribed victim identification procedures; they translated a commitment "to promote the universal values of human dignity" into a matter of compliance with minimum standards of institutional protocols.

As chapter 5 illustrates, this approach sidelines the input of NGO caseworkers who give more capacious assessments of which migrants deserve support and assistance based on more extensive and open-ended interviews, conversations, and observations that consider the broader structural conditions of migrants' lives. As mentioned, the *IOM Handbook* clearly states that the input of direct service providers, such as NGOs that assist migrants and IOM caseworkers, is essential for accurate appraisals of trafficked persons. It explains that the general identification framework "can be enhanced" by these providers based on their experience and knowledge.[72] However, even though the *IOM Handbook* recommends incorporating the views of service delivery organizations in this determination, the weight given to these organizations' input is at the discretion of the Japanese government, which makes the determination as to whether a migrant qualifies as a victim of human trafficking. NGO staff assisting migrants expressed endless frustration regarding clients whom they viewed as meeting UN Trafficking Protocol criteria but whose claims the Japanese government rejected. Some staff at migrant-support NGOs complained about cases in which different women were rescued from the same establishment and had experienced the same abuse and exploitation but received different designations, with some being recognized as victims of human trafficking and others not. These staff members lamented that even though procedures had been standardized, the government was completely opaque in how it was applying them and ignored NGO input.

Compliance Measures Also Miss the Role of Cultural Norms

The adoption of the *IOM Handbook*'s victim identification protocols was part of a broader swath of procedural changes that the Japanese government undertook to accommodate the Roadmap. *TIP Reports* and US embassy cables had in the past focused on the Japanese government's sponsorship of law enforcement trainings and its use of immigration control to reduce the number of undocumented foreigners as successes and signs of compliance and progress in fighting human trafficking. For instance, in 2005, a confidential cable from the US embassy in Manila maintained that "the reduction in the number of Filipinas going to Japan under the 'entertainer' rubric is a positive development that will likely lead to fewer incidences of trafficking."[73] A 2006 cable sent from the

US embassy in Tokyo to other US embassies in Asia and the secretary of state concluded, "Increased vigilance by police and immigration officers as well as new legislation has brought positive change to the trafficking-in-persons (TIP) situation in Japan. These measures have forced traffickers to change their business model and move deeper underground." This trend was recognized by the US embassy as "a sign of progress."[74] A 2007 cable from the embassy also cited such efforts as concrete, calculable bureaucratic steps: "One of Japan's greatest successes in combating trafficking has been the tightening of requirements for entertainer visas."[75]

This immigration-control approach has had several effects in Japan, none of which has resulted in a significant long-term increase in the number of migrant workers assisted as trafficking victims.[76] First, NGO caseworkers and Filipina migrants in Japan with whom I spoke expressed concern that police raids prompted by US pressure to increase the number of identified trafficking victims had made foreign women in the sex industry *more* vulnerable. Rather than living in groups and working in bars, where they could look out for one another, foreign women in the sex industry had increasingly started doing "delivery health"—that is, being dispatched to private residences and hotel rooms, where they were alone with clients whom they had not previously met. Stricter immigration regulations also meant that trafficking operations moved further underground, becoming more invisible, controlling, and coercive.[77] Some migrant women, desperate for visas enabling them to go to Japan to find work, started coming to Japan on marriage visas, for which they were forced to pay both marriage brokers and Japanese husbands to sponsor their visas.[78] In some cases, their husbands force them into prostitution.[79] In the mid-aughts and 2010s, Filipina wives in the region of rural Nagano, where I previously conducted research, explained that changes in immigration policy in response to the government's counter-trafficking efforts had made getting an entertainer visa increasingly difficult in the Philippines. Consequently, they had noted an influx of Filipina brides into the area, some of whom had paid their Japanese husbands to marry them so that they could obtain spousal visas and enter Japan for work; these women were indebted to, and completely at the mercy of, the Japanese men.[80] The tightening of immigration policy in Japan also does nothing to change the political-economic and cultural conditions that lead Filipina migrants there.

Moreover, the transposition of migrants' accounts of violence and abuse into checked boxes on a form not only ignores the political-economic realities of foreign migrants' lives but also ignores problems with police, prosecutor, and labor culture in Japan. In addition to encouraging the Japanese government to adopt a formal victim identification protocol, the US embassy in Tokyo had begun to hold training sessions geared at teaching formal identification procedures, such as those in the *IOM Handbook*, to law enforcement. Whereas in the past the embassy had worked primarily with the MOFA, the issue of human trafficking had also gotten them involved with the NPA and the DOJ. One US embassy staff member characterized these trainings as involving direct, procedural instruction geared for "professionals." He explained, "Even though the specific investigation rules and techniques are different [in the two countries], you can get a way of addressing a problem that will translate." In his words, they focused on the "very, very nitty-gritty: How do you identify a victim? What are the signs? How do you talk to a victim?" Courses on recognizing and investigating trafficking cases also started being offered at police colleges in Japan. At nationwide police conferences, the Japanese National Police Agency began providing guidance to local police forces on how to investigate human trafficking cases.[81] I learned through my interviews that during the mid-2000s, some members of the Japanese police force received language training in vernaculars used by migrant workers, such as Tagalog. During this training, they improvised how to approach migrant workers suspected of being victims of trafficking, acting out potential encounters and ways to sensitively engage with them. The Immigration Bureau also began offering trainings with lectures from IOM lawyers, NGO representatives, and scholars.

Yet just as the US State Department encouraged these efforts, it recognized that they would have limited impact on account of established police and prosecutor culture in Japan. Generally, Japanese police are responsible for initial investigations, apprehensions, and arrests of those suspected of penal code violations; the police then turn over cases to public prosecutors, who collect further evidence, file indictments, and bring cases to court. Not only have Japanese police officers been accused of racial profiling, sexism, and discrimination against migrants but, as mentioned previously, bureaucratic and prosecutorial priorities favor quickly closed and career-enhancing cases.[82] Moreover, Japanese police are documented to have close connections with organized crime, including receiving payoffs and being sympathetic to their conservative views.[83] Meanwhile, public prosecutors, who have complete discretion over indictment decisions, file formal indictments in a minority of cases, dropping charges for many reasons.[84] Beginning in the 1990s, these prosecutors began dealing with an increase in caseloads as crime in Japan also increased.[85] More straightforward and easily prosecutable cases presumably took precedence. The criteria for transfer into highly coveted posts rests more on avoiding mistakes, such as having cases acquitted, than on making a bold policy intervention or winning a big case.[86] Indictments are subject to approval by two or three superiors up an intuitional chain of command who review the adequacy of evidence.[87] Consequently, the overall conviction rate for all cases in Japan exceeds 99 percent, and prosecutors exercise extreme caution toward indicting suspects without decisive evidence.[88] Although one premise of the UN protocol is that victims of human trafficking can serve as witnesses for the state in criminal prosecutions against transnational organized crime syndicates, public prosecutors often rely on confessions, which are procured while suspects are detained and interrogated at length.[89] Without confession and other forms of hard evidence, which are difficult to obtain in trafficking cases, prosecutors often hesitate to indict.

The potential for stopping migrant labor exploitation in Japan is also complicated by embedded labor cultures in the country. Since the 1980s, there has been much demand for migrant labor in Japan. Because the Japanese government did not offer residence permits for unskilled migrant labor, in 1993 it began a Technical Intern Training Program (Ginō Jisshū Seido, hereafter the TITP or the Trainee Program), which quickly became a legal loophole for bringing low-paid migrant workers to Japan. (The program was ostensibly established so that workers from developing countries could come work in Japan to acquire skills to repatriate, thereby contributing to their home country's economic development.) Many abuses have been documented within the program. For instance, Japanese media and legal professionals have described conditions in which passports have been confiscated and workers became indentured, were forced to work excessive hours, or did not receive overtime pay.[90] Cases have also been documented in which migrants on trainee visas were literally worked to death.[91] In 2010, Jorge Bustamante, the UN special rapporteur on the human rights of migrants, produced an extensive report of abuses within the system.[92]

The Japanese government has acknowledged that egregious cases of labor exploitation are occurring through the program, and as I discuss in the book's conclusion, revisions to the program and the Immigration Control and Refugee Act have been made to address them.[93] However, as NGOs and news reports attest, these problems have persisted. Moreover, the treatment of workers who have entered Japan through the TITP also raises broader questions about cultural standards of labor and employment in Japan. Consider my interview with Rina, the project manager of the counter–human trafficking project at an international organization's Japan office. As soon as I mentioned the TITP, Rina offered, "Everyone knows the Trainee Program is a way to get cheap labor in Japan." I later heard the same from a law professor at a top Japanese university. He relayed that in a meeting with representatives from the Japanese Ministry of Justice, one civil servant openly admitted that the program was a matter of "*tatemae*" (face)—that is, a strategy for admitting cheap unskilled laborers without giving the appearance that was their intention. The government needed the laborers, some of whom were involved in building infrastructure for the 2020 Olympics. Indeed, the Japanese government had relied heavily on undocumented migrants to build the bullet-train tracks for the 1998 Nagano Olympics. Then, before the Olympics began, it launched "Operation White Snow," a police campaign aimed at deporting undocumented migrants, including those who had worked on the railroad extension.[94] Rina shared how troubled she had been by the campaign. We discussed how the Trainee Program shares much with guest-worker programs in the United States and Canada, which have been widely documented as rife with exploitation and abuse.[95]

Rina submitted that in some cases, discrimination based on race and class informs worker exploitation; however, in others, the problems reflect broader issues of work culture in Japan. For example, she brought up cases of small-scale employers in Japan, including mom-and-pop manufacturing businesses or farms, that commit what are categorized as "human trafficking abuses," though they do not recognize that they are exploiting their employees. These employers have, by necessity, worked themselves to the bone their entire lives, many laboring sixteen-to-twenty-hour days, seven days a week; they believe that they are holding foreign employees to the same standards to which they hold themselves. Indeed, overwork has been a domestic labor rights concern in Japan for decades—including being recognized as a problem in elite corporations and government offices in Japan. *Karōshi* (death from overwork) has been so common that the Japanese government keeps official statistics on it, just as they do for deaths from cancer or heart disease. More recently, popular media reports have emerged in Japan about *burakku kigyō* (black corporations), companies that employ Japanese citizens and engage in exploitative, sweatshop-like labor practices, such as requiring extensive overtime without offering overtime pay and permitting verbal abuse and harassment by superiors. Since 2012, journalists and rights activists have awarded an annual *burakku kigyō taishō* (Most Evil Corporation of the Year Award; literally "Black Corporation Award") to the worst offenders; nominees have included major corporations, such as NHK, Panasonic, and Taisei Corporation, the main contractor that built Tokyo's new Olympic stadium.[96]

Rina then shared her own experience. She had worked in a Japanese government ministry after she graduated college. Such positions are highly coveted, attracting graduates from Japan's top universities. When Rina was hired, she was informed by her superiors that her salary was based on a twenty-four-hour workday without overtime. She explained that while there, she regularly worked twenty-hour days on a six- and sometimes seven-day workweek. A law professor at Tokyo University—the preeminent law school in Japan and the program from which the most elite government bureaucrats are selected—shared similar stories about former students from his program who had held positions in Japanese government ministries. One had died of *karōshi* in his late forties. The other, also in his forties, had stopped working under doctor's orders because of concerns about the strain on his heart. He had been working around the clock and hardly sleeping. This law professor explained that many of the elite of the elite (e.g., Tokyo University law school grads) are putting in 450 billable hours a month—under intense pressure from their superiors and without overtime pay.[97]

Formal procedures for identifying victims of human trafficking based on indicators and standardized questionnaires offer uniform, concrete, measurable criteria for identifying victims of human trafficking. However, they do little to address the norms that structure this—to borrow Primo Levi's term—"gray zone" of labor violence or the police and prosecutor culture that makes the prosecution of trafficking cases so challenging.[98] Instead, the guidance culture surrounding the UN Trafficking Protocol offers procedural conformity as a banal means of addressing a complicated and entrenched set of problems, directing attention away from the complexities of history, geography, and culture that shape labor exploitation in Japan and around the globe.

Conclusion

This chapter has explored some of the banalities of the victim identification protocols recommended by the US State Department and the IOM and adopted by the Japanese government. It has described how the guidance culture that governs the global counter–human trafficking project translates the promotion of human dignity and the protection of human rights into a set of modular best practices and a checklist of bureaucratic tasks. This guidance culture makes compliance a matter of following protocols, turning procedural consistency into an end in itself. It instrumentalizes human rights, reducing political action to technical prescription and equating justice with institutional conformity. In this process, a global counter–human trafficking effort turns away from more nuanced and complex understandings of structural violence, cultural and geographic specificity, and larger political economic relations. This logic follows from the Trafficking Protocol itself, which is designed to establish a minimum standard for action. Here, the banality of good results not from mismatched or imposed standards, nor is it the product of the absence, lapses, or neglect of established protocols. Rather, it lies in the very insistence on a rote adherence to a protocol in the face of its recognized inadequacies and neglect of structural considerations.

Some may laud the US TIP Office for sticking to its guns and initially refusing to rank Japan among the Tier 1 when NGOs and third-party embassies in Japan expressed persistent concerns.[99] However, as I explain in this book's conclusion, when Japan finally did make Tier 1 in 2018, the rationale had little to do with any success in identifying foreign labor migrants as trafficking victims; indeed, their mistreatment was still recognized as a serious problem.[100] Rather, most of what was celebrated was Japan's criminalization of the compensated dating practices engaged in by Japanese teenage girls. Also, that year Japan had finally signed on to the UN Trafficking Protocol.

Political scientists have stressed the importance of international norms in shaping state behavior. However, if international guidelines are themselves problematic, little will be achieved by compliance with them. Indeed, these guidelines give UN member-state governments the impression and satisfaction that they are doing something even if they have little effect on the problem or are arguably making it worse. Moreover, what appears to be a mundane bureaucratic formula becomes an instrument of legal violence when we consider the fates of those women who do not receive this designation. Here, the banality of the protocol lies in its complete indifference to its own inadequacy.

In the remaining chapters, I explore how this self-serving logic informs the everyday practice of victim assistance in Japan and the Philippines. In some cases, bureaucratic violence can be chaotic and arbitrary.[101] However, in others, as I have been arguing, it can also be the product of a steadfast and pointed application of rules. Chapter 5 explores the banalities of the victim assistance process by considering how the technicalities of the victim identification protocol allows women who were exploited and abused to be denied protection as trafficking victims.

BANAL JUSTICE

───────────

I have reached a point where I have come to view the reason that I am here in Japan at the level of the spiritual. I'm not here because of "work." I'm here because God knows there is something I will have to do based on the idea of goodness. Regardless of religion, there must be equality, or love for people, or something like that. Because I cannot otherwise imagine my being here in Japan, working for 11 years. It helps me to see my job through the perspective of the spiritual, or else I would be quitting, leaving here, and working somewhere else.

—VICENTE, caseworker at a Japanese NGO

Vicente grew visibly upset when he began talking about the case. His voice trembled and rose, and his head shook back and forth in dismay. We were sitting in a small two-room apartment in an accessory building at the NGO where he had been a social worker for the past eleven years. The organization served as both a home for orphaned and abandoned children and a temporary residence for foreign mothers with Japanese children who had left abusive relationships. It also provided transitory housing for single foreign migrant women, including those who had been identified as trafficked.

The NGO's pastoral surroundings belied its location on the outskirts of Tokyo. From the local train station, I had ridden a public bus through miles of verdant hills and rice fields before arriving at an isolated convenience store, where Vicente, wearing a pale blue guayabera and a warm smile, picked me up in his NGO's van; we then drove an additional twenty minutes through more countryside, and up a steep sylvan grade, before arriving at the NGO property. As we sat at a small table beside the tatami room where a group of eleven Filipina migrants had recently stayed, Vicente shared his frustration with the outcome of their case.

His NGO had assisted the women in leaving what he clearly understood to be a "trafficking situation." However, the IOM, following the Japanese government's guidelines, had declined to help repatriate the women or provide for reintegration assistance. They told Vicente that the problem was that his NGO had reported the case through the prefectural police, as opposed to the National Police Agency. Moreover, the NGO had itself begun initiating arrangements for the women's return to the Philippines. Unbeknownst to Vicente, these steps were not consistent with Japanese government protocol for trafficking cases. Consequently, the women would be repatriated without formal recognition as victims of human trafficking. Vicente was infuriated by the official decision, and particularly by the lack of transparency in the process through which it had been made. He had tried to protest and had written a letter of complaint to the IOM and the Japanese Ministry of Justice. However, both agencies remained firm in their decisions. Vicente expressed deep remorse over what had transpired, which he viewed as a miscarriage of justice:

> *It was very painful for me to know that these women have been with us. We've talked to them. We know of them to have been interviewed by the police, and the police had all of the information about their case in their reports. And in the end the government would say, "Because you did not report immediately to the National Police, we cannot consider them as trafficking victims." I said, "Where in your process does it say that we cannot report to the prefectural level police? Because the prefectural police have a person in charge of trafficking. It would be the assumption that that person would inform the National Police along with the regional Women's Consultation Office. The Women's Consultation Office acted on the case and asked us to take care of the women, so we thought that everything had been cleared."*

Vicente's frustration was compounded both by his painful recognition that he had let down his clients and by how the IOM and Japanese government had responded to his complaint, which made him further question the rationale behind their decisions: "They said that they already closed the club [that had been holding the women], and the owner of the club was crying to them, and 'we are processing these people to go home, and they get their pay. All of them can go home safely.

What's the point of making a big issue of this thing?' Something like that. But this is a trafficking case! What really drove me mad is that the women cannot avail of the aftercare to which trafficking victims are entitled. I blew my top. I was angry. I'm angry with the system."

This chapter takes seriously the anger that NGO caseworkers like Vicente feel about the treatment of their clients under Japan's Action Plan as demonstrations of an alternative understanding of justice persisting within the global counter–human trafficking project. I build on scholars who have challenged the notion that justice manifests in a singular, prescriptive legal form. Rather, these scholars argue that justice is "an empty signifier."[1] Its meanings are multiple, situated, and culturally and geographically shaped by affective, judicial, and other forms of discretion, even within a single movement or organization.[2] Moreover, these scholars maintain that appeals to justice are implicit not only in the rules and institutions of law but also in the claims of those who contest them.[3] As Marianne Constable writes, "Claims on behalf of and within the 'system,' as well as claims made against it, appeal however silently, however strategically, however hypocritically, to justice."[4]

Here I decouple the understandings of justice articulated by NGO caseworkers like Vicente from the formal, juridified vision of justice—or what I call Justice—enacted through official protocol. I explore how and why the Justice endorsed by global counter–human trafficking campaigns neglects to address the structural violence shaping labor migrants' lives. I argue that the anger of NGO caseworkers like Vicente is a response to the intractable contradictions embedded in the vision of Justice underpinning the official counter–human trafficking protocol, which fails to both protect all foreign migrants who have been severely exploited and abused, and enable caseworkers like Vicente, who are deeply committed to supporting their clients, to do their jobs with integrity. For these NGO caseworkers, the Trafficking Protocol's Justice is banal, an unthinking articulation that serves the interests of national governments and international agencies more than the needs of those it purports to assist. Its failures do not result from lapses in its application but from rote adherence to it.

The protection of trafficking victims is a key tenet of the "Framework for Action" of the UN Trafficking Protocol, which is explicitly organized around "the three internationally recognized themes of prevention, protection and prosecution," also known as the "3Ps."[5] As mentioned in chapter 4, those migrants formally recognized as victims of human trafficking are eligible for a paid trip home, counseling and medical care, and rehabilitation funds. However, to qualify for this protection under the Japanese government's Action Plan, a foreign migrant must be officially recognized by representatives from Japan's Ministry of Justice, who determine, on a case-by-case basis, whether an individual meets the criteria for assistance.[6] As we have seen, despite the recognized expertise and experience of NGO caseworkers, their input is considered only one factor—an "indicator"—and in no way determining of the government's decision.[7] Moreover, although government decisions on specific cases are presumably based on the formal official criteria and established guidelines discussed in chapter 4, the rationales behind individual decisions is not ordinarily disclosed to caseworkers. For instance, another NGO caseworker cited a case in which nine of her clients had been working under the same abusive circumstances at a bar, but only one woman was recognized by the Japanese government as a trafficking victim. This caseworker could not understand why the other eight women were not, and she was not offered any explanation as to why. She, too, shared her frustration with the opacity of the Japanese government's determination process and, like Vicente, with her inability to secure resources for her clients as trafficking victims.

For these NGO caseworkers, the selective process by which some migrants receive protection under the protocol, while others subjected to the same conditions do not, calls into question the protocol's commitment to protect. As we have seen, the Trafficking Protocol's definition of human trafficking is at once capacious and vague, allowing for flexible interpretation by national governments and thus their diplomatic buy-in, and limited in what it recognizes as violence. In the remainder of the chapter, I explore the vision of Justice that underpins the Japanese state's enactment of the Trafficking Protocol, and I contrast it with the understanding of justice that motivates NGO caseworkers with whom I spoke. I begin with the very personal predicament Vicente faced in his endeavor to realize justice for his clients. I then consider the Japanese state's vision of Justice and how NGOs caseworkers' commitments at once enable and are sidelined by the official trafficking victim assistance process in Japan.

A Predicament of Justice

As indicated in this chapter's epigraph, Vicente viewed victim recognition as a matter not just of assisting his clients but also of personal accountability and a spiritual calling, a doing right by his clients and achieving justice for them in some small way "based on the idea of goodness." He told me on another occasion that he's "mellowed as [he's] aged" and now didn't think he could change the entire world but wanted "to contribute in [his] one small portion, to contribute in a given space." For Vicente this meant ensuring that his clients' rights were protected, in part by addressing the discrimination that they experienced in Japan, not only as Filipinas but also as women working in the sex industry, who were commonly disparaged and regularly had their rights dismissed. He explained, "Of course, you have to feel something as a Filipino, but not just because they are Filipinos. They are people, human beings. What makes them lower than you or me? They are the same." He explained that his job was exhausting, but "it's more than just work. It's, in a way, a meaning of why I am here." He continued by adding that if it were just a job, he could not manage it; "there would be so much pain, so much pressure, so much disappointment, despair." It was something that he did in the name of "equality" and "love for people."

Motivated by such commitments, Vicente had spent days talking on the phone to the eleven women he had assisted before the women had felt comfortable leaving their situation. He explained that they had taken risks each time they contacted him, knowing that they could be punished if the calls were discovered. He recalled that when they first phoned his NGO, he had had to establish rapport with them and gain their trust. He shared that he spoke to them in Tagalog, identifying himself as Filipino, and told them, "You can call me *Kuya* [big brother] Vince." After that, he explained, "They started pouring out their pain, all those things." He listened and tried to evaluate how to best advise them. He relayed that half of the group had been staying in an ordinary apartment, but the other half was living "in inhuman conditions." This half of the group was housed in a filthy, run-down shack with little more than insect-infested futons. None of the women were given sufficient food. Vicente explained, "They were promised they would get 3,000 yen (about US$25) a day as a food allowance, but they don't have any money." They sometimes relied on receiving secret gifts of rice from customers to have enough to eat. The women housed in the shack did not have a toilet. They were expected to relieve themselves outside in the fields. He relayed how at night, when they were too scared to go outside, the women used plastic garbage bags to urinate and defecate. They had told him, "Even if we come from a poor area of the Philippines, we do not live in this kind of situation; it's very inhuman." Vicente also shared that a number of the women were regularly being raped or sexually assaulted by the club owner. They had been living in these conditions for several months before they called Vicente's NGO.

Before advising the women to leave, Vicente had weighed many factors. He recognized that the women were concerned about not only the immediate dangers that they would face if they were caught trying to escape but also the broader social and economic consequences of leaving an income opportunity, however abusive and exploitative. He thought about the political-economic circumstances in the Philippines that had motivated them to go to Japan, considering that the women's families and communities likely expected them to return with money and that many had incurred significant debt to travel abroad. He was concerned that encouraging them to leave could have negative long-term consequences for them. He explained that before feeling comfortable encouraging them to leave, he needed to both understand the situation they were in and the risks involved with their leaving it: "I had to lay the groundwork first. How far would they be willing to sacrifice or take the risk? The women who called said that some of the group does not want to go home. They are here to earn money, and what would happen if they didn't have their salaries? Their parents would beat them." He explained the significance of the rapport that he had established in shaping their decision and the sense of responsibility that he felt toward them. "They know that I can be trusted, that I will not leave them hiding, for example. So that is a very crucial thing there. And it's of course a burden on me. I have to see them through the best method that I can." He was pained by the outcome of these women's case because he felt a sense of personal responsibility to them.

Because the women were located far across the country, Vicente had arranged for them to go to the nearby prefectural police, who had contacted a local Women's Consultation Office (WCO) (Fujin Sōdan Sentā; Fujin Sōdanjo) to shelter and assist them. The WCO then requested that the women be transferred to Vicente's shelter because it had better capabilities, after which the prefectural police brought the women to Vicente's NGO. When the women arrived, Vicente asked them if they would be uncomfortable staying in the small two-room apartment, as the space would be tight for all eleven of them. He relayed that they had told him, "We will be comfortable; we are used to the hard life in the Philippines." They added that they wanted to stay at the NGO because they trusted him, saying, "We want to stay here because you're here."

It pained Vicente that these women had not received the assistance that he believed to be their due. The technicalities on which the Japanese government had refused to grant the women status as trafficking victims forced Vicente to face the limitations of his ability to help them. As cited in the chapter epigraph, Vicente had learned to cope with the everyday frustrations of his job by making sense of his work as part of a larger calling by God. Like many NGO workers from the Philippines that I met in Japan, Vicente identified as Catholic and followed a tradition similar in spirit to that of liberation theology. After he graduated from college, he had worked as a university chemistry instructor in Manila. He had then switched to social work, getting an MBA and working as a project supervisor at a big agency that funded community-based projects in poor communities throughout the Philippines. On one of these projects, he had met the Japanese head of the National Association of Social Welfare Officials, who had invited him to join a training program to study the social welfare system in Japan. Through it, he met the head of the NGO where he was now working. She had petitioned the Japanese government for him to receive a skilled-labor visa so that he could work with her organization.

Vicente's frustration with the outcome of the migrants' case stemmed not only from his "spiritual" commitment to helping others but also from a conviction that the women were entitled to assistance and to having their rights protected. He had been bothered by what he viewed as the cynicism of the Japanese government's position toward the women, and he questioned the rationale for refusing to consider the women as victims of trafficking. He sardonically summed up what he understood to be the government's position on the case: "'Well, she went home with her salary, that's good enough. She should be happy with it.'" This position angered him. "Forget about her rights, forget about these things. This is the wall that I have to face. What happens to the worker in that kind of situation?" For Vicente, the Japanese government's refusal to recognize the women as trafficking victims was a refusal to recognize both the immediate and the broader social and political-economic injustices shaping their lives. He said, "Theirs is a very flimsy excuse. We are talking about lives here. We are talking about victims." Vicente was furious with how the Trafficking Protocol allowed the Japanese government to reduce his clients to bare life, dismissing the quality of their lives or their well-being beyond the immediate circumscribed terms. He refused to simply concede to the protocol's jurisdictional distinctions and formal technicalities and accept the qualified relief offered to these women—the mere release from their contract so that they could return home with their earned salary—as the Japanese government insisted that he do. He saw how these conventions deprived his clients of the protections and assistance that he believed they should be accorded as a matter of human rights, assistance such as aftercare and the financial resources to make lives for themselves in the Philippines.

For Vicente, the women's experiences at the club in Japan were the product of both the pervasive discrimination that migrant workers face in Japan and the women's structural vulnerability in the Philippines, which had led them to an abusive and exploitative work situation. The outcome of their case was an extension of the Japanese state's indifference to migrants' rights and of the Philippines' lack of resources and political will to contest it. As Vicente thought about his clients' feelings and futures, he saw the disjuncture between the women's needs and the distinctions and conventions of the Trafficking Protocol. He was angered by the "unprotection" of his clients allowed by the Trafficking Protocol, the Japanese government, and the IOM's ongoing, active failure to protect abused and exploited migrants even while it claimed not to want to expose them to harm.[8] He felt that this unprotection was a miscarriage of justice.

Experiences like these placed Vicente in a predicament over whether to continue to refer clients to the Japanese government for recognition as victims of trafficking. For him, victim recognition was not just a matter of assisting clients through a protocol; it was a serious and emotional matter of personal investment and accountability. Vicente was deeply pained by what had happened with this case: "I really feel bad about their not being recognized. We are here to help them, not because it's our work, but because we are human beings, we're Filipinos, and they deserve to be helped. Why should they be lost in the process?" Like Mrs. Saito in chapter 3, Vicente defined his own humanity by ensuring that his clients received the assistance that he believed they were due. He worried also that he had betrayed the women's trust. He felt that by trusting that the protocol would serve them, he had ultimately failed them.

Later in the conversation, Vicente mentioned an ongoing case involving two teenage girls, seventeen and eighteen years old, who had been exploited and sexually abused while working in a club and who wanted to finish high school when they returned to the Philippines. On the one hand, if these girls were recognized as victims of trafficking, they would be eligible for funds for their repatriation and to finish their schooling; his small NGO and the NGOs with which he worked in the Philippines lacked the resources to offer such support without Japanese government assistance. On the other hand, if Vicente referred these girls to the Japanese government, he had no guarantee that it would accept his assessment that the girls qualified as victims of trafficking; it could decide for one reason or another to simply deport them without any assistance. Moreover, as I discuss in chapter 6, because of need-to-know protocols, he would also be kept in the dark about their fate. He would have to completely let go of the case, meaning he would not have any say in if or how the girls would be assisted, and he would not know what happened to them once they returned home. Vicente's past experiences had made him uncertain as to whether the Japanese government would recognize the girls as trafficking victims and provide them with the appropriate resources and support. He explained, "Yeah, I have doubts. . . . They don't even tell me what will happen. They do not trust me to tell them that here is a victim. So it goes round and round."

The vision of Justice embraced by international actors and powerful national governments, like Japan's, is defined by legal doctrine and enacted by government representatives. Under this juridified Justice, naming a victim requires identifying a perpetrator. This vision relies on juridical and carceral strategies for controlling individualized criminal behaviors through courts, payments, and prisons. The language of the Trafficking Protocol subtly but clearly privileges this juridical and carceral vision of Justice over others. Although it includes specific provisions for prosecuting traffickers, it lacks them for ensuring social and economic justice for victims.

The protocol does include recommendations for protecting victims and preventing human trafficking. Item (b) of the Statement of Purpose of the Trafficking Protocol identifies the need to "protect and assist" victims of human trafficking, "with full respect for their human rights."[9] As detailed in chapter 6, the first item in Article 6 of Section II gives clear instruction that states must ensure privacy and confidentiality of victims' identities and circumstances.[10] The second item in Article 6 requires that State Parties adopt measures that "ensure" that trafficking victims are informed and enabled to participate in court and administrative procedures, including criminal prosecution of their traffickers. However, the items that address direct assistance and protection are much vaguer and more tentative. They do not require that state parties *ensure* anything; they only recommend that state parties "*consider* implementing measures to provide for the physical, psychological and social recovery of victims," and that "in appropriate cases" they cooperate with NGOs to do so.[11] The protocol does not specify what particular provisions would be considered sufficient; it asks state parties only to "consider" a range of possible ones: "appropriate housing" (as opposed to incarceration); the provision of "counselling and information, in particular as regards their legal rights, in a language that the victims of trafficking in persons can understand"; "medical, psychological and material assistance"; and "employment, educational and training opportunities."[12] As part of these measures, the protocol also asks parties to consider offering trafficking victims' permanent residence, and even potentially citizenship, in the countries to which they were trafficked on account of "humanitarian and compassionate factors."[13] A signatory state government can consider taking such steps and then decide, for one reason or another, not to do so and not be in violation of the agreement. Using noncommittal and vague language regarding victim assistance was a strategy for encouraging UN member-state governments to sign on to the Trafficking Protocol by leaving room for different governments to interpret the protocol as they saw fit. More specific, directive, and constraining standards would increase the likelihood that potential signatories would opt out. In other words, garnering a maximum possible number of signatories on the protocol necessarily took precedence over adopting one that guaranteed protection and assistance to those whose rights were violated.

The vision of Justice articulated in the Japanese government's Action Plan hews closely to that of the UN Trafficking Protocol. Both assume that juridified victims will testify against their traffickers in court and thereby support national government efforts to prosecute crimes and lock up criminals.[14] Both documents are also premised on the notion that insofar as trafficking survivors' testimony helps governments prosecute traffickers, the interests of victims of trafficking are, in at least some sense, aligned with those of national governments, despite the fact that many trafficking survivors are technically undocumented and thus in violation of national immigration laws when they apply for status. As discussed in earlier chapters, the history of the anti-trafficking movement in Japan is in part a history of *some* migrants' testimony coming to be viewed as credible and advantageous to the national government, while the testimony of other migrants who have suffered abuse and exploitation, such as Vicente's clients, is dismissed as unreliable, useless, or insignificant. Once a potential trafficking victim is identified by the Japanese government, police agencies and public prosecutors can be tasked with investigating the case—for instance, by looking for material evidence of crimes that support the victim's testimony, such as locks on the outside of the doors of the buildings where they lived or worked.[15] In this regard, the testimony of trafficking victims becomes a tool for government prosecutions of transnational organized crime. Indeed, receiving protection as a victim of human trafficking can rest on an individual's willingness to testify on behalf of the national government—a quid pro quo that instrumentalizes trafficking survivors to serve criminal justice objectives for member-state governments.

To better understand how the Japanese government was enacting Justice through the Action Plan, I formally requested an interview at the Ministry of Justice (MOJ), the Japanese state agency that administers Japan's judicial and penal system, including prosecuting human traffickers. The MOJ also oversees the registration of citizens and foreign visitors and residents. My efforts to meet with police agencies were repeatedly deflected, so I was surprised by how quickly and readily I was granted this visit.[16]

I enter the Ministry of Justice complex through the stately edifice of its famous "Red-Brick Building." The imposing neo-baroque structure was first completed in 1895 as part of the Meiji government's efforts to transform Tokyo into a modern national capital. Just as the Meiji government had modeled the Meiji Civil Code after west-ern Europe's codes, and Germany's in particular, it looked to two German archi-tects, Hermann Ende and Wilhelm Böckmann, to design the structure that would house its justice ministry. The style of the building self-consciously echoes European capitals like Paris and Berlin, where Ende had designed numerous buildings. Ar-chitecture embodies cultural meanings, and this grand one at once announces the ministry's oversight of Justice on the archipelago and asserts its membership in an international community of advanced nations.

Ironically, the redbrick structure that I enter is a replica of the original build-ing, which was nearly destroyed by the United States during the World War II firebombing of Tokyo. Although in the early 1950s the complex was returned to use, the building was only restored to its original form in 1991 as part of a plan to re-create the appearance of the Kasumigaseki government district during the Meiji era. I remember that in 2000, when Ambassador Lauriola officially pre-sented the report of his Ad Hoc Committee to the UN General Assembly, he stressed that the accomplishment of the convention was a matter of "sort(ing) through" the "basic differences" in nation-states' juridical concepts, legal systems, and domestic and foreign policy positions. He credited the relatively quick and successful conclu-sion of the negotiating process to "an emerging political will, driven by newspaper headlines and public opinion . . . to search for a global response to organized crime on a global level." However, it was not just political will that enabled so many na-tional governments to reach a formal consensus. Just as nationalisms take modular forms, so do government bureaus.[17] The Japanese MOJ parallels other government departments and ministries across the globe charged with administering the rule of law; these analogous national government bureaucracies facilitate the administra-tion of international Justice as a modular project on a global scale.

As one might expect, security to enter the building is tight. After an officer permits my entry, I am escorted through the complex by a choreographed relay of guards with earpieces and microphones, each of whom salutes before leading me to the next attendant, who has been informed via his earpiece where I am going and to whom I am to be handed off next. I am ushered down hallways, into a tunnel, across a sunken garden, and over to the Public Prosecutors' Office, a modern high-rise on the other side of the compound.

After I sign in with the security guards there, I am greeted by a smiling young man wearing a suit who, before indicating that he will bring me upstairs to my scheduled interview, confirms that I will limit my questions to those that I was required to submit as a condition of my being granted the meeting. I reaffirm my compliance, and he then hands me a printout of my questions, adding that a selection of them have been marked with x's and will not receive responses because they are "not directly related to the ministry's work." I restate my willingness to comply. Only then does the man tell me that he will take me upstairs to the interview, and he leads me to a conference room on the nineteenth floor. A desk is set up for me at one end, and across from it stands a row of tables, with five chairs for the public prosecutors and representatives from the Immigration and Criminal Affairs Bureaus who have been selected to speak with me. All appear young—in their thirties, like me—and they seem enthusiastic about their work. Their responses to my questions move seamlessly between discussions of human trafficking as a human rights violation, to the need for criminal prosecution of traffickers, to the challenge of determining which migrants are really trafficked and which are simply trying to take advantage of the system:

> "Human trafficking violates human rights, and we must make clear to all that each life is invaluable."

> "In the attorney general's office, our department covers all cases of prosecution, from murder to narcotics, with human trafficking as one such crime."

> "Of course, there are people who cannot be determined to be victims. In that case, we proceed with regular deportation steps. . . . We try to look at their cases and determine whether or not someone is a 'victim' using wide criteria."

> "The difficulty is that investigations are time-consuming. The time frame for an investigation is limited, and there have been cases in which the investigation was not completed within an established time frame."

> "If reaching out for help involves telling a story, humans don't always tell the truth. So even though a migrant is actually a victimizer, they claim to be a victim to get out of the country. How to deal with that is a major issue. We determine the validity of the claim that one was trafficked at the scene. . . . We need to determine whether this person's claim is valid or not by objectively looking at the situation and the evidence. That's the most difficult part."

The preceding stock responses, selected from a longer interview that included more of the same, did not surprise me; rather, they reminded me of the informational barriers that shelter the bureaucratic state. The interview was a self-consciously choreographed affair, and these statements easily align with the MOJ's official mandate, which centers on judiciary procedure and the importance of regulations to a functioning society. It seemed possible that after I had submitted my interview questions, my interviewees had coordinated their responses with the official ministry website, where the bureaucracy's official role is clearly explained in English for a foreign audience: "In order to live in this community it is necessary to have rules and regulations. . . . It is also essential for the maintenance of peace and order in society that when someone causes an injury or steals property, that person is appropriately punished. The Ministry of Justice not only prescribes such basic rules applicable in society but also [creates the] basic judicial framework under which these rules are faithfully observed."[18]

Based on earlier experiences at Japanese and US government offices, I could have anticipated the textbook answers that I received. My interviewees were professionals, behaving in accordance with their institutional positions, and we were in a professional setting with their colleagues present. The job of prosecutors under the Action Plan is to work with potential witnesses to trafficking crimes, separating them out from those migrants whose testimony would not be helpful in court, whether because of an insufficiency of hard evidence supporting their claims, because the case would be difficult to win for some reason or another, or because pulling it together would simply take more time than a conviction would be worth for them. Period. Considering why these migrants found themselves in such vulnerable and abusive conditions to begin with, or ensuring the long-term well-being of these witnesses, who are not Japanese citizens, is far outside their occupational purview. So, too, is ensuring on a day-to-day basis that work conditions for all foreign migrants in Japan are fair and safe.

I was surprised, however, by the warmth, youthful enthusiasm, and sincerity of the MOJ staff that I met, particularly considering the bureaucracy's rules-based, law-and-order mission and some of the stiffer interviews that I had previously conducted in other government agencies in Japan and the United States. Like Kato-san in chapter 3, who had come from the National Police Agency to coordinate the national offices working together to enact Japan's new anti-trafficking action plan, these civil servants seemed firm in their conviction that they were enacting justice, and they understood their jobs in the context of cosmopolitan aspirations and commitments to contributing to a global society and protecting human rights ("Human trafficking violates human rights, and we must make clear to all that each life is invaluable"). They either did not recognize or did not find it appropriate to mention in the context of discussing their work the suffering of migrant workers in Japan or the broader structural inequalities shaping these migrants' lives. As I prepared to leave the interview, a man from the Immigration Bureau approached me to connect personally about his experience as an exchange student in the United States a few years earlier, noting that he had enjoyed his stay tremendously. While I appreciated the friendly gesture, I was disoriented by his facile shift to such a breezy topic of conversation. A public prosecutor also came up to say that he wanted a researcher (me) to know that even though the number of recognized victims of human trafficking had been decreasing, the Japanese government was really trying to enact justice, protect human rights, and help trafficking victims. In stark contrast to the vision of justice shared by NGO caseworkers like Vicente, he made no mention of the vulnerabilities and abuse that migrant workers face in Japan, no acknowledgment that the current system was imperfect at best and that more consideration of migrants' rights could be made. If these civil servants aspired to a sense of cosmopolitan humanitarianism, it was one, like that underpinning the UN Trafficking Protocol and Japan's Action Plan, that gave limited consideration to the everyday structural realities of migrant workers' lives.

Managing the Protection of Victims

In the first years after the Japanese government adopted its Action Plan, it relied on grassroots NGOs like Vicente's to shelter and assist migrants identified as victims of human trafficking while their papers were being processed.[19] Japan's Action Plan includes clear provisions for this assistance, including paying NGOs for costs incurred in housing and assisting those identified as trafficked. However, by 2007, the Japanese government began transitioning victim assistance to existing regional Women's Consultation Offices and public women's shelters. Part of government social welfare services, these offices were initially established by the Baishun Bōshi Hō (Prostitution Prevention Act) of 1956 to counsel Japanese women to leave sex work; in more recent decades, this mission has been set aside to focus on assisting Japanese women dealing with domestic violence, family conflict, and debt. These offices are found in each of Japan's forty-seven prefectures and metropolitan areas, staffed by women's counselors (*fujin sōdanin*) who serve as caseworkers and are usually employed part-time. Presumably, the Japanese government wanted to house trafficking victims in public shelters for reasons of both economy and control. Not only would relying on existing shelters keep down the cost for housing victims by not requiring additional outlays to migrant shelters, but it would also keep assistance local and in-house. NGO shelters tend only to be located in larger cities, whereas migrants are identified as trafficking victims across Japan, and tensions between migrant-support NGOs and the Japanese government are well known.

The shift to relying on Women's Consultation Offices was not fully successful, at least according to US embassy employees, NGO staff, and a women's counselor with whom I spoke. US embassy staff did, however, recognize some positive aspects of relying on WCOs to house identified victims of trafficking, as one staff member explained, "At least you're taking trafficking victims to shelters where you have people who are … aware of PTSD." The US State Department also expressed reservations about the Japanese government's reliance on public shelters. The 2007 *TIP Report* notes that public shelters are inadequate for the care of foreign trafficking victims insofar as they offer in-house counseling only in Japanese and do not have staff trained to address "the unique trauma of trafficking and the cultures of the victims."[20] Embassy cables from that time also relay concerns that WCOs were set up to encourage speedy repatriation rather than victim assistance in investigating and prosecuting traffickers.[21]

Moreover, women's counselors were uncomfortable with WCO public shelters being used to house trafficking survivors. They publicly argued that they had their hands full with domestic violence cases and did not have the staff necessary to handle trafficking cases.[22] As the Japanese government was initiating this transition, a women's counselor spoke with me at length about her and her colleagues' reservations. With sweat beading across her furrowed brow, she prefaced her comments by saying that she was aware that speaking openly about her concerns could result in negative consequences for her or other WCO staff, but she felt so strongly about the issues that she was determined to make her feelings known. Shaking, she explained that women's counselors did not feel confident that they had the language and cultural skills—to say the least of appropriate training—to assist foreign women that had just left trafficking situations. She also shared concerns that the presence of these women in public women's shelters—the locations of which are not necessarily private—could endanger both staff and other residents. She did not understand why the government was asking WCOs to shelter foreign trafficking survivors, and she and many of her colleagues were not supportive of the move.

The US embassy had repeatedly encouraged the Japanese government to work with local NGOs instead of relying on WCOs. It recognized that these NGOs had an established track record of successfully assisting foreign migrants, employed staff with cultural and linguistic expertise, and were part of established international grassroots assistance networks. However, the US embassy's support of the NGOs was not unqualified. One US embassy staff member complained to me, "Japanese NGOs are not, in a sense, professionalized. They're very much mom-and-pop operations, or usually just mom operations: one full-time staff and several volunteers. The finances are horrible." What NGO staff like Vicente viewed as necessary flexibility and individualized attention to clients' needs, US government officials understood as insufficiently bureaucratic.

Ultimately, the Japanese government settled on using some combination of WCOs and NGO shelters to house and assist trafficking victims and thereby manage their obligation under the Trafficking Protocol to protect trafficking victims. Public shelters are preferred for economy and convenience, but NGOs, which have language and cultural expertise, can be commissioned by WCOs on a case-by-case basis to house victims for logistical and practical reasons.[23] Consequently, grassroots NGO staff continued to be involved, but only in clearly circumscribed ways and by explicit government invitation or direction.

Another Vision of Justice

NGO caseworkers like Vicente were frustrated by their qualified incorporation into these efforts. They recognized that the official model of Justice underpinning these efforts would at best protect the bare life of foreign labor migrants; it in no way proposed a path to social and economic justice. These caseworkers also saw parallels between the dismissal of the rights and needs of migrants, whose labor is so essential to the Japanese economy, and foreign caseworkers' own sidelining within the counter–human trafficking project, despite the essential role that they were playing in it.

Vicente and I kept in touch when I was in the United States, and some years later, over email, he spelled out some of his commitments to migrants' rights. I had written him and asked him to share how he understood "justice," and he first replied: "What a just world would look like? More migrant-friendly countries that are more respectful of migrants' dignities and rights. Such a country values the migrants' contribution to society and proactively provides them with means to attain their potentials as persons, in the form of trainings, education, and government support in the basic areas of health, housing, employment, pension, family life." He then offered an example of the experiences of members of the Filipina community with which he worked, thinking about their needs: "Among the Filipino [sic] migrants, many are now in the mid-forties-to-sixties age bracket. There is a decline in their health, and we see cases of women dying of cancer recently. Funerals are very difficult moments for many undocumented migrants because . . . they are confronted with their own mortality. Not being enrolled in the pension and health insurance system compounds that fear." He stressed how foreign workers' lack of access to social entitlements affected their lives.

Finally, he linked his work with his NGO to his broader vision of social and economic justice:

As a social worker, I am committed to this vision of justice as I have been doing my best for the past 21 years now. As a social worker, I do individual casework, group work and community organizing. Conditions here require that I be a generalist social worker, meaning that I should be able to respond to any given situation. In Japan, though we have an increasing number of foreigners, we do not have culturally competent, government employed social workers who can support them. My fervent hope is that that the Japanese government will be able to recognize this need and open the doors for foreigner social workers like what they are doing for the nurses, caregivers, household workers and now recently, for the farm workers.

With the proper support and corresponding opportunity, foreigners will not just be able to survive but thrive in Japan.

Vicente found intolerable the Japanese government's treatment of migrant workers as disposable. In this treatment, he saw a willingness to sap foreign migrant labor and move on and an unwillingness to recognize these workers as part of Japanese society and provide them with social entitlements—such as pensions and health care—despite their contributions to the Japanese economy. Although the Japanese government's Action Plan has a provision for identified victims of human trafficking to remain in Japan long-term, in practice they are, almost without exception, repatriated.[24] Of course, Vicente knew that many migrants want to return home after what they'd experienced in Japan; however, he took issue with the practice of repatriating migrants to situations in which they lacked resources to support themselves and often carried significant debt. He connected this treatment of migrant workers to forms of ethnic discrimination in Japan that took a "blame the victim" attitude toward migrants who are exploited and abused. He explained, "There's a general feeling in Japan that there are superior and inferior societies. Asian societies are inferior. That's why they will say, 'This woman met her problems because she came here. So it's her responsibility. If she did not come, she would not have this problem.'" Vicente viewed the sidelining of foreign caseworkers, like himself, within the counter-trafficking project as connected to this treatment of foreign workers. It lay on a continuum of violence in which the rights of "Asians" (*Ajia-jin*) in Japan were dismissed to varying degrees, with some, like his clients, suffering much more severely and brutally than he ever did. Vicente had wonderful relationships with his Japanese boss and colleagues. However, he had witnessed and experienced enough discrimination in Japan to speak critically of broader social attitudes and trends.

Vicente's vision of justice drew on a "moral imagination" at odds with that of Japanese government officials and the Trafficking Protocol more broadly;

in other words, he envisioned different "possibilities for a morally better or worse world" than the UN's global campaign allowed.[25] Vicente believed that social and political-economic change was necessary to address this discrimination and the structural vulnerability foreign migrants face. His vision of justice resonated with many other Philippine and some Japanese NGO caseworkers with whom I spoke in Japan. It also resonated with some staff at international organizations, both Japanese and foreign, but they had few avenues for transforming mainstream beliefs and government or international agency practices.

Alongside Vicente's anger about his clients' treatment was his frustration with NGO caseworkers' exclusion from official conferences and other discussions about how to handle human trafficking: "I feel that we who are in the field, who are working in the field, our voices are not even heard. We are not even invited to meetings or to sessions." Although NGOs had been invited early on to present on their observations and cases, they were often excluded from later meetings. Others with whom I spoke said that even if NGOs were invited to present on their work or give their opinions at conferences or meetings, Japanese government officials just smiled and nodded and then ignored their suggestions. One NGO staff member requested a meeting with police and immigration regarding their decision on a case. She was upset by their approach, but she soon realized that she could say nothing to change their decision. Her position was too far down the institutional hierarchy, and as a foreign national, her opinions would not be taken seriously. "They are so used to seeing these women as criminals that they can't really see them any other way," she seethed. Like Vicente, other NGO caseworkers with whom I spoke were frustrated by the sidelining and dismissal of their perspectives. For them, their work was tied both to a spiritual commitment to doing good by helping others and to a political commitment to structural change and fighting racism and labor exploitation. Yet because their views were often sidelined, these caseworkers were also regularly forced to recognize the limits, and even the failures, of their work.

These NGO caseworkers found themselves caught in the vagaries of official protocols and the anemic vision of Justice that informs them. They did not feel that justice was being served by these protocols, but if they refused to participate in them, they worried that the situation would be worse. Lives were at stake. So instead of stepping down in protest, these caseworkers scaled back their expectations, did what they could do for the time being, and held fast to alternative visions of justice that at once underpin and challenge official protocol. Meanwhile, in their anger and frustration, we see their refusal to accept the Justice for migrants offered by the Japanese state and the UN Trafficking Protocol. This anger is a form of unrest that refuses the banal institutional strategies of a global counter–human trafficking project, insisting instead that another way is possible.

Conclusion

Japan's Action Plan follows the model of legal-juridical Justice set out in the UN Trafficking Protocol. This model of Justice aspires to comprehensiveness and international translatability.[26] However, it does so at the expense of foreign labor migrants who have clearly been exploited and abused, like Vicente's clients, but who are duly deported or repatriated without any concern for the long-term impact of their suffering or their well-being. Justice under the protocol thus means managing certain kinds of violence while overlooking other kinds. It means that the Japanese state's refusal to protect those within its border from abuse and exploitation can now be readily displaced onto matters of protocol. It means migrants like Vicente's clients are left unprotected.

Moreover, for NGO caseworkers like Vicente, the Japanese government's victim identification protocols are unjust not only because they banally discount migrants deserving of assistance but also because they compromise the integrity of caseworkers committed to migrant assistance. For these caseworkers, realizing justice for their clients means being accountable to their clients' experiences and needs by putting themselves in their shoes and working from their perspectives. It means taking account not only of migrants' short-term safety but also of their long-term well-being and stability. These NGO caseworkers experience their clients' unprotection in two ways. First, they view it as a loss of what could have been possible in terms of migrant assistance. Second, they experience it in personal and ethical senses insofar as they, "abandoned by the state, feel they can no longer do their job to care [for] and protect" their clients.[27] Fearing repercussions for their organizations and their clients, caseworkers like Vicente were sometimes reluctant to openly express their frustration with government efforts because they feared being cut out of the official assistance process. At the same time, these caseworkers refused to conflate understandings of Justice as the administration of the rule of law with justice as the pursuit of what is right.

Because the Trafficking Protocol falls under the Convention on Transnational Organized Crime, it centers on a carceral model that recognizes only a juridified victim who can serve as a government witness to a crime with sufficient will and evidence to prosecute. Realizing Justice under the Trafficking Protocol does not entail eradicating the structural conditions that make migrants vulnerable to the violence it identifies as human trafficking; rather,

Justice means instrumentalizing bare life to prosecute crimes against centralized state governments. Migrants fall outside the official protocol if their testimony is not deemed useful for these purposes—for instance, if the government does not identify, or opts not to prosecute, any crimes perpetrated against them. Consider how Japanese officials addressed the abuse and exploitation of Vicente's clients not by recognizing them as victims of broader social and political-economic injustices but by simply getting them their contracted salaries. They maintained that any other action was unnecessary. A migrant worker can fall outside the protocol for many reasons beyond the procedural, including the simple fact that, as noted in previous chapters, prosecutors and police have little interest in pursuing a time-consuming case that will be challenging to win in court. Recall how the Japanese government told Vicente that the denial of resources to his clients was not something to make a "big issue" about. It showed little interest in prosecuting the bar owner, taking the (potentially temporary) closing of his business and his tears as a sufficient consequence.

Such a solution is justifiable under the official protocol. However, for Vicente and many other grassroots activists that I met in Japan and the Philippines, this Justice is insufficient. The alternative vision of justice imagined by Vicente is unattainable solely through laws, policies, and international treaties. Rather, it can only be realized through a reconceptualization of the social. It demands a shift in how the Japanese government and its citizens conceptualize their relationships to foreign migrant workers and the countries from which they come, including a reimagining of commitments to how Japanese people live with and relate to people in and from the Philippines. This is a vision of justice that asks national governments and their citizenries to see foreign workers as part of their imagined community.[28] Such recognition would require more than a set of institutional protocols to address violence against individual migrants. It would involve attention to the "afterlife" of imperialism in the Philippines, including the contemporary extraction of natural resources and the reliance on Philippine labor.[29] This understanding of the connections between unequal historical and contemporary geopolitical relationships underlies Vicente's call for justice, which echoes the call put forth by Matsui Yayori so many decades earlier.

Vicente and other NGO caseworkers I knew in Japan and the Philippines worked relentlessly to shift the course of official efforts, insisting on a different moral economy and endeavoring to realize the justice that they knew was due. Yet because they lacked the power and resources to fully realize their vision of justice, their efforts have thus far been only aspirational. Thus, we also see in Vicente's anger the unequal institutional relationships that structure official efforts. His anger reflects his lack of power in domestic and international arenas. Under such conditions, Vicente's alternative vision of justice is frustratingly caught in a holding pattern, trackable in the frustration and anger of caseworkers while official protocols ignore and dismiss it.

This chapter has traced the banality of the global counter–human trafficking project by focusing on the treatment of foreign labor migrants who suffer extreme abuse and exploitation but still do not qualify for protection and assistance under it. Yet those who do not meet the criteria for recognition as victims of human trafficking are not the only ones left unprotected under the UN Trafficking Protocol. Formally identified victims of trafficking often remain unprotected as well. In chapter 6, I turn to the banality of services provided to those who are granted official status as trafficking victims but are nonetheless inadequately assisted and supported through it.

6

THE NEED TO KNOW

———

Communication—at least meaningful, verifiable communication—cannot be
rendered into a sequence of protocol statements.

—PETER GALISON, "Removing Knowledge," 2004

Chapter 5 focused on the banality of the protocol in its failure to recognize
those migrants who suffer abuse and exploitation but do not technically qualify
for protection and assistance. This chapter turns to the banalities that inhere
in the assistance provided to those foreign workers who *do* officially qualify as
trafficking victims in Japan. Represented in flowcharts on the Japanese Ministry
of Foreign Affairs website, the protocol for "Protecting Victims of Trafficking
in Persons" is a pipeline organized around a formal division of labor involving
different public, private, and international agencies in Japan and trafficking victims' home countries (see figures 6.1 and 6.2).[1] Shelters in Japan house migrants
and provide for their day-to-day needs, such as counseling and daily support.
Foreign embassies issue travel documents for their nationals because many do
not have appropriate papers. Japanese immigration officials provide residency
permits and process departure documents so that victims of human trafficking will not leave Japan with undocumented status, which can carry a criminal

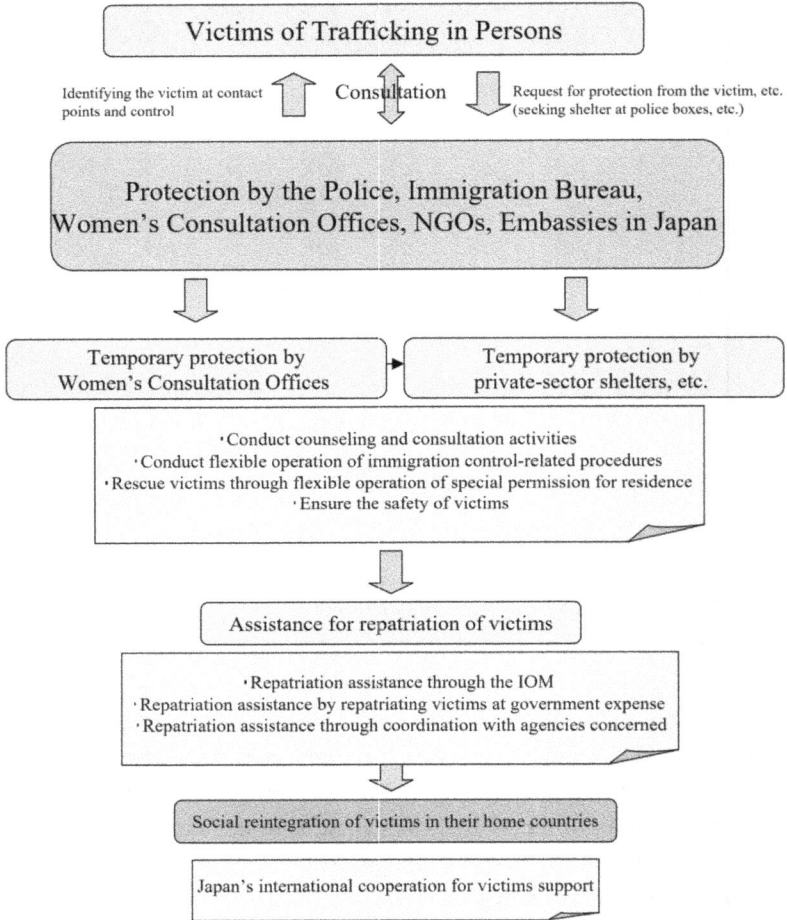

Process of Protecting Victims of Trafficking in Persons

Victims of Trafficking in Persons

Identifying the victim at contact points and control · Consultation · Request for protection from the victim, etc. (seeking shelter at police boxes, etc.)

Protection by the Police, Immigration Bureau, Women's Consultation Offices, NGOs, Embassies in Japan

Temporary protection by Women's Consultation Offices → Temporary protection by private-sector shelters, etc.

· Conduct counseling and consultation activities
· Conduct flexible operation of immigration control-related procedures
· Rescue victims through flexible operation of special permission for residence
· Ensure the safety of victims

Assistance for repatriation of victims

· Repatriation assistance through the IOM
· Repatriation assistance by repatriating victims at government expense
· Repatriation assistance through coordination with agencies concerned

Social reintegration of victims in their home countries

Japan's international cooperation for victims support

FIGURE 6.1. "Process of Protecting Victims of Trafficking in Persons" flowchart, from Ministry of Foreign Affairs, Japan, accessed July 10, 2023, https://www.mofa.go.jp/policy/i_crime/people/action-2.pdf.

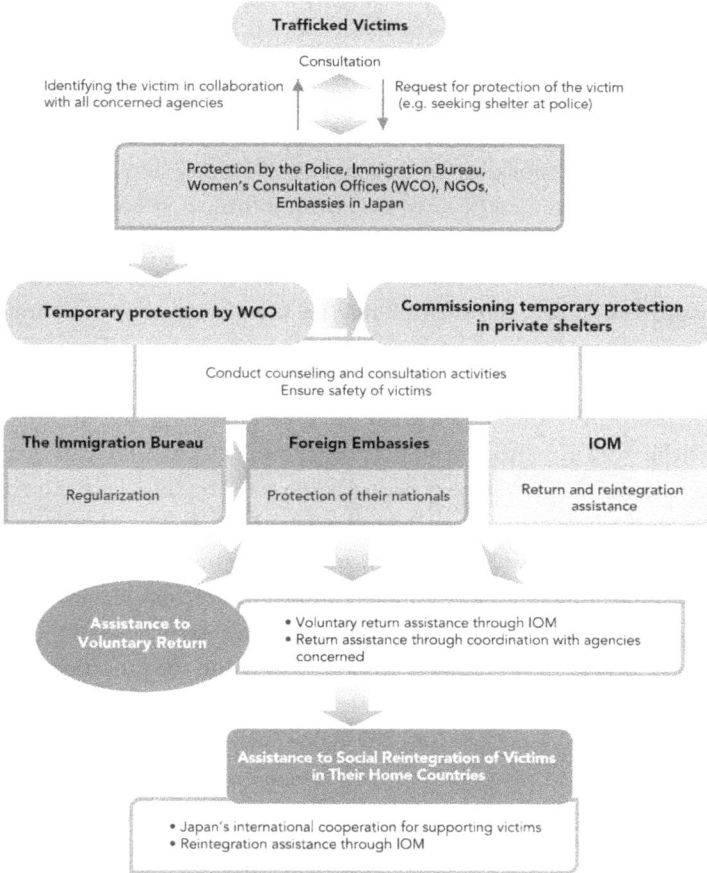

Protection

We are ensuring a system for victim identification and protection.

Trafficked Victims

Consultation

Identifying the victim in collaboration with all concerned agencies

Request for protection of the victim (e.g. seeking shelter at police)

Protection by the Police, Immigration Bureau, Women's Consultation Offices (WCO), NGOs, Embassies in Japan

Temporary protection by WCO

Commissioning temporary protection in private shelters

Conduct counseling and consultation activities
Ensure safety of victims

The Immigration Bureau	**Foreign Embassies**	**IOM**
Regularization	Protection of their nationals	Return and reintegration assistance

Assistance to Voluntary Return

• Voluntary return assistance through IOM
• Return assistance through coordination with agencies concerned

Assistance to Social Reintegration of Victims in Their Home Countries

• Japan's international cooperation for supporting victims
• Reintegration assistance through IOM

5

FIGURE 6.2. "Protection" flowchart, from Ministry of Foreign Affairs, Japan, *Japan's Actions to Combat Trafficking in Persons*.

penalty. The IOM Tokyo makes travel arrangements for a migrant's safe return home and helps coordinate qualifying medical and psychological care and the collection of any owed wages.[2] IOM Tokyo staff members also bring identified victims to the airport and sometimes escort them home. Once a trafficking survivor arrives home, staff from the IOM office in her home country, such as the IOM Manila, escort her from the airport to her family or to a local NGO. Local NGOs then provide reintegration assistance, which can include psychological counseling, vocational training, job assistance, or funding to complete high school, depending on available funds from the Japanese government, donations, or international sources.

As recognized trafficking victims move between these different organizations tasked with assisting and protecting them, information about their circumstances must be relayed as well. However, how this information is treated, and what can be relayed, is not left to the discretion of those involved in the assistance process. In fact, information management is one of the first topics covered in *The IOM Handbook on Direct Assistance for Victims of Trafficking*, which prescribes that all "data" concerning victims should be governed by "need-to-know" protocols.[3] It states, "The key principle governing the handling of confidential as well as more general data concerning victims and trafficking is the 'need to know.' Service delivery organization staff should follow this rule in all cases and disclose data internally and externally only to such persons whose need and right to receive such information is acknowledged."[4] In other words, whereas guidelines developed by international institutions like the IOM are expected to circulate on a global scale to systematize victim assistance protocols, specific information about trafficked individuals and the procedures for assisting them is highly restricted and controlled during the assistance process.

In this chapter, I explore how the IOM's information management protocols transformed the assistance process for caseworkers in Japan and the Philippines, affecting both their relationships with their clients and their ethical dispositions to their work. I contrast the IOM protocols with those that grassroots NGOs in these countries had developed to protect their clients before their incorporation into official counter–human trafficking efforts.[5] Before Japan adopted its Action Plan, all the NGOs with which I worked in Japan and the Philippines had intact policies for managing their clients' personal information. These policies centered on how to effectively and self-reflexively protect their clients' privacy while cooperating with other trusted NGOs in their transnational network to best support their clients in both the short and long term. However, Japan's official assistance pipeline segmented client support into discrete, isolated jobs. In this process, it parsed NGO clients' experiences and lives into bits of confidential data that could be selectively transmitted along an assistance chain.

Presented as a means of protecting trafficking victims, these protocols are justified as necessary and pragmatic, and NGOs participating in the Action Plan had to adopt them. However, insofar as these protocols endeavored to manage data about NGO clients only during the official assistance process, they also contributed to the detachment of victim assistance from the broader contexts of migrants' lives and their well-being as persons in the short and long term, considerations the NGOs stress. NGO caseworkers thus found themselves having to set aside their desire not only to know their clients as people but also to understand the broader social and political economic circumstances of their lives in order to follow official assistance guidelines. NGO caseworkers were to contribute a single link in the assistance chain and trust that all the links were adding up to a sufficient whole. For those like Vicente, this shift had troubling implications for how they could relate to their clients and understand the ethics of their work.

My conversations with NGO caseworkers illustrated how these protocols had unintended consequences and cumulative effects that undermined their commitments toward their clients. Scholars have argued that strategies of not-knowing or not-sharing information can figure as mechanisms of government control, in part by mediating its contradictions.[6] Peter Galison, for instance, has explored how the US government's need-to-know compartmentalization of knowledge as "classified information" works as a deliberate, if costly, strategy of government "antiepistemology."[7] Andrew Mathews has argued that the deliberate production of both knowledge and ignorance is a necessary part of the quotidian practice of state making in Mexico.[8] However, these studies tend to focus on intentional government strategies through which ignorance is cultivated to augment power. Here I show how banal logics of information management compromise projects that aspire to ethical forms of assistance and protection, resulting in anemic forms of care. I argue that for all the IOM protocols' focus on ethics and safety, they put migrants at greater risk by compartmentalizing information about them and diverting attention away from the structural violence that led them to Japan and that they will confront back home. At the same time, they stymie self-evaluation and critique of their inadequacies. Although NGO caseworkers with whom I spoke abided by these protocols out of necessity, some were also frustrated by them and tried to find ways to maintain their ethical commitments to their clients in spite of them.

"Confidential Personal Data" Is Not the Same as "Private Matters"

Before the Trafficking Protocol was adopted, caseworkers at all the NGOs where I volunteered and conducted research in Japan, the Philippines, and the United States had strict policies to protect their clients' privacy. These policies took a person-centered approach that considered clients' needs in both the short and long term. At the anti-human-trafficking NGO in the United States where I volunteered, information management policies were the most formalized and consistent with the IOM's need-to-know protocols. Before being accepted to work at the organization, I was required to attend an extensive training that focused on ethics protocols regarding victim assistance, including guidelines for privacy and confidentiality. I also received a volunteer handbook that clearly stated that confidential information obtained during my volunteer work with the organization could not be used to advance current or future employment or obtain personal gain or profit. The handbook explained that any breach of confidentiality policies would result in volunteer termination. It specifically instructed shelter volunteers not to ask questions out of curiosity, not to gossip, and always to maintain strict shelter-resident confidentiality. I had to sign a formal confidentiality agreement before being accepted as a volunteer with the organization.

Staff at this organization were especially concerned about how the disclosure of information outside the organization might affect public perceptions of their clients and thus how they would be treated. For instance, one NGO caseworker explained that her clients did not want other people to know that they were trafficking victims because they worried that they would be "looked at funny" on that account. This caseworker also shared concerns that her clients might be objectified. To protect clients and hide their background, this caseworker took precautionary measures. For example, she shared that she would identify herself simply as a "friend" if a bank clerk inquired about her relationship with the client when she accompanied the client to open a bank account. This caseworker also explained that she always resisted handing out her business card when she was with a client because it clearly said the name of the counter-trafficking NGO on it and thus might lead people to assume her client was a trafficking survivor. Organization staff also worried that victims' stories could have commercial value and thus be commodified or otherwise exploited for personal gain. Caseworkers and administrative staff complained about the many films and television specials that have been made about human trafficking, some of which featured survivors without their consent. They often refused to speak to reporters or researchers and regularly turned down requests to provide access to clients out of concern that their clients could be exploited.

At the organizations with which I worked in Japan and the Philippines, client confidentiality was taken no less seriously, but it was managed more informally and differently focused. Although, as discussed in chapter 3, these organizations strategically shared client information with US government officials to push for policy change, they were highly protective of information about their clients with researchers, journalists, and the public.[9] I was accepted as a volunteer at NGOs in both countries only after I verbally agreed to respect the organization's standards of confidentiality above and beyond what is conventional for ethnographic research ethics. Yet perhaps, as one caseworker at Tahanan explained, because researchers, journalists, and filmmakers were not trying to access their clients' stories at the time, staff at these organizations conceived of their policies less as strategies for protecting clients from self-interested and predatory others and more as matters of a commonsense respect for their clients as private citizens. For example, when I asked this caseworker about the organization's confidentiality policies, she described them as a straightforward matter of the discretion one would show any person and of people's basic entitlement to control their "personal information." She commented matter-of-factly, "Of course, these are people's private matters, so I don't really want to talk about them with others." When I asked this caseworker whether regular NGO employees signed confidentiality agreements, she said that she was unaware of such practices among organizations with which she worked in Japan. At the time, such agreements were unusual in Japan, which is not a litigious society relative to the United States; civil cases were infrequent, and formal written agreements among private parties regarding noneconomic matters were rare.[10] However, this caseworker also explained that within the organization, there was clear and explicit consensus not to discuss clients' cases. She stated that staff and volunteers at the NGO shared an understanding that it was "*jōshiki, atarimae*" (common sense) not to disclose information about clients. It was common sense—what one knows and accepts as a social being to be right and true—to protect clients' privacy.

Notably, however, before Tahanan was contracted for Japan's counter-trafficking project, its confidentiality policies did not ordinarily extend to members within the assistance chain, and certainly not within the organization. Rather, caseworkers worked directly and collectively with staff both in their own organizations and in NGOs that would be assisting their clients' in their home countries. For these NGOs, approaching their clients as whole people meant considering the broader circumstances of their lives and doing what they could to ensure their safety and well-being throughout and beyond the assistance process. To do so, it was important to be able to share knowledge about clients within an organization and with those NGOs in migrants' home countries that would be assisting them once they returned. This information was not in any way shared promiscuously; however, caseworkers worked collectively to support clients with an eye toward their well-being, including after they left the shelter. In an essay in the GAATW newsletter about the day-to-day workings of Saalaa, a women's shelter at a migrant-support NGO in Japan, Carina Morita, at the time a caseworker, explains how staff at the shelter take a team approach to cases and work collaboratively to share responsibilities. She describes how after a caseworker has a difficult telephone conversation or case intervention, coworkers make a point of being available to that caseworker for consultation and discussion to help offer perspective and clarification. She explains, "Working on a particular case requires a multidisciplinary approach. Some workers will have a better orientation in specific areas, such as legal or social welfare issues. Discussing the case after an especially difficult intervention with a staff manager/co-worker will give the counsellor/helper a better and more objective view of the issues in the case as well as a venue for exploring other entry points for intervention. It will also identify and clarify what can and what cannot be done. This also enriches self-knowledge for the counsellor/helper, identifying strong and weak areas in her interventions."[11] Morita identifies this approach as creating a "culture of comfortable openness" that encourages positive working relationships and mutual support among shelter staff. In her words, staff are "constantly sharing and exchanging information," not only about clients but also about themselves.[12] Doing so helps caseworkers acquire multiple perspectives on cases, refine their assistance strategies, and cope with the emotional strains of the work. NGOs assisting migrants before the Action Plan also shared information with partnering organizations in migrants' home countries, working directly with them to help strategize the best way to support clients who had suffered abuse or exploitation abroad and following up on them once they were home. The ethics that governed their confidentiality practice was not rooted in adherence to a fixed set of protocols. Rather, it was informed by an ongoing process of self-evaluation and self-questioning. As Morita explains in her essay, self-reflexivity was built into victim assistance at her NGO.[13] Caseworkers turned to one another to gain additional perspectives, to become aware of their own myopias, and to strategize together how to best serve a client overall.

These grassroots NGOs' approach to information management differed in subtle but significant ways from the one prescribed by the *IOM Handbook*'s victim assistance protocols. Whereas NGOs protected clients' "private matters" and "personal information" out of respect for their privacy as people, the *IOM Handbook* treated knowledge about trafficking victims as "confidential personal data."[14] The *IOM Handbook* defines this category as "any personal data, health record or description that might reveal the identity or location of a trafficking victim, or any private and personal detail concerning a trafficking victim in the organization's care."[15] A key distinction here lies in the nature and purpose of *data* as opposed to *information* or *matters*. Whereas *information* is knowledge centered on a person ("knowledge obtained from investigation, study, or instruction"), and private *matters* are "the events or circumstances of a particular situation" affecting a private individual, *data* are facts instrumentally centered on a task ("factual information [such as measurements or statistics] used as a basis for reasoning, discussion, or calculation").[16] If "personal information" and "private matters" must be protected so that the person in question is not objectified, exploited, or commodified, "confidential personal data" must be protected to properly execute a given duty, one delineated by a division of labor and a set of procedures.

While such distinctions might strike some as purely semantic, I would argue that they point to deeper, more pervasive priorities. Consider, for instance, how the official victim assistance protocol is organized through an assistance and protection pipeline (see figures 6.1 and 6.2). Within such a model, private shelters are a single section of a division of labor separated into carefully delineated pragmatic tasks, in this case those of "temporary protection" and limited "counseling and consultation activities." Under these protocols, caseworkers are those who execute these tasks, custodians who receive restricted bits of the "confidential personal data" necessary to perform their role in a circumscribed chain. Victims are acknowledged only through the pieces of data relevant for that segment of the pipeline. NGO caseworkers are not expected to consider their clients' lives beyond their temporary stay in the shelter. Rather, these caseworkers are expected to encounter "victims" only to the extent necessary to complete their segment of the chain.

The shift in treating knowledge about NGO clients as data marked a corresponding and significant shift in how NGO caseworkers could approach both their jobs and their relationships with their clients. Need-to-know protocols are presented first and foremost in the *IOM Handbook* as matters of safety, appearing in the first chapter, "Security and Personal Safety."[17] The chapter explains that these protocols are mandated out of concern that organized crime syndicates will make efforts to exact revenge not only on those who have escaped and gone to the authorities but also on those who assist them. It cautions, "Even though it is possible to cause staff anxiety through overstating the level of risk, all personnel who are required to interact with trafficking victims should be fully informed of the risks involved."[18] Risks to victims include kidnapping, violence, reenslavement, and other forms of retribution, including death. Those assisting victims are also believed to be at risk of retribution.

Certainly, some might argue that dangers exist to both trafficked persons and assistance staff if information about their whereabouts is known; keeping information about trafficked persons confidential serves some protective function. However, the handbook assumes that without very strict and military-style modes of information management, NGO caseworkers would not control the spread of information about their clients and endanger both their clients and themselves. One could argue that such concerns are unfounded. As we have seen, NGO caseworkers had managed to maintain client confidentiality for decades before the protocols were in place. Moreover, the handbook's focus is more limited than that of the NGOs. It addresses safety during the assistance process but not necessarily once the process is complete. Under the protocol, protection and assistance are offered only for the times and places in which trafficked persons are formally assisted. "Personal matters" that make migrants vulnerable to violence and abuse in their communities back home fall outside its purview. Recall, for instance, Vicente's concerns that the parents of some of the women he assisted might beat them if they were repatriated without sufficient resources. Consider, too, that brokers or traffickers may be knowledgeable about migrants' natal families and communities and may even belong to them. Protecting trafficking victims' confidential personal data while they are in the victim assistance pipeline does not address the dangers and vulnerabilities that they may face once they have been returned home, as discussed in chapter 8.

Meanwhile, the official protocol's transformation of information about trafficked clients into "confidential personal data" had implications for how those involved in assisting victims could understand and carry out their jobs. Under the official need-to-know protocols, NGO caseworkers received only enough information to perform a circumscribed delegated task. This practice restricted not only what caseworkers knew about their clients but also how they could interact with them. They were no longer expected to approach their work as assisting people who needed care and support but to focus on completing a given job. Indeed, need-to-know protocols in victim assistance ensured that those involved could perform *only* the circumscribed role that they received the information to execute. Further, NGO caseworkers could now not even share information about their clients with colleagues within their organization. The *IOM Handbook* explains: "Within each service delivery organization, the need to know should also apply between functions within the organization—no confidential data should be disseminated outside the counter-trafficking section and the security handling principles should be as diligently applied within the service delivery organization as without."[19] Consequently, NGO caseworkers' relationships with their clients were restricted to specific compartmentalized duties.

Need-to-know protocols also encouraged NGO caseworkers to adopt different ethical dispositions toward their work and clients. According to the *IOM Handbook*, protecting victims' confidential personal data is not simply a strategy for preventing harm and ensuring safety during the formal assistance process. It also contributes to the ethical value of assistance work. "Appendix 1: Ethical Principles in Caring for and Interviewing Trafficked Persons" lays out eighteen ethical protocols to be followed in victim assistance. "Ensure privacy" and "Ensure confidentiality" are numbers 3 and 4 on the list, after "Do no harm" and "Ensure safety, security and comfort."[20] These ethical principles are to be executed through a standardized, replicable procedure of "due diligence."[21] Although the concerns might seem to be exclusively meant to ensure client and caseworker safety, Bill Maurer tells us that due diligence is not geared toward establishing certainty so much as the warranting of "personal regard and ethical scrutiny."[22] Its primary concern is managing reputations by creating a system for verifying one's ethical practice to both oneself and others.[23] In other words, as part of need-to-know protocols ostensibly aimed to protect one's clients and oneself, due diligence offers a means for those involved in assisting victims of human trafficking to measurably verify that they are behaving ethically and that the organizations for which they work are ethical bureaucracies.[24] It provides a framework through which caseworkers can make sense of their day-to-day practices, their roles in counter-trafficking efforts, and the importance and "goodness" of their jobs in relation to practices of information management.

The *IOM Handbook* explains, "In view of the increased risk posed by organized criminal activities to trafficking victims and support staff, the service delivery organization must at all times use all due diligence in the management and disposal of confidential personal data."[25] The handbook then specifies the steps involved in using due diligence, including the following:

The provision of assistance will generate hard copies. . . . IOM suggests that the following guidance be applied to all printed material containing [confidential personal and confidential trafficking] data:

- All copies must be kept secure and under lock and key either at the office of the service delivery organization or shelter when not in use.
- When in use, they should never be left unattended, or left lying on desks, tables or in areas accessible to others.
- When paper copies are no longer required, they should be disposed of by being shredded or similarly destroyed.
- To that end, all service delivery organizations involved in assisting trafficking victims should try to ensure that a shredding machine is available and functioning on the premises.[26]

These practices of due diligence may seem to be necessary, pragmatic procedures for protecting identities. At a time when many people worry about identity theft, practices like shredding documents are commonplace. Yet such practices are adopted out of concern that identity thieves might rummage through one's garbage and use discarded documents for criminal ends. The likelihood that traffickers would do so, particularly given that the shelter locations are confidential, seems beyond small. Yet when framed as ethical requirements in victim assistance, practices such as shredding documents reframe the ethics of protecting another as a matter of procedural compliance. Moreover, the very enumeration of such steps offers a means of attesting to the IOM's adherence to practical ethics. What for Tahanan caseworkers had required a self-reflexive ethics of respecting and assisting clients as people at risk of a range of harms became a mechanical matter of managing documents to protect data. In other words, the *IOM Handbook*'s due diligence guidelines turned protecting clients' privacy into a matter of following rules and made caseworker ethics a quotidian practice of self-regulation to be pragmatically managed on a day-to-day basis. Ethically assisting clients went from engaging in a collective and self-reflective practice of caring for a person to being a procedural practice of executing tasks according to protocol.

Due Diligence Disciplines Curiosity

All the NGO caseworkers with whom I spoke took the formal, prescribed protocols seriously. Yet the adoption of them also transformed how NGO caseworkers understood their role in the assistance process and the ethics guiding their work. These caseworkers were not simply expected to follow need-to-know protocols but also to internalize them as part of the ethics of their jobs. Individual caseworkers responded to this compulsion in different ways, ranging from complete acceptance to outright mistrust.

On the one hand, the need-to-know protocols encouraged NGO caseworkers to identify as a group with privileged access, and some internalized this access as a burden of responsibility. For instance, when I asked about the rationale behind the protocols, one caseworker explained, "'Need to know' is born out of the requirements of assistance. You need to anticipate the repercussions of making certain information public. You get to receive information that is not really for public consumption." Others internalized the protocols to the extent that they had forgotten they were explicitly mandated by IOM guidelines. For instance, when I asked one IOM staff member in Manila where she had learned the importance of the need-to-know policy, whether or not she had read it in the organization's manual, she tried to remember and then said, "It might be written in our counter-trafficking manual, but for me, it also comes out of a very deep recognition and appreciation and understanding of trafficking: that it involves a lot of people that you cannot trust, you know, that you have to be very careful. So for me it comes out of there." For this staff member, the keeping of secrets had become a form of self-discipline—a means through which she performed her credibility, commitment, and ethical proficiency on an everyday basis.

On the other hand, when internalized as ethical practice, these protocols had the consequence of limiting the kinds of information some people involved in these efforts expected—and even wanted—to receive about their clients. For instance, the aforementioned IOM staff member explained that the need-to-know policy not only affected what information she released but also what information she expected, or even wanted, to receive from coworkers about the clients she escorted from the Manila airport. When I asked during our conversation about the partnering organizations in Japan that were assisting her clients there, she explained tentatively: "What I know is that, for example, we work with an NGO." When I named a few of the NGOs in Japan that I knew assisted trafficking victims there and asked which one they were partnering with, the staff member confessed that she didn't know which organizations her clients came through. She said that she had only a vague sense of the operations ongoing in Japan and the assistance the women had received there. She explained matter-of-factly: "We . . . operate on a need-to-know basis. I don't need to know where they're staying [in Japan]. I don't need to know if it doesn't impact what we do here. I don't need to know which [Japanese] agency is arranging for the security of the traffic victim. What I need to know is, for example, does she have an irate boyfriend or husband here? Does she have kids here? Did her parents force her into this? Those are the things I need to know. But in terms of the modalities, everything is need-to-know basis, just for security." At the time of our interview, I had not read the *IOM Handbook*, and I was surprised by her response. I had managed to learn the specifics of the assistance chain between Japan and the Philippines through my research, so I had reasoned that the information could not be that closely guarded. But the IOM caseworker shared that she *avoided* accessing the information so that she would not know too much about an identified victim when she went to the airport to meet her:

> If I know some bits of information, and I work with some bureau of information officials at the airport very closely, I go up to them while waiting for the returnees and all that. And when you're chitchatting . . . you know, they could ask you, Oh where do[es the person you're meeting] come from? And, you know, I'll never know if [the official has] been paid a bit out of the trafficker's payroll. And if I know something . . . It's better you don't know. So you'll say, 'I don't really know . . . I just know the flight.' And of course [I know] this flight comes from Nagoya or something. But I don't even know if these girls traveled from Kobe to Nagoya. So it's a security measure.

Out of an abstract "security" concern that she might accidentally reveal information about where her client was traveling from, this IOM staff member had come to question her own discretion and, correspondingly, to discipline her curiosity. To comply with need-to-know protocols, she intentionally tried to avoid knowing anything about her clients' experiences in Japan, setting aside the possibility that having more knowledge about their situation might enable her to better support them. She explained the logic behind her approach, stating, "We are very paranoid"—a claim that implicitly acknowledged the irrationality of the practice. At one point in our interview, I asked, "Is there any danger to you or to staff at [your organization] because of the kind of work you do? Do you ever worry about traffickers coming after you?" She quickly responded, "A lot. Not traffickers coming after us per se, but recognition [by someone] that just destroys your confidentiality thing altogether." For her, concern about breaking official ethics protocols of confidentiality went beyond concerns for her and her client's bodily safety.

Others involved in the assistance process were more pragmatic about the need-to-know protocols, recognizing them as necessary parts of their jobs but demonstrating less personal investment in them. For instance, when I asked one staff member at an international organization in Japan about her office's need-to-know policy, she explained that she could only speak to her organization's official position. She restated published guidelines, "There is 'information management.' You only reveal certain things to certain people." This staffer affirmed, as officially stated, that her office had a baseline rule that they are not allowed to cite cases under any circumstances and that doing so to forward personal interests would be considered both unethical and a violation of organization standards. Of her job, she explained, "One of the things you learn is handling information."

I heard similar comments from NGO workers in Japan and the United States that partnered with the IOM. On another occasion, I attended a meeting for social service providers of victims of trafficking in the United States in which one NGO caseworker shared a story that illustrated the importance of information management to protect survivors' privacy. This caseworker explained that she had recently visited a public assistance office to request a sample application letter so that she could submit one for her client. This caseworker was shocked when the public assistance staff member gave her a sample letter in which personal information about the applicant had not been blocked out. The caseworker recognized the letter, which had been circulated around the government office in its unredacted state, as belonging to a former client of her NGO. She was extremely upset. Anyone in the office would now know that this woman had been a victim of trafficking, information the former client may have not wanted revealed. The caseworker advised the group, "This is why you submit as little information as necessary."

However, other NGO caseworkers in the United States also explained that they discouraged their clients from telling them too much out of pragmatic concerns that they might be forced to unwittingly compromise their clients, who would be required to testify against their traffickers. They did not trust the US legal system to protect their clients. For instance, one caseworker, Jasmine, worried that she could be called on to testify against her client. Although new state laws protected caseworker-client privilege, she expressed concerns that the laws were still untested and uncertainty remained regarding how much they covered. She explained, "We don't let them tell us too many details about their experiences. Because sometimes they waive caseworker-client privilege because they are claiming psychological damages, and so opposing council can subpoena our notes. We don't know what will happen in court, and opposing council has gotten some files that we've tried to keep away." Consequently, Jasmine actively tried to prevent her clients from telling her much about their experiences—even if it might affect how she assisted them—while their cases were being adjudicated.

These examples illustrate how need-to-know protocols encourage NGO caseworkers to not only pragmatically accept the need to not reveal or share too much but also internalize it as a desire to not ask too much, or even want to know too much, for fear of hurting their clients and compromising their assistance projects. Acting ethically per the protocol meant remaining siloed in their knowledge about their clients. Yet paradoxically this could compromise their ability to understand their clients' needs or critically reflect on the assistance process. Whether or not the assistance process was effective on the whole or whether changes could be made to it to better support their clients were not questions NGO caseworkers were supposed to be equipped to ask.

Vicente's Catch-22

Not all caseworkers were ethically comfortable with the need-to-know protocols. Some shared reservations about them and even openly rejected their premise. They refused to accept that to act in the best interest of their clients they should set aside their desire not only to know them as people but also to understand the scope of violence in their lives. Consider a conversation that I had with Vicente. At one early point during my research, I shared with him that I was trying to trace the contact points among different organizations that assist women who have been identified as trafficked. I was hoping that he might be able to shed light on the process. He responded that technically, he was not supposed to know about what happens at these points "because of the protocol; the standard operating procedure of the IOM is that once we pass them the case, we don't know what happens next. We are not supposed to know, and they are not supposed to tell us." At this time, I had not yet learned about the need-to-know protocols governing the process. Surprised by Vicente's response, I asked him why he didn't know. My work with the Tokyo-based migrant support organizations during the 1990s had taught me, as Morita explained, that as part of their assistance strategies, NGOs assisting migrants in Japan routinely and discreetly share details about cases both within an organization and with caseworkers in NGOs that would be assisting these clients back home.[27] Parodying a robotic voice, Vicente recited the rationale behind the need-to-know protocols: "Because they are trafficking victims; they need to be protected." Confused, I asked, "So what does it mean to protect them?" Vicente continued dryly, "There will be the least number of people who knew what happened to them." Still confused and noting the skepticism in his voice, I pressed on, "And why does that protect them?" He began flatly, "They said it would be better that you don't know where they are, where they were sheltered, what happened to them in their return countries, when they return." At that point, Vicente could no longer contain his outright annoyance and frustration with this strategy. He explained that he was personally invested in what happened to those that he assisted, and he felt accountable to them. He could not just treat them as cases to pass on. He felt the need to ensure that his clients were OK, not only in the short term but also in the longer term. He then shared that at a conference on human trafficking attended by representatives of the Japanese government, he had spoken out, explaining to the officials present:

> Very concretely, I want to trace the flow of how the victims should be handled, from my point to the end, to home, to aftercare, to the reintegration component. Because of course you [in the government] present a lot of very good reports and you present a lot of very good programs, but you are not the one who is facing the victim. I am the one facing the victim. And I am the one who has to tell them, "You have to trust me, you have to trust the system, and things will be better." If, at the start, I don't know what is wrong with the system, then I can't trust the system. Even at the start, I have to be very direct about it, very frank about it to the victim.

For Vicente, knowing what happened to his clients throughout and beyond the assistance process was a matter of being accountable to them. It was also a matter of constantly scrutinizing assistance practices in the interest of making them more attuned to the needs of migrants. The division of labor and need-to-know protocols that governed the Action Plan's assistance process—in which he was expected to blindly follow procedures in a chain—left him feeling alienated from his clients and unable to ethically do his job. Moreover, Vicente had other practical reasons for wanting to follow through on his clients' situations. For instance, he explained, the women might ultimately return to Japan, and if not, others from their families or communities could follow similar migration paths. The more he knew about their outcomes and situations at home, the better prepared he would be to support these migrants in the future. He shared that he had also complained to the IOM about this practice: "I said, 'At least we, the original people who were involved in the case, at least we should be given the feedback, what happened to them.'" Yet his entreaty had no effect.

Vicente then shared how he got around need-to-know protocols so that he could make ethical peace with his work. He disclosed that because he personally knew staff at the organizations in the Philippines that assisted migrants repatriated from Japan—his NGO had for years collaborated with them as part of the same assistance network—he would learn from these staff about where his clients wound up and how they were doing. He explained, "We get the feedback informally, because we know where some of the victims will be (because there are a limited number of NGOs working with migrants in different regions). But it's unofficial." Vicente appreciated this information and found it helpful in enabling him to do his job by allowing him to think about the well-being of his clients within the broader scope of their experiences and lives. However, the fact that this information was shared informally—and outside official protocols—also levied restrictions on how it could be used to improve the assistance process, creating a dilemma for Vicente. As he explained, "We aren't even able to say that we got the feedback from [that organization in the Philippines], because [that organization in the Philippines] is not allowed to share that information." Vicente found himself caught in a catch-22. The need-to-know protocols meant that established caseworkers like him had to rely on personal networks and back channels to follow up and get information about their clients in order to best support them. However, because he was not supposed to have this information, he was constrained in how he could use it to support his clients and lobby for change.

Vicente's exasperation with the channeling and compartmentalization of information was connected to his broader frustration with the inadequacy of existing channels for incorporating feedback from those working on the front lines to improve migrant outcomes. "There should be a way of feedback to improve the system," he insisted. He felt that channels for incorporating feedback and improvement were formally lacking in "the overall process of the whole system." He elaborated, "If the process is not clear, if the process cannot be trusted, or the process is not open for criticism or suggestions, how will it be improved?" He also expressed concerns that because the Japanese government and the IOM did not follow the women long term, little was known about the successes or failures of assistance efforts. Indeed, little practical attention was paid to the fates of these women after they returned home, a topic to which I return in chapters 7 and 8.

In fact, the UN does have official channels for feedback, including formal program reviews and reports by special rapporteurs. The decision to appoint a special rapporteur on trafficking in persons, especially women and children, was made by the UN in 2004; these special rapporteurs serve for three-year terms and submit annual reports to the UN Human Rights Council and the General Assembly. However, caseworkers like Vicente saw little effect of such reports, which are channeled and discussed high up the bureaucratic and governmental ladders; it takes years for even small, highly diluted impacts to be felt downstream. In contrast, NGO caseworkers like Vicente relied on intimate and long-standing relationships based in mutual concern and on reliable, ongoing direct channels of communication. These channels enabled the exchange of information in real time and adjustments to assistance strategies on an immediate case-by-case basis. Vicente explained, "For example, we can work directly with [an NGO in the Philippines] because we trust them, and they trust us. We've been working with them for many years in many cases.... So there is already that given relationship; it's a relationship built on trust and on knowing the other organization, the people in the other organization, for so many numbers of years."

Conclusion

Different strategies of information management enable different forms of personal assistance. Need-to-know protocols are compatible with a trafficking victim assistance program governed by a division of labor in which different parties have circumscribed responsibilities and communicate minimally with one another to carry out a set of limited, prescribed tasks. Such an approach facilitates a modular victim assistance program in which a shared protocol forms the unifying link among different countries and agencies. However, it demonstrates little commitment to the long-term well-being of clients as people. Need-to-know protocols allow NGO caseworkers to know that a painful experience exists, but they render the specific nature of this experience, and thus any potential future needs of the client, inaccessible. They also present challenges for any ongoing assessment of the assistance process. Those involved only have information relevant to their practically and temporally circumscribed role. Outside periodic reviews from special rapporteurs or other audits, adjustments to the process to better support clients becomes difficult, hampering efforts to improve it. Such protocols also prohibit the collective forms of thought and action so crucial to NGOs' effectiveness, supplanting them with liberal notions of individual privacy, a utilitarian approach to knowledge, and a distributed approach to responsibility organized through a division of labor. Insofar as official need-to-know protocols make maintaining client confidentiality an ethical practice in the process, it becomes an end in itself.

NGO caseworkers like Vicente who are committed to a client-centered approach felt stymied by these information management strategies, which made it difficult to have a comprehensive and diachronic understanding of an individual client's well-being. They were told that to act in the best interest of a client, they must set aside their desire not only to know her as a person but also to understand the broader social and political economic circumstances that had brought her to this point. In addition, despite these caseworkers' central role in victim assistance, they were encouraged, ostensibly in the interest of both the project and victim protection, to uncritically trust the bureaucratic division of labor and to assume that all was going smoothly. They were told that to help their clients, they must separate themselves from them as people and regard them only as bits of "confidential personal data" to be passed on to the next point in the chain.

NGO caseworkers like Vicente found this shift in available client knowledge painful and counterproductive. For them, a client-centered approach to information management involved sharing information among trusted and equally invested parties in ways that would enable them to best support people in both the short and long term. It also meant engaging in an ongoing process of self-evaluation and self-questioning with respect to how best to assist a person in need—in other words, constantly *thinking* about how to best serve another. Recall how Morita explained that self-reflexivity was built into victim assistance at her NGO: caseworkers turned to one another to gain additional perspectives, to become aware of their own myopias, and to strategize together to best support their clients as people.[28] Caseworkers like Vicente struggled with the compulsion to conceive of the ethics of their work as a matter of following protocol. For them, these mandated practices clearly did more ethical—and practical—harm than good.

7

FUNDING FRUSTRATION

———————

The most innovative and proactive of Japan's attempts to fight TIP has been the funding for a number of anti-TIP programs in source countries. Often contained in its Human Security development programs, Japan has annually contributed about USD 8.7 million to specific anti-TIP programs in source countries.

—EMBASSY TOKYO, "Japan, the U.S., and TIP: At a Tipping Point?"

The UN's emphasis on collaboration meant that grassroots NGOs in the Philippines were pulled into what were called "partnerships" with international organizations and centralized governments to assist repatriated trafficking survivors. Widely touted on UN websites, these partnerships offered cash-strapped NGOs (and their clients) access to new financial resources. However, NGO staff soon learned that the money came with agendas and mandates that constrained and sometimes conflicted with their commitments. Staff at the organizations with whom I spoke felt compromised by, and ambivalent about, the bureaucratic strings attached to their inclusion in these projects.

This chapter and chapter 8 follow Japan's assistance and protection pipeline for trafficking victims to the Philippines to consider the experiences of NGO caseworkers and their clients. I focus on a grant administered by the

International Labour Organization (ILO) to assist women returning home as victims of human trafficking. Funded at nearly US$2,000,000 by the UN Trust Fund for Human Security (UNTFHS), the Economic and Social Empowerment of Returned Victims of Trafficking in the Philippines and Thailand project ran between May 2006 and April 2009. Per the grant application, the ILO Philippines would select three grassroots NGOs in Metro Manila to help execute the project.[1] Here I consider how the subcontracting relationships that structured this grant disempowered NGO staff while ostensibly supporting them. I argue that the restrictive protocols of available grants, such as funding constraints and accounting requirements, set aside the priorities and commitments of NGOs, ultimately channeling resources toward international-organization and centralized-government agendas. Moreover, not only did the institutional structure of these efforts ignore NGO caseworkers' insight and expertise, which was based on years of assisting migrants, but it also ultimately pushed some of them out of the movement at the cost of losing their experience, knowledge, and perspectives altogether. I explore how NGO staff struggled with the burden of these requirements, in some cases burning out and leaving the project. This pushing out of committed yet frustrated activists is another way that meaningful critique is banally evacuated from these projects.

My focus on the consequences of funding for grassroots NGOs in the Philippines builds on the work of feminist scholars who have explored how NGO work both enables and constrains feminist activism, at once empowering and subjugating women.[2] These scholars have taught us that feminist NGOs are not outside the state or market and not only adopt transnational models and strategies of governance but also appropriate, embrace, and deploy these models for their own ends.[3] However, less attention has been paid to how economic incorporation in global governance projects compromises the commitments of grassroots NGOs or how NGO caseworkers cope with the frustration that accompanies their participation.[4]

In the remainder of this chapter, I explore how international funding protocols contribute to NGO staff frustration by at once reinforcing and disguising inequities among NGOs, national state governments, and international organizations as they sideline NGO commitments. I begin by introducing Sibol, one of the NGOs that applied for funding from the UNTFHS-ILO project. I then explore how, why, and to what ends the project's funding hierarchies constrained the activities of NGOs contracted through it.

Sibol's office was in an accessory building of a church compound on a congested and dusty thoroughfare running through a neighborhood in the southeast corner of Metro Manila. To reach the office, one climbed three flights of cracked and grimy wooden stairs and then walked down a dim hallway with peeling stucco and pitted tile before reaching a heavy, locked yellow wooden door. The office itself could only be described as modest, even relative to other NGOs I visited in the city. A total of, at most, 100 square feet, the crowded space was divided by a bookcase, which created two narrow work zones that were hedged by plywood shelves, cabinets, and desktops, all painted pale blue. What appeared to have originally been a closet, an attached even smaller room, all but filled by a metal 2' × 3' table and two chairs, was used when staff met privately with a client. A small air-conditioning unit completely occupied the office's lone window. Wads of folded newspapers sealed the gaps around the unit, blocking out any natural light but permitting reminders of the world outside: traffic noise and, occasionally, the chirping of birds.

Sibol was part of the lively, transnational, grassroots migrant-assistance network that included Tahanan and other Japanese NGOs. Known for working with Filipina migrants who had returned from Japan—it had assisted thousands—the organization was among those commissioned by the IOM to assist returned trafficking survivors after the Japanese government adopted its Action Plan. I first visited Sibol in 2000 as part of my earlier research on Filipina migrants in rural Nagano. When I began this project, I contacted Jem, Sibol's assistant director, to arrange another visit between December 2006 and January 2007, requesting permission to conduct research with the organization and offering to provide any assistance that I could.

One morning toward the end of my stay, Jem greeted me at the Sibol office door in her usual uniform of a navy skirt, a crisp white blouse, and brown loafers. She had requested my input on the proposal that she was submitting to the ILO for a grant it had received from the UNTFHS. As Jem and I sat on two folding chairs in front of a folder stuffed with papers, she explained that Sibol was requesting a little more than US$100,000 for three years of assistance and outreach activities. She asked me to look over the "activities" section of the application, which detailed their plans and budget. She added that of the approximately US$2M that the ILO had received from the UN, a total of US$380,000, had been allocated for direct assistance and outreach project activities in both the Philippines and Thailand. I asked where the funds not used for these purposes would go—the bulk of the money *and more than US$1.2M. Jem raised her eyebrows skeptically and shrugged. She shared that she had repeatedly observed that funding for anti-human-trafficking efforts in the Philippines went to the Philippine government's "operations costs." She surmised that this money went to administrative salaries, because "the government offers few social services" for trafficking survivors. Then, referencing the ILO budget, Jem ventured with guarded annoyance, "Some of the money might have gone to the grant orientation meeting in Bangkok." She explained that she had not attended the meeting but had heard from others that the entire group of NGO applicants and ILO representatives had been billeted in a four-star hotel to learn about the grant application process. Jem was glad that NGOs had a venue to meet project partners and exchange information; however, she explained, staying at a hotel like that was "way above her NGO staff's standards." Bangkok has a lot of good two- and three-star hotels. She did not understand why the group had not stayed in one of those. "It surprised me that they were staying in such a fancy hotel. We're not used to that, and I don't want us to get used to that. Sibol perennially faces a crisis of not having enough money." She gestured to the office's two antiquated computers, which still relied on dial-up internet access. She explained that many of Sibol's clients struggle to feed their families, to say nothing of accessing medical care. Sibol had few financial resources to offer them. She added that groups working for women's rights, not only in the Philippines but also in other Southeast Asian countries, were especially having funding problems these days. "Maybe," she added, "we need to take a closer look at how we distribute funds."*

Jem's frustration with funding priorities in UN-sponsored anti-human-trafficking efforts points to a dilemma for many grassroots activists who, like her, had long pushed for international attention to human trafficking and had initially been hopeful about the Trafficking Protocol. On the one hand, Jem recognized the strategic benefits of collaborating with international organizations and governments to accomplish Sibol's aims. Jem viewed international organization and government support as necessary for fighting the exploitation of transnational labor migrants. Moreover, Jem explained, organizations like hers are characteristically cash-strapped. Working within national or international organization agendas offers them access to money and political power. On the other hand, NGO staff like Jem recognized the challenges that accompany working with national governments and international organizations, which often stipulated that NGOs adapt to their agendas and program requirements to access funds.

Sibol is one of a number of organizations in the Philippines established in the 1980s and 1990s to support Filipinx migrants returning from overseas, including those coming back from Japan in, as Jem described, "distressed conditions." Staff at Japanese women's shelters had observed the challenges that their clients faced when they returned home, from difficulty becoming financially stable, to struggles with trauma experienced abroad, to family conflicts, to difficulty getting financial support from the Japanese fathers of their children. They had reached out to the Philippine National Council of Churches to help establish centers in the Philippines that could provide, in Jem's words, "a continuity of services." Initially, Sibol's funding came from churches in Japan and other parts of the world, which raise money through donations. However, Jem explained, "Because churches provide assistance to a lot of organizations, these are not huge funds, just small funds that enable us to maintain our operations. It doesn't necessarily mean that we have the funds to do everything we want to do." Occasionally, the organization received limited funding for specific projects from the Philippine government's Department of Social Welfare and Development.

When staff at Sibol were contracted by the IOM to provide repatriation and reintegration assistance to "victims of human trafficking," they viewed the work as consistent with their mission: many women whom the organization assisted during the 1980s and 1990s would have qualified as trafficking victims under the new UN definition. What changed was Sibol's relationships with the IOM and the Japanese government. New funding agreements formalized and institutionalized these arrangements. As Jem explained, "We started entering into a new kind of partnership [with the IOM] wherein Sibol would be an NGO service provider for victims of trafficking when they return to the Philippines." Under these partnerships, state and international bodies would oversee their activities. Not only would Sibol have to adapt to these bureaucracies' standards of practice, including attending oversight meetings and submitting specifically formatted financial-accounting reports, but participating NGOs would have to adjust their programs to what the national governments funding these efforts were willing to support (see chapter 8). Jem's frustration with the UNTFHS-ILO grant reflected a broader set of concerns regarding both funding priorities and the subsumption of NGO expertise and commitment by more powerful government-run bodies. Much like Vicente and the other NGO caseworkers in chapter 6, the staff at Sibol found themselves in a catch-22: at once indebted to international agencies for much-needed funds and constrained by them. A meeting that I had at the ILO in Manila with a man whom everyone at Sibol affectionately called "Attorney Larga" brought these dynamics into clear relief.

I met with Attorney Larga in the new ILO office on the nineteenth floor of the recently completed RCBC Plaza, an office skyscraper complex with one of the most prestigious addresses in one of the highest-rent districts of the Philippines. I went with Girlie, one of Sibol's former clients, who was there to deliver Sibol's grant application for the ILO project. Security to enter RCBC Plaza is tight. We had to pass through four security checkpoints on our way to the office. Before even entering the RCBC complex, we had to pass through a metal detector and have our bags checked by armed guards. Our bags were checked again as we entered the specific building where the ILO office was located. Once inside the building, we had to register at a special counter for the UN and surrender our identification, phones, and cameras to get visitor badges. We then rode an elevator to the nineteenth floor. In the hallway outside the elevator landing, another armed guard and metal detector protected the door to the ILO office. My bag was once again scanned before I was permitted entry.

Recently remodeled, the entire office smelled of fresh paint. An ILO staffer welcomed us and escorted us through the sparsely furnished reception room down a long hallway to Attorney Larga's office, which had expansive views of the city and was vacant apart from some empty bookcases and a large new desk covered with a mess of papers. Attorney Larga welcomed us. He was professionally dressed in slacks and a well-pressed dress shirt. I noticed that he was particularly warm toward Girlie; other bureaucrats and officials that I had met during my stay seemed somewhat dismissive of Sibol's former clients during our meetings.

During our interview, I asked Attorney Larga about the UN grant that his office was administering. He responded, "Most trafficking victims come home empty-handed. They are heavily indebted. They suffer stigmatization." He explained that these factors made them vulnerable to "re-trafficking." The Japanese government was keen on projects that might help prevent trafficking victims from returning to Japan and discourage additional migrants from entering trafficking situations there. He continued, "But instead of herding direct grants to agencies of the Philippine government, they prefer to channel it to the UN Trust Fund for Human Security. And the ILO was chosen as the implementer of the project." I asked why the Japanese government decided to go through the UN and not just give the funds directly to NGOs. Attorney Larga explained that the Japanese government wanted to be included (and thus acknowledged) as part of a larger UN project. Moreover, Attorney Larga surmised, "They'd prefer to have something more institutional . . . in the sense that it will be for the UN with strict monitoring, etc., and bounded by certain UN regulations. They're looking perhaps upon more standardized and more institutional ways of managing the issue in the context of the United Nations."

I then asked Attorney Larga about the ILO's role. He responded vaguely that the organization would mediate between the UN and receiving governmental and nongovernmental agencies. It is the "glue connecting the different segments," he offered. It would "pull in partner agencies" and "make sure that everything goes smoothly." It would provide the "technical inputs" (what he later explained as the "tools") to set up a smooth referral system and a database. Also, it would distribute the funds, overseeing how they were spent by NGOs and ensuring that they were not wasted or used inappropriately—that is, outside the parameters the Japanese government had established for the trust fund's grants.

By many accounts, Attorney Larga, who passed away in 2017, was sincerely committed to fighting for migrants' rights and channeling money to local NGOs. He seemed to have been well-intentioned in applying to the UNTFHS for funds for the ILO empowerment project. An obituary for him in the *Manila Times* claimed that "the non-government organizations that are active in the labor migration front saw him as a friend and ally."[5] It described him as "both intellectually and financially honest" and as someone who "would never tolerate mercenary pursuits disguised as public service."[6] Both characterizations rang true to comments I heard about him from NGO staff and clients. His application to the UNTFHS was prompted by an ILO study that had identified the need to extend services to trafficking survivors beyond repatriation.[7] The study had found that the return and reintegration project was "inadequately attended to" and that this inadequacy made "returnees vulnerable to re-trafficking."[8] At the same time, on account of changes in migration policy and law enforcement following the adoption of the UN protocol, the ILO anticipated an increase in repatriation of trafficking survivors.[9]

The UNTFHS accepts funding applications only from organizations that are bound by UN Financial Regulations and Rules, requiring these organizations to collaborate with non-UN agencies and individuals to execute their grant. Attorney Larga saw the grant as an opportunity to use his institutional position at the ILO to channel resources to grassroots groups for their work with trafficking survivors. He also endeavored to incorporate NGO and survivor perspectives into the project plan. In a stakeholder presentation that he gave at the beginning of the grant tenure, he listed as priorities "listen[ing] and learn[ing] carefully from returnees about their concerns, needs and ideas" and "foster[ing] a rights-based, bottom up approach."[10] He described his intention to develop a "flexible approach that provides real solutions to the individual (versus a 'one size fits all solution')."[11] He even began his presentation by high-lighting the voices of trafficking survivors, playing a ten-minute video clip from a play about their experiences working as entertainers in Japan that they had developed and performed to build community and engage in political activism in their communities. (I discuss this play in chapter 8.)

However, despite Attorney Larga's desire to incorporate the perspectives of NGOs and trafficking survivors, the subcontracting relationship structuring both ILO and NGO funding through the UNTFHS grant would, by design, prioritize Japanese government interests and agendas. The Japanese government had established the UNTFHS in 1999 with a pledge of US$4.2 million to promote human security projects through UN agencies around the world.[12] As I explain in chapter 8, Japanese government officials had come to see the promotion of human security as central to its foreign policy interests and had begun committing foreign policy resources to its wider adoption within the UN.[13] By February 2005, the Japanese government—the sole donor to the fund since its inception—had given approximately US$256 million to the fund, and it ultimately set the agenda for how monies should be spent.[14]

One focus was on reducing undocumented labor migration to Japan by promoting human security in Asia.[15] After the Asian currency crisis of 1997, the Japanese government was concerned about increasing numbers of migrant workers from the region entering the country. The UNTFHS-ILO empowerment project was one of several projects funded by the Japanese government over the aughts that aimed to reduce undocumented migration to Japan, in this case by preventing "re-trafficking."[16] Per grant guidelines, the Philippine government would also have a say in any programs funded in its territory. (All UNTFHS-funded projects are required to have the consent of the recipient government.)[17] However, most countries that receive development aid from Japan, such as the Philippines, lie within Japan's sphere of influence, and their governments are to some degree beholden to it.[18]

In our conversation, Attorney Larga recognized that the Japanese government wanted to discourage unregulated Filipina migration to Japan; the funding it provided for "reintegration" aimed to deter the re-migration of trafficking survivors who were viewed as vulnerable to it. He also acknowledged that the Japanese government had specific parameters for how the funds it had donated to the UN for trafficking assistance should be spent. For instance, the guidelines for UNTFHS-funded programs, like the ILO's guidelines, explicitly state that the fund will not consider "stand-alone programmes" that do not include "concrete plans to mainstream the human security approach" or requests to address a "resource gap for existing initiatives which do not apply the human security approach."[19] It will not consider funds for "large-scale infrastructure" projects, "large-scale micro-credit and/or grant schemes," or "emergency assistance that does not ensure self-sustainability at the community-level."[20] It will not accept applications from individuals or non-UN organizations, and it requires "substantive involvement of the applying UN organization(s)" for programs carried out by non-UN organizations.[21] It also requires partnering NGOs to follow institutional protocols, employing a formal referral system and database and submitting a line-by-line accounting of spending.[22] Such a funding structure leaves NGOs with limited discretion to use the monies as they best see fit. For instance, they could not use funding to help clients develop work collaboratives or as short-term resources to tide over clients who found themselves in health or work emergencies.

For its part, the ILO, as the officially funded party, was required to follow a predetermined reporting schedule and financial-statement template to closely monitor spending for all activities implemented during the reporting period. These expectations of grantee accountability are standard, intended to ensure that funds are not misappropriated and are used according to approved parameters. However, they also require following a rigid model that leaves little room for contingencies or unforeseen needs. In this regard, Attorney Larga, even with his good intentions and efforts to listen to NGO staffers, was still limited by the terms of the grant and the Japanese government's interests in funding it; similarly, if funded, Sibol would become at once the beneficiary of, *and the instrument for accomplishing*, the Japanese government's objectives. In other words, the incorporation of NGOs like Sibol into larger international funding practices involved their instrumentalization as tools for accomplishing the ends of international organizations and national governments that provided the funding. Insofar as NGOs in the Philippines participated in the project, they would implicitly be helping link the Japanese government's aspirations for international leadership with its strategic objectives for migration control, which in part informed its funding agenda. What choice did they have?

The NGO Burden of Bureaucratic Glue and Strings

Given Attorney Larga's vague response about the ILO's role as the "glue connecting the different segments" that would offer "technical inputs" and "tools," it's hard not to perceive an uncomfortable irony in the insistence, on the part of both the UN and the Japanese government, that the ILO was needed to ensure that contracted NGOs do not waste or inappropriately use funds. Most governments and international organizations charge overhead costs for grant administration to cover office and staff expenses, and the ILO is no exception. Recall Jem's frustration with the ways that she believed the Philippine government used anti-trafficking funding almost exclusively for administration costs. Remember, too, that Jem was opposed to the ways the ILO wasted money on luxuries such as four-star hotel rooms. She would have preferred to use the funds to assist clients. I heard other NGO staff in Japan and the United States offer related critiques. For instance, one lamented that so little of available funding goes to "direct assistance" for the women and instead goes to researchers, education, training, law enforcement, and expensive Japan Airlines plane tickets instead of less expensive tickets on other airlines (for identified victims' return home).

As discussed in previous chapters, Sibol and other NGOs in Japan and the Philippines came to the attention of international organizations and government agencies because their bare-bones operations had track records of doing effective work with migrants despite operating on shoestring budgets. These organizations have been resourceful, gutsy, and creative in their ability to access funds, even if their strategies did not always formally correspond to international protocols. Grassroots NGO workers in Manila spoke to me about how they had previously found ways to circumvent the institutional restrictions of international grants and channel additional funds to their clients by depriving themselves. For example, as mentioned in chapter 2, Gloria Reyes shared that during the 1990s, her grassroots feminist organization had taken portions of the salaries they had been paid as "experts" by international grants and invested the money back in their NGO so that they could give interest-free loans to the women they were assisting. She described their strategy: "See, as an NGO, we don't really pay our salaries as they are on paper. We save. We put it away." She explained that in their grant application, "Because we were 'experts,' we could actually put that I am worth P50,000/month [about US$1265.00/month in 1993]. But instead of getting P50,000, I get probably P20,000 [about US$506.00/month]." The organization could then use the remaining P30,000/month (about US$759.00/month) to help their clients. In other words, these women donated more than half of their grant-funded "expert" salaries to direct assistance. Gloria explained that their organization also saved money that had been designated in the grant for "catering" and nonnecessary items, using those funds instead to help their clients. These activists were not necessarily from wealthy backgrounds; many came from middle-class or lower-middle-class backgrounds in the Philippines. Their decisions regarding how they spent grant funds derived from their discomfort with the spending priorities of granting agencies and their commitment, first and foremost, to supporting their clients.

In our conversations, NGO staff not only questioned the spending priorities of these projects but also voiced frustration with the increased bureaucratic demands that accompanied them, demands they viewed as misguided, wasteful, and sometimes demeaning. Some of these frustrations became clear to me through my volunteer work with an anti-human-trafficking NGO in the United States. One day, Beth, a caseworker with whom I was friendly, asked me to assist in filling out donor forms, which were due that day. The organization relied on funding from different sources for a variety of purposes, and each donor required different forms to account for how donations were spent. Soon after we began working, I realized that I had helped Beth fill out the same forms the previous week. She explained that because clients' names were redacted on the forms, and because we had been cutting and pasting set phrases across forms, we had made mistakes that had to be corrected. As we worked, she complained that filling out the forms was a waste of time and a hassle, and she often felt overwhelmed by what amounted to a slew of extra paperwork. Because of some granting agencies' new requirements, she had to use different forms for different clients, which was confusing and time-consuming to manage. In addition, Beth approached her clients as people, not data to input; thus, she found the process to be dehumanizing. Moreover, donors often changed their required accounting forms, forcing Beth to spend days redoing templates and inputting information instead of working with clients. She explained that "it's normal to have to submit all receipts, but now 15%–20% of my time is going to financial accounting and grant paperwork instead of client services."

National governments and international organizations had initially relied on the input and expertise of grassroots groups as they established a global counter–human trafficking project. However, rather than providing resources for them to use as they saw fit, these funders now aimed to further incorporate the NGOs into an international bureaucratic hierarchy. They expected NGO staff to train themselves to accommodate government and international agencies' standards of compliance and audit.[23] Moreover, instead of celebrating the work that these organizations managed despite their small budgets, funders saw their lack of sufficient resources as a sign of their being insufficiently professional and thus in need of oversight. As we have seen, adopting standardized global institutional practices was often framed as professionalizing NGOs. Recall that a US embassy staffer complained that NGOs assisting migrants in Japan were "mom operations" and not sufficiently professionalized. In addition to requiring onerous accounting procedures, the US government and international organizations promoted the production of guidelines, workshops, and conferences aimed at professionalizing the organizations.

Such was the case with the UNTFHS-ILO empowerment project. As Attorney Larga mentioned, standardization and professionalization were objectives of channeling the money through the ILO and having NGOs formally apply through it. At the same time, in official presentations and documents, participating NGOs in the Philippines were variously referred to as "partners" and "sub-contracts" or "subcontractors." For instance, the subsection titled "The Project Partners" under the heading "Implementating Modality" in the project brochure states, "The implementation of the programme components will be mainly subcontracted to partner government agencies, non-government organizations and other stakeholders."[24] In his PowerPoint presentation to stakeholders, Attorney Larga also used the term "sub-contracts" to refer to the budget allocation for direct assistance in the Philippines and Thailand: "Sub-contracts amount to approx. $380,000 per country."[25]

This subcontracting dynamic reflects the conditional incorporation of NGOs in these efforts. In capitalist expansion, subcontracting is a cost-cutting practice that enables scalar expansion by taking advantage of existing resources.[26] It allows for fictions of responsibility while letting contracting parties off the hook for labor violations or other project failures.[27] In UN project funding, the logic works a bit differently, allowing entities like UNTFHS, working through the ILO, to subsume the agendas of local NGOs while having them do work that prioritizes Japan's foreign policy interests. The ILO, as lead agency, would oversee and mediate, integrating and directing coordination among implementation organizations toward "the shared objectives of the human security programme."[28] It was "responsible for the overall management and technical guidance, financial and technical reporting to the donor," and it would be expected to establish "the appropriate governance structures and coordinating mechanisms" at the UN, government, and local community levels.[29] The NGOs would provide labor and resources to carry out direct assistance and develop training materials, and staff would undergo training themselves so that they could sustain and expand the project's objectives beyond the grant tenure to realize the UNTFHS's objectives of producing "concrete and sustainable benefits" and developing tools "for replication and expansion."[30]

These guidelines have real implications for how direct assistance organizations can conceive of their work. Grassroots NGOs in Manila applied to be part of the project because it offered much-needed funds to sustain their direct assistance programs. Yet to receive funding, they would need to accommodate UNTFHS criteria. By treating NGOs as subcontractors, the project imposed a neoliberal logic of flexible labor onto human rights assistance; this structure also served as a means of control, keeping NGO activity in line with government and international agency interests regardless of caseworkers' experiential knowledge and perspectives. At the same time, as I next explain, financial contributions enabled national governments to participate in global counter–human trafficking efforts without expecting changes in their policies regarding migrants' home countries or the behaviors of corporations in them; in this way, short-term funding became a proxy for real structural change.

The "UN Graveyard Is Full of Trust Funds"

NGO critiques of the funding priorities of global counter–human trafficking efforts did not escape the UN. By the late aughts, the UN was facing criticism from within and without the organization that its efforts to fight human trafficking were insufficiently victim-centered. In response, in late 2010 the UN Voluntary Trust Fund for Victims of Trafficking in Persons (UNVTF) was launched by then secretary-general Ban Ki-moon as part of the UN's 2010 Global Plan of Action to Combat Trafficking in Persons. This trust fund was founded on the premise that it would provide "Member States, the private sector and individuals with an opportunity to show their solidarity with the victims of trafficking in persons in a concrete way."[31] Specifically, it would support "the implementation and delivery of activities and services that both enhance the psychological recovery and social reintegration of victims and empower survivors to reclaim their rights to justice and fair compensation, as part of the global fight against trafficking. This includes through the identification of victims, legal, prosecution assistance, coordination and information sharing across relevant actors."[32] Like the UNTFHS, one of the key aims of the UNVTF was "to reduce the vulnerability of victims being discriminated, re-victimized and re-trafficked."[33] This agenda appealed to the governments of many migrant-receiving countries, which would be the primary donors for the fund and, like Japan, wanted to discourage undocumented migration. To prevent re-trafficking, the UNVTF proposed to help "step up global efforts" and "provide tangible assistance."[34] This time, contributions to it would be focused on the protection of and direct assistance to victims of trafficking, including the provision of essential services. These efforts included providing funding for a range of services: shelter, food, medical care, legal aid, access to justice, and psychosocial support. Grassroots NGOs would be the primary channels for these funds. The trust fund would be administered by UNODC staff, and thus only 10 percent of funds would be applied to direct operational costs.[35]

Yet despite this provision for increased resources for direct assistance to trafficking survivors, a closer look at the fate, responses to, and reviews of this new trust fund point to some of the problems that plague a bureaucratically based model for effecting meaningful political change. For instance, the establishment of the UNVTF meant that NGOs could apply directly to the UN for funding; however, few actually receive money, and funding for direct assistance is dwarfed by that spent by the UN for administrative purposes. Consider that by June 2022, the fund had distributed over US$6 million split among 140 projects in sixty countries to support a total of approximately five thousand individuals per year.[36] These numbers are paltry considering that the UN estimates that the number of victims of human trafficking worldwide is in the tens of millions and the UN secretariat's budget is in the billions.[37] Moreover, the fierce competition for funding means that NGOs must ensure that they can assimilate and adapt to the bureaucratic strategies of international organizations in order to be competitive. For instance, in the first call for proposals in 2011, the fund received over 250 applications, out of which 11 were selected. In the third round, announced in 2017, 29 projects were selected from 183 proposals; and in its fourth round in 2020, it received 268 proposals, funding 32.[38] Clearly, existing need is far greater than distributed resources.

Reviews of the program, which have been mixed at best, also draw attention to the problems in the allocation of funding. For instance, a 2014 program review noted that the wording of the General Assembly resolution that established the fund "was extremely broad and provided no guidance on how the UNVTF was to be set up and run, and from where administrative resources should be drawn."[39] Others highlighted the challenge of raising money for victims, let alone funds to cover the secretariat's costs.[40] Respondents believed that more administrative funds were needed for "project monitoring" yet recognized that this would affect "the already limited resources available for distribution to grantees."[41] The fund was already struggling to cover the direct and indirect management costs that the UNODC charges for "program support." The 2014 review concluded, "Across all stakeholder groups, a lack of sufficient funding was identified as a major constraint to the UNVTF fulfilling its objective to assist victims of trafficking. To date, the Trust has been unable to generate a critical mass of funds that would allow for all administrative costs to be met, while remaining true to the spirit of Article 38 in providing humanitarian, legal and financial aid to victims of trafficking in persons, with low overheads."[42] One respondent to the 2014 midyear evaluation of the trust fund noted that the "UN graveyard is full of Trust Funds."[43]

More troubling, the UNVTF instrumentalizes human rights and the lives of trafficking survivors as a means through which individuals, corporations, and centralized states can assert themselves as being committed to change through self-interested strategies. Donations to the fund have been solicited with the slogan HAVE A HEART!, appealing to people to have compassion and act out of humanitarian benevolence.[44] Contributions are celebrated as a successful form of participation by national governments and private donors. Certainly this money is needed and could be put to good use. However, the needs of those whom the fund was set up to assist have remained incidental to its purpose, a point explicitly, if unwittingly, articulated at the official press conference announcing the fund. Held at the UN's New York headquarters on November 4, 2010, the press conference featured as speakers the US-based celebrities Ashton Kutcher and his former spouse, Demi Moore. The two were introduced by Yuri Fedotov, executive director of the UNODC, as "deeply committed to the struggle against human trafficking," on account of their founding of an organization focused on child pornography and sex trafficking.[45] In approximately three minutes of extemporaneous comments, Kutcher offered: "Today, we are here with the good fortune of trying to change . . . sixty-two years of neglect. Because either we are ignoring the issue, or we don't care. And as an optimist," he continued, his voice quavering, "I care, and I want to believe that everybody cares. . . . These people have a right to freedom, they have a right to be loved, they have a right to be rehabilitated."[46] After explaining that the same supply chains that traffic humans also traffic drugs and arms, supporting organized crime and terrorism, he cynically concluded:

> Human beings that are trafficked can talk. They have voices. They may be the greatest assets that we have in fighting drugs, organized crime, terror, because they know who is trafficking them. They know the supply lines. And with love, support, and rehabilitation, they are assets. So instead of criminalizing these people, today we have an opportunity to support a fund that will give them the resilience, the strength, and the determination within themselves to maybe come forward and become some of the greatest assets that we have in the world. And along the way, while we are fighting for our own national security, maybe someone will find freedom.[47]

As Kutcher described it, the fund, like the Trafficking Protocol, offered donors an opportunity to kill two birds with one stone, so to speak. Not only could they feel good about "hav[ing] a heart" and supporting a humanitarian project for assisting trafficking victims, they could also improve their own national security because victims would be required to testify against their traffickers. NGO caseworkers complain that testifying retraumatizes their clients and some simply do not feel comfortable doing so. However, the question of how trafficking survivors might feel about having to repeatedly bear witness to, and thereby relive, their experiences to serve US security interests seemed not to have crossed Kutcher's mind. He at once celebrated the moral goodness of those who support the UN project and cynically suggested that we should also support the fund out of a self-interested desire for national security. He articulated himself as a caring person while also suggesting that trafficking victims were strategic instruments for US national security agendas.

Kutcher may seem an easy target.[48] Nevertheless, his speech well captures the instrumentalist logic that pervades UN efforts to fight human trafficking and that frames financial donations by national governments as a means of taking "innovative and proactive" steps to fight trafficking in persons.[49] These solicitations, as Elizabeth Bernstein pointedly explains, problematically suggest that one can address the violence that has come to be identified as human trafficking simply through financial donations.[50] Such an approach makes money a proxy for real political engagement in ways that are both consumer and media friendly and amenable to the status quo.[51]

This donation logic is not an innovation of counter human–trafficking efforts. It was pioneered during the mid-1970s by Amnesty International and other human rights organizations, which developed direct-mail fundraising strategies to grow their resources and following.[52] The strategy appealed to AI because it freed the organization from depending on a large, actively engaged membership base. Instead, it could cut costs by restricting solicitation to preselected audiences and tailor messages to them accordingly.[53] By 1977, the organization was funded largely by white-collar professionals—lawyers, doctors, academics, businesspeople—who never attended meetings, gathered in public forums, or engaged in letter-writing campaigns. For these members, supporting human rights meant simply writing a check.[54] Also in the 1970s, as human rights developed cachet, large foundations began to finance human rights causes.[55] In 1975, the Ford Foundation gave a half million dollars to support human rights work, and this was soon followed by donations from the Rockefeller Foundation and others. Soon many organizations were centering their attention on convincing foundation officials instead of engaging with a large membership base.[56] A further shift to national governments or international organizations for funding was not a far stretch.

Human rights organizations justified the move away from grassroots mobilization toward an information activism in the name of alleviating suffering even at the expense of tactical purity. The shift toward influencing media, policy elites, and wealthy donors as opposed to grassroots engagement was part of a broader international shift in the focus of activism in the United States during the 1970s.[57] However, the result was a new, graphic, and sensationalized style of communicating political causes that combined fact reporting with direct-mail and foundation funding and included media publicity aimed at a broad humanitarian appeal—approaches that moved human rights and humanitarian work away from the self-reflective and socially and politically engaged approach that activists like Matsui envisioned.[58] One consequence of this shift away from hands-on grassroots mobilizing toward more detached forms of activism, such as financial donations and data collection, has been the equation of such disconnected forms of political action with protecting human rights. For instance, the United Nations Global Plan of Action to Combat Trafficking in Persons has included little in the way of promoting grassroots engagement or victim assistance beyond recognizing that "poverty, unemployment, gender-based violence, discrimination, and marginalization are among contributing factors" to human trafficking and establishing the donor-funded UNVTF.[59] This programmatic neglect of the cultural and political economic contexts within which migrants are abused and exploited is part of what creates frustration among those, like Jem, who have long worked as direct service providers for exploited migrant workers and who see the funding structure as part of the problem.

Caseworkers Burn Out

As I mentioned, Jem had initially been hopeful about the formal expansion of Sibol's mission and the accompanying international recognition and new funding streams opened up by the NGO's formal relationship with the IOM. She had hoped that UN-sponsored anti-human-trafficking campaigns would bring attention to the issues many Sibol clients face and help accelerate social change. She was well aware of the economic conditions that pushed Filipina women to go to Japan as migrant laborers and the abuses that they faced while there. Jem had come to work at Sibol the day after she graduated from college. She told me that she had been motivated by a personal commitment to social justice. As a college student, she had been active in student movements, including protesting US military bases in the country. She explained that she had been "trying to, in a way, change the world, change society." In this respect, Jem was not unlike other caseworkers I met at direct assistance NGOs in Japan, the United States, and the Philippines. The overwhelming majority of these NGO workers expressed similar commitments regarding social inequality and gender-based violence. Some of them had come out of the domestic violence or migrants' rights movements; others had backgrounds in intersectional feminism, Marxian theory, and postcolonial theory; and some drew on personal or familial experiences. Many had long advocated for women's and migrants' rights, and some had attended the Beijing conference, where the issue was foregrounded.

Like Cherie, Vicente, and others with whom I spoke, Jem had gradually grown frustrated with the UN-sponsored anti-trafficking efforts on account of both her personal commitments and her observations of their impact on Sibol's clients. She was enthusiastic about what Sibol had accomplished on its own, sharing with pride how the organization had helped its clients not only reestablish their lives in the Philippines but also establish a grassroots collective that provided them opportunities for support, leadership, and activism. Given what she believed was possible, Jem was frustrated with the ways in which the new funding practices and bureaucratic hierarchies were restructuring Sibol's operations. She worried that the Japanese government and the UN were not prioritizing the interests of Sibol's clients, which would require more sustained attention to their political-economic vulnerabilities. While in some ways helpful, the UNTFHS-ILO project seemed insufficient in the face of the deep structural changes that were needed. Jem was also dismayed by government and international organization spending priorities planned for the project. She explained of Sibol's clients' financial situations: "I've seen how difficult life gets every year." In this regard, her ambivalence derived from her political stakes in creating a more just and equal society and her frustrations with the discrepancies she witnessed moving between the elite and grassroots worlds. She was concerned that current globalized anti-trafficking operations were being compromised by geopolitical and institutional priorities and not accomplishing what they professed to do.

As I have shared, many involved in direct assistance in contemporary anti-human-trafficking efforts suppress their frustration because they believe that their work is necessary and they hope to make a difference. Many also identify personally with the migrants that they assist. However, despite, or perhaps on account of, their commitments to their jobs, I often heard staff at these organizations speak of burnout and complain of being overworked. For example, even after the Action Plan was established, the director of an NGO in Japan that assisted trafficking victims shared how her organization's lack of funds was a serious cause of stress for her, which I included in my field notes:

> Noriko shared that she is so stressed out that she needs to drink to get to sleep at night. She joked that her sleep formula is 2 × 4.5%, or two beers. Her organization is underfunded and understaffed. She said that on some Sundays she is the only one there. Another staff member in the room mentioned the new ILO funding project, adding skeptically that only the UNTFHS (and thus, by

proxy, the Japanese government) will be able to decide how the money is spent. Noriko replied with a sarcastic comment about its position toward migrants: "Here's some money, now go home." She explained that the Japanese government just wants to get the women out of Japan as quickly as possible—and as cheaply. Keeping them in Japan was more expensive so the government was anxious to get them to leave.

In addition to the significant stress caused by persistent funding and staff shortfalls (even with UNTFHS support), NGO staff are also subject to the ongoing stress of working with people experiencing severe emotional distress. Studies of service providers have shown that they "are often traumatized both by the heavy work burden and additionally by the cases that they are not able to assist to a better life."[60] As discussed in chapter 3, NGO caseworkers shared how their constant exposure to "vicarious" and "secondhand" trauma deeply affected them. On occasion, too, they became the targets of their distressed clients. For instance, during one interview in Tokyo, I learned about a shelter case in which a group of residents was having dinner, and one trafficking survivor started running toward a shelter staff person with a knife. She had been triggered upon hearing one of the other residents call the staff person "Mama" out of affection. She associated the term with the mama-san of her brothel, and she feared that this woman was coming back to get her. She held the knife like she was going to kill the shelter staff person because she never wanted to go back to the brothel again.

For NGO caseworkers coping with such trauma, the added burdens imposed by international and government involvement sometimes felt intolerable. As discussed in chapter 6, these caseworkers experienced feelings of impotence as those in more powerful administrative positions (both government and international organization officials) ignored their input about cases. Constrained by government policies and funding, these caseworkers sometimes questioned the help that they were able to provide, while some complained that their work was not recognized as skilled labor by international organization staff or government officials.

The demands of participation weigh on NGO staff until some can no longer bear them. During the course of my research, I noted the departure of a number of staff members at the grassroots service providers that I followed in Japan, the United States, and the Philippines. While many with whom I spoke have been caseworkers for years, I was also struck by the high level of turnover that I observed at some organizations over the years of my fieldwork. I began to get the impression that some of these NGOs had revolving doors for support staff in which idealistic caseworkers passed in and then, after a few years, came out in resigned exhaustion. Because the jobs do not pay well, even single adults find surviving on their wages difficult. Some of the big well-funded organizations in the United States offer benefits and competitive salaries to top administrators. However, regular staff, including caseworkers, are not always offered these incentives. Smaller organizations often have tight budgets and sometimes can only afford to hire staff on a part-time basis at close to minimum wage. NGO workers not infrequently decided to move on after a certain number of years. Although some choose to stay long term, a number of those whom I met at these shelters experienced burnout, and many more spoke of desires to do other work, even if they ultimately remain in their jobs. A few move on to positions with international organizations or government agencies, which offer better pay, full-time employment, benefits, and job security. Indeed, a few years after my visit to Manila, Jem left Sibol for a professional position with better conditions and prospects for working with migrants, taking her record of accomplishments, skills, and expertise with her. She had told me during my stay that she was planning to leave. Her voice flat with exhaustion, she explained that after so many years with the organization, she was ready for something new.

Conclusion

Constructivist scholars in international relations have pointed to the new roles that NGOs are playing in shaping global norms. However, despite assertions by both national governments and the UN of their desire to collaborate with NGOs in addressing human trafficking, the relationship is in no way egalitarian. Dependent on funds from centralized governments, international organizations, and private donors that place constraints on how resources can be used, NGO staff find themselves compromised and stymied in what they can achieve.[61] Moreover, although the UN is based on a principle of sovereign equality, funding practices are one way that hierarchies among nation-states, and between nation-states and NGOs, are maintained.[62] If the availability of new funding for local NGOs was heralded as one success of the adoption of the UN Trafficking Protocol, it came with the trade-off of being subcontracted labor.

In a study of highly educated professional women who leave successful careers when they become mothers, sociologist Pamela Stone disproves the claim that these women leave their careers out of choice; rather, she shows that these women are pushed out of the workforce by the structure of labor in this country and by workforce policies.[63] In an analogous sense, committed NGO caseworkers like Jem, who have long been involved in working to assist exploited migrants, have been pushed out of this work by funding priorities and labor hierarchies. They became disillusioned with the distribution of funds and burned out by subcontracting dynamics and began to question what they could accomplish with such an arrangement.

One might expect staff at grassroots direct-assistance NGOs like Sibol to express frustration with the allocation of funds in anti-human-trafficking projects. NGOs have a history of critiquing UN projects, and as was the case with Gloria Reyes, some grassroots feminist organizers in the Philippines have long histories of activism against the government, including having been imprisoned for it.[64] Based on these histories, they may be less willing to set their frustrations aside. However, I also interviewed international organization staff in Japan, the Philippines, and the United States, as well as a handful of government officials, who expressed reservations about their work for similar reasons. Recall, too, the five-page "Informal Note" (discussed in chapter 2) that then UN high commissioner for human rights Mary Robinson distributed to the UN General Assembly on June 1, 1999. She had expressed both high hopes about the prospects of an international protocol on human trafficking and reservations that the Trafficking Protocol would simply become a tool for immigration enforcement by national governments. In her capacity as high commissioner for human rights, Robinson's suggestions were limited to the inclusion of specific references, provisions, and language that affirmed signatories' commitments to maintaining and protecting the human rights of not only those recognized as victims of trafficking but also, and more broadly, migrant workers and those seeking refugee status. Her suggestions were efforts to maximize their consideration as a subsidiary issue, despite her preference that human rights be prioritized.

Fewer than two years after Mary Robinson submitted her comments, she left her position as UN high commissioner. In her opening remarks at the annual session of the UN Human Rights Commission in Geneva, she made no secret of her frustration with the mismatch between the rhetoric and the reality of the UN's human rights project, stating, "I believe it is one of the major disconnects between the eloquence and fine language used by so many representatives of governments in speaking about human rights and the fact that the core budget allocates less than 2% to human rights work."[65] She explained, "I believe that I can, at this stage, achieve more outside of the constraints that a multilateral organisation inevitably imposes."[66]

Despite their misgivings, many feminists and human rights activists, like Robinson and Jem, had strategically supported the Trafficking Protocol in the hopes that it would do some good. They had also worried that if they did not participate, issues of migrants' rights would be completely overlooked. However, some committed to migrants' rights found that their participation in the day-to-day operations of the UN counter–human trafficking program required too much compromise of these commitments. They had had enough of national governments and international organizations instrumentalizing their work with their clients. The funding issues that frustrated Jem were not simply the consequence of a less-than-ideal convention that was nonetheless worthy of support. These issues were also symptoms of the unequal access to money and power that institutionally structured NGO collaborations with the UN and other international organizations. In chapter 8, I offer more detail on how these inequalities shaped the execution and banal outcomes of the enactment of the UNTFHS-funded, ILO-run project introduced here. We will see how receiving these funds not only compromises the work of grassroots NGOs but also fails trafficking survivors.

8

CRUEL EMPOWERMENT

For women to be empowered, they have to be aware of their social situation and their rights, especially knowing how to fight for them.

—ANDREA LUISA C. ANOLIN AND LARA SALUD C. JAVIER,
"Empowering Returned Filipino Women Migrants and Their Children:
The Batis Center for Women Experience"

This chapter continues to focus on the incorporation of grassroots NGOs in the Philippines into the nearly US$2,000,000 UNTFHS-ILO Economic and Social Empowerment of Returned Victims of Trafficking in the Philippines and Thailand project, introduced in chapter 7. According to the UNTFHS-ILO project report, a key challenge for NGOs in the Philippines and Thailand was "convincing the women not to re-migrate" and to "try their hand in engaging in entrepreneurial activities in the country."[1] One way that the project aimed to address this challenge was by "giving the women credible and reliable career advice to help them achieve economic stability."[2] To these ends, the project's strategies in the Philippines were twofold. First, it would fund "immediate services" in the form of psychosocial counseling, health care, career coaching, occupational guidance, vocational training, and "access to small-credit and savings schemes" for a select group of repatriated migrants (150–200 per year, or a total of 450–600 over three years).[3] This targeted group would include not only "official returnees" (i.e., those formally repatriated as victims of trafficking) but also "unofficial returnees" who were identified through existing NGO networks as having suffered abuse and exploitation akin to trafficking victims.[4] In an effort "to ensure the sustainability of the project's impact as a whole," these interventions would be designed not simply to provide direct assistance to those involved in the program but to offer models for future efforts insofar as they would be documented in order "to disseminate them for possible adjustment and replication by other agencies and mainstream them into the policy framework of relevant agencies and institutions."[5] Second, the program was designed to have long-term impacts by pioneering new forms of "institutional development" in the form of "technical advisory and capacity building services."[6] The project brochure summed up its objectives this way: "At the end of the project, targeted returned victims of trafficking will have been assisted, empowered and protected from re-trafficking and the capacities of service providers to reintegrate victims of trafficking will have been improved."[7]

A focus on empowerment in official efforts to assist and protect trafficking victims is not exclusive to the UNTFHS-ILO grant but a central feature of counter–human trafficking efforts across the globe. These efforts present empowerment as a strategy not only for trafficking survivor recovery but also for preventing human trafficking more broadly. However, international agencies and centralized governments that fund such programs may hold different understandings of empowerment than the NGO caseworkers and clients who enact and are targeted by them. Empowerment is not a singular unified discourse; the concept brings together multiple intellectual genealogies that can be articulated in different ways.[8] This chapter compares the vision for trafficking survivor empowerment engaged by the UNTFHS-ILO project with that of the Women Empowerment Project (WEP)—an empowerment program independently established in 1995 by Batis, a grassroots NGO in Metro Manila that was later subcontracted under the UNTFHS-ILO project. As will be clear, the two projects took very different approaches to survivor empowerment. Funded as a short-term enterprise, the UNTFHS-ILO empowerment project endeavored a limited but reproducible and scalable intervention focusing on targeted coaching tools and training models for NGOs and government agencies to use into the future. In contrast, the WEP was established as a long-term project to support Batis clients both in their individual recovery and as they developed, what organization staff called, a "people's organization" to collectively advocate for their rights and transform the political-economic status quo.

Anthropologists and feminist scholars have explored how individualized, market-centered empowerment approaches like that of the UNTFHS-ILO empowerment project articulate with neoliberal government strategies through their emphasis on individual self-sufficiency, small government, and market-based competitiveness.[9] Rather than addressing the political-economic circumstances that disempower those they endeavor to assist, these strategies serve as forms of governance.[10] Through them, centralized states and international organizations participate in a convenient and cost-effective humanitarianism, relying on NGOs with stripped-down budgets and volunteer or low-paid part-time labor to fulfill their agendas while doing little to address the structural inequalities of the status quo.[11] Building on these studies, I highlight both the banality and the cruelty of the UNTFHS-ILO project in the Philippines by contrasting its approach to empowerment with that of the WEP. I describe the model of empowerment endorsed by the UNTFHS-ILO project as "cruel" following Lauren Berlant, whose notion "cruel optimism" foregrounds the painful experience of hopeful fantasies for those who do not have control over the material conditions of their lives.[12] Building on Berlant, I argue that the UNTFHS-ILO project offered a form of cruel empowerment in the sense that its approach to empowering trafficking survivors ignored the structural conditions that prompted their labor migration and made them vulnerable to abuse and exploitation in the first place. Consequently, as the project solicited the commitments and hopes of both repatriated trafficking survivors and the grassroots NGO workers dedicated to supporting them, it invariably created "a relation of attachment to compromised conditions of possibility."[13]

Moreover, I demonstrate that the cruelty of the project was tied to its banality through a bureaucratically thoughtless disregard of the needs of those it purported to assist. As we will see, the WEP's rights-based, community-focused empowerment strategies prioritized Batis clients' economic needs, commitments, and stakes. At the same time, Batis staff were painfully aware of their organization's inability to fully empower their clients given both its limited financial resources and the structural constraints of their clients' lives. However, rather than ignoring these limitations, they responded to them head-on by encouraging trafficking survivors to build economic collectives and engage in political action geared toward structural change that could hopefully make a material difference in their lives.

I first draw on published reports and documents to examine the vision of empowerment informing the UNTFHS-ILO project, considering how and to what ends it enlisted grassroots NGOs like Batis to execute its agenda. I then turn to the Batis WEP and its alternative understanding of empowerment, which the UN-sponsored project sidelined and neglected. I end by drawing on interviews with former Batis clients to consider what they gained from the WEP and why the approach to empowerment taken by the UN project was so inadequate for addressing their needs.

The Empowerment Politics of Human Security

Selection for funding from the UNTFHS is competitive; to be eligible, the ILO had to design its empowerment project to fit under the trust fund's banner of advancing "human security." The UNTFHS website cites the definition of human security adopted under General Assembly resolution 66/290: "an approach to assist Member States in identifying and addressing widespread and cross-cutting challenges to the survival, livelihood and dignity of their people."[14] This understanding of human security was endorsed by Sadako Ogata, a Japanese diplomat who was the first woman to serve as the UN high commissioner for refugees, holding the position from 1991 to 2000. The daughter of a career Japanese diplomat and educated at Georgetown and UC Berkeley, Ogata promoted the approach as a "bottom-up" strategy that emphasized people as "actors and participants in defining and implementing their vital freedoms."[15] For her, this focus on individual agency and autonomy moved beyond protection-focused, top-down "rule of law" strategies that had come to dominate international aid and development.[16] Rather, a human security framework shifted the focus of security from the state to the individual.[17] In this regard, a human security vision of empowerment was easily compatible with individualistic, and arguably neoliberal, models of development. Ogata and her coauthor Johan Cels write, "Human security means . . . empowering individuals and communities to develop the capabilities for making informed choices and acting on their own behalf."[18]

Encouraged by Ogata, the Japanese government promoted human security during the 1990s as part of its efforts to play a larger role in international society under the framework of "proactive pacifism."[19] It began committing considerable resources to human security in its foreign policy and encouraging wider application of the approach by the UN and NGOs.[20] As a concept, human security both resonated with the emphasis on peace in Japan's postwar constitution and was consistent with its long-standing practices of ODA and attention to nonmilitary forms of security building.[21] The concept also served domestic interests. As explained in chapter 7, "empowered" populations in Asia were believed to be less likely to become labor migrants in Japan.

When the Japanese government funded the establishment of the UNTFHS in 1999, it did so with the understanding that empowerment could serve as a strategy to address inadequacies of existing development models and economic threats to people's lives in Asia.[22] In 2001, after Ogata left her position as UN high commissioner for refugees, the Japanese government appointed her and Amartya Sen to co-chair an independent Commission on Human Security.[23] The Commission on Human Security aimed to mainstream human security in the work of global, regional, and national organizations. Commissioned by the Japanese government, Ogata and Sen authored a report, "Human Security Now" (2003), which they presented to then UN secretary-general Kofi Annan to promote public understanding and develop human security as "an operational tool for policy formulation and implementation."[24] In 2003, Ogata was appointed president of the Japan International Cooperation Agency (JICA) (a position that she held until 2012), where she began to incorporate considerations of human securitization and empowerment into strategies for Japan's official development assistance.[25]

An extension of Ogata's vision, the UNTFHS's objectives include developing "preventative responses" that could address the "root causes" of risk and vulnerability.[26] Its website explains that it aims to "translate the human security approach into practical actions and provide concrete and sustainable benefits to vulnerable people and communities threatened in their survival, livelihood and dignity."[27] The words "concrete" and "sustainable" in the project description are key. Over the past few decades, as philanthropic work has come to be measured according to the "performance" standards of venture capitalism, grant and donation recipients have increasingly been expected to demonstrate the "cost-effectiveness" of their projects.[28] The ability to offer a practical, reproducible, and expandable model that promotes a human security approach is a central funding criterion for the UNTFHS grant. Projects are expected to create lasting solutions, and applicants are asked to "avoid duplication" in the programs.[29] As the submission guidelines explain, "Submissions are reviewed for their salience in applying the human security approach . . . to deliver concrete and sustainable benefits. . . . Programmes with clear and feasible strategies for replication and expansion beyond the proposal will be given priority attention."[30] Not only are applications screened "to ensure replication and mainstreaming of the human security approach beyond the proposed programme," but grantees are monitored on a quarterly basis to this end.[31] In other words, the fund was oriented toward efficiently developing targeted, cost-effective strategies that could produce scalable and reproducible models. By situating the focus of "security" at the level of the autonomous "human," the vision of empowerment promoted under human security was one that ultimately focused on interventions at the level of the individual as opposed to even incremental larger-scale political-economic change.[32]

Aiming for "the long-term economic reinsertion of returnees with a view to achieving self-reliance," the ILO's proposed project fit neatly within Ogata's human security framework.[33] As previously mentioned, the direct assistance programs would be documented and disseminated as models for future efforts, and the program would additionally include knowledge and capacity-building strategies for NGOs and government agencies that would extend beyond the grant period. Of the approximately $380,000 grant funds allocated to sub-contracted agencies in the Philippines, 40 percent (approximately $152,000) was allocated for "knowledge development" and "capacity building," with 15 percent (approximately $57,000) going to the former and 25 percent (approximately $95,000) to the latter.[34] Not surprisingly, much of this money went to experts and government agencies. For instance, the Philippine government's Department of Social Welfare and Development was funded to "develop and institutionalize a system and a tool on reporting, referral, and documentation of the cases of trafficking."[35] (Specifically, it used project funds to create a new Referral System on the Recovery and Reintegration of Trafficked Persons and a National Recovery and Reintegration Database, which centralized and standardized information about repatriated trafficking survivors in part to facilitate their monitoring.) Other monies were allocated to Metro Manila–based NGOs to expand their outreach capabilities. For instance, these grassroots NGOs were funded to develop networks with grassroots nonprofit organizations and government units in their clients' communities of origin. The rationale was that these local organizations had already assisted thousands upon thousands of returned migrants using innovative strategies on shoestring budgets and thus could be further relied on to cost-effectively assist trafficking survivors. They would also be most familiar with potential livelihood opportunities for returned migrants in their home communities and could be mobilized to help repatriated trafficking survivors find work. Finally, working with these networks would enable Metro Manila–based NGOs to conserve resources because their caseworkers would not have to travel to follow up with clients living in other parts of the country.[36]

Also with an eye toward future expansion, the UNTFHS-ILO project aimed to train NGO caseworkers to become career coaches and advisers and to teach financial literacy to trafficking survivors. Most social workers and case managers at NGOs and government agencies have experience in psychosocial counseling. However, to extend the project in line with UNTFHS goals of creating long-term impacts with short-term interventions, the ILO proposed developing expert tools and training resources so that NGO caseworkers could "help the trafficked migrants find better social and economic options to aid them with their reintegration" after the project ended.[37] To ensure that these resources would be scalable and reproducible, the UNTFHS-ILO project included funding for the development of expert-produced manuals that would "prepare service providers to acquire the necessary coaching skills in order for them to be competent coaches when they walk the women towards the path of economic reintegration."[38] The guidebooks would outline best training and coaching practices that could be used across individual cases, reinforcing that the UNTFHS-ILO project would offer sustainable and expandable results per the fund guidelines.

To produce the guidebooks, the ILO hired experts. First, to produce a career-coaching manual for NGO staff, it hired Loree Cruz-Mante, a human resources and organization development practitioner and a longtime collaborator with the ILO, who had consulted for government agencies, employers' and workers' groups, and faith-based and private corporations.[39] Titled *Coaching Returned Victims/Survivors of Trafficking toward Gainful Careers*, the guide's "ultimate goal" was "to equip service providers with appropriate skills to help victims and survivors of trafficking get back to a world of work that is realistic, safer and satisfying."[40] The manual offers tools and a framework that could presumably guide NGO caseworkers to coach trafficking survivors, including "basic principles, concepts, strategies, practical tips and tools on coaching as they are used to help victims/survivors of trafficking become economically and socially empowered."[41] The contents focus on "six key factors that are critical in building gainful careers": "realistic self-assessment, skills-building, updatedness, networking, communication skills, and human relations."[42] Cruz-Mante stresses the significance of caseworkers' roles as "coaches" as compared to their roles as "counselors."[43] In her introduction, she explains:

> The preferential use of the term "coach" is very critical. Imagine a basketball game, football or soccer game where coaches are quite a visible figure on the court or field. What do coaches do? Before the game, they pep up the team for the game ahead. They repeat the game plan, making sure each one understands what to do. They dwell on what winning the game means for the team. They harp on the lessons learned from countless hours of practice and learning how to be a team. They tell the team that they can and will win this game.[44]

Here the guidebook assumes that trafficking survivors are playing the "game" of financially supporting themselves and their families on a level playing field and can readily and easily acquire the training and skills that they need to prevail. However, as we will see, elsewhere the program explicitly documents this not to be the case.

A second manual, titled *Catalogue of Skills and Livelihood Training Programmes and Other Support Services*, was produced to complement the coaching guidebook.[45] To develop this manual, the UNTFHS-ILO project hired another professional, Dr. Divina M. Edralin, a professor of business management in the College of Business and Economics at De La Salle University in Manila.[46] Intended as a reference guide for caseworkers and survivors, the catalog includes an exhaustive list of contact information for various support services—counseling, legal assistance, medical care, microfinance, networking and advocacy, scholarships, temporary shelter—that could serve as resources for NGO coaches and their "coachees."[47] It also includes a directory of participating organizations, both government and employer based, that offer training and support services, and it lists existing training courses in fields ranging from "Agricultural and Aquatic Business" to "Textiles and Garments."[48]

Conceivably, such resource lists could be useful for people building careers in the Philippines. However, the cruelty of the UNTFHS-ILO model comes into stark relief when one considers the strategies offered to NGO coaches to identify livelihood possibilities and necessary training for trafficking survivors. To develop the manual, Edralin conducted research, including focus groups with returned survivors and NGO staff, as well as surveys of training programs, government agencies, caseworkers, employers, and trade unions. She concluded that returned trafficking survivors needed several forms of support: better entrepreneurial guidance to identify an appropriate livelihood, and the available training to pursue it; clear information about available resources; access to loan/credit facilities; information on other possible sources of income in their communities; and assistance on how to set up their businesses.[49] To address these clearly articulated needs, the catalog aimed to provide "realistic options for skills trainings, livelihood opportunities and other remunerative activities including support services for returned victims of trafficking towards their full economic reintegration."[50] Throughout, Edralin stresses that the catalog will help NGO coaches identify which livelihood strategies are most appropriate and suitable for individual trafficking survivors, "consistent with the trafficked person's personal aspirations and in accordance with his/her competencies."[51]

To this end, the catalog offers two assessment tools, in both English and Tagalog, for NGO staff to use as tools for career coaching. The first is a Personal Entrepreneurial Competencies Assessment, derived from the work of Harvard psychologist David McClelland. A self-administered questionnaire consisting of fifty-five brief statements, the assessment evaluates "entrepreneurial readiness" based on scores on ten personal qualities that can "be translated into actions," or competencies: opportunity seeking, persistence, commitment to work contract, risk taking, demand for efficiency and quality, goal setting, systematic planning and monitoring, information seeking, persuasion and networking, and self-confidence.[52] These competencies are understood as characteristics of successful entrepreneurs that transcend culture and geography. Through self-evaluation with the assessment, women who aspire to be entrepreneurs learn what personal qualities they are lacking and need to further develop in order to achieve entrepreneurial success.

The second assessment tool is a Career Interest Assessment based on the Holland vocational preferences model, first proposed in the 1950s by Johns Hopkins sociologist and psychologist John Holland. This assessment is based on the notion that personalities seek out and flourish in career environments best suited for them. It focuses on six "vocational themes": realistic, investigative, artistic, social, enterprising, and conventional. Depending on an individual's "occupational personality" score, it recommends career choices.[53] The listings are numerous and almost exclusively professional, white-collar careers. For example, potential careers for those who score highly in "realistic" competencies include air traffic controller, archaeologist, athletic trainer, cartographer, and correction officer. For those who are "investigative," it recommends careers such as actuary, agronomist, airplane pilot, anthropologist, and architect. For those who are "enterprising," it suggests advertising executive, attorney, banker, campaign manager, lobbyist, school principal, stockbroker, and so on.[54]

Indeed, financial counseling and training could provide a useful foundation for these women's future endeavors. Moreover, these women may indeed have the aptitude to become attorneys, stockbrokers, architects, or archaeologists, and with sufficient additional support and job availability in the Philippines, they could presumably find ways to support themselves and achieve upward mobility for their families in such capacities without going abroad. However, to make such prospects realities would arguably require providing NGOs considerably more resources to distribute to their clients than those allocated through the UNTFHS-ILO program. Sixty-five percent ($247,000) of the approximately $380,000 allocated to subcontracted agencies in the Philippines was allocated for direct assistance to returned migrants. This allocation amounted to *only about US$450–$548 per migrant over three years.*[55] Caseworkers well knew that most of their clients who were targeted by the program were already struggling to single-handedly support children or natal families and lacked education beyond the secondary level. The guidebooks completely ignored these realities, instead cruelly advising caseworkers to coach their clients to aspire to careers that they had little practical hope of achieving.

The cruelty—and banality—of the UNTFHS-ILO project's empowerment model is all the more striking given that the UNTFHS-ILO project report explicitly recognized the challenges these women would face trying to realize its recommended proposals, stating that the women "may be heavily in debt" and "may have no source of income or livelihood upon their return given their low educational attainment and the lack of skills that fit the needs of industries." Moreover, it recognized up front that they have "little access to credit."[56] Other sections of the report noted that "many found themselves in a precarious economic situation, often with little or no source of income after their return. Many times these women were thrust into a worse economic situation than their pre-migration experience because the migrants often do not have the requisite education nor experience to find well-paying jobs after their return."[57] These challenges were also acknowledged elsewhere in program documents. For instance, the introduction to the project brief for the Philippines component of the program states, "More often than not . . . victims of trafficking come home empty-handed, with inadequate savings, or heavily indebted. Much as they want to work in their countries of origin, they possess inadequate skills or lack qualifications, aside from the scarce local job opportunities."[58] Echoing this point in his PowerPoint presentation, Larga explained, "Most returnees find their opportunities on return are rarely any better than when they originally migrated."[59]

The severity of these women's immediate financial challenges can be grasped when one considers that Batis AWARE—the "people's organization" formed by Batis clients—made optional its membership fees of P50 (less than $1.25 at the time), asking members to pay "from the heart" only what they could afford, because they knew that the women would struggle to come up with even that much money to contribute. One former Batis client explained, "Because, you know, we don't have a job. We are single parents, etc." In the project report, one participating NGO pointed out the challenge of teaching the concept and skills of financial management included in the coaching manual because "most of their clients actually do not have sources of income nor savings to manage."[60]

Despite this awareness of NGO clients' financial struggles, the UNTFHS-ILO project report justified offering financial management skills training and professional career coaching on the grounds that "the economic lot of the women could change in the future especially because they are starting to learn to engage in enterprise. Putting it this way, preparing the women for the eventuality of them having monetary resources to manage would then be seen as a useful exercise rather than a waste of time and resources. It would be defeatist to think that the women should not learn financial management just because they are currently penniless. It will not be any different from the thought that the women do not have the capacity to make improvements in their financial status."[61] The well-intentioned thoughtlessness of this approach becomes clear when one considers the women's own livelihood aspirations, which were tucked into a footnote in the catalog. Much more makeshift and modest, and arguably more immediately feasible given the women's circumstances, these include small-scale and ad hoc businesses that the women nonetheless struggled to undertake on account of a lack of resources and experience, including starting a business doing subcontracted garment work; starting a small piggery, meat-processing service, or fishpond; engaging in farming, rice retailing, selling meat at the public market, or raising poultry; making and selling coconut wine, *suman* (rice cake), or coconut jam; making and selling rags or ceramics; operating a tricycle (passenger motorbike); or opening a *sari-sari* store (small neighborhood sundry shop) or a *carinderia* (small eatery).[62]

One could read the catalog's suggestions as a simple example of geographical, cultural, and class-based misunderstanding on Edralin's part. Yet the problem is also rooted in the funding parameters of the UN program. Recall that the UNTFHS placed constraints on how grants could be used, prioritizing projects that could offer targeted and short-term but reproducible and expandable models for fostering human security. The small-scale enterprises suggested by the women would not necessarily resolve their economic precarity without broader structural shifts. In this light, the catalog offers an example of how the UNTFHS-ILO project cruelly ignored the broader political-economic realities shaping these women's lives, suggesting instead that adopting professional career coaching and training could prevent migrant re-trafficking without broader structural change. It offered aspirational, individualistic solutions that ignored the actual political-economic circumstances of these labor migrants' lives.

Failures of Inadequate Training and Funding

This banal and cruel logic of empowerment played out in other components of the UNTFHS-ILO project, including those that were oriented toward providing direct assistance for more immediately realistic livelihood endeavors. For instance, one contracted NGO, Kanlungan, used some of its UNTFHS-ILO funds to offer "mini-grants" to its clients for small-scale business ventures. Within the first two years, eighty women participated in the program, with sixty receiving seed capital ranging from $125 to $313.[63] To qualify for the grants, the women first had to be certified through psychological assessment and counseling as having emotionally moved on from their trafficking experiences to the point where they were ready to "plan for their future" and "start picking up the pieces."[64] This condition was required as one of a number of "safeguards" to "ensure that the grant money given to the trafficked women to set up a social enterprise or livelihood will be put to good use by the women, that the women will succeed with their socioeconomic venture, and that the grant will not turn into a dole-out venture."[65] Once certified, the women were eligible to attend a nine-day training program, spread over the course of two-and-a-half months, to learn about themselves and their business aptitudes as well as their weaknesses. The training was intended to help the women begin charting a vision for their future and engage in activities geared toward developing their confidence in themselves and their capacity to change their lives. The final five sessions introduced the women to entrepreneurship, including "market research, business planning, pricing, knowing the competition, business management, and financial reporting."[66] The capping exercise of the training was coming up with a plan for a feasible business, which would serve as the basis for a business development grant. However, at the end of the grant period, although the women who participated in the training program had been able to keep their capital intact and sustain their businesses, the overwhelming majority were able to save only minimal amounts of money, if they had saved anything at all.[67] The program thus demonstrated little potential to make participants economically self-sufficient. Moreover, because women who received grants were encouraged to believe that they had been certified and trained to succeed in their business endeavors, they were left to blame themselves for their continuing struggles—just as they had blamed themselves for their earlier ones (discussed further in next section).

Another training program—established through a collaboration between a different participating NGO and the corporate social development arm of Splash Corporation—had a similar outcome. Splash Corporation is a personal-care company in the Philippines that specializes in products such as skin whiteners and hair color. Its social development organization, Splash Foundation Inc. (now Ang Hortaleza Foundation Inc.), offered a five-day cosmetology training to fifteen clients of the NGO. These women received basic training in hair cutting and perming, manicures, pedicures, foot spa, and reflexology. According to the project report, the Splash training inspired confidence in the women, who felt that they had learned livelihood skills.[68] However, on account of budgetary constraints, the training offered to the women was insufficient for them to become licensed cosmetologists, and none had the capital to open a beauty salon. The women were left without a means to put their limited new skills to use. In an effort to support the women, the NGO used remaining funds from the UNTFHS-ILO project to convert part of its office into a beauty parlor that could provide employment opportunities to the women; however, the business struggled to gain clients.[69] Again, the women were left without adequate means to support themselves and their families.

In other words, with few exceptions, the UNTFHS-ILO project provided insufficient resources to truly transform these women's lives. A survey of 164 women who were assisted through the reintegration portion of the program showed that 80 percent of them still preferred to re-migrate.[70] Part of the problem was that the project's vision of empowerment was tied to the UN Trafficking Protocol's understanding of human trafficking as a circumscribed, compartmentalized event carried out by those viewed as individual bad actors. From this perspective, helping a trafficking survivor is a simple matter of removing her from a particular situation and helping her as an individual recover and reintegrate into her home community. The possibility that the violence experienced by a trafficking survivor might be structural and thus might have preceded her decision to migrate and persist after she returns home is ignored, if not dismissed. Remember that the *IOM Handbook* characterizes exploitation as a "phase" of the trafficking experience rather than as reflective of larger structurally and historically embedded vulnerabilities that labor migrants face.[71]

The UNTFHS-ILO project report recognized that despite women's participation in the program, they were emotionally dealing with feelings of "failed migration, the prospect of being unable to provide for their families and failing again for the second time, and a whole gamut of other fears, disappointments, concerns, and trepidations."[72] However, the project implicitly framed these women's struggles as personal issues and thereby arguably compounded the very feelings of failure and disappointment that the report acknowledged. It approached their economic challenges as matters of inadequate personal training that could be resolved with a model of individual empowerment. It assumed that enabling their reintegration and preventing their re-trafficking were simple matters of identifying economic opportunities for individual women and providing business training to them. Little was said about the immediate political-economic circumstances of their families and communities and how these connected to larger national and global political-economic dynamics and histories. Rather, the project cruelly assumed that these socioeconomic issues could be addressed through targeted strategies and on an individual basis apart from local, national, and international political-economic change.[73]

When one considers the independent efforts of Batis and its WEP, one sees even more clearly how the UNTFHS-ILO project banally sidelined other visions for empowering trafficking survivors. Batis was chosen to be part of the UNTFHS-ILO project on account of its reputation, experience, and track record assisting returned migrants from Japan. Established in the late 1980s, the organization had served more than two thousand returned Filipina labor migrants before it joined the project.[74]

Batis staff had established the WEP in 1995 based on their observations of their clients' needs. They had listened repeatedly to former migrants share feelings of failure, disappointment, regret, fear, and uncertainty. They noted that these women faulted themselves not only for the violence, abuse, and exploitation that they experienced in Japan but also for the challenges that they confronted after they returned to the Philippines. Most of the women were Catholic (and the others, Protestant Christians), and many felt shame—and were shamed by their families and communities—about their experiences in the Japanese sex industry. Moreover, organization staff recognized that few resources existed to help these women reestablish themselves at home.

Batis staff began the WEP to augment the psychosocial and welfare services that the NGO was already providing by adopting a "rights-based framework" aimed at both individually and collectively empowering its clients.[75] As part of the program, staff held seminars to counsel the women to stop blaming themselves and to see their experiences in the context of broader patterns of social and political inequality. The organization maintained that to be empowered, the women needed "to be aware of their social situation and their rights, especially knowing how to fight for them."[76]

For Batis, supporting their clients in this endeavor involved working with the women "beyond the personal and individual levels, and to work with the women collectively."[77] They considered clients as partners in promoting human welfare and development, not just as service recipients. They also encouraged their clients to develop a "shared identity as survivors" and "to see the links among their experiences." By crafting a sense of collective identity and communicating their shared experiences, the organization hoped that the women would see themselves in the context of larger social and political processes and work to "address, and work for the transformation of, social conditions that perpetuate the continued migration of Filipinos for overseas work and the increasing feminization of Philippine labor migration."[78]

Batis leadership first encouraged the women to learn to assist and support each other. They set a goal of helping the women develop their own independent and self-run "people's organization" that would provide them with a venue to discuss issues that confronted women migrant workers. Batis staff fostered organizational independence for the community, sponsoring trainings and workshops to help the women develop their capabilities as public speakers, advocates, writers, project managers, and peer counselors, among other things.[79] In 1996, a group of clients and former clients established Batis AWARE (Association of Women in Action for Rights and Empowerment) to develop, run, and advocate for their own agenda. As part of Batis AWARE, former clients learned to serve as peer counselors for newer returnees, accompanying them for medical visits, helping them in reintegration activities, and supporting their involvement in advocacy activities.[80]

Noting the economic struggles that the women faced in rebuilding their lives, Batis also supported the development of cooperative livelihood projects, including a sewing shop and a vigil candle shop. Although the initial livelihood projects never became self-sufficient economic enterprises, the organization's long-term support built up the women's self-confidence, gave them experience running a cooperative, and inspired them to develop other projects. Building on this model, the women of Batis AWARE later established a burger stand (2005), a small restaurant (2007), and a small laundry shop (2007), which have helped some members become more financially stable. The group has also published two zines, *Daloy* 1 and 2, which include writing, art, and poetry by Batis AWARE members and serve as creative and personal outlets for them.[81]

In late 2006 and early 2007, I regularly met with and interviewed a group of Batis AWARE members who spoke passionately about how their work with the organization had "empowered" them. They described both the relief and the enthusiasm inspired by their work with Batis. They began one extended conversation by sharing how the organization had helped them come to terms with their experiences in Japan. Women shared how they had initially blamed themselves for the abuse and exploitation that they experienced as labor migrants because they were unaware that their legal rights were being violated. One woman explained, "Deep inside, we're angry and we felt ashamed in ourselves." Another shared, "Because, as we said, when we first went to Japan, we didn't know our rights. And we didn't know that is a violation of our rights. Of course, we get hurt, we get angry, but we don't know that is harassment, that is violation, and everything."

They shared how seminars and workshops that they received through Batis had helped them understand their experiences not as isolated instances of personal misfortune but as incidents rooted in broader patterns of structural inequality and gender and racial discrimination. Women reflected on how they had previously suppressed their anger when customers at the clubs where they worked in Japan would touch their breasts and other parts of their bodies. They described their fear working in establishments owned by organized crime syndicates, where they felt disrespected and were exploited and sexually abused. However, because they also felt so vulnerable as migrant workers, they did not think they could do anything about their treatment. Instead, some women believed that they had invited the behavior or deserved it. The WEP seminars and workshops had changed their understanding of their experiences. One woman explained, "Because of the seminars, we found out so many rights . . . of women and . . . children . . . that we didn't know." Another added, "When we came back here, when we approached Batis, we found out that . . . they are violating our rights as women, as human beings, and as a Filipino. It was discrimination." Knowing that their anger was justified and that they had been unjustly violated liberated the women and empowered them to share their experiences with others. In this regard, their empowerment was about educating not only themselves but also others about migrants' and workers' rights. For instance, one woman shared the importance of passing on what she had learned to other Filipina migrants, noting, "There are also many women in Japan who do not know that their rights as women have been violated. Because they don't have such seminars given to us, seminars here [at Batis]."

Women shared how hard it was for them to talk about their experiences in Japan before they worked with Batis. One woman explained, "Most of the members, we don't tell our parents what happened in Japan. They don't know." Another added, "Like me. I hid it for so many years. I did not tell my family. . . . I hid it from my family. And from myself also." Another woman began, "We do not tell the whole story about what happened. Because . . ." as another completed her sentence, "Nahihiya ka [You are embarrassed]." The first woman agreed: "Because we're very much ashamed of what happened. At first." Yet another added, "And afraid also to tell. They might laugh at me. They might have a bad impression about me. Something like that."

By giving them the support and confidence to talk about their experiences collectively, Batis had helped these women heal and move on. One woman eloquently explained, "It's my experience that when you bring out problems and experiences that you can't tell your family, you get peace of mind. It is the healing process of a person. Because when you don't let it out, that's all you've experienced. When you don't tell it to other people, it's like you're locked up. You are trapped in a situation where . . . you will think and think about what happened to you until . . . you lose yourself. That's right. Based on our experiences, we need to listen to [others'] grievances and stories of their lives." Slowly, by building rapport and trust, they shared their stories with one another. This identification of commonalities in their experiences became part of an empowering, healing process.

The women spoke of how the WEP enabled them to draw on the pain of their experiences in Japan to become advocates and activists, making a difference in their communities. Empowerment here meant going beyond being an individual victim and survivor to offering support and inspiration for others. As Cecille Pauline Sanglap Montenegro, a president of Batis AWARE, explains, "I really want victim survivors to not only be a victim and not only be a survivor, but to also be an inspiration for women."[82] Several of the women discussed how becoming peer counselors enabled them to come to terms with the pain of their own experiences. They explained that using their experiences to help and inspire others enabled them to see themselves as both victims and empowered survivors. One woman explained, "[We are] now empowered. Because before we stayed in one room and cried and thought about our problems." Yet another illustrated the importance of mutual exchange with someone who had similar experiences, describing a case in which she was taken to interview a woman who had returned from Japan, but "she wasn't sharing much of her experiences in the interview. . . . Just question and answer. Question and answer." After the interview, in a less formal context when they went outside to eat, "She shared the whole of what happened to her. Because I also shared my experience."

Batis AWARE members also shared that as their involvement with Batis helped them contextualize their experiences in Japan within broader shared patterns of inequality, they became able to channel their anger into political engagement, which they understood as another manifestation of their empowerment. One Batis AWARE member explained, "Empowerment means, well, you can face the world. We can advocate, we can share with you what we have learned. We can talk to the congress. We can talk to the senate and fight for women's rights and human rights!" Another spoke with pride of her activism, saying, "Even the friends of my son, they know. Ay, your mother is an activist."

Several women highlighted their theater advocacy project, Teatro Batis, as an important form of political activism for them. One woman explained, "We became advocates through our testimonies. Number one is through theater advocacy." Through the project, which was established in 2000, the women developed a play based on their experiences in Japan, and they performed it for Philippine policymakers, public audiences in various parts of Japan, and Philippine secondary schools and communities.[83] The play was a deliberate vehicle for political action, aiming to educate both government officials and members of the public about the patterns of abuse they experienced and prospective migrants about their labor and human rights and what to do if they found themselves in similar situations abroad. The play at once presented women's individual experiences in Japan and collectively linked them as the product not of personal bad luck but of broader shared forms of gender-based political-economic vulnerability and exploitation that needed to change.[84] The women explained how the theater piece worked to empower prospective migrants; as one shared, "If you enter a country illegally or legally, you must know your rights. And you must know where to ask [for] help, assistance. . . . If you can't get assistance from the government, you can from the consuls. . . . In other countries, you can get assistance from NGOs. . . . Through the performance, we are giving them what to do if ever they will encounter what we have encountered. . . . They will know that. Everything."

Other women shared how they now confidently analyze and take positions on migration issues. They shared that both Batis and Batis AWARE had worked as members of the Alliance of Migrant Workers and Advocates to participate in legislative advocacy to repeal the deregulation provision in the Migrant Workers Act of 1995. In 2005—as Japan was developing its counter–human trafficking project—officers of Batis AWARE served as resource persons during legislative hearings of the Japanese government for policy changes on entertainer visa requirements.[85] They criticized the Philippine government for the way it treated labor migrants, calling them "national heroes" but offering them little protection and support. One woman commented cynically, "You become a hero if you're dead already." Another added, "We're not ashamed of being Filipino but we're ashamed of the government. The government is very lazy."

When I asked the women of Batis AWARE what they wanted from their government, they shared modest desires. One woman simply answered, "A chance to have a good job here so we won't go abroad . . . because we need to support our children." Another woman added, "Of course, number one is good government." Yet another said that she hoped the government would "pay attention to the people. They wouldn't just keep getting richer and richer. Everywhere, that's what those at the top do." Another joined in, "We're begging, please listen. Because our government is deaf [*bingi*]." She explained, "The government, they take money from us. Taxes. And also remittances. And money for papers." However, she lamented that despite this, "Our government does not give any help to us. We ask, but they do not listen."

When I asked what the women desired for their future, they said that first and foremost, on a personal level, they hoped for more financial stability for themselves and their children. One said she hoped her children would not "replicate what we experienced," explaining further, "We are trying to give them the best education and values." They also had broader political dreams.

One woman said, "My dream for the world is to have equal rights from men. And to recognize the rights of the women."

These women also took their commitment to political change into their everyday lives. Another Batis AWARE member shared that she now calls out people, such as bus drivers, when they use sexist expressions. Others agreed that they now speak out and fight for women to be respected in their daily routines. Yet another woman, Nora, explained that because she only made it through her second year of high school, she had always felt inferior to others and deferred to them even if they mistreated her. She shared that she was no longer intimidated by those who are wealthier or more educated than she is. I had witnessed her confidence firsthand during my stay when Nora had escorted me to meet with a government official and a prominent feminist scholar at the University of the Philippines, the nation's preeminent university. Frankly, I had sometimes been nervous in these meetings; Nora, however, had enthusiastically initiated conversations, asking questions and offering her opinions.

For Batis and Batis AWARE, empowerment involved individual personal growth, but it was not centered on it. Rather, empowerment was focused on community building, recognizing the patterns and roots of inequality, and working for broader political-economic change—all of which were understood as objectives in and of themselves and necessary for personal empowerment. In other words, Batis staff and Batis AWARE members saw empowerment as intimately linked to participation in social worlds, to peer and community relationships that helped them identify as a group and see themselves as collective agents of social and political transformation. Batis staff recognized the organization's limitations with respect to changing their clients' lives exclusively by supporting the women as individuals—the NGO lacked both financial resources and sufficient political pull. However, through the WEP it endeavored to give its clients the tools and the confidence to begin working for structural change and to encourage others to join their movement. Ironically, Batis's success with its WEP was part of what made it an appealing and viable subcontractor for the UNTFHS-ILO project, which then banally sidelined the organization's focus on political activism and structural transformation in the interest of having it promote a modular, scalable, individual-centered response.

Conclusion: Empowerment's Limits

Discussions about empowering trafficking survivors pervade counter–human trafficking efforts. NGOs, government offices, and international agencies around the world often frame their objectives in such terms. Empowerment approaches were developed under the assumption that oppressed and underprivileged populations occupy a world of political-economic opportunity, which they simply need more confidence and better skills to access.[86] In such a model, the potential for improving lives depends on providing individual members of vulnerable groups the necessary tools for taking advantage of available resources. However, such an approach runs up against its own limits in a world in which resources and opportunities are unequally distributed through long-standing structural inequalities both within and among nation-states. The focus of empowerment approaches on individuals' will, hope, and agency, even in the face of exploitation and violence, is important; however, we also need to be able to see the limits of agency and dreams in the face of structures of power and forms of domination.[87]

Batis staff and Batis AWARE members were well aware of these limits, which were tied not only to the organization's limited resources for assistance but also to the positioning of the Philippines in the global political economy and the positioning of returned Filipina migrants within the Philippines. Its WEP offered a model of empowerment that tried its best to address these limits head-on. It encouraged its clients both to individually develop skills and confidence and to collectively work to advocate and lobby for their civil, social, and economic rights. The Batis and Batis AWARE vision approached individual empowerment as part of a broader collective process for social and political-economic change.

Yet the broader context—and the expertise and visions of Batis staff and Batis AWARE members—was precisely what the UNTFHS-ILO project thoughtlessly ignored, even while it depended on the NGO's subcontracted labor. Instead, the UNTFHS-ILO project focused on a model of individual, market, and career-focused empowerment divorced from the political-economic realities of Batis AWARE members' lives. The UNTFHS-ILO project presented individual empowerment alone as the solution and focused on developing neatly packaged pilot programs that could offer what administrators hoped would be sustainable benefits with limited, targeted investments and no additional resources. Its individualized, market-logic approach of maximizing profit with minimal investment was both cruel in its failure to acknowledge the political-economic constraints of trafficking survivors' lives and carelessly unthinking in its approach to the predicament it endeavored to address.

Consider one final illustration of the limitations of any assistance project that does not also endeavor to address the broader structural constraints of these women's lives. On one of the last days of my stay in the Philippines, Nora began to cry as we ate lunch in a small barbecue restaurant near the women's center where I was staying. As mentioned in the last section, Nora was one of the women who had assisted me in my research during my stay in Manila, taking me around the city; introducing me to government officials, international agency staff, and academics; and sometimes joining my interviews. I had been humbled by her self-confidence and her thoughtful and outspoken opinions on personal and political issues. She had spoken enthusiastically about her self-empowerment through her work with Batis. Until that moment, I had experienced her as irrepressibly forward-looking, upbeat, and optimistic. That afternoon, she shared another side of herself. Through tears, she told me that for weeks her five-year-old son had been passing large amounts of blood in his bowel movements. She had taken him to a doctor, who had recommended a scan. She needed US$200 for the procedure alone, and she did not know how she would come up with the money for her son's medical care. She had purchased a small lot and house with her savings from Japan, but lacking a steady income, these expenses would be more than she could handle. She was terrified for her son. She simply lacked the financial resources to help him.

Based on the summary sheet of the UNTFHS-ILO project on the UNTFHS website, one would never guess that a woman targeted by the project, such as Nora, might continue to suffer after participating so successfully in the program. According to the sheet, the project "successfully provided assistance to more beneficiaries than initially envisaged."[88] The sheet estimates that the project directly benefited 480 women and 150 children in the Philippines (Manila, Pampanga, and Central Luzon). It described the successes of the project this way: "Through home visits, legal and psychosocial counselling services, as well as referrals to health, non-formal education and law enforcement assistance, returned trafficked victims were empowered to regain control of their lives. In addition, their respective communities were mobilized to support their full reintegration back into social and communal life. Lastly, in order to promote long-term empowerment and to reduce the risk of re-trafficking, returnees received educational and employment services which resulted in significant improvements in their economic security."[89] Yet nothing in the program addressed the high cost of medical care relative to incomes in the Philippines, which enable medical and pharmaceutical companies across the globe to profit at the cost of children's lives. Nothing in the UNTFHS-ILO project's accounting of achievements suggests that forms of structural inequality in the Philippines might continue to bear on the lives of trafficking survivors, leaving them so vulnerable that they have little choice but to risk returning to abusive and exploitative labor situations abroad to afford medical treatment for sick family members. In a world of unequally positioned nation-states, where profit for some trumps the well-being of many, empowerment strategies like those endorsed by the UNTFHS-ILO project will continue to run up against their own limits. In this instance, we might ask if the millions of dollars used for empowerment programs like the UNTFHS-ILO project would be better spent guaranteeing medical care for families in the Philippines and ensuring that women like Nora can support their children through collective economic endeavors. Until official projects "pay attention to the people" and their needs as such, any empowerment that they fund will be to at least some degree both banal and cruel.

Conclusion

THE MISPERFORMANCE OF THE TRAFFICKING
PROTOCOL, OR THE LESS THINGS CHANGE,
THE MORE THEY STAY THE SAME

The adoption in 2000 by the United Nations General Assembly of the Protocol to Prevent, Suppress and Punish Trafficking in Persons, Especially Women
and Children marked a significant milestone in international efforts to stop
the trade in people. As the guardian of the Protocol, UNODC addresses human
trafficking issues through its Global Programme against Trafficking in Persons.
A vast majority of States have now signed and ratified the Protocol. But translating it into reality remains problematic. Very few criminals are convicted and
most victims are probably never identified or assisted.

—UNODC, "UNODC's Response to Human Trafficking"

Getting results was no substitute for doing things the proper way.

—AKHIL GUPTA, *Red Tape: Bureaucracy, Structural Violence,*
and Poverty in India

In some respects, this book is a snapshot of a moment in time, documenting
the adoption and early enactment of the UN's global counter–human trafficking project in Japan. Institutional development is part of the organization's
working logic, and over the past twenty years the UN has continued to modify
its approach, establishing new groups and developing additional programs
for its counter–human trafficking efforts. As I discussed in chapter 7, the UN

launched in 2010 the Global Plan of Action to Combat Trafficking in Persons, establishing with it the Voluntary Trust Fund for Victims of Trafficking in Persons (UNVTF), which solicits contributions to provide grassroots NGOs funds for direct assistance to trafficking survivors. Before that, in 2007, it established the Inter-agency Coordination Group against Trafficking in Persons (ICAT) to improve coordination among relevant international organizations and monitor the implementation of existing instruments and standards pertaining to human trafficking.[1] Since 2017, the UN has worked with Alliance 8.7 to catalyze action and "scale up solutions" for its 2030 Sustainable Development Goal Target 8.7, which includes eradicating forced labor and ending modern slavery and human trafficking.[2] These developments are among those meant to augment and strengthen UN efforts, including identified shortcomings.

However, despite the updating of earlier strategies, the institutional structures and logics underpinning these efforts have not changed. Bureaucratic proceduralism, assumed to be apolitical, remains their organizing logic.[3] Global scalability, as a form of universalizing progress and endless growth, remains their celebrated objective and mode of improvement.[4] Indicators remain the measures of success, continuing to present policy solutions as quantifiable technical matters.[5] Structural inequality still receives insufficient attention, with consideration of the inequities wrought by colonial histories and contemporary geopolitical relationships set aside in the interest of a modular generalizable program conducive to governance at scale.

Not surprisingly, these new strategies are still not making a significant impact in ending the violence and abuse now glossed as human trafficking. Indeed, the United Nations Office on Drugs and Crime (UNODC) openly recognizes the limitations of its ongoing program, as evident in the opening epigraph, which was for years published on the organization's website. At that time, the UNODC asserted that the Trafficking Protocol was a "significant milestone" even while recognizing it as "problematic" and nearly ineffective in practice. More recently, the UNODC's *Global Report on Trafficking in Persons, 2020* maintained that because the COVID-19 pandemic has made increasing numbers of people economically vulnerable, it "is likely to increase trafficking in persons."[6] In a December 2022 report, the UNODC's Inter-agency Coordination Group against Trafficking in Persons (ICAT) stressed a rise of trafficking cases on account of recent humanitarian crises and conflict situations.[7] Similarly, the most recent report to the UN Human Rights Council (HRC) by Siobhán Mullally, UN special rapporteur on trafficking in persons, especially women and children, documented serious ongoing concerns with trafficking in persons in the agricultural sector, and her latest report to the UN General

Assembly identified heightened risks of trafficking tied to climate change and rooted in "existing and persistent inequalities, in poverty, in racism, and in discrimination."[8] Former special rapporteur Maria Grazia Giammarinaro's final report to the HRC in 2020 argued, "Profound changes are needed in the current approach to anti-trafficking action, which predominantly tends to prioritize investigation and prosecution of traffickers over victims' support, empowerment and long-term social inclusion."[9]

Paradoxically, this regular public acknowledgment of the limitations and inadequacies of the UN's counter–human trafficking strategies has yet to inspire a significant rethinking of its approach. Instead, token achievements of current efforts are celebrated even as progress is recognized as inadequate, ploddingly slow (and per Alliance 8.7, "slowing"), and largely ineffective in addressing the broad scope of this violence.[10] Current efforts assume a self-rationalizing and self-serving logic, offering the promise of ongoing amendments as cover for maintaining the status quo by adhering to an institutional model that obviates a full reckoning with the political-economic and sociological conditions of human trafficking. Even when a change of approach seems to be signaled, as with a new set of IOM guidebooks that acknowledge that smuggled migrants are also vulnerable and deserving of assistance, the recommendations remain abstract and generic, avoiding binding commitments or any extended engagement with political-economic conditions.[11] The result is a highly funded, systematized effort at global governance that is ultimately banal in its endeavor to do good.

Some readers might contend that I am being too ungenerous in my characterization of these efforts and discounting the positive changes set in motion by the Trafficking Protocol. These readers might argue that the failures of the global effort to fight human trafficking simply reflect the limitations of international law, which lacks a formal enforcement mechanism and thus must depend on national government compliance. They might argue that now at least *some* resources exist for victims of trafficking, even though only a nominal number of gravely abused and exploited individuals qualify for them. Some may also see progress in the fact that after years of pressure from the US State Department, the Japanese government has reformed some of its immigration laws, is now publicly acknowledging labor migrant abuse, and is making efforts to conduct inspections of some migrants' worksites. For instance, under the Obama administration, *TIP Reports* began to increasingly cite NGO testimony regarding the mistreatment and abuse of migrants in Japan's Trainee and Technical Internship Program, noting that the program "continued to lack effective oversight or means to protect participants from abuse."[12] In response, in 2016 the Japanese government passed the Act on Proper Technical Intern Training and Protection of Technical Intern Trainees, and in 2017, it established the Organization for Technical Intern Training (OTIT), which began conducting inspections of trainee worksites and documenting labor abuses.[13] Should not such steps be applauded?

Certainly, such moves toward reform are important, and direct assistance to migrant workers who have suffered abuse and exploitation needs to continue and be expanded. The IOM Tokyo office's 2019 *Tracer Survey*, an assessment of the effectiveness of Japan's assistance program for repatriated trafficking victims in the Philippines, found that the short-term direct aid provided to repatriated victims did indeed make a difference in helping the women find housing and economic support and deal with the trauma of their experiences.[14] However, the report also concluded that these benefits remain short-term and that broader, more flexible, and longer-term aid is needed for these women to contend with the economic precarity of their lives; it found that 77 percent of respondents expressed a desire to re-migrate for work, citing as reasons low income, the difficulty of finding jobs in the Philippines, and family needs.[15] Meanwhile, despite these findings, Japanese-government funding of the program was cut by more than half between 2008 and 2021.[16]

Indeed, any improvements born from current counter–human trafficking campaigns have been paltry in the context of the recognized scale of the problem. From the time when the Japanese government began enforcing its Action Plan in 2005 through March 31, 2022—a period of seventeen years—it provided repatriation and reintegration support to a mere 354 foreign migrants.[17] Meanwhile, Japan's declining population has made its economy increasingly dependent on foreign labor.[18] In addition to the tens of thousands of foreign women who have entered Japan to work in the sex industry, hundreds of thousands of migrant workers have been coming to Japan on an annual basis through the TITP alone.[19] Even with the new TITP regulations, violations of Japan's Labor Standards Act have been cited in 70 to 80 percent of OTIT inspections, and worksites hiring migrant workers who come through other channels (the majority) are hardly monitored at all.[20] *TIP Reports* continue to cite NGO reports of migrant debt bondage and state that TITP interns are still being detained, criminally charged, and in some cases deported when they attempt to leave abusive and exploitative contracted positions.[21]

In fact, the most notable shift in Japan's counter–human trafficking efforts over the past decade has been an increase in the number of *Japanese nationals* being identified as domestic sex-trafficking victims on account of the government's crackdown on *enjo kōsai* practices, in which Japanese high school girls engage in compensated dating with older Japanese men.[22] Concerned about the moral decay of Japanese youth and encouraged by the US State Department's flagging of this practice as sex trafficking, the Japanese government has, since 2011, investigated between 600 and 842 cases per year of "child prostitution" involving Japanese nationals—numbers far outpacing investigations of foreign labor trafficking.[23] These investigations were a key rationale for Japan's Tier I *TIP Report* rankings in 2018 and 2019 despite the fact that both years, the reports noted that few foreign trafficking victims had access to government-provided social services.[24] To wit, in 2018, only seven foreign trafficking victims received repatriation assistance, and this number dropped to five in 2019.[25]

While this book has focused primarily on foreign migrant labor exploitation and abuse in Japan, these problems are endemic around the world, although the country of origin of different labor migrants, and thus also the political-economic histories through which their migration paths have emerged, may vary. In the United States, the Southern Poverty Law Center has described guestworker programs as "close to slavery."[26] Severe abuse, exploitation, and indenture are regularly found in agriculture, meat processing, and other industries, and the numbers of government worksite inspectors are far below what is needed to regularly monitor employers of migrant workers.[27] The US government, like the Japanese government, offers assistance to only a small portion of those foreign workers suffering abuse and exploitation in its territories. Since its inception in 2007 through June 2023, the National Human Trafficking Hotline identified 164,839 victims of trafficking.[28] However, between January 2008 and June 2022, the US government granted fewer than ten thousand T visas (approximately six hundred per year) to allow victims of human trafficking to legally remain in the United States, receive social services, and testify against their alleged traffickers.[29]

Meanwhile, international programs that provide NGOs funding for direct assistance to victims of trafficking continue to struggle for resources and can help very few. Grants from UNVTF to NGOs conventionally range from $20,000 to $60,000, and as mentioned in chapter 7, receiving awards is competitive. Funded NGO projects are generally able to assist only dozens of individuals at a time, with occasional projects reaching up to 100–150 people. As it stands, the trust fund does not even consistently receive the $2,000,000 in annual funding that it needs to maintain a predictable and stable level of grants; in 2021, it received contributions of only $911,881 from private donors and UN member states. Meanwhile, as stated earlier, the UN estimates that the number of human trafficking victims is in the tens of millions worldwide.[30]

Clearly the UN's global counter–human trafficking campaign offers a very partial triage that stands in for the banal neglect of the root causes of migrant exploitation and abuse. One could say that it achieves more for international organizations and national governments—which benefit from funding and institutional development to administer these projects and the moral satisfaction and cultural capital that accompany doing something "good"—than it effectively contributes to stopping this violence on a global scale. Indeed, as current efforts stand, they are focused on getting countries to merely do a *bare minimum*. A Tier I *TIP Report* ranking literally means that a country meets the TVPA's "minimum standards" of efforts to address human trafficking—not that the country is "doing enough to address the problem."[31] As Luigi Lauriola, chair of the Ad Hoc Committee on the Elaboration of a Convention against Transnational Organized Crime, stated in his UN General Assembly presentation of the committee report, international agreements like the Trafficking Protocol simply offer "a framework and the tools for better international cooperation" on the issue.[32]

Sara Ahmed coins the word "nonperformative" to identify official declarations of redress that are unable to enact the actions that they name because the structural conditions necessary for their realization are not in place.[33] She develops the term in her ethnography of diversity practices in higher education to refer to the oxymoronic impotence of these practices, which perform idealized institutional commitments to diversity while deflecting attention away from the structural realities that stymie these commitments' realization. One could similarly say that the UN Trafficking Protocol is nonperformative insofar as it declares an intent to fight human trafficking while neglecting to address the colonial histories and contemporary political-economic inequalities that make labor migrants vulnerable to it. However, the Trafficking Protocol has created teeming effects, not only in new forms of collaboration but in the proliferation of guidelines, legal innovation, and funding flows that have had real—although not always beneficial—effects on people's lives. When hundreds of millions of dollars dedicated to a project, and an assembly of national governments and international organizations are committed to it, to be ineffective is not simply to be nonperformative. Rather, the banality of the UN protocol lies in its *misperformance* of its stated aims—its banal proliferation of a modular global program that ultimately reinforces a structurally violent status quo. The Trafficking Protocol misperforms its stated goals in two intertwined ways. First, it neglects to address, and thus allows and perpetuates, the political-economic conditions that make migrants vulnerable to the violence and exploitation now glossed as human trafficking in the first place; and second, it introduces new resource-devouring bureaucratic programs that, becoming ends in themselves, distract attention from, and thereby reinforce, the underlying problem.

This book has traced the misperformance of the UN's counter–human trafficking project through its day-to-day enactment in Japan. It has shown how the modular scalable bureaucratic protocols necessary to enact a global counter–human trafficking project also deeply compromise it. As these protocols banally prioritize compliance on a global scale, they neglect to consider what exactly this compliance achieves and for whom it achieves it. Participation in this misperformance does not require malfeasance; rather, it reflects the absorption of official, accepted practice to the extent that one neglects to consider its implications for the realities of others' lives. Instead, lilliputian pockets of improvement are hailed as justification for a globalized, institutional response that ignores the underlying fabric of political-economic vulnerability faced by migrant workers.

Bureaucracies are technologies for maintaining a stable and consistent status quo. They offer forms, standards, and guidelines for managing large numbers of people by creating modular systems for compliance that can function as forms of rule at scale.[34] Bureaucratic administration is not designed to be an instrument of social or political-economic change; we are misguided in expecting it to be. The inadequacy of the UN-sponsored global counter–human trafficking project is not a matter of the as-of-yet inability of a limited number of cooperating institutional actors to overcome a growing problem. Rather, the project's inadequacy stems from its very assertion that the forms of violence now glossed as human trafficking can be addressed through its modular institutional global governance strategy. This modular strategy in fact ignores and reproduces the structural conditions underlying the violence it purports to fight, all the while sidelining the insight and input of experienced grassroots caseworkers who are attuned to it. It conditions a banal neglect of the root of the problem that it ostensibly endeavors to solve.

The Trafficking Protocol's modular approach is vested by the notion that human trafficking calls for a humanitarian response and that global governance can accomplish such ends on a global scale.[35] The Japanese government's annual report on its measures to combat trafficking in persons is a case in point, assailing trafficking in persons as "a grave violation of human rights" that "requires a prompt and appropriate response from a humanitarian perspective."[36] Yet as legal scholar Janie Chuang has argued, approaching human trafficking as a global humanitarian issue depoliticizes and absolves national governments and their citizens from the roles that they play in creating the conditions of foreign migrant labor abuse.[37] As I have shown, the Trafficking Protocol's humanitarian focus—which centers on protection and assistance after the fact of abuse—enables labor migrants' countries of origin to ignore their responsibility for creating jobs at home and entering international trade and labor agreements that econom- ically and personally protect their citizens. Similarly, this focus allows migrant- destination countries, such as Japan and the United States, to ignore how their colonial histories and contemporary policies in migrant-sending countries, as well as their immigration laws, guest-worker policies, and lax enforcement of labor laws at home, leave foreign workers at risk of violence, while aiding only a select group that has suffered harm.

More than providing humanitarian assistance to migrants *after they have been severely abused and exploited*, efforts to fight human trafficking need to focus on *preventing their abuse in the first place* by addressing the conditions that enable this abuse to persist.[38] Under the Trafficking Protocol, efforts to prevent human trafficking have been narrowly imagined and given limited at- tention. They have primarily centered on modular institutional strategies such as tightening visa requirements and border oversight and engaging in basic forms of public information sharing, such as circulating posters and leaflets to educate workers, government officials, and the public about human traffick- ing.[39] Certainly, educating employers and workers about labor standards and ensuring that they are being followed is important. However, strategies such as tightening immigration control have often made migrants *more* vulnerable to exploitation, as they push migrants to take riskier measures to find work.

In a first for efforts by the United States, the Biden administration has fore- grounded prevention in its 2021 National Action Plan to Combat Human Traf- ficking. The plan appears well intentioned, recognizing gaps in current efforts and aspiring to take appropriate measures, including by consulting with an ad- visory council composed of trafficking survivors, considering the specific ways that "systemic racism intersects with [participating agencies'] antitrafficking work," and focusing on "decreasing systemic disparities that marginalize cer- tain communities."[40] Its list of "priority actions" includes initiatives to reduce demand for products produced under conditions of forced labor, including by mandating greater transparency in supply chains, considering how current nonimmigrant workers' programs facilitate labor exploitation, and increasing protections for migrant workers who leave exploitative labor situations.[41] In early 2023, Vice President Kamala Harris announced a public-private initiative in which private corporations such as Nestlé, Target, and Columbia Sports- wear would invest billions of dollars in northern Central America to address the "root causes of migration" from the region.[42] The initiative commendably aspires to not only address "economic drivers of migration" but also focus on "good governance and labor rights."[43] Yet questions have already been raised about the vision and oversight of these plans.[44] In the past, multinational corporations have used overseas factories and subcontractors to eschew stricter labor and environmental regulations in the United States, resulting in deteriorating labor and environmental conditions abroad. How will such patterns be prevented in this case? Multinational corporations expand by prioritizing shareholder profit and corporate growth above worker and environmental well-being. What incentives do corporate shareholders and executives have for ensuring that workers are not exploited if doing so will cut into profits?

In practice, the Biden administration's plan has not departed from the current UN-sponsored model, which enables national governments and international organizations to avow that they are working to fight human trafficking while ignoring the geopolitical imbalances, trade agreements, and histories of resource and labor extraction that have rendered labor migrants vulnerable in the first place. By highlighting the banality of these contemporary efforts, this book exposes the contradictions embedded in the national economies of migrant-receiving states like Japan and the United States. Even as these UN member states continue to fund and support UN anti-human-trafficking efforts, their economies depend on and benefit from both predatory relationships with foreign laborers' home communities and their work abroad. A professed concern for migrants' well-being is inevitably belied by gatekeeping borders, restrictive immigration policies, and unmonitored worksites, all of which result in migrant workers' conditional incorporation into these national economies as vulnerable and disposable laborers. Ninety percent of the UNODC budget comes from UN member-state donations. Member states thus have the final say in available resources and how they are allocated. Citizens in these countries, insofar as they are democratic, ultimately hold responsibility for how our governments make these resources available. To push our governments to do better, those of us who live in migrant-destination countries need to *think* about how and to what ends these resources are made available. In other words, we need to *think* about our dependencies on and relationships with workers in and from these countries, including those who play critical roles in supporting our economic well-being while our immigration policies, trade relations, and labor market conditions make them vulnerable to violence. These relationships beg for new understandings of the banal and misperformative workings of global institutional practice that reinforce dynamics so in need of transformative change. We will need to move away from collecting data and producing expert knowledge in the form of prescriptive guidelines and globalizable plans and move toward thinking about, and then addressing in practice, the specific historical and political-economic relationships that create and perpetuate such grave inequalities and vulnerabilities for some. We will need to confront deeply rooted and tightly woven geopolitical and economic relationships, including the logics of commodity production, international wage and currency gaps, and trade policies.

It is time to think about new strategies for addressing the structural factors that make migrants vulnerable to human trafficking. It is time to reconsider the global institutional models that have thus far constrained our visions for transformative action. In this case, not only will "the master's tools never dismantle the master's house," but the compulsion to use these tools will keep us from developing other available, and more effective, plans.[45] We must start by insisting that citizens of migrant-destination countries think about their direct and indirect relationships to those in migrant-sending ones, including how these relationships are tied to migrants' suffering and how changing these relationships can prevent it. Such an endeavor cannot center on isolated individual prosecutions or be driven by humanitarian benevolence for those who have already been abused. Rather, it will require listening to grassroots caseworkers who assist migrants—and to labor migrants themselves—and collectively recognizing what Arendt called the "responsibility" that citizens in migrant-destination countries bear for foreign workers' well-being in an economically interconnected world.[46] It will entail examinations of existing systems of inequality, even when changing these systems will be inconvenient, uncomfortable, and require sacrifices. The first step will be to "unfreeze" taken-for-granted definitions, doctrines, and concepts underpinning the current UN global project so that we can recognize them for what they are: fodder for the misperformance of justice.[47] Only then can we interrupt the flow of programmatic action to see what has been neglected, sidelined, missed, and forgotten by its banality of good.

Notes

1. In this book, I use the expression "NGO" to refer to a group of local organizations in the United States, Japan, and the Philippines that assist foreign migrant workers—in this case, particularly foreign migrant women—following these organizations' self-practice of identification. These NGOs varied in terms of their history, size, and funding. However, in broad strokes, the NGOs that provide direct assistance to migrants in Japan and the Philippines were very small grassroots groups; in the United States, they were larger, better funded, and more bureaucratically organized but still relatively modest organizations. For more on NGOs as a diverse category of organizations with a range of political orientations and missions, see Bernal and Grewal, *Theorizing NGOs*.

2. See Agustin, *Sex at the Margins*; Bernstein and Shih, "Erotics of Authenticity"; Doezema, "Loose Women or Lost Women?"; Mahdavi, *Gridlock*; Suchland, *Economies of Violence*; Yea, "Towards Critical Geographies of Anti–Human Trafficking."

3. See Bernstein, *Brokered Subjects*; Chang and Kim, "Reconceptualizing Approaches to Human Trafficking"; Cheng, *On the Move for Love*; Chuang, "Beyond a Snapshot"; Feingold, "Playing the Numbers"; Kempadoo, Sanghera, and Pattanaik, *Trafficking and Prostitution Reconsidered*; Lloyd and Simmons, "Framing for a New Transnational Legal Order"; Mahdavi, *Gridlock*; McGrath and Watson, "Anti-slavery as Development"; Musto, *Control and Protect*; Suchland, *Economies of Violence*; Vanderhurst, *Unmaking Migrants*; Warren, "Troubling the Victim/Trafficker Dichotomy in Efforts to Combat Human Trafficking."

4. By bare life, I mean, following Giorgio Agamben, the sheer fact of biological existence absent any consideration of the quality of that life. See Agamben, *Homo Sacer*. To understand the stakes for counter–human trafficking work of the discrepant sets of human rights covered in the International Covenant on Economic, Social and Cultural Rights (ICESCR) and the International Covenant on Civil and Political Rights (ICCPR), see Chuang, "Beyond a Snapshot."

5. Seyla Benhabib argues that legal concepts and human rights discourse are juris-generative in the sense that their universe of meaning is transformed and enhanced as they are successively iterated by different people in ever new and contested deployments. See Benhabib, *Dignity in Adversity*. For further discussion see Osanloo, *The Politics of Women's Rights in Iran*; Osanloo, "Redress"; Osanloo, *Forgiveness Work*.

6. Pangalangan, "Human Rights Discourse in Post-Marcos Philippines." Marcos ratified the ICESCR in 1974 and the Convention on the Elimination of All Forms of Discrimination against Women in 1981 while also unapologetically suppressing civil and political rights by declaring martial law, dissolving Congress, adopting a constitution granting vast presidential powers, jailing and murdering political opponents, engaging in extrajudicial killings and disappearances, and completely suppressing free press and union organizing. After Marcos's overthrow in 1986, the new Aquino administration publicly re-established civil liberties and entrenched support for human rights, ratifying the ICCPR and mandating human rights education for students, government officials, and law enforcement. Nonetheless, under subsequent administrations, extrajudicial killings and disappearances, and the suppression of free press, government opposition, and union organizing have persisted. For further discussion, see Claude, "Human Rights Education."

7. Pangalangan, "Human Rights Discourse in Post-Marcos Philippines."

8. For discussion of how legal transparency opens governments to critique, see Osanloo, "Islamico-Civil 'Rights Talk'"; Osanloo, *Politics of Women's Rights in Iran*.

9. For discussion of a parallel process in Iran, see Osanloo, "Islamico-Civil 'Rights Talk'"; Osanloo, *Politics of Women's Rights in Iran*.

INTRODUCTION

1. Except for one, now deceased, public figure, I use pseudonyms to refer to all whom I interviewed and all organizations with which I worked, and I have altered or removed identifying details to protect peoples' identities. To this end, I have also created composite figures based on interviews with multiple people. No named person discussed in this text should be assumed to be a single, identifiable individual.

2. Chuang, "Beyond a Snapshot."

3. DeStefano, *War on Human Trafficking*.

4. UNODC, *International Framework for Action to Implement the Trafficking in Persons Protocol*, 3.

5. Lloyd and Simmons argue that during the 1990s, a "transnational legal order" focused on fighting human trafficking began to emerge through processes of norm convergence solidified by linking human trafficking to transnational crime. See Lloyd and Simmons, "Framing for a New Transnational Legal Order," 400. Related, Laura Gómez-Mera argues that over the past decade, governance of TIP has shifted from being a state-centered set of rules and institutions to a decentralized and increasingly fragmentary transnational regime complex. She points to the proliferation of public and private initiatives that promulgate new rules for state and nonstate actors. She attributes this proliferation of public-private initiatives to the issue's complicated and multidimensional nature. See Gómez-Mera, "Global Governance of Trafficking in Persons." For further discussion, see Foot, Toft, and Cesare, "Developments in Anti-trafficking Efforts."

6. See Dottridge, "How Is the Money to Combat Human Trafficking Spent?"; Hoff, "Where Is the Funding for Anti-trafficking Work?"; Napier-Moore, "Global Funding Information Sheet Anti-trafficking Review"; Ucnikova, "OECD and Modern Slavery."

7. For a discussion of the stakes of efforts to quantify human trafficking on a global scale, see Merry, *Seductions of Quantification*.

8. See, for example, ILO, *Human Trafficking and Forced Labour Exploitation*; IOM, *IOM Handbook on Direct Assistance for Victims of Trafficking*; UNICEF, *Guidelines on the Protection of Child Victims of Trafficking*; UNODC, *Toolkit to Combat Trafficking in Persons*; Zimmerman and Borland, *Caring for Trafficked Persons*; Zimmerman and Watts, *WHO Ethical and Safety Recommendations for Interviewing Trafficked Women*; UN Economic and Social Council, Report of the United Nations High Commissioner for Human Rights to the Economic and Social Council; UNHCR, Guidelines on International Protection, No. 7."

9. See UN General Assembly, Resolution 53/114.

10. Shamir, "Anti-trafficking in Israel," 152. Note, too, that between 2000 and 2013, the number of states that established domestic laws criminalizing sex and labor trafficking increased from 10 percent to about 73 percent (Lloyd and Simmons, "Framing for a New Transnational Legal Order"). By 2014, a minimum of 146 countries had introduced criminal legislation against human trafficking (UNODC, *Mid-Term Independent Project Evaluation for the Management of the Voluntary Trust Fund for Victims of Trafficking, Especially Women and Children*). Regional initiatives include the European Union's Framework Decision on Combating Trafficking in Human Beings (2002); the Council of Europe's Convention against Trafficking in Human Beings (2005); the Economic Community of West African States' (ECOWAS) Plan of Action against Trafficking in Persons (2002); the South Asian Association for Regional Cooperation (SAARC) Convention on Preventing and Combating Trafficking in Women and Children for Prostitution (2002); the Association of South East Asian Nations' (ASEAN) Declaration against Trafficking in Persons (2004); the Coordinated Mekong Ministerial Initiative against Trafficking Process (2004); and the Organization of American States' (OAS) General Assembly Resolution on Trafficking in Persons (2003, 2005).

11. Cited in US Department of State, *Trafficking in Persons Report, June 2007*, 124.

12. See Parreñas, *Illicit Flirtations*; US Department of State, *Trafficking in Persons Report, June 2001, 2002, 2003, 2004*, and *2005*. For in-depth discussion of the abuse and exploitation faced by migrant women in the Japanese sex industry, see JNATIP and F-GENS, "'Nihon ni okeru jinshin baibai no higai ni kan suru chōsa kenkyū' hōkokusho"; Migrant Women Worker's Research and Action Committee, *NGOs' Report on the Situation of Foreign Migrant Women in Japan*.

13. Repeated discussion of this program can be found in the Japan country narratives of the US Department of State's *Trafficking in Persons Report* for every year between 2011 and 2022.

14. Kelley, *Scorecard Diplomacy*.

15. See Cameron and Newman, "Trafficking of Filipino Women to Japan"; Caouette and Saito, *To Japan and Back*; Dinan, *Owed Justice*; ILO, "Human Trafficking for Sexual Exploitation in Japan"; Lim, *Sex Sector*.

16. Kelley, *Scorecard Diplomacy*; Shamir, "Anti-trafficking in Israel." The publication of the annual *Trafficking in Persons Report* is mandated under the US Trafficking Victims Protection Act of 2000 (hereafter TVPA; div. A of the Victims of Trafficking and Violence Protection Act of 2000, Pub. L. No. 106–386, 114 stat. 1466 [2000]). The US State Department's Office to Monitor and Combat Trafficking in Persons website has described it as a "diplomatic tool to engage foreign governments on human trafficking"

(US Department of State, Office to Monitor and Combat Trafficking in Persons, "Trafficking in Persons Report," last updated June 15, 2023, https://www.state.gov/j/tip/rls/tiprpt/). The reports summarize the status of efforts to fight human trafficking around the globe, including identifying progress made and new concerns that have developed in different parts of the world. They also include country summaries of these efforts, ranking countries on three tiers according to their government's efforts to meet TVPA standards. Placement on the Watch List in the 2004 *Trafficking in Persons Report* threatened Japan with an automatic downgrade to Tier 3, the lowest tier, which meant possibilities of sanctions if more concentrated efforts were not made within two years. It also grouped Japan with countries such as Zimbabwe, the Philippines, Guatemala, Nigeria, and Thailand. Placing a close and strategic ally like Japan on the Watch List was controversial, as I discuss in chapter 2.

17. Cited in Embassy Tokyo, "Japan, the U.S., and TIP"; see also Kelley, *Scorecard Diplomacy*.

18. Cited in Embassy Tokyo, "Japan, the U.S., and TIP"; see also Kelley, *Scorecard Diplomacy*. The Task Force included representatives from the Cabinet Secretariat, the Cabinet Office, the National Police Agency, the Ministry of Justice, the Ministry of Foreign Affairs, and the Ministry of Health, Labour and Welfare. It was later enlarged to include representatives from the Gender Equality Bureau and the Human Rights Bureau.

19. US Department of State, *Trafficking in Persons Report, June 2004*, 14. Parreñas explains that according to the 2004 and 2005 reports, "Filipina hostesses in Japan constituted the largest group of sex-trafficked persons in the world, making up more than 10 percent of the 800,000 estimated victims of human trafficking worldwide." See Parreñas, *Illicit Flirtations*, 4.

20. Embassy Manila, "Number of Filipino 'Entertainers' Going to Japan Declines"; Parreñas, *Illicit Flirtations*, 4. On a monthly basis, the number of Filipina women entering the country between 2004 and 2005 dropped from 7,000 in 2004 to 1,000 in 2006. The US embassy concluded that new visa restrictions had made workers more valuable, forcing employers to provide better salaries and working conditions. It also concluded that fewer Thai women were working in brothels and that clubs in Japan and the number of establishments selling sex under coercive conditions had declined in response to these efforts. See Embassy Tokyo, "Review of Japan's Anti-TIP Policy." By 2019, according to Immigration Services Agency of Japan statistics, the number of Filipina women entering Japan on *kōgyō* (entertainer) visas was 5,632; however, the number of Philippine nationals who entered as *haigūsha* (spouses or dependents of Japanese nationals) stood at 26,699. As I later discuss, this latter residency category has been identified as one that Filipina women have begun to use in order to find jobs in Japan; however, because the visa category is so broad, it is impossible simply based on the numbers to identify how many such individuals do so.

21. Over the past several years, this ranking has dropped back down to Tier 2. I discuss this further in the book's conclusion.

22. See, for example, Aoyama, "Gurōbaru-ka to sekkusu wāku"; Tolentino, "Migrant Women in Japan"; JNATIP and F-GENS, "'Nihon ni okeru jinshin baibai no higai ni kan suru chōsa kenkyū' hōkokusho."

23. Nowhere is this clearer than in UNODC, *Global Report on Trafficking in Persons, 2020*.

24. IOM, *Tracer Survey*.

25. See Faier, *Intimate Encounters*; Faier, "Planetary Urban Involution in the Tokyo Suburbs"; Montañez, Nuqui, and Sicam, *Pains and Gains*; Parreñas, *Illicit Flirtations*; Piquero-Ballescas, "Philippine Migration to Japan"; Sassen, "Economic Internationalization."

26. Dauvergne, *Shadows in the Forest*; Tadiar, *Things Fall Away*; Trinidad, "Japan's Official Development Assistance (ODA) to the Philippines."

27. Bello et al., *Anti-development State*.

28. Dauvergne, *Shadows in the Forest*; Chanbonpin, "Holding the United States Accountable for Environmental Damages"; Gutierrez, "International Environmental Justice on Hold."

29. Dauvergne, *Shadows in the Forest*.

30. Neitzel, *The Life We Longed For*.

31. See Basel Action Network, "Building Toxic Waste Colonies." A full inventory can be found in Senate Economic Planning Office, Philippines, "Japan-Philippines Economic Partnership Agreement (JPEPA)," 16.

32. Bello et al., *Anti-development State*; Dauvergne, *Shadows in the Forest*; Tadiar, *Things Fall Away*.

33. For discussions of labor migration from the Philippines as a strategy by which Filipinxs endeavor to manage the structural violence shaping their lives, see work by Asis, Huang, and Yeoh, "When the Light of the Home Is Abroad"; Cheng, *On the Move for Love*; Faier, *Intimate Encounters*; Faier, "Planetary Urban Involution in the Tokyo Suburbs"; Guevarra, *Marketing Dreams, Manufacturing Heroes*; Montañez, Nuqui, and Sicam, *Pains and Gains*; Parreñas, *Illicit Flirtations*; Piquero-Ballescas, "Philippine Migration to Japan"; Pratt, *Families Apart*; Rodriguez, *Migrants for Export*; Yea, *Trafficking Women in Korea*.

34. Rodriguez, *Migrants for Export*.

35. Adriano, "Agrarian Reform, Populism and Agrarian Debacle"; Hawes, *Philippine State and the Marcos Regime*; Chandran, "Philippine Peasants Fight for Land 30 Years after Reform."

36. Faier, *Intimate Encounters*.

37. Faier, "Planetary Urban Involution in the Tokyo Suburbs."

38. For how the reliance on middlemen and Japan's strict immigration policies negatively impacts the lives of Filipina migrants in Japan, see Parreñas, *Illicit Flirtations*.

39. For a discussion of the abuses these women face, see JNATIP and F-GENS, "'Nihon ni okeru jinshin baibai no higai ni kan suru chōsa kenkyū' hōkokusho"; Schmetzer, "Japan's Sex Industry Can Be Lethal for Asian Women."

40. JNATIP and F-GENS, "'Nihon ni okeru jinshin baibai no higai ni kan suru chōsa kenkyū' hōkokusho"; Southern Poverty Law Center, "Close to Slavery." As discussed in this book's conclusion, the Japanese government's Organization for Technical Intern Training has conducted inspections of TITP worksites since 2017; however, technical interns are just one group of foreign labor migrants in Japan, and these inspections occur sporadically at only a fraction of the sites where they are employed.

41. Guevarra, *Marketing Dreams, Manufacturing Heroes*; Rodriguez, *Migrants for Export*.

42. Biocentric ideas about race were introduced to Japan from Europe and the United States in the nineteenth century and then interpreted through discourses of Japanese nationalism. For a discussion of racism in Japan, including intra-Asian racisms, see Condry, *Hip-Hop Japan*; Dower, *War without Mercy*; Faier, *Intimate Encounters*; Fujitani, *Race for Empire*; Kang, *Traffic in Asian Women*.

43. UN, Protocol to Prevent, Suppress and Punish Trafficking in Persons, art. 9, item 4.

44. Waly, preface, 5.

45. "Human Trafficking—Our Response," UNODC, accessed January 2, 2023, https://www.unodc.org/unodc/en/human-trafficking/our-response.html (emphasis in original).

46. UNODC, *Global Report on Trafficking in Persons, 2020*, 5.

47. For example, under the current model, violations ranging from the forced labor of Mexican migrants in Florida's tomato fields; labor abuses faced by Filipina women in Japan's sex industry; and the labor exploitation of Togolese boys who, fed stimulants, work sixteen-hour days for a year on Nigerian farms in exchange for only a motorbike are all approached as analogous crimes in which private individuals have been subject to exploitation by other private individuals under specific conditions of migration defined as human trafficking. The specific histories, geographical and cultural factors, and geopolitical relationships shaping these migration trends fall out of the picture. For a discussion of these abuses as forms of human trafficking, see, respectively, Estabrook, *Tomatoland*; Parreñas, *Illicit Flirtations*; Piot, "'Right' to Be Trafficked."

48. During the Cold War, this bipolar dynamic was challenged by the Non-Aligned Movement's anticolonial push for equal rights. After the Cold War ended, the movement shifted its focus to developing multilateral ties and fostering unity among countries, particularly those in the Global South.

49. This notion of globality emerged in the 1960s and 1970s and is geographically and historically specific. For a discussion of how differently situated people and groups can articulate overlapping understandings of globality in geographically and culturally contingent ways, see Heise, *Sense of Place and Sense of Planet*.

50. See Heise, *Sense of Place and Sense of Planet*; Ingold, "Globes and Spheres"; Cosgrove, *Apollo's Eye*. In the 1960s and 1970s, the Gaia hypothesis suggested that all of the planet's life-forms were linked as a single, world-encompassing, self-sustaining feedback system. This new global sensibility also offered new ways for framing the intensification of transnational migration and political-economic relations as globalization. During the 1960s, allegories of the global village became popular in the United States, romanticizing global connectedness (Heise, *Sense of Place and Sense of Planet*). Ideas about global human rights developed in the context of these emerging narratives of planetary connectedness.

51. See Bradley, *World Reimagined*, 137.

52. Buergenthal, "Evolving International Human Rights System"; Walzer, *Toward a Global Civil Society*.

53. See, for example, Commission on Global Governance, "Our Global Neighborhood"; Finkelstein, "What Is Global Governance"; Keck and Sikkink, *Activists beyond Borders*; Weiss and Wilkinson, "Rethinking Global Governance?"; Weiss and Gordenker, *NGOs, the UN, and Global Governance*; Weiss and Thakur, *Global Governance and the UN*. To capture the dynamics among private actors and subnational, governmental, and inter-

governmental organizations in international governance, international relations scholars have introduced concepts such as "regime complex" (Raustiala and Victor, "Regime Complex for Plant Genetic Resources," 279), "transnational governance networks" (Andonova, Betsill, and Bulkeley, "Transnational Climate Governance," 57), and "transnational regime complexes" (Gómez-Mera "Global Governance of Trafficking in Persons," 305). Other scholars have also written about the possibilities of a "global civil society" (Keck and Sikkink, *Activists beyond Borders*, 33) and a "world polity" (Boli and Thomas "World Culture in the World Polity"; Ruggie, *Constructing the World Polity*).

54. Weiss and Thakur, *Global Governance and the UN*. Theories of global governance developed in part in response to understandings of the limitations of UN power. By the 1990s, establishing a single global government seemed increasingly improbable. Political scientist James Rosenau used the term "governance"—as opposed to "government"—in international relations to refer to "the regulation of interdependent relations in the absence of overarching political authority" (cited in Weiss and Thakur, *Global Governance and the UN*, 6). Global governance would involve the collective affairs of a range of stakeholders—not only state authorities but also intergovernmental organizations, civil society, and private sector entities—who both work together and independently strategize to maintain order and control. Proponents of global governance aspired to "provide international government-like services in the absence of a world government" (Weiss and Thakur, *Global Governance and the UN*, 3).

55. See UN General Assembly, Resolution 53/114. For further discussion, see Gómez-Mera, "Global Governance of Trafficking in Persons."

56. "United Nations Launches Global Plan of Action against Human Trafficking," UNODC, September 1, 2010, https://www.unodc.org/unodc/en/frontpage/2010/September/un-launches-global-plan-of-action-against-human-trafficking.html.

57. My understanding of "disentanglement" is indebted to Hannah Appel, who demonstrates how modular forms of expertise, labor organization, and infrastructure enable an aspirational disentanglement of capitalist practices from the specificities of place. See Appel, *Licit Life of Capitalism*, 5. For related discussions on the friction and gaps that enable capitalist practice to proceed, see Clarke, "Transnational Yoruba Revivalism and the Diasporic Politics of Heritage"; Tsing, *Friction*.

58. See Appel, *Licit Life of Capitalism*; I. Feldman, *Governing Gaza*; Gupta, *Red Tape*; Herzfeld, *Social Production of Indifference*; Hortman and Heyman, *Paper Trails*; M. S. Hull, *Government of Paper*; Hyndman, *Managing Displacement*; Mountz, *Seeking Asylum*; Navaro-Yashin, *Make-Believe Space*; Scott, *Seeing Like a State*; Weber, *Economy and Society*.

59. Strathern, *Audit Cultures*.

60. See Larsen, "Politics of Technicality," 75.

61. My understanding of Arendt's notion of banality follows Benhabib, "I. Judgment and the Moral Foundations of Politics in Arendt's Thought"; Benhabib, "Identity, Perspective and Narrative in Hannah Arendt's 'Eichmann in Jerusalem'"; R. J. Bernstein, "Reflections on Radical Evil."

62. Arendt, *Responsibility and Judgment*, 159. See also Arendt, *Eichmann in Jerusalem*.

63. Arendt, *Responsibility and Judgment*, 159.

64. Arendt, "Thinking and Moral Considerations," 444.

65. See R. J. Bernstein, "Reflections on Radical Evil."

66. Benhabib, "I. Judgment and the Moral Foundations of Politics in Arendt's Thought"; Benhabib, "Identity, Perspective and Narrative in Hannah Arendt's 'Eichmann in Jerusalem.'"

67. See Benhabib, "Identity, Perspective and Narrative in Hannah Arendt's 'Eichmann in Jerusalem,'" 44–46; R. J. Bernstein, "Reflections on Radical Evil." Arendt did not aim to characterize evil in a metaphysical sense so much as describe the banality of a specific form of evil that had emerged with the introduction of totalitarianism into the world. Her correspondence with Karl Jaspers highlights her specific focus on "*this* evil, not evil per se." See Arendt and Jaspers, *Correspondence, 1926–1969*, 542; Benhabib, "Identity, Perspective and Narrative in Hannah Arendt's 'Eichmann in Jerusalem,'" 46.

68. See Arendt, *Responsibility and Judgment*, 159.

69. See Mbembe, "Provisional Notes on the Postcolony"; Mbembe, "Banality of Power and the Aesthetics of Vulgarity in the Postcolony."

70. Many decades ago, sociologist Johan Galtung stressed the need to attend to the ways that durable harm in people's lives is caused by two interconnected forms of violence: personal and structural. He distinguished between these two types of violence by their source. "Personal" or "direct" violence can be attributed to individual agents, such as abusive employers or customers. In contrast, he described as "structural" or "indirect" those forms of violence that are caused by durable social structures: racisms, sexisms, political-economic inequalities, legal structures, and colonial legacies, among others. Galtung argued that because these two forms of violence work in tandem—structural violence can result in increased vulnerability to personal forms of violence, and vice versa—both require our attention. See Galtung, "Violence, Peace, and Peace Research," 170. Scholars have since built on Galtung's framework. Sociologist Randall Collins described "bureaucratic violence" as that form of violence that eliminates "any personal sense of moral responsibility." See Collins, "Three Faces of Cruelty," 433. Sarah Milne and Sango Mahanty describe a form of "bureaucratic violence" in global environmental governance that is rooted in "the implementation of mundane technical rules that hide local contestation, sideline criticism, and deny justice." For them, bureaucratic violence is a form of "symbolic violence" that derives from governing bureaucracies' "persistent deployment of and adherence to bureaucratic constructs, which simplify and conceal what is going on." See Milne and Mahanty, "Value and Bureaucratic Violence in the Green Economy," 133, 141. Cecelia Menjívar and Leisy Abrego define legal violence as the harmful effects on migrants' lives of immigration laws, which obstruct and derail immigrants' paths to incorporation by creating a new axis of social stratification based on legality as a social position. With this notion, they include those forms of structural and symbolic violence that are legally codified and produce social suffering. See Menjívar and Abrego, "Legal Violence." Wendy Vogt illustrates how legal violence "funnels migrants into dangerous and clandestine routes." See Vogt, "Crossing Mexico," 765; Vogt, *Lives in Transit*.

71. See Collins, "Three Faces of Cruelty"; Herzfeld, *Social Production of Indifference*. Collins identified the "Eichmann syndrome" of Nazis—"the routinized following of orders"—as the "epitome" of what he referred to as "callousness: brutality routinized and bureaucratized, cruelty without passion." See Collins, "Three Faces of Cruelty," 419.

72. Herzfeld, *Social Production of Indifference*.

73. Weber, *Economy and Society*.

74. See Vaughn, *Challenger Launch Decision*.

75. See Ministry of Foreign Affairs, Japan, *Japan's Actions to Combat Trafficking in Persons*, 4.

76. Koh, "Why Do Nations Obey International Law?"

77. Müller, "Introduction: Lifting the Veil of Harmony," 2.

78. In contrast, in a domestic legal context, the expression "legal instrument" generally refers to legally binding documents, such as contracts, leases, and deeds, which can be guaranteed by law enforcement according to established bodies of law.

79. Agnew, *Globalization and Sovereignty*; Falcón, *Power Interrupted*; Mazower, *No Enchanted Palace*.

80. Agnew, *Globalization and Sovereignty*.

81. Chuang, "United States as Global Sheriff"; Clarke, *Fictions of Justice*.

82. See, for example, Allen, *Rise and Fall of Human Rights*; Clarke, *Fictions of Justice*; Clarke, *Affective Justice*; Ferguson, *The Anti-politics Machine*; Li, *Will to Improve*; Mosse, *Cultivating Development*; Merry, *Human Rights and Gender Violence*; Merry, *Seductions of Quantification*.

83. Consider Clarke, *Affective Justice*; Englund, *Prisoners of Freedom*; Ferguson, *Anti-politics Machine*; Mosse, *Cultivating Development*; Yea, "Mobilising the Child Victim."

84. Sally Engle Merry has theorized the vernacularization of human rights. See Merry, *Human Rights and Gender Violence*. Notable work on resistance to international legal and human rights regimes includes Allen, *Rise and Fall of Human Rights*; Clarke, *Fictions of Justice*; Englund, *Prisoners of Freedom*; Piot, "'Right' to Be Trafficked"; Tate, *Counting the Dead*.

85. See also Roces, "Prostitution, Women's Movements and the Victim Narrative in the Philippines."

86. This term is famously James Scott's. See Scott, *Domination and the Arts of Resistance*, 13–16.

87. As discussed in chapter 6, the UN Human Rights Commission has appointed a special rapporteur on trafficking in persons, especially women and children, who is tasked with undertaking country visits, producing an annual report, and taking action against complaints regarding the failure to protect trafficked persons' human rights. The UN also undertakes independent evaluations of the effectiveness of it projects. However, these reports, filed on annual or multiyear cycles through official UN or government channels, have limited, if any, immediate effect on the everyday realities of caseworkers' jobs and migrants' lives.

88. Sharma and Gupta, "Introduction—Rethinking Theories of the State in an Age of Globalization," 11. For further discussion, see Sharma, *Logics of Empowerment*; Gupta, *Red Tape*. Others have expanded their work through attention to the cultural logics that govern the everyday practice of state bureaucracies, such as M. S. Hull, *Government of Paper*; Mathews, "Power/Knowledge, Power/Ignorance"; Mathews, "State Making, Knowledge, and Ignorance"; Mountz, *Seeking Asylum*.

89. Riles, *The Network Inside Out*. Others have built on Riles in examining the daily routines through which human rights, humanitarian, and other international laws are articulated in disparate local settings. Sally Engle Merry and Arzoo Osanloo have considered how human rights laws are adopted and transformed as vernacular discursive

practices. For instance, Osanloo demonstrates how women in contemporary Iran negotiate both liberal and Islamic subjectivities as they make rights claims in family court. These Iranian courts are imbued with multiple ideologies, and women, as legal agents, negotiate multiple subjectivities—liberal, religious, and other—as they appeal for their civil and human rights. See Merry, *Human Rights and Gender Violence*; Osanloo, *Politics of Women's Rights in Iran*; Osanloo, *Forgiveness Work*. Additionally, studies by Jennifer Hyndman and Kamari Clarke have considered the contradictions underpinning international efforts to enact justice and humanitarianism in, respectively, the United Nations High Commission for Refugees' refugee camps and the International Criminal Court. See Hyndman, *Managing Displacement*; Clarke, *Fictions of Justice*.

90. See Bornstein, *Spirit of Development*; Hemment, *Empowering Women in Russia*; Scherz, *Having People, Having Heart*.

91. See Billo and Mountz, "For Institutional Ethnography."

92. Butler, *Bodies That Matter*, xii. Butler famously uses the expression "come to matter" to refer to how objects of knowledge, such as "the global," are performatively articulated as simultaneously material and semiotic processes.

93. Laura Nader famously introduced the notion of "studying up" as an ethnographic method. See Nader, "Up the Anthropologist," 284.

94. See Barnett, *Eyewitness to a Genocide*; Falcón, *Power Interrupted*; Merry, *Human Rights and Gender Violence*; Riles, *The Network Inside Out*; Bradley, *World Reimagined*; Kelley, *Scorecard Diplomacy*; Keck and Sikkink, *Activists beyond Borders*; Mazower, *No Enchanted Palace*; Moyn, *Last Utopia*; Eckel and Moyn, *Breakthrough*; Prügl et al., "Whistleblower."

95. Berlant, "Cruel Optimism," 21.

96. See Arendt, *Responsibility and Judgment*.

97. Arendt, *Responsibility and Judgment*, 163.

98. Arendt, *Responsibility and Judgment*, 167.

99. Arendt, *Responsibility and Judgment*, 175.

100. Arendt, *Responsibility and Judgment*.

101. Annan, "Address at the Opening of the Signing Conference for the United Nations Convention against Transnational Organized Crime."

1. A GLOBAL SOLUTION

1. A public statement of the financial struggles faced by NGOs in Japan that assist abused migrant workers can be found in Tamai, "Jinshin baibai higai konzetsu, NGO to ittai de."

2. See Halley, "Rape at Rome"; Lobasz, *Constructing Human Trafficking*; Musto, *Control and Protect*; Suchland, *Economies of Violence*.

3. For a discussion of CATW and the global feminist movement against human trafficking, see Halley, "Rape at Rome"; Kang, *Traffic in Asian Women*; Lobasz, *Constructing Human Trafficking*. Note also that Barry's bio on the Women's Media Center website describes its publication as having "launched a new global movement against trafficking in human beings." See "Kathleen Barry Bio," Women's Media Center, accessed June 21, 2023, https://www.womensmediacenter.com/profile/kathleen-barry.

4. Barry began working on *Female Sexual Slavery* in 1975, several years after women's groups in Korea and Japan began organizing and publishing about the treatment of Korean women by Japanese men. For perspective on this time frame, see Barry, *Female Sexual Slavery*; Klemesrud, "Personal Crusade against Prostitution"; Matsui, "Watashi wa naze kīsen kankō ni hantai suru no ka"; Matsui, cited in Russell and Van de Ven, *Crimes against Women*, 177–79. Bunch also learned from and collaborated with these Korean and Japanese activists. See Bunch, foreword. For further discussion of how relationships between feminists in the United States and activists in Asia were rooted in the objectification of "Asian women" as a gendered and racialized category of personhood, see Kang, *Traffic in Asian Women*.

5. Cited in Matsui, "Sexual Slavery in Korea," 68. See also Bunch, *Passionate Politics*; Mackie, *Feminism in Modern Japan*; Malony, "Crossing Boundaries"; Matsui, *Women's Asia*; Matsui, "Josei hogo jigyō to josei no jinken"; Matsui, *Ai to ikari tatakau yūki*; Park, "Nanajū-nendai no Kankoku to Nihon ni okeru kīsen kankō hantai undō"; Roces and Edwards, *Women's Movements in Asia*; Takahashi, "Josei no jinken to kīsen kankō hantai undo"; Takahashi, *Baibaishun mondai ni torikumu*.

6. Mackie, *Feminism in Modern Japan*.

7. Bunch, for instance, makes strong statements about the need to account for structural issues and diversity among women in forging a global feminist movement. She critiques the Western media for characterizing feminist movement as being exclusively focused on issues important to middle-class white women in the United States. However, in advocating for a global approach, she overlooks the complicity of women in the United States in perpetuating structural inequalities between themselves and women in the Global South and thus the need for political-economic change to address them. See Bunch, *Passionate Politics*, 332–44.

8. I borrow the notion of encapsulation from Susan Friend Harding, who writes of "narrative encapsulation" as a form of "cultural domination" in which one group's story "is reframed by the terms of another." See Harding, *Book of Jerry Falwell*, 65. More recently, Kamari Clarke has built on Harding to discuss "legal encapsulation," a "discursive technocratic practice that, in the negotiation of justice, turns attention from structural inequality to the language of the law." See Clarke, *Affective Justice*, 17.

9. Like other similar shelters in Japan, Tahanan developed as the global anti-domestic-violence movement, which modeled the establishment of domestic violence shelters, converged with a regional women's movement to address the sexual exploitation of Asian women by Japanese men. For further discussion, see Babior, "Women of a Tokyo Shelter"; Kuwajima, "Purosesu to shite no 'jiko kettei'"; Morita, "Caring for Caregivers"; Shipper, *Fighting for Foreigners*.

10. This case is not isolated. For further discussion of how global framings of violence against women have displaced local understandings of events and deflected attention from structural forces that oppress women, see Hemment, "Global Civil Society and the Local Costs of Belonging"; Kang, *Traffic in Asian Women*; Ong, "Strategic Sisterhood or Sisters in Solidarity?" These studies have demonstrated that the pretense of strategic sisterhood assumed by women in metropoles ignores differences and inequalities among women, instead asserting individualistic notions of transnational feminine citizenship.

11. For discussion of the role of scale in shaping political movement, see Moore, "Rethinking Scale as a Geographical Category"; Tsing, "The Global Situation."

12. Unlike myopias, which blur out all but that which is nearby, hyperopias are refractive errors that make immediate objects difficult to see, fixing on a single abstracted view from a distance.

13. Halley, "Preface: Introducing Governance Feminism," ix.

14. See Barry, *Female Sexual Slavery*; Suchland, *Economies of Violence*. Campaigns against what was then labeled "white slavery" and the "traffic in women" during the late nineteenth and early twentieth centuries had resulted in several multilateral conventions: the 1904 International Agreement for the Suppression of the White Slave Traffic, the 1910 International Convention for the Suppression of the White Slave Traffic, the 1921 International Convention for the Suppression of the Traffic in Women and Children, and the 1949 Convention for the Suppression of the Traffic in Persons and of the Exploitation of the Prostitution of Others. However, none of these international agreements had political consequence or lasting effect on popular opinion in the United States, western Europe, or elsewhere.

15. For books on the topic in the 1960s, see Barlay, *Sex Slavery*; O'Callaghan, *The Slave Trade Today*; O'Callaghan, *The White Slave Trade*.

16. The book was the product of a collaboration between British aristocrat-turned-socialist-author Robin Maugham and Sean O'Callaghan.

17. Weiler, "*Slave Trade in the World Today*, a Documentary, Arrives."

18. hooks, *Feminism Is for Everybody*. See also Freidan, *The Feminine Mystique*.

19. Barry documents many instances of this in her book, including the following: In 1973, the United Nations Human Rights Commission took up the case of Nasreen Hussein, one of three Persian girls who had been kidnapped, forced into marriage, and enslaved in Zanzibar; although a fully documented appeal was sent to the Tanzanian government, it simply died from inaction when the government did not respond. Out of twenty-three thousand complaints of human rights violations filed with the UN under a new 1973 procedure for dealing with slavery practices, only eight cases survived the bureaucratic evaluation and procedures. In both 1965 and 1974, INTERPOL refused to permit the public circulation of its reports on the sexual traffic of women involving Europe, the Middle East, South America, and Africa. See Barry, *Female Sexual Slavery*, 53–67.

20. Barry, *Female Sexual Slavery*.

21. In the fall of 1960, Prime Minister Ikeda Hayato initiated a long-term economic development plan that he called the Income Doubling Plan (*Shotoku Baizō Keikaku*). Aiming to double the size of Japan's economy in ten years, the plan called for a combination of tax breaks, targeted investment, incentives to increase industrial development and exports, and an enlarged social safety net. Over the course of the plan, Japan's annual economic growth averaged over 10 percent, and the size of the economy more than doubled.

22. See "South Korea: The Seoul of Hospitality"; Korea Church Women United, "Kisaeng Tourism"; Lie, "Transformation of Sexual Work in 20th-Century Korea"; Matsui, cited in Russell and Van de Ven, *Crimes against Women*, 177–79. By 1973, 80 percent of Japanese tourists to Korea were men; 98 percent of them were unaccompanied by women. For further discussion, see Lie, "Transformation of Sexual Work in 20th-Century Korea."

23. Yun Chai, "Asian-Pacific Feminist Coalition Politics"; Lie, "Transformation of Sexual Work in 20th-Century Korea."

24. Lie, "Transformation of Sexual Work in 20th-Century Korea."

25. Lie, "Transformation of Sexual Work in 20th-Century Korea." Lie cites an un-named sex tour *kisaeng* reported to have said, "It's hard for us to accept some—but we must work hard not only for ourselves and our families but for our country's future. Our country needs more money for its economic development." See Lie, "Transformation of Sexual Work in 20th-Century Korea," 319.

26. Lie, "Transformation of Sexual Work in 20th-Century Korea."

27. Lie, "Transformation of Sexual Work in 20th-Century Korea."

28. See N. Lee, "Negotiating the Boundaries of Nation, Christianity, and Gender"; M. Lee, "Japan-Korea Solidarity Movement in the 1970s and 1980s"; Matsui, cited in Russell and Van de Ven, *Crimes against Women*, 177–79; Matsui, "Watashi wa naze kīsen kankō ni hantai suru no ka."

29. Misook Lee describes how women's groups in Japan and Korea established a "women's solidarity movement" centered on Japanese sex tourism in Korea. See M. Lee, "Japan-Korea Solidarity Movement in the 1970s and 1980s," 7. This solidarity movement centered on issues of human rights, labor rights, and the ongoing legacies of the colonial past. Similarly, Alice Yun Chai writes of an "Asian-Pacific feminist perspective" that developed through solidarity networks among grassroots women activists in Asia. See Yun Chai, "Asian-Pacific Feminist Coalition Politics," 67.

30. In the 1950s and 1960s, international Christian networks linked Japanese and Korean churches as Korean Christians began studying at Japanese theological seminaries. These networks formed an important base, particularly among progressive Christians, for activism against the Park dictatorship in Korea and the neo-imperialist role that Japan was playing in Korea. See M. Lee, "Japan-Korea Solidarity Movement in the 1970s and 1980s."

31. M. Lee, "Japan-Korea Solidarity Movement in the 1970s and 1980s."

32. Kim, cited in Matsui, "Sexual Slavery in Korea," 22.

33. Shigematsu, *Scream from the Shadows*.

34. See Matsui, *Ai to ikari tatakau yūki*; Matsui, "Josei hogo jigyō to josei no jinken"; Matsui, "Sexual Slavery in Korea"; Matsui, *Why I Oppose Kisaeng Tours*; Matsui, *Women's Asia*.

35. Matsui, *Ai to ikari tatakau yūki*.

36. Matsui, "Sexual Slavery in Korea," 25.

37. Russell and Van de Ven, *Crimes against Women*, 179. See also Park, "Nanajū-nendai no Kankoku to Nihon ni okeru kīsen kankō hantai undō."

38. Park, "Nanajū-nendai no Kankoku to Nihon ni okeru kīsen kankō hantai undō."

39. Park, "Nanajū-nendai no Kankoku to Nihon ni okeru kīsen kankō hantai undō."

40. Cited in Stokes, "Sex Package Tours." The leaflets read:

> We appeal to the conscience of the Japanese and to your sense of shame. When the word "economic animal" was invented to criticize the Japanese did we feel shame? The territory the "sex animals" are departing for coincides, surprisingly enough, with that once occupied by the Japanese Army. People there must be reminded of the arrogant clump of Japanese military boots only too clearly. Don't you feel pain to be part of this assault force? Almost all the tours to South Korea are for so-called "kisaeng parties," i.e., to buy women. How insensitive can you be? Forming up in squads like this to go off to buy girls? Let's find a new way to live together with

Asians. We have to remember that the future can only be built after sincere inner reflection on the past.

For further discussion, see Stokes, "Sex Package Tours."

41. Park, "Nanajū-nendai no Kankoku to Nihon ni okeru kīsen kankō hantai undō."

42. Norma, *Japanese Comfort Women and Sexual Slavery*.

43. Matsui, "Sexual Slavery in Korea," 23. See also Norma, *Japanese Comfort Women and Sexual Slavery*. Matsui's position on prostitution was complex and seemed to shift some over time. Although she participated in events with prostitution-abolitionists like Barry and Bunch, Matsui also wrote supportively of the movement in Thailand to decriminalize prostitution (Matsui, *Women's Asia*, 70). She later stressed the importance of women's "right to sexual self-determination" (*seiteki jiko ketteiken*) as part of "women's human rights" (*josei no jinken*). See Matsui, "Josei hogo jigyō to josei no jinken," 23. When Matsui discussed what was often referred to as "forced prostitution" in Asia, she consistently insisted that economic and geopolitical inequalities be considered as determining factors. She summarizes feminist debates on prostitution and positions herself in relation to them in Matsui, "Pekin kaigi no igi to 21-seiki e no kadai."

44. Matsui, "Sexual Slavery in Korea," 23.

45. Matsui, *Women's Asia*, 71.

46. In this way, her attention differed from other *ribu* activists, who tended to focus on issues confronting Japanese women. See Shigematsu, *Scream from the Shadows*.

47. M. Lee argues that Matsui's self-reflexive activism was part of a new kind of civic activism that developed in Japan in the 1960s and 1970s, beginning with the mass anti–US-Japan Treaty movement (*Anpo Tōsō*), developing through the anti–Vietnam War movement in Japan, and taking form in the Japan-Korea solidarity movement that pushed for the democratization of South Korea in the 1970s and 1980s. These civic movements led to a shift away from a comfortable mythology of Japanese victimhood to a new morality grounded in a sense of individual responsibility for both the past and the present. Through these movements, solidarity came to be understood "as a process of listening to and learning from the voices of the struggling others toward the goal of self-reformation" (6). In regard to Korea, this self-reformation included questioning Japan's role in Korea and addressing its foreign policy toward the country. See M. Lee, "Japan-Korea Solidarity Movement in the 1970s and 1980s."

48. Matsui wrote,

> Had I seen the poverty of Asia without having experienced the overwhelming wealth of Western Europe and the United States during my two-year stay there, perhaps I would have been less profoundly affected, but I felt intuitively that somehow this wealth had been taken from Asia. In my mind's eye, I could see Asia exploited, deprived, impoverished by centuries of colonial rule, and, as an Asian myself, I felt intense pain and anger. We are all human beings, inhabiting the same planet, so why must some of us suffer so. As this question tumbled around in my head it seemed to me that the idea of human equality before God is a reality that can be applied only to white Westerners.

Matsui, *Women's Asia*, 1.

49. Matsui, *Women's Asia*, 3

50. Mackie, *Feminism in Modern Japan*.

51. AWA members aimed to listen to and learn from women in other parts of Asia and to join them in solidarity against contemporary colonial legacies and ongoing violations of human rights and labor rights involving Japanese corporations and citizens. The first issue (1977) of the organization's bulletin, *Asian Women's Liberation* (in Japanese, *Ajia to josei kaihō*), featured a photo of Korean women protesting Korea's repressive military regime. The bulletin's opening statement declared, "We want to express our sincere apologies to our Asian sisters. We want to learn from and join in their struggles. We declare the establishment of a new women's movement on March first. This day when Korean women risked their lives for national independence from Japanese colonial rule marks the start of our determined efforts." Cited in Mackie, *Feminism in Modern Japan*, 203. Matsui used the category of "Asian women" to build de-imperialist and anti-capitalist forms of solidarity. However, as Laura Hyun Yi Kang argues, the category can be problematic insofar as it erases differences among women in the region and has been a tool of both US and Japanese imperial projects. See Kang, *Traffic in Asian Women*. For a discussion of how the category of "Asian women" was born through the "entanglement of Japanese empire and the U.S. empire," see Yoneyama, *Cold War Ruins*, 140.

52. *Onna Erosu* (Woman Eros) offered a forum for critical discussions of marriage, sexuality, prostitution, labor, and politics. The title of Matsui's *Onna Erosu* essay was later translated into English as "Why I Oppose Kisaeng Tours: Exposing Economic and Sexual Aggression against South Korean Women." See Matsui, *Why I Oppose Kisaeng Tours*.

53. Mackie, *Feminism in Modern Japan*.

54. Bunch, foreword.

55. The event was coordinated by Diane Russell, a colleague of Barry's in the anti-pornography movement. Barry worked with Russell to cofound the San Francisco–based Women against Violence in Pornography and Media in 1977.

56. Russell and Van de Ven, *Crimes against Women*, xv.

57. Barry, "Network Defines Its Issues," 44.

58. Barry, *Female Sexual Slavery*, 6. See also Suchland, *Economies of Violence*, 31.

59. Matsui, "Watashi wa naze kīsen kankō ni hantai suru no ka," 68. Matsui was not alone in citing, and being moved by, this assertation by Korean women activists. In a 1974 essay, Takahashi Kikue, who was also involved in the anti-sex-tourism movement, cites Korean women's groups as having written, "Nihon dansei wa keizai-teki yūetsu o tanomi ni mizukara yokubō o manzoku saseru tame ni Kankoku josei o sei no dorei to shiteiru" (Relying on their economic superiority, Japanese men use Korean women as sex slaves to satisfy their own desires). See Takahashi, *Baibaishun mondai ni torikumu*, 12. In a 1996 interview, Takahashi describes being approached by Korean activist Kim Yoon-ok at the 1973 Korea-Japan National Council of Christian Churches conference. Kim appealed to her to take action, saying, "Nihon no dansei wa wagakuni no josei o sei no dorei ni shiteiru" (Japanese men are making women in our country their sex slaves). See Takahashi, "Josei no jinken to kīsen kankō hantai undō," 315.

60. Barry, *Female Sexual Slavery*.

61. Matsui engaged with US-based globalist feminists through her activism, and she did later use the expression "sexual slavery" to describe the experiences of Asian migrant

women working in Japan's sex industry. See, for instance, Matsui, *Women in the New Asia*, 19. However, when Matsui used this term, she insisted first and foremost that the women's experiences be understood in relation to specific geopolitical histories and political-economic relations between Japan and their countries of origin. She did not frame sexual slavery as a singular form of universal oppression against women as Barry and Bunch did. Matsui also refused to see Filipina entertainers in Japan "only as victims," explaining that she was "amazed by their strength" and "impressed" by their "great vitality" in following their dreams of finding success in Japan. See Matsui, *Women in the New Asia*, 49.

62. Barry explains that she offered the framework of female sexual slavery precisely because it could encompass "international traffic in women *and* forced street prostitution taken together." See Barry, "Network Defines Its Issues," 7 (emphasis in original). For further discussion, see Suchland, *Economies of Violence*.

63. Kondō Uri, a member of Matsui's Asian Women's Association, worked with Barry to organize five sessions on female sexual slavery, trafficking in women, and sex tourism (see Bunch and Castley, introduction). Barry had initially endeavored to get jurisdiction for complaints on what she called "sexual slavery" moved to the UN Status of Women Commission, angered that these complaints were under the jurisdiction of the Human Rights Commission, which was, in her words, "backlogged and male-dominated" (Barry, "International Feminism," 49). She also lambasted the UN, arguing that it "will not interfere with its member nations' abusive practices toward women when its officials are themselves privately carrying out these practices" (Barry, *Female Sexual Slavery*, 67).

64. Bunch and Castley, introduction, 9.

65. Bunch and Castley, introduction, 10.

66. Bunch, "Network Strategies and Organizing against Female Sexual Slavery," 58.

67. Bunch, "Network Strategies and Organizing against Female Sexual Slavery," 58. Matsui was supposed to attend; however, at the last minute she could not, and another representative from the AWA took her place.

68. See Matsui, "Why I Oppose Kisaeng Tours," 64–72.

69. Bunch and Castley, introduction, 10.

70. During the 1980s and early 1990s, feminists in the United States also began to write critically about the treatment of women as a unified group at the expense of considering how the category was crosscut by race, class, sexuality, citizenship, and other categories of difference. See Crenshaw, "Demarginalizing the Intersection of Race and Sex"; Hull, Scott, and Smith, *All the Women Are White*; Mohanty, *Third World Women and the Politics of Feminism*; Moraga and Anzaldúa, *This Bridge Called My Back*.

71. Bunch, cited in Keck and Sikkink, *Activists beyond Borders*, 177.

72. Kang, *Traffic in Asian Women*, 7.

73. See Bunch, *Passionate Politics*, 335–44.

74. Bunch, *Passionate Politics*, 341.

75. Bunch, "Network Strategies and Organizing against Female Sexual Slavery," 53.

76. Russell and Van de Ven, *Crimes against Women*, xi.

77. St. James, cited in Russell and Van de Ven, *Crimes against Women*, 179, 180.

78. See Russell and Van de Ven, *Crimes against Women*, 175–77.

79. Russell and Van de Ven, *Crimes against Women*, 175.

80. Bunch, "Network Strategies and Organizing against Female Sexual Slavery," 55.

81. Bunch, "Network Strategies and Organizing against Female Sexual Slavery," 53 (emphasis in orginal).

82. Keck and Sikkink, *Activists beyond Borders*, 166.

83. Cmiel, "Emergence of Human Rights Politics in the United States."

84. Moyn, *Last Utopia*, 275. Duncan Bell argues that what is widely glossed as liberalism is upon closer look an invented tradition that lacks a historically stable core (Bell, "What Is Liberalism?"). Samuel Moyn similarly maintains that the term has been used to refer to an internally diverse range of competing and sometimes contradictory claims by those identifying as socialists, democrats, republicans, conservatives, feminists, and even anarchists (Moyn, *Last Utopia*). Others have demonstrated that in different times and places, liberalism has been used to justify both imperialist logics and forms of racial, gendered, sexual, and national exclusion, and to reject these positions (see Bell, "What Is Liberalism?"; Brown, *States of Injury*; Mehta, "Liberal Strategies of Exclusion"; Mehta, *Liberalism and Empire*; Povinelli, *Cunning of Recognition*; Povinelli, *Empire of Love*). Unlike earlier statist liberal traditions, which tended to reject appeals to extrasocial and nontemporalized norms, the new liberalism that emerged from the ideological wars fought against totalitarianism during the Second World War and the Cold War relied on global universals to fill the vacuum created by the loss of confidence in imperialism as a mode of good governance (see Moyn, *Last Utopia*).

85. Moyn, *Last Utopia*, 275. See also Bell, "What Is Liberalism?" Until the mid-twentieth century, Locke had been widely viewed as a Whig apologist rather than as part of a liberal tradition. See Moyn, *Last Utopia*.

86. Bell, "What Is Liberalism?"; Brown, "'The Most We Can Hope For . . .'"; Moyn, *Last Utopia*.

87. Cmiel, "Emergence of Human Rights Politics in the United States."

88. Eckel, "International League for the Rights of Man, Amnesty International, and the Changing Fate of Human Rights Activism."

89. Buergenthal, "Evolving International Human Rights System"; Cmiel, "Emergence of Human Rights Politics in the United States"; Kelly, "1973 Chilean Coup and the Origins of Transnational Human Rights Activism."

90. Cmiel, "Emergence of Human Rights Politics in the United States."

91. Keck and Sikkink, *Activists beyond Borders*; Merry, *Human Rights and Gender Violence*.

92. Bunch, "Women's Rights as Human Rights," 487.

93. This shift parallels a broader shift among feminist activists in the United States toward international advocacy and NGO-ization in the later decades of the twentieth century. See Alvarez, "Advocating Feminism'"; Bernal and Grewal, "Introduction"; Halley et al., "From the International to the Local"; Lang, "The NGOization of Feminism."

94. Russell and Van de Ven, *Crimes against Women*, 218.

95. Gold, *Passionate Politics*.

96. Matsui's activism derived from her deep identification as a Japanese citizen. Yet her sense of Japanese identity was very different from those promulgated by the Japanese state or Japanese corporations. She strove to create a sense of Japanese identity that was deeply self-reflexive, open, cosmopolitan, and committed to acting in ways that were socially,

politically, and economically responsible to all. See Matsui, "Josei hogo jigyō to josei no jinken"; Matsui, *Ai to ikari tatakau yūki*.

97. Mackie, *Feminism in Modern Japan*. By 1987, the AWA had five hundred members, including attorneys, students, housewives, scholars, entertainers, and nuns. See Iyori, "The Traffic in Japayuki-San." In addition to publishing *Asian Women's Liberation*, the organization also held monthly public study meetings, engaged in protests, and networked with other women's groups in Japan and abroad. See Iyori, "The Traffic in Japayuki-San."

98. Faier, *Intimate Encounters*.

99. Chan-Tibergien, *Gender and Human Rights Politics in Japan*; Douglass and Roberts, *Japan and Global Migration*; Shipper, *Fighting for Foreigners*; Yun Chai, "Asian-Pacific Feminist Coalition Politics."

100. Iyori, "The Traffic in Japayuki-San"; Yun Chai, "Asian-Pacific Feminist Coalition Politics."

101. Ajia Josei Shiryō Sentā, *Pekin hatsu, Nihon no onnatachi e*; Babior, "Women of a Tokyo Shelter"; Ohshima and Francis, *Japan through the Eyes of Women Migrant Workers*.

102. Founding member Ninotchka Rosca brought the phrase to the 1993 UN World Conference on Human Rights in Vienna, where it gained international prominence. It was later popularized at the Beijing conference by then first lady of the United States, Hillary Clinton. Moreover, women's groups in Japan and the Philippines are not alone in asserting claims based on women's rights. Many women's groups in the Global South have lobbied governments and international organizations for recognition of them. See Falcón, *Power Interrupted*; Merry, *Human Rights and Gender Violence*, 65.

103. Ohshima and Francis, *Japan through the Eyes of Women Migrant Workers*, 184. See also Babior, "Women of a Tokyo Shelter"; Shipper, *Fighting for Foreigners*.

104. Iyori, "The Traffic in Japayuki-San."

105. For many women's groups in the Global South, the fight for women's rights is inseparable from the fight against racism and national and global political-economic inequalities. See Falcón, *Power Interrupted*; Suchland, *Economies of Violence*.

106. Ajia no onnatachi no kai [Asian Women's Association], "Ajia kara no dekasegi onnatachi naze Nihon ni kuru no ka? (Tokushū)"; Yun Chai, "Asian-Pacific Feminist Coalition Politics."

107. Ajia no onnatachi no kai, "Ajia kara no dekasegi onnatachi naze Nihon ni kuru no ka? (Tokushū)."

108. De Dios, cited in Imam, "The Diplomat," 34.

109. See also Aguilar, "Export of Philippine Women"; Pascual and Glipo, "WTO and Philippine Agriculture."

110. Bello et al., *Anti-development State*; Pascual and Glipo, "WTO and Philippine Agriculture."

111. Aguilar, "Export of Philippine Women"; Pascual and Glipo, "WTO and Philippine Agriculture."

112. Imam, "The Diplomat," 34.

113. Imam, "The Diplomat," 34.

114. De Dios, cited in Imam, "The Diplomat," 34. See also De Dios, "Revisiting the Trafficking of Women." De Dios and others involved in CATW-AP were drawn to a

human rights model in part because Amnesty International had pressured the Philippine government to observe their human rights while they were imprisoned during the Marcos regime. See Imam, "The Diplomat."

115. See Barry, "International Feminism."

116. Barry, "International Feminism," 40.

117. Kang, *Traffic in Asian Women*, 15.

118. Russell and Van de Ven, *Crimes against Women*.

119. Barry, "International Feminism," 37.

120. Barry, "International Feminism," 37.

121. Suchland, *Economies of Violence*.

122. Bunch and Reilly, *Demanding Accountability*, 4.

123. Bunch, "Network Strategies and Organizing against Female Sexual Slavery," 58.

124. Bunch and Reilly, *Demanding Accountability*, 14. Testimonies were offered both by women who wished to speak about their own experiences and by advocates. Each participant prepared a ten-minute statement and, when possible, also forwarded written testimonies, biographies, and photographs to be included in media packets. Representing different regions of the world, the panel moderators who introduced each session had been active in the Global Campaign. They included, in order of the sessions: Monica O'Conner (Irish Women's Aid); Nelia Sancho Liao (Asian Women Human Rights Council); Gladys Acosta (Latin American Institute for Alternative Legal Services); Florence Butegwa (Women, Law and Development in Africa); and Charlotte Bunch (Center for Women's Global Leadership). See Bunch and Reilly, *Demanding Accountability*, 13.

125. The Center for Women's Global Leadership helped form an International Coordinating Committee (ICC) to collaborate in selecting Global Tribunal speakers. The ICC included representatives from thirteen NGOs in countries across the world, including the Sudan, Zimbabwe, the Bahamas, the Netherlands, Costa Rica, Pakistan, the Philippines, Canada, and the United States. The Committee included Asma Abdel Halim (WiLDAF, Sudan); Marion Bethel (CAFRA, Bahamas); Florence Butegwa (WiLDAF, Zimbabwe); Roxanna Carrillo (UNIFEM); Winde Evenhuis (HOM, Netherlands); Alda Facio (ILANUD, Costa Rica); Hina Jilani (AGHS Legal Aid, Pakistan); Nelia Sancho Liao (Asian Women's Shelter Network); Annette Pypops (Match International Centre, Canada); Ana Sisnett (Fund for a Compassionate Society, USA); Maria Suarez (FIRE, Costa Rica); and Anne Walker (IWTC). See Bunch and Reilly, *Demanding Accountability*, 13).

126. Chew explained in her presentation that after this woman's job in the shipbuilding industry evaporated with the economic crisis in Poland, she had gone to work in a restaurant in Yugoslavia, where she was approached by a man offering her the same kind of work in Germany for much higher pay. She had given him her passport and traveled with him into Germany, where she was told she had to work as a prostitute. The man had raped her and taken photographs, which he threatened to send to her mother if she did not comply. The man then sold her to another man who brought her to the Netherlands, beat her, and forced her to work in a "window." She eventually escaped, but the Dutch government refused to recognize her as a political refugee. Finally, with the help of STV, she pressed charges against the men who had trafficked her and was permitted to stay in the Netherlands through the trial. See Bunch and Reilly, *Demanding Accountability*, 51–52.

127. Although many human rights NGOs viewed the Vienna conference as a failure, the Global Tribunal prompted important shifts in conceptualizations of human rights with significant implications for a global feminist movement against human trafficking. See Boyle, "Stock-Taking on Human Rights"; Finn, "Human Rights in Vienna."

128. Keck and Sikkink, *Activists beyond Borders*, 184.

129. Thomas and Beasley, "Domestic Violence as a Human Rights Issue."

130. Keck and Sikkink, *Activists beyond Borders*, 172.

131. This definition was established with Nuremberg. In the wake of the Holocaust, the possibilities of state-sponsored violence against a state's own citizens seemed most compelling and urgent. Beginning with the UN Charter, international human rights law developed to protect individual rights from limitations or abuse imposed on them by national governments. The human rights movement then developed to enforce governments' obligation to protect individual human rights by drawing attention to their violations of these duties under international law. International human rights covenants bind signatory states to respect all persons' human rights and to be accountable to the abuses of those rights. However, although international human rights law was ostensibly gender neutral—protecting all human beings—the origins and focus of the body of law on the behavior of centralized states had confined the practice of international human rights law to the public sphere. See Thomas and Beasley, "Domestic Violence as a Human Rights Issue."

132. Keck and Sikkink, *Activists beyond Borders*, 172–73. This shift was enabled by rulings on human rights over the previous decades and particularly from three significant cases decided by the Inter-American Court of Human Rights: *Velásquez-Rodríguez v. Honduras*, *Godínez-Cruz v. Honduras*, and *Fairén-Garbi and Solís-Corrales v. Honduras*. Before this point, under international law, government accountability for human rights abuses had been limited by the concept of state responsibility, which arose only when an act by an individual could be imputed to the state. Consequently, in traditional human rights practice, state governments were held accountable only for what they did directly or through an agent. Acts of purely private individuals against other private individuals, such as human trafficking, were outside the scope of international human rights law. Similarly, existing international bans on slavery and trafficking were difficult to enforce against acts of enslavement, indenture, labor exploitation, and servitude carried out by independently acting private citizens.

133. Bunch and Reilly, *Demanding Accountability*, 10.

134. Bunch and Reilly, *Demanding Accountability*, 10.

135. N. Lee, "Negotiating the Boundaries of Nation, Christianity, and Gender," 78.

136. Keck and Sikkink, *Activists beyond Borders*, 178. See also Pheterson, *Vindication of the Rights of Whores*. At the time of the Rotterdam Workshop, Barry had recognized that feminists should not be intervening in the lives of women who could leave sex work of their own accord. However, she soon adopted a position maintaining that a woman could never consent to prostitution; it was always coerced and sexually exploitative by a universal patriarchal system. With this position, Barry not only put herself at odds with those who claimed that their participation in sex industries was agentive but also alienated sex workers' rights activists. See Barry, *Prostitution of Sexuality*; Halley, "Rape at Rome."

137. Chew, "Reflections by an Anti-trafficking Activist."

138. Ralston and Keeble, *Reluctant Bedfellows*.

139. Roces, *Women's Movements in Asia*.

140. Ralston and Keeble, *Reluctant Bedfellows*, 64.

141. Roces, *Women's Movements in Asia*.

142. Roces, *Women's Movements in Asia*.

143. Roces, *Women's Movements in Asia*.

144. Delfin, Enriquez, and Jajurie, *A Primer on Prostitution*, 22, cited in Roces, *Women's Movements in Asia*, 274.

145. Keck and Sikkink, *Activists beyond Borders*, 186. Soon after, in 1994, the Organization of American States created the first "official" definition of "violence against women," which included not only rape, battery, sexual abuse, and torture but also forced prostitution and trafficking in persons. Keck and Sikkink, *Activists beyond Borders*, 173.

146. Coomaraswamy, *Report of the Special Rapporteur on Violence against Women*.

147. Coomaraswamy, *Report of the Special Rapporteur on Violence against Women*.

148. Charnysh, Lloyd, and Simmons, "Frames and Consensus Formation in International Relations."

149. Bunch and Douglas, "Interview."

150. Bunch and Douglas, "Interview," 12.

151. Keck and Sikkink, *Activists beyond Borders*.

152. Matsui, *Ai to ikari tatakau yūki*. In response, Matsui held a meeting before the Beijing conference for women in Asia to plan their agenda for the meeting together.

153. Keck and Sikkink, *Activists beyond Borders*, 198.

154. Matsui, *Women's Asia*, 4.

2. THE PROTOCOL'S COMPROMISES

1. This provision was important to activists like Gloria because the industry is unregulated by the government, and much abuse and exploitation occurs within it. Activists in the Philippines like Gloria believe that current political economic inequalities between most Philippine nationals and tourists, many of whom are Japanese and American men, render sex workers—the overwhelming majority of whom are women and children—too vulnerable to this abuse. Under the act, sex tourism is defined as "a program organized by travel and tourism-related establishments and individuals which consists of tourism packages or activities utilizing and offering escort and sexual services as enticement for tourists. This includes sexual services and practices offered during rest and recreation periods for members of the military." The act provides that it is illegal "to undertake or organize tours and travel plans consisting of tourism packages or activities for the purpose of utilizing and offering persons for prostitution, pornography or sexual exploitation." The act is also unique in that it outlaws "any act, transaction, scheme or design involving the use of a person by another" for the purposes of pornography, defined as "any representation, through publication, exhibition, cinematography, indecent shows, information technology, or by whatever means, of a person engaged in real or simulated explicit sexual activities or any representation of the sexual parts of a person for primarily sexual purposes." See Anti-trafficking in Persons Act of 2003, Republic Act No. 9208, Twelfth

Congress of the Republic of the Philippines, May 26, 2003, https://www.wcwonline.org/pdf/lawcompilation/PhilippinesRepublicActNo9208AntiTrafficking.pdf.

2. See Halley, "Preface: Introducing Governance Feminism," ix.

3. Bernstein, *Brokered Subjects*.

4. Shamir, "Anti-trafficking in Israel."

5. See Basu, "Globalization of the Local/Localization of the Global"; Hemment, "Global Civil Society and the Local Costs"; Ong, "Strategic Sisterhood"; Bernal and Grewal, "Introduction."

6. DeStefano, *War on Human Trafficking*; Charnysh, Lloyd, and Simmons, "Frames and Consensus Formation in International Relations."

7. Neudek, Zyhlarz-Shaw, and Lovell, "World Ministerial Conference."

8. Charnysh, Lloyd, and Simmons, "Frames and Consensus Formation in International Relations."

9. UN General Assembly, Resolution 55/25.

10. Kaye, "Contemporary Forms of Slavery in Argentina."

11. Kaye, "Contemporary Forms of Slavery in Argentina."

12. DeStefano, *War on Human Trafficking*.

13. UN General Assembly, "Draft Elements for an Agreement on the Prevention, Suppression and Punishment of International Trafficking in Women and Children, Supplementary to the Convention against Transnational Organized Crime," 1.

14. UN General Assembly, "Draft Elements for an Agreement on the Prevention, Suppression and Punishment of International Trafficking in Women and Children," 3.

15. Suchland, *Economies of Violence*.

16. The 1970s and 1980s had witnessed an expansion of sex tourism across the globe on account of several factors: the presence of US military bases overseas, and increases in tourism in some parts of the world, especially on account of the rise of the civil aviation industry and rising prosperity in some countries, coupled with debt crises and structural adjustment policies in others. See Suchland, *Economies of Violence*.

17. IOM, *Trafficking and Prostitution*, 3, cited in Suchland, *Economies of Violence*, 63.

18. See Suchland, *Economies of Violence*.

19. UN General Assembly, "Draft Elements for an International Legal Instrument against Illegal Trafficking and Transport of Migrants," 2.

20. DeStefano, *War on Human Trafficking*.

21. Suchland, *Economies of Violence*.

22. For further discussion, see Skinner, "Fight to End Global Slavery."

23. For further discussion of this history, see Suchland, *Economies of Violence*.

24. Stolz, "Educating Policymakers and Setting the Criminal Justice Policymaking Agenda."

25. Stolz, "Educating Policymakers and Setting the Criminal Justice Policymaking Agenda."

26. See Lobasz, *Constructing Human Trafficking*. As Jennifer Lobasz explains, despite the recognition of these forms of migrant labor exploitation as human rights violations, the Clinton administration's approach still externalized the problem, understanding it as originating outside the United States and not tied to US political-economic policies, and representing traffickers as foreign and often co-nationals of their victims.

27. UN General Assembly, "Draft Protocol to Combat International Trafficking in Women and Children Supplementary to the United Nations Convention on Transnational Organized Crime."

28. UN General Assembly, "Draft Protocol to Combat International Trafficking in Women and Children Supplementary to the United Nations Convention on Transnational Organized Crime," 2 (my emphasis).

29. UN General Assembly, "Draft Elements for an Agreement on the Prevention, Suppression and Punishment of International Trafficking in Women and Children, Supplementary to the Convention against Transnational Organized Crime," 2, 5.

30. Lobasz, *Constructing Human Trafficking*.

31. UN General Assembly, "Draft Protocol to Combat International Trafficking in Women and Children Supplementary to the United Nations Convention on Transnational Organized Crime."

32. UN General Assembly, "Draft Protocol to Combat International Trafficking in Women and Children Supplementary to the United Nations Convention on Transnational Organized Crime."

33. Although not discussed in this book, a third supplementary protocol against the illicit manufacturing of and trafficking in firearms was also attached.

34. US domestic policy on prostitution would shift under the George W. Bush administration, which prioritized the prostitution-abolitionist position taken by evangelical Christians and radical feminists. Prostitution-abolitionists such as Laura Lederer were appointed to key advisory positions within the State Department dealing with human trafficking. Policy decisions within the United States shifted toward abolishing prostitution, and organizations receiving government funding were required to sign an anti-prostitution pledge. This shift would eventually put the US position in some ways at odds with the UN Trafficking Protocol, the negotiations for which had visibly included sex workers and sex workers' rights activists. See Hughes, "Combating Sex Trafficking"; Lobasz, *Constructing Human Trafficking*.

35. DeStefano, *War on Human Trafficking*; Charnysh, Lloyd, and Simmons, "Frames and Consensus Formation in International Relations."

36. UN General Assembly, Resolution 55/25, 32.

37. UNICRI and AIC, *Human Smuggling and Trafficking from the Philippines*, 4. The program was developed by the Centre for International Crime Prevention (CICP) and the United Nations Interregional Crime and Justice Research Institute (UNICRI). The former was tasked with organizing technical cooperation activities; the latter oversaw the development of a standardized research methodology and the coordination of research across various projects involved in the program.

38. For discussion of liberal internationalist understandings of human rights, see Brown, "'The Most We Can Hope For...'"; Bell, "What Is Liberalism?"; Moyn, *Last Utopia*.

39. Suchland, *Economies of Violence*.

40. DeStefano, *War on Human Trafficking*; Joutsen, "Four Transitions in the United Nations Crime Programme."

41. Joutsen, "Four Transitions."

42. Joutsen, "Four Transitions."

43. Joutsen, "Four Transitions."

44. UNICRI and AIC, *Human Smuggling and Trafficking from the Philippines*, 4. See also UN General Assembly, Resolution 54/131; UN Economic and Social Council, *Report on the Eleventh Session*. The program also initiated for governments, NGOs, and other concerned institutions a "series of 'demonstration projects'" that were implemented in different countries (see UNICRI and AIC, "Human Smuggling and Trafficking from the Philippines," 2). These projects aimed to assist governments to (a) counteract groups involved in human smuggling and trafficking, (b) strengthen crime prevention strategies, and (c) improve victim witness protection and assistance. The first of the demonstration projects was a pilot project in the Philippines, the initial activity of which was a "Rapid Assessment" report about human trafficking and smuggling in the country, with an eye toward identifying the role of transnational organized criminal groups so that "appropriate technical cooperation activities" could be identified. See UNICRI and AIC, "Human Smuggling and Trafficking from the Philippines," 5.

45. UNICRI and AIC, "Human Smuggling and Trafficking from the Philippines," 4.

46. UNICRI and AIC, "Human Smuggling and Trafficking from the Philippines," 3.

47. UN, "UN Convention against Transnational Organized Crime—General Assembly, 62nd Plenary Meeting."

48. Lauriola, "Address on the Elaboration of a Convention against Transnational Organized Crime."

49. Annelise Riles has argued that in the realm of international law, formal aesthetic conventions of pattern and design can generate consensus in ways that content and doctrine never can. Consequently, these conventions have come to be accepted means of generating agreement among states on a global scale. See Riles, *The Network Inside Out*, 70–91.

50. For further discussion, see Chuang, "United States as Global Sheriff."

51. UN General Assembly, Resolution 55/25, 32.

52. Traces of the disagreement among feminists are palpable in the protocol's inclusion of the redundant "women and children" in its title, as mentioned previously. The phrase was added to satisfy feminists focused on sex trafficking. By including this and other circuitous phrasings, the definition remained sufficiently ambiguous about forced prostitution to satisfy people on both the CATW and the GAATW sides. For a discussion of these debates, see Musto, *Control and Protect*; Gallagher, *International Law of Human Trafficking*.

53. Falcón, *Power Interrupted*.

54. The note was distributed just ahead of the fourth of eleven sessions of the Vienna Process, through which the convention and its protocols were drafted.

55. UN General Assembly, "Informal Note by the United Nations High Commissioner for Human Rights," 3.

56. UN General Assembly, "Informal Note," 1, 3.

57. See Bunch, "Women's Rights and Gender."

58. Bunch, "Women's Rights and Gender," 6–7.

59. Raymond, "Guide to the New UN Trafficking Protocol," 4.

60. Raymond, "Guide to the New UN Trafficking Protocol," 7.

61. Raymond, "Guide to the New UN Trafficking Protocol," 3.

62. Hughes, "Combating Sex Trafficking," 28; Lederer, "Addressing Demand"; Raymond, "Guide to the New UN Trafficking Protocol."

63. Chew, "Reflections by an Anti-trafficking Activist," 74.

64. Gallagher, "Human Rights and the New UN Protocols," 1004.

65. For further discussion see Gallagher, *International Law of Human Trafficking*.

66. Gallagher, "Human Rights and the New UN Protocols," 1004. Some feminists and human rights activists have resisted the use of indicators, expressing concerns about lack of data, oversimplification, and bias. For instance, see Alston, "Ships Passing in the Night"; Green, "What We Talk about When We Talk about Indicators," 1082–84; Merry, *Seductions of Quantification*; Rosga and Satterthwaite, "Trust in Indicators." However, during the 1990s, interest in them grew among committees monitoring human rights compliance and corporate social responsibility. Some, including the UN's Office of the High Commissioner of Human Rights, aimed to use these measurements to facilitate the analysis of information and increase accountability. For a discussion of how indicators make policy solutions appear to be simple and objective technical matters of measuring a problem, establishing standards, and developing appropriate protocols and procedures, see Merry, *Seductions of Quantification*.

67. Gallagher, "Two Cheers for the Trafficking Protocol," 1.

68. Gallagher, "Human Rights and the New UN Protocols," 1004.

69. UN General Assembly, "Informal Note by the United Nations High Commissioner for Human Rights," 1.

70. UN General Assembly, "Informal Note," 1.

71. UN General Assembly, "Informal Note," 2.

72. UN General Assembly, "Informal Note," 2.

73. UN General Assembly, "Informal Note," 3.

74. UN General Assembly, "Informal Note," 4.

75. UN General Assembly, "Informal Note," 5.

76. UN General Assembly, "Informal Note," 4.

77. Human rights and labor rights activists often expressed more complex understandings of human trafficking than those articulated in the protocol. For instance, in a presentation at the ILO Symposium on Trafficking in Human Beings in Tokyo, Japan, in September 2003, Roger Plant, then the head of the ILO's Special Action Programme to Combat Forced Labour, stressed the complexity of the issue of human trafficking, the importance of addressing all forms of forced labor, and the "huge structural problems" that underlay them. He explained, "We cannot delude ourselves that a plethora of ministerial meetings, declarations and action plans is in itself the answer to the gruesome problem of trafficking in Europe as in the rest of the world." Plant, "Trafficking in Destination Countries," 2. However, the ILO had been criticized for its position on sex work and thus maintained a low profile during the negotiations. Chuang, "United States as Global Sheriff." Ultimately, despite his reservations, Plant stressed the "urgent need to reach consensus" and to "develop comprehensive and integrated programmes across the board in both origin and destination countries." Plant, "Trafficking in Destination Countries," 2–5.

78. George W. Bush was then president of the United States, and fighting human trafficking was a key component of a larger agenda embraced by his evangelical base, which included abolishing prostitution.

79. See Merry, *Seductions of Quantification*; Warren "Trafficking in Persons."

80. Gloria Reyes's secondhand story should not be dismissed as isolated, nor should we assume that the grassroots NGO staff in the Philippines acted exceptionally. The difficulty of calculating these numbers came up in other interviews that I had as well. For instance, US State Department employee Amy O'Neill Richard shared the challenges that she faced in the late 1990s when she worked with the CIA's Center for the Study of Intelligence to produce a report assessing the scale and scope of human trafficking in the United States to support the drafting of the US Trafficking Victims Protection Act of 2000. Richard's findings, published in her 1999 report *International Trafficking in Women to the United States: A Contemporary Manifestation of Slavery and Organized Crime*, became the baseline for assessing anti-human-trafficking efforts by the US government. In our interview, Ms. Richard openly and on the record spoke of the difficulties that she faced estimating the phenomena, the irregularities inherent in the process, and the diplomatic and geopolitical considerations that affected US trafficking reporting and policy. Similarly, a UNESCO study concluded, "Numbers take on a life of their own, gaining acceptance through repetition, often with little inquiry into their derivations. Journalists, bowing to the pressures of editors, demand numbers, any number. Organizations feel compelled to supply them, lending false precisions and spurious authority to many reports." Cited in DeStefano, *War on Human Trafficking*, 13.

81. Falcón, *Power Interrupted*.

82. Falcón, *Power Interrupted*, 158.

83. Cited in Falcón, *Power Interrupted*, 160.

84. See Falcón, *Power Interrupted*, 158.

85. Mazower, *No Enchanted Palace*.

86. Kelty, "Against Networks," 10.

87. See Ahmed, *On Being Included*.

88. See, for example, Piot, "'Right' to Be Trafficked"; Vanderhurst, *Unmaking Migrants*.

3. THE INSTITUTIONAL LIFE OF SUFFERING

1. Grugel and Peruzzotti, "Domestic Politics of International Human Rights Law," 179. See also Flowers, *Refugees, Women, and Weapons*, 87.

2. Raustiala and Slaughter, "International Law, International Relations and Compliance," 539.

3. Finnemore and Sikkink, "International Norm Dynamics and Political Change," 892. See also Flowers, *Refugees, Women, and Weapons*; Flowers, "International Human Rights Norms in Japan."

4. Flowers, *Refugees, Women, and Weapons*; Flowers, "International Human Rights Norms in Japan"; Tsutsui, *Rights Make Might*.

5. Dawes, *That the World May Know*; I. Feldman, *Governing Gaza*; Navaro-Yashin, "Affect in the Civil Service"; Ticktin, *Casualties of Care*.

6. Dawes, *That the World May Know*; I. Feldman, *Governing Gaza*; Malkki, *Need to Help*; Navaro-Yashin, "Affect in the Civil Service"; Ticktin, *Casualties of Care*.

7. See Bradley, *World Reimagined*; Fassin, *Humanitarian Reason*; Ticktin, *Casualties of Care*.

8. Fassin, *Humanitarian Reason*, 247. See also Bradley, *World Reimagined*; Ticktin, *Casualties of Care*. Fassin and Rechtman explain that in the 1980s and 1990s, forms of testimony and witnessing introduced with the Nuremberg trials came to inform new understandings of trauma. In 1980, post-traumatic stress disorder (PTSD) was first entered into the DSM. The development of this diagnosis signaled a growing conviction in the psychological sciences of the long-lasting and consequential imprint that trauma could leave on an individual. This understanding of suffering became a cause for necessary intervention and created an equivalence of victims who could then be treated according to established protocols. See Fassin and Rechtman, *Empire of Trauma*. For a discussion of how these assumptions about the universality of suffering have come to inform humanitarianism and certain movements for human rights, see Ticktin, *Casualties of Care*.

9. Mrs. Saito permitted me to take notes on her comments but asked that I not record her. Mr. Lopez permitted me to record him.

10. The Japanese government has a long documented record of dismissing the rights of undocumented migrants. See Sellek and Weiner, "Migrant Workers"; Hatsuse, "Reciprocity and Migrant Workers"; Zuo, "Migrant Workers 'Exploited' in Japan." One impetus behind migrants' rights activism in Japan during the 1990s was a series of cases reported in the newspapers in which undocumented Thai women were criminally prosecuted without adequate interpretation during their interrogations and trials for killing their Thai *mama-san* (bar manager) while trying to escape because she had locked them in an apartment and forced them to sexually service customers. See Dinan, *Owed Justice*; Fukami, *Tsūyaku no hitsuyō wa arimasen*. Japanese activists, including Matsui, specifically mentioned these cases as key illustrations of both the exploitation faced by migrant women in the Japanese sex industry and the injustices that these women experience under Japanese law. See Kainō, "Hajimeni"; Matsui, "Josei hogo jigyō to josei no jinken"; Mutō, "Hogo wo motometa josei-tachi no genjitsu"; Ōtsu, "Minkan sherutā kara mieru Nihon shakai no jinshin baibai no jittai"; Ōtsu, "Hajimeni"; Saito, "Jinshin baibai higaisha to wa dare ka?"

11. This phrasing was Mr. Lopez's translation, which I wrote in my notebook during the interview. The emphasis was in the original.

12. See Ahmed, "Affective Economies"; Clarke, "Transnational Yoruba Revivalism and the Diasporic Politics of Heritage"; Faier, "Filipina Migrants in Rural Japan and Their Professions of Love"; Mankekar, *Unsettling India*; Stoler, *Carnal Knowledge and Imperial Power*. Like what Raymond Williams has called "structure[s] of feelings," these intensities precede and exceed subjectification; they are instead carried in signs and circulate among bodies. For Williams's discussion of "structure[s] of feeling," see Williams, *The Long Revolution*, 64–88. For a discussion of affect that extends Williams, see Mankekar, *Unsettling India*.

13. See Ahmed, "Affective Economies"; Mankekar, *Unsettling India*; Clarke, *Affective Justice*.

14. For studies of the cultural specificity of suffering, see Scheper-Hughes, *Death without Weeping*; Kleinman, Das, and Lock, *Social Suffering*. For work on the cultural and historical specificity of empathy, see Throop, "Latitudes of Loss."

15. Throop, "Latitudes of Loss."

16. Ahmed, "Affective Economies," 120.

17. Vance, "Innocence and Experience," 204.

18. Dawes, *That the World May Know*, 25. See also Ticktin, *Casualties of Care*.

19. James, *Democratic Insecurities*, 33.

20. Fregoso, "For a Pluriversal Declaration of Human Rights"; Speed, *Incarcerated Stories*.

21. Speed, *Incarcerated Stories*.

22. Fregoso, "For a Pluriversal Declaration of Human Rights."

23. See Agustin, *Sex at the Margins*; Bernstein, *Brokered Subjects*; Chapkis, "Trafficking, Migration, and the Law"; Doezema, "Loose Women or Lost Women?"; Mahdavi, *Gridlock*; Musto, *Control and Protect*; Parreñas, *Illicit Flirtations*; Kempadoo, Sanghera, and Pattanaik, *Trafficking and Prostitution Reconsidered*; Soderlund, "Running from the Rescuers"; Ticktin, *Casualties of Care*; Vance, "Innocence and Experience."

24. Ticktin, *Casualties of Care*.

25. The precedent for using testimonies of personal suffering as a strategy for compelling political and legal change was established with the Nuremberg trials. Personal accounts of life in Nazi concentration camps set the stage for the formal development of international human rights law by serving as evidence of the Nazis' crimes against humanity. In the 1960s and 1970s, Amnesty International built on this precedent by using personal testimonials to argue against torture and for the release of prisoners of conscience. For instance, in its country reports, the organization began to combine objective data from its fact-finding missions with direct testimonials by victims of human rights abuses, relying on personal narratives—including photos, names, and graphic descriptions of torture, rape, and killing—to encourage readers to identify with the suffering of others. During the 1980s and 1990s, globalist feminists borrowed from these models and began using testimonies and oral histories in political protest as forms of evidence of women's trauma, abuse, and victimization to lobby the UN and state governments to address violence against women. The Global Tribunal in Vienna, described in chapter 1, is a key example of the use of this strategy by feminists. Lin Lap Chew's presentation of the testimony of a Polish woman who had been trafficked set the stage for such accounts to be used as political tools. For a discussion of the history of how Amnesty International built on the precedents set by the Nuremberg trials, see Bradley, *World Reimagined*. For a discussion of how feminists borrowed from this model and began using personal testimonies to lobby the international community, see Barry, Bunch, and Castley, *International Feminism*; Bunch and Reilly, *Demanding Accountability*; Roces, "Prostitution, Women's Movements and the Victim Narrative in the Philippines."

26. For a discussion of how the international human rights regime has altered the political landscape of social movements in Japan by empowering domestic actors, shifting their self-understanding, and reorienting their goals, see Tsutsui, *Rights Make Might*.

27. Lynn Hunt argues that the emergence of the epistolary novel in England during this time helped foster a new emotional regime of empathy that became a basis for the development of notions of universal human rights. This new narrative form transformed the ways that people made sense of themselves in relation to others by inviting readers to identify with the protagonist of the text. See Hunt, *Inventing Human Rights*. Similarly, Thomas Laqueur argues that humanitarianism has roots in late eighteenth-century

Europe, when "human" came to be a shorthand not simply for a bearer of rights but also for "the ethical subject." See Laqueur, "Mourning, Pity, and the Work of Narrative in the Making of 'Humanity,'" 38.

28. Mr. Lopez's comments reminded me of the position toward human rights taken by many in the Global South, who stress the need for greater recognition of those rights protected under the International Covenant on Economic, Social and Cultural Rights (ICESCR), as opposed to those that fall under the International Covenant on Civil and Political Rights (ICCPR) prioritized by countries in the Global North. The ICCPR protects civil and political rights, ensures the liberty and security of persons, and protects against cruel and unusual punishment and forced labor or servitude, among other protections; however, the ICESCR maintains entitlement to a quality of life, including an adequate standard of living, rights to the highest attainable standards of mental and physical health, and the right to fair and just work conditions. Violations of the latter human rights are oven overlooked and even dismissed, even when they can make people vulnerable to violations of their civil and political rights. For a discussion, see Chuang, "United States as Global Sheriff."

29. Tolentino, "Migrant Women in Japan," 25.

30. Tolentino, "Migrant Women in Japan," 25.

31. Tolentino, "Migrant Women in Japan."

32. Tolentino, "Migrant Women in Japan," 25.

33. Cited in Kelley, *Scorecard Diplomacy*, 223.

34. 150 Cong. Rec. S9213–S9214 (September 14, 2004) (statement of Sen. Kennedy).

35. For a discussion of how immigration and visa laws make migrants personally and financially vulnerable, see Menjívar and Abrego. "Legal Violence"; Parreñas, *Illicit Flirtations*.

36. See, for instance, Brysk, *Speaking Rights to Power*.

37. See Hartman, *Scenes of Subjection*, 19–20.

38. See also Gupta, *Red Tape*.

4. A ROADMAP

1. See US Department of State, *Trafficking in Persons Report, June 2007*, 42.

2. See Embassy Tokyo, "MOFA Presents Talking Points for Upcoming G/TIP Visit of Amb. Lagon"; Embassy Tokyo, "G/TIP Ambassador Lagon's July 2 Meeting with the Japanese Government." Compiling the *TIP Report* is a tedious process of assimilating data gathered from various sources, including, by necessity, the Japanese government. To produce its 2007 *TIP Report* on Japan, the US embassy in Tokyo documented that it had dedicated 207 hours of variously ranked staff time to researching trafficking issues, developing and implementing TIP programming and training, and coordinating with contacts. For details, see Embassy Tokyo, "2007 *TIP Report*: Japan (March 9)."

3. The 2007 *TIP Report* had not been entirely critical of the Japanese government. Reports issued before 2005 had faulted Japan for uniformly deporting trafficking victims as "illegal immigrants," failing to provide any assistance to victims, and not prosecut-ing traffickers. In 2004, the *TIP Report* also noted that Japan lacked an official, clearly designed policy to address human trafficking, had a large trafficking problem that

involved organized crime, and was not employing resources to address the issue. It again maintained that the Japanese government "offered victims of sexual slavery little in the way of legal advice, psychological or financial support" and instead deported them as "illegal aliens." See US Department of State, *Trafficking in Persons Report, June 2004*, 97. After Japan adopted its Action Plan, the Japanese government had begun recognizing as "trafficking victims" a small cross-section of migrants whose circumstances came to the attention of police or immigration authorities. The 2005 TIP Report applauded Japan for this effort, and the 2007 TIP Report similarly and diplomatically stated that Japan showed "modest progress in advancing anti-trafficking reforms" (124). However, in 2006, the TIP Report returned to concerns that traffickers were not being prosecuted, and by 2007, when numbers of identified victims dropped on an annual basis, concerns were raised about victim identification. See the Japan narratives in US Department of State, *Trafficking in Persons Report, June 2005*, 132–33; US Department of State, *Trafficking in Persons Report, June 2006*, 149–51; US Department of State, *Trafficking in Persons Report, June 2007*, 124–26.

4. The 2007 TIP Report had concluded, "Some victims were not appropriately identified by Japanese authorities and, as a consequence, were treated as violators of Japanese immigration or prostitution statutes and penalized instead of being protected as victims of human trafficking." See US Department of State, *Trafficking in Persons Report, June 2007*, 125. Specifically, the report expressed concerns about the decline in the number of victims identified by Japanese authorities: "The 58 victims found by the government in 2006 were less than half the number identified in 2005." See US Department of State, *Trafficking in Persons Report, June 2007*, 124. The concerns expressed in the TIP Report were reiterated in internal cables sent from the US embassy in Tokyo, which also discussed Japan's "inconsistent victim identification and protection." See Embassy Tokyo, "G/TIP Ambassador Lagon's July 2 Meeting with the Japanese Government." The State Department maintained that it had "heard reports of women otherwise classifiable as victims of human trafficking being deported as violators of immigration law by Japanese authorities." See Embassy Tokyo, "Advocating for TIP Victim Identification Procedures in Japan."

5. US Department of State, "U.S. Relations with Japan: Bilateral Fact Sheet."

6. Embassy Tokyo, "G/TIP Ambassador Lagon's July 2 Meeting with the Japanese Government." The cable was sent to all China posts; the Association of Southeast Asian Nations; the Labor Collective; the Departments of Health and Human Services, Homeland Security, and Justice; and the secretary of state. The Japanese government's Interministerial Task Force included high-ranking representatives from a range of Japanese offices, including the Cabinet Office; the National Police Agency; and the Ministries of Foreign Affairs, Justice, and Health, Labor, and Welfare.

7. Embassy Tokyo, "Advocating for TIP Victim Identification Procedures in Japan."

8. Embassy Tokyo, "Advocating for TIP Victim Identification Procedures in Japan." TVPA and UN Trafficking Protocol standards are very similar, although not identical. For a discussion of the similarities and differences, see Musto, "What's in a Name?"

9. Embassy Tokyo, "G/TIP Ambassador Lagon's July 2 Meeting with the Japanese Government."

10. For further discussion, see Koh, "Why Do Nations Obey International Law?"; Raustiala and Slaughter, "International Law, International Relations and Compliance."

11. Flowers, *Refugees, Women, and Weapons*; Flowers, "International Human Rights Norms in Japan"; Leheny, *Think Global, Fear Local*; Tsutsui, *Rights Make Might*. Japan's postwar constitution, which established Japan as a parliamentary democracy, explicitly guarantees both individual rights and "fundamental human rights" (see Article 97). However, as in the United States, little attention was paid to the issue in Japan until the 1970s and 1980s. While some in Japan are fierce advocates of international human rights today, for others, current conceptualizations of human rights are a Western imposition, incorporated into law during the Allied occupation. For a discussion of how human rights law has been approached in Japan, see Chan-Tiberghien, *Gender and Human Rights Politics in Japan*; Maki, "Constitution of Japan"; S. Matsui, "Fundamental Human Rights and 'Traditional Japanese Values'"; Port, "Japanese International Law 'Revolution'"; Repeta, "International Covenant on Civil and Political Rights and Human Rights Law in Japan"; Repeta, "U.N. Committee Faults Japan Human Rights Performance."

12. Flowers, *Refugees, Women, and Weapons*.

13. Keck and Sikkink, *Activists beyond Borders*, 12. Keck and Sikkink use the expression "boomerang" diplomacy to describe a new tactic for shifting global norms in which domestic NGOs work with foreign NGOs and governments to pressure their home government. This tactic is explicitly acknowledged in the 2001 *TIP Report*: "In preparing this report, the Department of State in Washington asked for information from our embassies and consulates around the world. Worldwide 186 U.S. embassies and consulates in consultation with host governments devoted substantial time and attention compiling and reporting information about the extent of trafficking in their host countries and efforts undertaken by host governments to address the problem. The embassy reports reflect discussions with host governments, local non-governmental organizations ("NGOs"), immigration officials, police, journalists, and victims, in addition to reviews of government, press, and NGO reports." US Department of State, *Trafficking in Persons Report, June 2001*, 4.

14. Kelley, *Scorecard Diplomacy*, 6.

15. Kelley, *Scorecard Diplomacy*, 17. Kelley uses the *TIP Report* to evidence the notable increase in the number of countries that have adopted anti-human-trafficking policies and legislation since 2001.

16. See Government Accountability Office, *Human Trafficking*.

17. Embassy Tokyo, "Japan Submission for *TIP Report*." This IOM handbook continues to be a guide and resource for the Japanese government, as attested by recent reports. For instance, the Japan country narrative of the 2017 *TIP Report* states, "National Police Agency (NPA) officials used an IOM-developed handbook and the Inter-Ministerial Liaison Committee's manuals to identify victims and refer victims to available services." See US Department of State, *Trafficking in Persons Report, June 2017*, 226. The 2018 *TIP Report* similarly states, "National Police Agency (NPA) officials continued to use an IOM-developed handbook and the Inter-Ministerial Committee's manuals to identify and refer victims to available protective services." See US Department of State, *Trafficking in Persons Report, June 2018*, 246.

18. See Kelley, *Scorecard Diplomacy*.

19. See Kelley, *Scorecard Diplomacy*.

20. See Kelley, *Scorecard Diplomacy*, 12–13

21. See Zimmerman and Borland, *Caring for Trafficked Persons*; Zimmerman and Watts, *WHO Ethical and Safety Recommendations for Interviewing Trafficked Women*. Not only does the Roadmap draw on and refer to the *IOM Handbook on Direct Assistance for Victims of Trafficking*, but the handbook itself references parts of the *WHO Ethical and Safety Recommendations for Interviewing Trafficked Women*. By overlapping and referencing each other, these guidebooks establish an internal sense of consistency and a shared language of consensus in the same ways that international agreements quote language from previous agreements. For a discussion of how international agreements do this, see Riles, *The Network Inside Out*.

22. Larsen, "Politics of Technicality," 75. Effected through the proliferation of guidelines and guidebooks, guidance culture has become an important strategy over the past four decades for encouraging compliance with international law where constraint and obligation cannot be imposed. A public call for the production of global guidelines can be traced back to the Stockholm Declaration, which presented their production as a moral imperative. For a discussion, see Larsen, "Politics of Technicality."

23. Sharma and Gupta, "Introduction," 11. See also Weber, *Economy and Society*.

24. Larsen, "Politics of Technicality." As Larsen explains, whereas a search for guidelines published before 1978 in the UN library produces 129 hits, a similar search between 1978 and 2009 exceeds the maximum list results of 8,287. See Larsen, "Politics of Technicality," 97n3.

25. Hecht, "Interscalar Vehicles for an African Anthropocene," 115.

26. IOM, *IOM Handbook on Direct Assistance for Victims of Trafficking*, 18, 16. This system, it continued, "applies equally to female and male individuals . . . and is especially important for minors" (16).

27. I borrow the notion of "audit culture" from Marilyn Strathern, who uses it as "an ironic reflection" on "proliferating objects of self-scrutiny." Strathern, "From Improvement to Enhancement," 1; see also Strathern, *Audit Cultures*. Sally Engle Merry has traced, in particular, how audit culture has come to be viewed as a tool for persuading publics and influencing governance decisions by drawing on assertions of social science expertise and claims to objectivity to assert credibility and legitimacy. She explains that quantifiable indicators make policy solutions appear to be simple technical matters of measuring a problem, establishing standards, and developing appropriate protocols and procedures. By establishing a formal definition of human trafficking and then collecting data on it at a global scale, the protocol promised to recognize human trafficking as a global phenomenon for states to measure and institutionally address. Merry, *Seductions of Quantification*; for exploration of other audit cultures, see Scherz, *Having People, Having Heart*; Shore and Wright, "Audit Culture Revisited"; Strathern, *Audit Cultures*.

28. IOM, *IOM Handbook on Direct Assistance for Victims of Trafficking*, 17.

29. IOM, *IOM Handbook on Direct Assistance for Victims of Trafficking*.

30. Embassy Tokyo, "Advocating for TIP Victim Identification Procedures in Japan."

31. IOM, *IOM Handbook on Direct Assistance for Victims of Trafficking*, 20. See also the UN Trafficking Protocol.

32. Per my conversations with NGO workers, in other cases potential trafficking victims may appear at *kōban* (police kiosks) on their own or be brought to the police by customers or concerned citizens.

33. Embassy Tokyo, "Advocating for TIP Victim Identification Procedures in Japan."

34. Embassy Tokyo, "Advocating for TIP Victim Identification Procedures in Japan."

35. IOM, *IOM Handbook on Direct Assistance for Victims of Trafficking*, 16.

36. Embassy Tokyo, "Advocating for TIP Victim Identification Procedures in Japan."

37. Embassy Tokyo, "Advocating for TIP Victim Identification Procedures in Japan." See also IOM, *IOM Handbook on Direct Assistance for Victims of Trafficking*, 4.

38. IOM, *IOM Handbook on Direct Assistance for Victims of Trafficking*, 26.

39. IOM, *IOM Handbook on Direct Assistance for Victims of Trafficking*, 50–52. The version of the form in figure 4.1 is from a hard copy of the handbook, dated May 21, 2009. The version of the form in the PDF of the handbook available online differs from it and is dated October 2, 2007.

40. Embassy Tokyo, "Advocating for TIP Victim Identification Procedures in Japan."

41. For instance, in 2020, the IOM office in Nigeria published a handbook on identifying victims of human trafficking that contained the same form. See IOM, *Trafficking in Persons*, 66–70.

42. IOM, *IOM Handbook on Direct Assistance for Victims of Trafficking*, 50–52.

43. IOM, *IOM Handbook on Direct Assistance for Victims of Trafficking*, 51.

44. IOM, *IOM Handbook on Direct Assistance for Victims of Trafficking*, 52 (emphasis in original).

45. IOM, *IOM Handbook on Direct Assistance for Victims of Trafficking*, 34.

46. IOM, *IOM Handbook on Direct Assistance for Victims of Trafficking*, 17.

47. Embassy Tokyo, "Advocating for TIP Victim Identification Procedures in Japan."

48. IOM, *IOM Handbook on Direct Assistance for Victims of Trafficking*, 32–33.

49. IOM, *IOM Handbook on Direct Assistance for Victims of Trafficking*, 32.

50. IOM, *IOM Handbook on Direct Assistance for Victims of Trafficking*, 32.

51. Embassy Tokyo, "Advocating for TIP Victim Identification Procedures in Japan."

52. IOM, *IOM Handbook on Direct Assistance for Victims of Trafficking*, 34.

53. IOM, *IOM Handbook on Direct Assistance for Victims of Trafficking*, 32.

54. IOM, *IOM Handbook on Direct Assistance for Victims of Trafficking*, 47.

55. IOM, *IOM Handbook on Direct Assistance for Victims of Trafficking*, 47.

56. Embassy Tokyo. "Review of Japan's Anti-TIP Policy."

57. US Department of State, *Trafficking in Persons Report, June 2006*; US Department of State, *Trafficking in Persons Report, June 2007*.

58. IOM, *IOM Handbook on Direct Assistance for Victims of Trafficking*, 19.

59. IOM, *IOM Handbook on Direct Assistance for Victims of Trafficking*, 32.

60. IOM, *IOM Handbook on Direct Assistance for Victims of Trafficking*, 18.

61. IOM, *IOM Handbook on Direct Assistance for Victims of Trafficking*, 18.

62. IOM, *IOM Handbook on Direct Assistance for Victims of Trafficking*, 19 (emphasis in original).

63. IOM, *IOM Handbook on Direct Assistance for Victims of Trafficking*, 17.

64. IOM, *IOM Handbook on Direct Assistance for Victims of Trafficking*, 22.

65. IOM, *IOM Handbook on Direct Assistance for Victims of Trafficking*, 18.

66. IOM, *IOM Handbook on Direct Assistance for Victims of Trafficking*, 17.

67. Kendall and Nouwen, "Representational Practices at the International Criminal Court," 241.

68. For a discussion of how bureaucratic standards work to disqualify people from assistance, see Herzfeld, *Social Production of Indifference*.

69. See Brenneis, "Reforming Promise"; Hull, *Government of Paper*.

70. Scherz, *Having People, Having Heart*.

71. Embassy Tokyo, "TIP: Final Clarification of Japan's Roadmap to Tier 1" (emphasis in original).

72. IOM, *IOM Handbook on Direct Assistance for Victims of Trafficking*, 18.

73. Embassy Manila, "Number of Filipino 'Entertainers' Going to Japan Declines."

74. Embassy Tokyo, "Review of Japan's Anti-TIP Policy."

75. Embassy Tokyo, "2007 TIP Report: Japan (March 9)."

76. As I discuss in the book's conclusion, such is the case not only in Japan but also in the United States.

77. Tolentino, "Migrant Women in Japan."

78. Tolentino, "Migrant Women in Japan."

79. Tolentino, "Migrant Women in Japan." Although the numbers of Filipina women entering Japan on entertainer visas dropped in 2005, the number of Philippine nationals entering Japan through other visa categories has remained high, suggesting that Filipina women are now using other visa categories to enter Japan to work.

80. For a discussion of how *haigūsha* visas (visas for spouses or dependents of a Japanese national) are being used to facilitate human trafficking, see Fujimoto, "'Gisō kekkon' no jirei kara jinshin torihiki no gurei zōn o kenshō suru." For a discussion of how the strategies of "flexible intimacy" engaged by some migrant women blur the lines between cross-border marriage and cross-border sex work, see Chen and Wang, "Flexible Intimacies in the Global Intimate Economy," 260.

81. Embassy Tokyo, "2007 TIP Report: Japan (March 12)." Although police are the primary investigative agency in Japan for suspected penal code violations, they arrest fewer than 20 percent of suspects, in part out of concerns about caseload pressure and jail capacity; the remainder is turned over to prosecutors without arrest. See Johnson, "Japan's Prosecution System."

82. See Japan NGO Network for the Elimination of Racial Discrimination. *Joint Civil Society Report on Racial Discrimination in Japan*; Kim and Lies, "U.S. Embassy in Tokyo Warns of 'Suspected Racial Profiling' by Japanese Police."

83. Johnson, "Above the Law?"; Kobayashi, *Nihon keisatsu: Fuhai no kōzō*.

84. See Gōhara, "Japanese 'Prosecutors' Justice' on Trial"; Johnson, *Japanese Way of Justice*; Johnson, "Japan's Prosecution System." Gōhara and Johnson offer statistics for formal indictments ranging from 7.2 percent to 37 percent of processed cases.

85. See Johnson, "Japan's Prosecution System." According to Johnson, hiring prosecutors did not keep pace with increased caseloads, intensifying the problem.

86. See Johnson, *Japanese Way of Justice*; Johnson, "Japan's Prosecution System."

87. See Gōhara, "Japanese 'Prosecutors' Justice' on Trial"; Johnson, *Japanese Way of Justice*; Johnson, "Japan's Prosecution System."

88. See Johnson, "Japan's Prosecution System."

89. See Gōhara, "Japanese 'Prosecutors' Justice' on Trial"; Johnson, "Japan's Prosecution System."

90. See Ito, "Japan's Foreign Trainee System Said Still Plagued by Rights Abuses"; Ibusuki, *Tsukaisute gaikokujin*; Denyer and Kashiwagi, "Japan Wakes Up to Exploitation of Foreign Workers as Immigration Debate Rages"; Urano, "Gaikokujin jisshūsei nana-wari, saitei chingin shitamawaru."

91. See Ibusuki, *Tsukaisute gaikokujin*; Ryall, "Overwork Accepted as Cause of Trainee's Death"; Uchiyama, "Ginō jisshūsei, hachi-nen de 174-nin shibō."

92. See Bustamante, *Report of the Special Rapporteur on the Human Rights of Migrants, Addendum.*

93. See Kamibayashi, "Gaikokujin ginō jisshū seido seiritsu no keii"; Watanabe, "Concerning Revisions in the Foreign Trainee and Technical Intern System."

94. *Japan Times*, "Illegal Aliens Who Built Nagano Games Sites Facing Sweep," 3.

95. For a discussion of the abuses of guest workers in the United States and Canada, respectively, see Southern Poverty Law Center, "Close to Slavery"; Pratt, *Families Apart.*

96. Osumi, "Nominees Announced for Japan's Sixth Annual Black Company Awards." See also "'Most Evil Corporations' Award 2012 Presentation & Symposium," *Black Corp Award Blog*, accessed June 24, 2023, http://blackcorpaward.blogspot.com/p /english.html.

97. Of course, such practices of overwork are not limited to Japan. Elite Wall Street traders are also expected to put in intense hours (see Ho, *Liquidated*). The head of mission at an international organization in Tokyo, a Philippine national, spoke with me about working twenty-hour days and sleeping in the office during the years he was working for a Catholic NGO and as the head of a refugee camp. He said that passion and commitment had motivated him.

98. See Levi, "The Gray Zone," 26. For an application of Levi's term to the situation of migrant laborers, see Holmes, "'Oaxacans Like to Work Bent Over.'"

99. Two thousand seven was not the last time the Japanese government was upset about its TIP ranking. In 2008, after once again finding itself on Tier 2, the US embassy received complaints from high-ranking officials in the MOFA who maintained that they had exerted great pressure on other government agencies to cooperate with the United States but that "these efforts have come to naught." Embassy Tokyo, "Deputy Vice Minister Objects to TIP Report Ranking." In response, staff at the US embassy privately expressed concerns that the Japanese government was experiencing "cooperation fatigue." Embassy Tokyo, "Japan Reacts Negatively to TIP Report Tier Ranking." In 2009 as well, the US embassy in Tokyo reported that the Japanese government again felt that its Tier 2 ranking was unwarranted. The government believed that it had made "an unprecedented multi-year, multi-agency effort to meet TVPA minimum standards," and the embassy was concerned that the issue could affect bilateral relations between the countries. That year, the embassy proposed taking more of a cooperative than an adversarial approach. Embassy Tokyo, "Japan, the U.S., and TIP: At a Tipping Point?" Still, Japan was again ranked at Tier 2. By the 2010s, NGO workers in Japan with whom I spoke shared that the Japanese government seemed to be waning in its efforts. These

NGO workers surmised that the Japanese government had resigned itself to being ranked at Tier 2.

100. US Department of State, *Trafficking in Persons Report, June 2018*.

101. For further discussion, see Gupta, *Red Tape*.

5. BANAL JUSTICE

1. See Clarke and Goodale, "Introduction," 11.

2. See Clarke, *Affective Justice*; Clarke and Goodale, *Mirrors of Justice*; Rosen, *Anthropology of Justice*; Sarfaty, "Why Culture Matters in International Institutions."

3. See Clarke, *Affective Justice*; Constable, "Law as Claim to Justice."

4. Constable, "Law as Claim to Justice," 636.

5. UNODC, *International Framework for Action to Implement the Trafficking in Persons Protocol*, 3. As mentioned in chapter 2, the 3Ps were adopted in the United States under the Clinton administration before they became part of the UN Trafficking Protocol. In 2008, the UN secretary-general encouraged that a fourth P, "partnership," be added. See UN Department of Public Information, "Add 'Partnership' to 'Three P' Agenda of United Nations Anti-trafficking Protocol, Deputy Secretary-General Urges General Assembly Thematic Debate," press release DSG/SM/397-GA/10713-HR/4956, June 3, 2008, https://www.un.org/press/en/2008/dsgsm397.doc.htm.

6. Mahmood Mamdani calls this authority "the power of naming" to highlight the political implications of who has the power to name forms of violence and how they are categorized. See Mamdani, "Politics of Naming."

7. IOM, *IOM Handbook on Direct Assistance for Victims of Trafficking*, 26.

8. I borrow the notion of "unprotection" from Noémi Tousignant, who characterizes it as "an ongoing, active process that fails to protect, even though it may not aim to expose." See Tousignant, *Edges of Exposure*, 16.

9. UN, Protocol to Prevent, Suppress and Punish Trafficking in Persons. Section II of the protocol focuses explicitly on the "protection of victims"; article 6 addresses "assistance to and protection of victims"; article 7 covers the "status of victims . . . in receiving States"; and article 8 addresses victim repatriation.

10. Article 6, item 1, of the Trafficking Protocol clearly mandates that "to the extent possible under its domestic law, each State Party shall protect the privacy and identity of victims of trafficking in persons, including, inter alia, by making legal proceedings relating to such trafficking confidential." UN, Protocol to Prevent, Suppress and Punish Trafficking in Persons.

11. UN, Protocol to Prevent, Suppress and Punish Trafficking in Persons (emphasis added), art. 6, item 3.

12. UN, Protocol to Prevent, Suppress and Punish Trafficking in Persons, art. 6, item 3.

13. UN, Protocol to Prevent, Suppress and Punish Trafficking in Persons, art. 7, items 1 & 2. The Trafficking Protocol also provides that "the State Party of which a victim of trafficking" is a national or permanent resident "shall facilitate and accept" the safe and lawful "return of that person," including by issuing legal travel documents (see art. 8). However, the protocol also provides for victims of trafficking to remain in receiving

countries to participate in criminal prosecution against their traffickers; it prefers that the individual's return be voluntary.

14. See Bernstein, *Brokered Subjects*.

15. The notion that trafficking victims' testimony is considered legitimate contrasts strikingly with the recent treatment of refugees, the testimony of whom has so lost legitimacy over past decades that medical and psychiatric measures have come to take on the burden of evidence in arguing their cases. See Fassin and d'Halluin, "Critical Evidence."

16. Police agencies in Japan are famous for refusing to speak with researchers and journalists, who run into what has been called the "police wall of secrecy." See Kobayashi, *Nihon keisatsu no genzai*, vi, cited in Johnson, "Above the Law?," 27.

17. Consider some analogues of Japan's Ministry of Justice: The US Department of Justice was established in 1870. In Germany, what is now the Bundesministerium der Justiz und für Verbraucherschutz (The Federal Ministry of Justice and Consumer Protection) was initially formed as the Imperial Justice Office (Reichsjustizamt) in 1877. It became a federal ministry, the Reichsministerium der Justiz or Reichsjustizministerium, after Germany became a republic in 1919. Both borrowed from the French Ministère de la Justice, which was established in 1790. For a discussion of the modular form of nationalism, see Anderson, *Imagined Communities*.

18. "Preface," Ministry of Justice, accessed July 1, 2023, https://www.moj.go.jp/ENGLISH/preface.html.

19. Support networks for Filipina migrants in Japan are especially well-established, in part because they were built through existing church networks in Japan and the Philippines and in part because long and well-recognized histories of organizing and social activism in the Philippines meant that migrants readily turned toward them.

20. US Department of State, *Trafficking in Persons Report, June 2007*, 125.

21. See Embassy Tokyo, "G/TIP Ambassador Lagon's July 2 Meeting with the Japanese Government"; Embassy Tokyo, "TIP: Final Clarification of Japan's Roadmap to Tier 1."

22. "Tekihatsu kara hogo e tenkan hitsuyō," *Asahi Shimbun*, July 23, 2004.

23. Shifts in spending demonstrate this move. In 2005, the Japanese government subsidized NGOs to house fifty-two identified victims. See Embassy Tokyo, "MOFA Presents Talking Points for Upcoming G/TIP Visit of Amb. Lagon." In 2006, the Japanese government earmarked $100,000 to subsidize victims' stays in private NGO shelters; however, that year they began to shift to WCOs, and only two individuals were referred to NGOs that year (Embassy Tokyo, "2007 TIP Report: Japan [March 9]"; Embassy Tokyo, "MOFA Presents Talking Points for Upcoming G/TIP Visit of Amb. Lagon"). By 2017, the numbers had shifted again. WCOs reported sheltering sixteen of the forty-six victims identified by the Japanese government; an "unknown number" (and presumably at least the balance of the forty-six) received assistance in NGO shelters. US Department of State, *Trafficking in Persons Report, June 2018*, 246.

24. As I explain in note 2 of chapter 6, a small number of those recognized as trafficking victims remain in Japan, usually receiving residency permits through marriages with Japanese men.

25. The term "moral imagination" is from Livingston, *Debility and the Moral Imagination in Botswana*, 19. For further discussion, see Scherz, *Having People, Having Heart*, 7.

26. See also Clarke, *Affective Justice*.

27. Tousignant, *Edges of Exposure*, 16.

28. E. Tendayi Achiume offers such a political possibility in her reconceptualization of migration as decolonization. Her work stresses the need for national political recognition of the ways that current migration patterns are products of postcolonial political-economic relationships that are rooted in colonial histories. See Achiume, "Reimagining International Law for Global Migration."

29. I use the term "afterlife" following Saidiya Hartman. See Hartman, *Lose Your Mother*, 6.

6. THE NEED TO KNOW

1. See also Ministry of Foreign Affairs, Japan, *Japan's Actions to Combat Trafficking in Persons*, 5.

2. IOM assistance is offered on a voluntary basis to those who are officially referred to the organization by the Japanese government as victims of trafficking. A small number of those receiving this referral decline IOM repatriation assistance because they prefer to remain in Japan to work and are eligible for a residency permit, most frequently through marriage to a Japanese man. The fact that some who qualify as trafficking victims decline repatriation assistance is itself revealing of these migrants' prospects back home.

3. This discussion follows a consideration of "security issues and risk assessment" to which it is closely tied. See IOM, *IOM Handbook on Direct Assistance for Victims of Trafficking*, 3–7. As explained in chapter 5, only two protections for trafficked persons are ensured by the Trafficking Protocol, one of which is maintaining the confidentiality of their identities and circumstances.

4. IOM, *IOM Handbook on Direct Assistance for Victims of Trafficking*, 9.

5. The IOM was initially brought in to help facilitate the logistics of the repatriation process for trafficking survivors. Those identified as trafficking victims must have their repatriation expenses covered, and some foreign embassies had faced challenges raising these funds for their nationals. The involvement of the IOM enabled the Japanese government to channel funding for repatriation and reintegration expenses through the organization.

6. See Galison, "Removing Knowledge"; Hecht, "Interscalar Vehicles for an African Anthropocene"; Masco, *Nuclear Borderlands*; Mathews, "Power/Knowledge, Power/ Ignorance"; Mathews, "State Making, Knowledge, and Ignorance"; McGoey, "Strategic Unknowns"; Proctor and Schiebinger, *Agnotology*.

7. Galison, "Removing Knowledge," 229, 236.

8. Mathews, "State Making, Knowledge, and Ignorance."

9. Such understandings about confidentiality have precedents in the work of earlier activists in Japan. For instance, in a 1996 keynote lecture at a conference for publicly employed women's counselors, Matsui expressed her frustration and dismay at the callous self-interestedness of Japanese news reporters who had broadcast the name, footage, and hometown of a Thai woman who had contracted HIV while working in the sex industry in Japan. She argued that this was a violation of this woman's human rights. See Matsui, "Josei hogo jigyō to josei no jinken."

10. See Ramseyer and Nakazato, "Rational Litigant"; Yasunaga, "Legal Intervention against Medical Accidents in Japan."

11. Morita, "Caring for Caregivers," 8.

12. Morita, "Caring for Caregivers," 8.

13. See Morita, "Caring for Caregivers."

14. IOM, *IOM Handbook on Direct Assistance for Victims of Trafficking*, 8.

15. IOM, *IOM Handbook on Direct Assistance for Victims of Trafficking*, 8.

16. *Merriam-Webster*, s.v. "information," 1a(1), accessed July 1, 2023, https://www .merriam-webster.com/dictionary/information; *Merriam-Webster*, s.vv. "matters," accessed July 1, 2023, https://www.merriam-webster.com/dictionary/matters; *Merriam-Webster*, s.v. "data," 1, accessed July 1, 2023, https://www.merriam-webster.com/dictionary /data.

17. The lead author of the chapter, Paul Holmes, had headed up a vice department with Scotland Yard until he began training law enforcement on investigative techniques for human trafficking. In addition to working on the *IOM Handbook*, Holmes also participated in the writing of related manuals for other international organizations, including the UN, the IOM, the Organization for Security and Co-operation in Europe, and INTERPOL. In 2013, the US State Department named him a *TIP Report* Hero for his contributions. Holmes's focus on safety in the face of transnational organized crime syndicates is consistent with the UN framing of the issue as a matter of transnational organized crime. Need-to-know protocols are standard strategies of knowledge compartmentalization in information security; such practices originated in antiquity as a military intelligence strategy to keep military secrets from falling into enemy hands. Their objective is risk management; they rest on the assumption that if fewer people know the details of a mission or task, information is less likely to be compromised. They work through a division of labor in which a mission can be broken into isolated tasks that can then be managed with limited understanding of the overall plan. For a discussion of the military roots of need-to-know protocols, see Roland, "Secrecy, Technology, and War."

18. IOM, *IOM Handbook on Direct Assistance for Victims of Trafficking*, 12–13.

19. IOM, *IOM Handbook on Direct Assistance for Victims of Trafficking*, 9.

20. IOM, *IOM Handbook on Direct Assistance for Victims of Trafficking*, 308. These principles were adapted from Zimmerman and Watts, *WHO Ethical and Safety Recommendations for Interviewing Trafficked Women*. Zimmerman and Watts, both scholars at the London School of Hygiene and Tropical Medicine trained in health policy and epidemiology, are founding members of the university's Gender Violence and Health Center. As discussed in chapter 4, the referencing of the WHO guidebook in the *IOM Handbook* creates a citational chain that connects the ethics of trafficking victim assistance with other expert standards of applied ethics.

21. IOM, *IOM Handbook on Direct Assistance for Victims of Trafficking*, 8.

22. Maurer, "Due Diligence and 'Reasonable Man,' Offshore," 477.

23. Maurer, "Due Diligence and 'Reasonable Man,' Offshore."

24. Jacob and Riles, "New Bureaucracies of Virtue Symposium."

25. IOM, *IOM Handbook on Direct Assistance for Victims of Trafficking*, 8.

26. IOM, *IOM Handbook on Direct Assistance for Victims of Trafficking*, 9–10.

27. See Morita, "Caring for Caregivers."

28. See Morita, "Caring for Caregivers."

1. The UNTFHS prioritizes projects that involve partnerships with civil society, faith-based organizations, NGOs, and local entities. See UNTFHS, "United Nations Trust Fund for Human Security Guidelines," 4. For further discussion, see Ogata, "The Human Security Commission's Strategy"; Sumi, "Human Security and Health."

2. See Basu, "Globalization of the Local/Localization of the Global"; Bernal and Grewal, *Theorizing NGOs*; Hemment, "Global Civil Society and the Local Costs of Belonging"; Hemment, *Empowering Women in Russia*; Ong, "Strategic Sisterhood or Sisters in Solidarity?"

3. See Bernal and Grewal, *Theorizing NGOs*; Hemment, "Global Civil Society and the Local Costs of Belonging."

4. For a related discussion of how government and international agency funding can push NGOs to adopt donors' priorities, rendering ineligible those issues to which they are committed but that fall outside donors' frameworks, see Hemment, "Global Civil Society and the Local Costs of Belonging." She describes similar feelings of ambivalence and frustration among feminist activists in Tver, Russia, regarding donor agency policies and the amount of bureaucratic activity required per transnational guideline to establish a crisis center for women.

5. Ople, "Notice to the World."

6. Ople, "Notice to the World."

7. Larga, "ILO-HSF Project Overview for Stakeholders," slide 1 notes.

8. Larga, "ILO-HSF Project Overview for Stakeholders," slide 1 notes.

9. Larga, "ILO-HSF Project Overview for Stakeholders," slide 1 notes.

10. Larga, "ILO-HSF Project Overview for Stakeholders," slide 16.

11. Larga, "ILO-HSF Project Overview for Stakeholders," slide 16.

12. Soeya, "Japanese Security Policy in Transition."

13. For further discussion, see Sumi, "Human Security and Health"; Timothy, "Human Security Discourse at the United Nations."

14. Sumi, "Human Security and Health."

15. The Japanese government funded similar projects in other parts of the world. For instance, in 2005 it also contributed to an EU project focusing on a Colombian NGO working to foster public awareness among potential migrants, some of whom go to Japan, about the dangers of overseas work. See Warren, "Trafficking in Persons," 218–20.

16. In the years before and after this project, the UNTFHS funded four other projects focused on assisting trafficking survivors in Southeast Asia, including ones in Vietnam (2003–6), Cambodia (2003–6), and Indonesia (2011–13). See "Cambodia," UNTFHS, accessed June 28, 2023, https://www.un.org/humansecurity/country/cambodia/; "Indonesia," UNTFHS, accessed June 28, 2023, https://www.un.org/humansecurity /country/indonesia/; "Viet Nam," UNTFHS, accessed June 28, 2023, https://www.un.org /humansecurity/country/viet-nam/.

Also, between February 2009 and May 2012, the UNTFHS funded the ILO and the European Economic Community to undertake a similar program to the one described in this chapter but that focused on migrants who had returned from the EU and neighboring countries. The program, Going Back—Moving On: Economic and Social Empowerment of Migrants including Victims of Trafficking Returned from the EU and Its Neighboring Countries, received more than $2.5M to work with returning migrants from Thailand and the Philippines. See "Going Back—Moving on," ILO, accessed June 28, 2023, https://www.ilo.org/global/topics/forced-labour/WCMS_142949/lang--en/index.htm. Moreover, the UNTFHS funds programs through a range of different UN agencies (including, among others, the United Nations Development Programme; the United Nations Educational, Scientific and Cultural Organization; and the WHO).

17. UNTFHS, "United Nations Trust Fund for Human Security Guidelines," 5.

18. See Warren, "Trafficking in Persons, 227. Japan's Official Development Assistance has tended to be sensitive to the interests of Japanese firms and stressed national economic growth, responding to not only international pressure but also domestic objectives. For example, in the years after World War II, the Japanese government endeavored to use reparations treaties to access raw materials, markets, and governments in Southeast Asia. During the 1970s and 1980s, development aid to Asia became a key strategy of a Japanese diplomacy that stressed "economic cooperation" (*keizai kyōryoku*), endeavoring to develop strategies in Asia independent of the United States, while limiting those efforts to bilateral ties unlikely to upset the United States. See Leheny and Warren, "Introduction," 5–7.

19. UNTFHS, "United Nations Trust Fund for Human Security Guidelines," 6.

20. UNTFHS, "United Nations Trust Fund for Human Security Guidelines," 6.

21. UNTFHS, "United Nations Trust Fund for Human Security Guidelines," 6.

22. UNTFHS, "United Nations Trust Fund for Human Security Guidelines."

23. See also Scherz, *Having People, Having Heart*.

24. ILO, *Economic and Social Empowerment*, 1.

25. Larga, "ILO-HSF Project Overview for Stakeholders," slide 14.

26. Tsing, "Supply Chains and the Human Condition."

27. Tsing, "Supply Chains and the Human Condition," 163.

28. "FAQs," UNTFHS, question 14, accessed June 28, 2023, https://www.un.org/humansecurity/trustfund/faqs/.

29. ILO, *Economic and Social Empowerment*, 1; "FAQs," UNTFHS, question 14.

30. "FAQs," UNTFHS, question 6.

31. UNODC, *From Victim to Survivor*, 6.

32. UNODC, *From Victim to Survivor*, 3.

33. UNODC, "UN Voluntary Trust Fund for Victims of Trafficking in Persons: Basic Facts."

34. UNTFHS, *From Victim to Survivor*, 5.

35. UNTFHS, *From Victim to Survivor*, 7.

36. UNODC, "UNVTF: 20 New NGO Projects Selected for Emergency Grants under the Sixth Grant Cycle."

37. "Overview," Alliance 8.7, accessed January 1, 2023, https://www.alliance87.org/about/.

38. See UNODC, "29 NGOs Selected for Funding from UNVTF Third Grant Cycle"; UNODC, "UNVTF Awards Grants to Six Additional NGOs under Fourth Grant Cycle."

39. UNODC, *Mid-Term Independent Project Evaluation*, 20.

40. UNODC, *Mid-Term Independent Project Evaluation.*

41. UNODC, *Mid-Term Independent Project Evaluation*, 21.

42. UNODC, *Mid-Term Independent Project Evaluation*, 20.

43. Cited in UNODC, *Mid-Term Independent Project Evaluation*, 21.

44. UNTFHS, *From Victim to Survivor*, back cover.

45. UN, "Launch of the UN Trust Fund for Victims of Human Trafficking."

46. UN, "Launch of the UN Trust Fund for Victims of Human Trafficking."

47. UN, "Launch of the UN Trust Fund for Victims of Human Trafficking."

48. For more in-depth analysis of the involvement of Ashton Kutcher and his former spouse, Demi Moore, in anti-human-trafficking efforts, see Majic, "Real Men Set Norms?" Kutcher's work can also be understood as part of the "charitable industrial complex" that enables the wealthy to engage in "conscience laundering." See Buffett, "The Charitable-Industrial Complex."

49. Embassy Tokyo, "Japan, the U.S., and TIP." See also Chuang, "Exploitation Creep and the Unmaking of Human Trafficking Law."

50. See Bernstein, "Sexual Politics of the 'New Abolitionism,'" 140.

51. See Bernstein, "Sexual Politics of the 'New Abolitionism,'" 140.

52. Cmiel, "Emergence of Human Rights Politics in the United States."

53. Cmiel, "Emergence of Human Rights Politics in the United States."

54. Cmiel, "Emergence of Human Rights Politics in the United States."

55. Keck and Sikkink, *Activists beyond Borders*, 98.

56. Cmiel, "Emergence of Human Rights Politics in the United States."

57. Cmiel, "Emergence of Human Rights Politics in the United States."

58. Cmiel, "Emergence of Human Rights Politics in the United States."

59. Shahid, "Remarks."

60. Brunovskis and Surtees, "Agency or Illness," 72.

61. NGOs in the Philippines are not alone in their frustration. For a discussion of the funding constraints faced by NGOs working with trafficking survivors in other parts of the world, see Clancey, Khushrushahi, and Ham, "Do Evidence-Based Approaches Alienate Canadian Anti-trafficking Funders?"; Dottridge, "How Is the Money to Combat Human Trafficking Spent?"; Hoff, "Where Is the Funding for Anti-trafficking Work?"; Surtees and de Kerchove, "Who Funds Re/integration?"

62. See Agnew and Crobridge, *Mastering Space*; Falcón, *Power Interrupted.*

63. See Stone, *Opting Out?*

64. For further discussion, see Enrile and Levid, "GAB[Riela]Net[Work]."

65. Robinson, cited in Capella and MacAskill, "Robinson Quits UN Job Citing Lack of Funds." After Robinson left, human rights–focused work increased to about 3 percent of the UN's annual budget; however, the increases came through extrabudgetary resources. Discretionary resources continued to surpass those from the regular budget, resulting in a shift of office priorities toward donors' interests. Weiss and Thakur, *Global Governance and the UN*, 271.

66. Robinson, cited in Capella and MacAskill, "Robinson Quits UN Job Citing Lack of Funds." See also Fahim, "Education of Mary Robinson."

8. CRUEL EMPOWERMENT

1. ILO, *Rays of Hope*, 42.

2. ILO, *Rays of Hope*, 42.

3. See "Targets and Results" and "The Project Components" in ILO, *Economic and Social Empowerment*.

4. See "Targets and Results" in ILO, *Economic and Social Empowerment*.

5. See "Strategy for Sustainability" in ILO, *Economic and Social Empowerment*.

6. See "Institutional Development" under "The Project Components" in ILO, *Economic and Social Empowerment*.

7. See "Targets and Results" in ILO, *Economic and Social Empowerment*.

8. See also Cruikshank, *Will to Empower*; Sharma, *Logics of Empowerment*.

9. See Gupta, *Red Tape*; Sharma, *Logics of Empowerment*.

10. Cruikshank, *Will to Empower*; Gupta, *Red Tape*; McKee, "Sceptical, Disorderly and Paradoxical Subjects"; Sharma, *Logics of Empowerment*.

11. Bernal and Grewal, "Introduction"; Gupta, *Red Tape*, 242.

12. Berlant, "Cruel Optimism."

13. Berlant, "Cruel Optimism," 21.

14. UN General Assembly, Resolution 66/290, cited at UNTFHS, "What Is Human Security."

15. Ogata, "Human Security Commission's Strategy," 26. On her mother's side, Ogata was the great-granddaughter of former prime minister Inukai Tsuyoshi and granddaughter of foreign minister Kenkichi Yoshizawa. She was one of the few women of her generation to be appointed to high-level government positions in Japan.

16. Ogata, "Human Security Commission's Strategy," 26.

17. Bosold and Werthes, "Human Security in Practice."

18. Ogata and Cels, "Human Security," 274.

19. Soeya, "Japanese Security Policy in Transition," 108. Beginning in 1995, the expression "human security" started appearing in Japanese government documents and UN and Asia-Pacific Economic Cooperation speeches given by Japanese prime ministers and foreign ministry officials. See Bosold and Werthes, "Human Security in Practice"; Soeya, "Japanese Security Policy in Transition." Other countries have also taken up the framework; for instance, Canada and Norway created a Human Security Network to focus on specific issues, such as land mines. Feminists, such as Charlotte Bunch, have also advocated for the idea. However, although diplomats made numerous references to the idea at the UN's 1995 World Summit for Social Development in Denmark, it did not gain sufficient support to warrant a new overarching human-security framework. See Timothy, "Human Security Discourse at the United Nations."

20. Timothy, "Human Security Discourse at the United Nations."

21. Edström, "Japan and Human Security."

22. Ogata, "Human Security Commission's Strategy."

23. Ministry of Foreign Affairs, Japan, "Plan for Establishment of the Commission on Human Security."

24. Mahlert, "Needs and Satisfiers," 1463.

25. JICA, or the Japan International Cooperation Agency, is the governmental agency that coordinates official development assistance (ODA) for the Japanese government.

26. "FAQs," UNTFHS, question 1, accessed June 28, 2023, https://www.un.org/humansecurity/trustfund/faqs/.

27. See "About the Trust Fund," UNTFHS, accessed June 28, 2023, https://www.un.org/humansecurity/.

28. Scherz, *Having People, Having Heart*, 102.

29. "FAQs," UNTFHS, question 12.

30. "FAQs," UNTFHS, question 6.

31. "FAQs," UNTFHS, question 15.

32. This focus on the individual is paradoxical given that human security appealed to Ogata as a framework because she believed it would include not only the civil and political rights protected under the International Covenant on Civil and Political Rights but also the economic, social, and cultural rights listed under the less recognized International Covenant on Economic, Social and Cultural Rights; for her, human security included economic security, health, and universal basic education as human rights. See Ogata, "Human Security Commission's Strategy." As Ogata and her coauthor Johan Cels explain, a human security approach "requires overcoming the compartmentalization of security, humanitarian, human rights, and development strategies by focusing on the protection and empowerment of people." Ogata and Cels, "Human Security," 276.

33. "Economic and Social Empowerment of Returned Victims of Trafficking in Thailand and the Philippines," ILO, accessed June 28, 2023, https://www.ilo.org/global/topics/forced-labour/WCMS_082047/lang--en/index.htm.

34. Larga, "ILO-HSF Project Overview for Stakeholders," slide 14.

35. ILO, *Rays of Hope*, 33.

36. ILO, *Rays of Hope*, 49.

37. ILO, *Rays of Hope*, 29.

38. ILO, *Rays of Hope*, 42.

39. Cruz-Mante, *Coaching Returned Victims/Survivors of Trafficking*, 104.

40. Wirth, foreword, i.

41. Cruz-Mante, *Coaching Returned Victims/Survivors of Trafficking*, 1.

42. Cruz-Mante, *Coaching Returned Victims/Survivors of Trafficking*, 1.

43. Cruz-Mante, *Coaching Returned Victims/Survivors of Trafficking*, 3. According to Cruz-Mante, counselors "seek understanding of the past, including acceptance and closure" (3), whereas coaches see the "present as a springboard towards ensuring a more desirable future" (2).

44. Cruz-Mante, *Coaching Returned Victims/Survivors of Trafficking*, 4.

45. Edralin, *Catalogue of Skills and Livelihood Training Programmes*.

46. Edralin, *Catalogue of Skills and Livelihood Training Programmes*, ii.

47. Cruz-Mante, *Coaching Returned Victims/Survivors of Trafficking*, 1.

48. Edralin, *Catalogue of Skills and Livelihood Training Programmes*, 1.

49. Edralin, *Catalogue of Skills and Livelihood Training Programmes*, ii, 12.

50. Edralin, *Catalogue of Skills and Livelihood Training Programmes*, 11.

51. Edralin, *Catalogue of Skills and Livelihood Training Programmes*, 12.

52. Edralin, *Catalogue of Skills and Livelihood Training Programmes*, 123–25.

53. Edralin, *Catalogue of Skills and Livelihood Training Programmes*, 122.

54. Edralin, *Catalogue of Skills and Livelihood Training Programmes*, 139–40.

55. Larga, "ILO-HSF Project Overview for Stakeholders," slide 14. The slide, titled "Project Funding," reads: "Approximate budget breakdown: 15% on knowledge; 25% capacity building; 65% direct assistance." Because Attorney Larga had passed away before I wrote this chapter, I was unable to follow up and ask him about these approximate percentages, which add up to 105 percent.

56. ILO, *Rays of Hope*, 1.

57. ILO, *Rays of Hope*, 6.

58. ILO, *Economic and Social Empowerment*.

59. Larga, "ILO-HSF Project Overview for Stakeholders," slide 7 notes.

60. ILO, *Rays of Hope*, 44.

61. ILO, *Rays of Hope*, 44–45.

62. Edralin, *Catalogue of Skills and Livelihood Training Programmes*, 12n1.

63. ILO, *Rays of Hope*, 9.

64. ILO, *Rays of Hope*, 8.

65. ILO, *Rays of Hope*, 6.

66. ILO, *Rays of Hope*, 8.

67. ILO, *Rays of Hope*, 8.

68. ILO, *Rays of Hope*.

69. ILO, *Rays of Hope*, 20–21.

70. ILO, *Rays of Hope*, 40.

71. IOM, *IOM Handbook on Direct Assistance for Victims of Trafficking*, 43.

72. ILO, *Rays of Hope*, 1.

73. Cruel empowerment is not limited to this case in the Philippines. For instance, Denise Brennan and Elena Shih have written critically about how counter–human trafficking campaigns in, respectively, the United States and in Thailand and China channel trafficking survivors into low-wage service work. See Brennan, *Life Interrupted*; Brennan and Plambech, "Editorial"; Shih, "Price of Freedom;" Shih, "Mission of Development."

74. Anolin and Javier, "Empowering Returned Filipino Women Migrants and Their Children."

75. Anolin and Javier, "Empowering Returned Filipino Women Migrants and Their Children," 47.

76. Anolin and Javier, "Empowering Returned Filipino Women Migrants and Their Children," 49.

77. Anolin and Javier, "Empowering Returned Filipino Women Migrants and Their Children," 47.

78. Anolin and Javier, "Empowering Returned Filipino Women Migrants and Their Children," 44.

79. Anolin and Javier, "Empowering Returned Filipino Women Migrants and Their Children."

80. Anolin and Javier, "Empowering Returned Filipino Women Migrants and Their Children," 44, 51–52.

81. Yllang Montenegro, "DALOY, Wealth of Batis-AWARE Women," World Pulse, April 30, 2019, https://www.worldpulse.com/community/users/yllang/posts/88289.

82. Montenegro, cited in Jackie Enzmann, "Migrant Labor and Human Rights: Building Connections between Civil Society in Japan and Southeast Asia," Sasakawa Peace Foundation, January 11, 2019, https://www.spf.org/en/spfnews/information/20190111_01.html.

83. Written by actor and writer Rody Vera, the play, titled *Mizushobai*—a euphemism for the sex industry in Japan where many Filipina migrants work—is based on interviews and improvisational exercises with women in the group. The first half of the play focuses on the paths that led the women to Japan. During the second half, information is presented on the health issues, such as reproductive health and issues related to drug use; the social strain of migration on families; and the poor labor conditions that undocumented workers face. See Vera, *Mizushobai*. The play was performed for Philippine communities in Dagupan City and Pangasinan, and in secondary schools in Pampanga, Laguna, Samar, and Davao.

84. The performers of Batis AWARE were proud of how the play had changed their audience's opinion about overseas migration. For instance, during one sequence of the play, a group of six women recite in turns, line by line, "Although there are many stories of success about Filipinas who go to Japan, many others also experience physical and sexual abuse from their employers and partners. The experiences of these women can happen to anyone, whether they went abroad through legal or illegal processes. You call us 'Japayukis,' a term loaded with judgment about our character and experiences. But like many of you, all we wish for is to find a better life for our families. But even though these things happened to us, even if our lives are hard, we continue to press on for ourselves and the sake of our children. We hope that what we have shared will help you avoid the mistakes that we made. We hope for a time when things like this no longer happen." See Vera, *Mizushobai*, 55. One woman relayed that before the performance, they asked the audience if any of them wanted to go abroad. Everyone raised their hand. However, when asked the same question after the performance, nobody did. These women took this shift as validation that the audience, as one explained, "appreciated the play."

85. Anolin and Javier, "Empowering Returned Filipino Women Migrants and Their Children," 50.

86. Empowerment was initially developed by social workers as an assistance strategy to help inner-city Black families develop more effective skills for dealing with the social institutions—schools, police, welfare, offices, the courts—shaping their lives. Inspired by the civil rights movement, Barbara Bryant Solomon argued that empowerment should be the goal of social workers working with Black families in the inner cities of the United States. She was working against dominant conceptualizations of psychosocial problems of these communities as deriving from internal intrapsychic factors. Rather, she wanted to draw attention to the role of "external, oppressive social institutions" in shaping these communities' lives (81). See Solomon, "Empowerment."

Her assumption was that through empowerment, "oppressed communities" could overcome feelings of powerlessness that they had internalized on account of "negative valuation by the larger society" (81). Solomon focused on "power blocks"—acts, events, and conditions that stymied individuals to develop effective personal and social skills (80). She identified these as acting both indirectly, having been incorporated into family processes, and directly, insofar as they were also applied by agents of social institutions. She believed that once these communities developed better skills for dealing with social institutions, they would be better equipped to take advantage of opportunities available to them. See Solomon, "Empowerment." Later, women in development projects picked up empowerment as a strategy that bridged feminist activism and development work, enabling activists in the Global North to build bridges with those in the Global South. For further discussion, see Afshar, *Women and Empowerment*; Mehra, "Women, Empowerment, and Economic Development."

87. Farmer, "Anthropology of Structural Violence"; Hartman, *Scenes of Subjection*; Mbembe, "Provisional Notes on the Postcolony."

88. See "Notable Achievements" under "Programme Overview" in UNTFHS, *Economic and Social Empowerment*.

89. See "Notable Achievements" under "Programme Overview" in UNTFHS, *Economic and Social Empowerment*.

CONCLUSION

1. For further information, see ICAT, "About Us," accessed January 1, 2023, https://icat .un.org/about.

2. Alliance 8.7 is a global partnership established in 2016 to respond to Target 8.7 of the UN's Sustainable Development Goals; the ILO currently serves as its secretariat. See ILO, *Alliance 8.7*.

3. For a discussion of bureaucratic proceduralism as apolitical, see Sharma and Gupta, "Introduction."

4. For a discussion of global scalability as a form of universalizing progress and endless growth, see Tsing, "On Nonscalability."

5. For a discussion of how indicators present policy solutions as quantifiable technical matters, see Merry, *Seductions of Quantification*.

6. UNODC, *Global Report on Trafficking in Persons, 2020*.

7. See ICAT, *World in Crisis*.

8. See Mullally, *Report of the Special Rapporteur on Trafficking in Persons*, A/HRC/50/33 (April 25, 2022); Mullally, *Report of the Special Rapporteur on Trafficking in Persons*, A/77/170 (July 15, 2022), 2.

9. Giammarinaro, *Report of the Special Rapporteur on Trafficking in Persons*, 1. The UN special rapporteur on trafficking in persons, especially women and children, submits annual reports to the General Assembly and the Human Rights Council/Commission on Human Rights. These reports are public documents that summarize the special rapporteur's communications with governments and other related material. They are based on two- to three-week-long trips in which the rapporteur interviews a range of actors—victims, government officials, and NGO workers—and then makes recommendations. For NGOs, visits by special rapporteurs offer opportunities to bring international visibility to their issues. For further discussion, see Merry, *Human Rights and Gender Violence*, 57–61.

10. Alliance 8.7, *Alliance 8.7*.

11. See IOM, *IOM Guidance on Referral Mechanisms*; IOM, *IOM Guidance on Response Planning for Migrants Vulnerable to Violence, Exploitation, and Abuse*; IOM, *IOM Handbook on Protection and Assistance*. These publications were motivated by the "operational challenges" that IOM staff and NGO caseworkers had been confronting in their

counter–human trafficking work, regularly encountering migrants who were clearly in distress and had been abused and exploited but did not qualify for assistance as victims of trafficking based on official criteria (see IOM, *IOM Handbook on Protection and Assistance*, 4). They also build on the "migrant vulnerability model" developed in the Global Compact for Safe, Orderly and Regular Migration, which was endorsed by the UN General Assembly in December 2018 (IOM, *IOM Handbook*, ix). Yet the Global Compact is a nonbinding agreement, and the programmatic, institutional models offered in the new IOM texts do little to either expand direct assistance for migrant workers or address the political-economic structures that condition the structural violence that makes these migrants vulnerable in the first place. Even when the guidebooks cite structural factors, the discussion is minimal and nonspecific. For instance, only two of the 284 pages of the *IOM Handbook on Protection and Assistance* (197–98) are dedicated to a discussion of "structural-level determinants of migrant vulnerability," including them as part of a quadripartite model of migrant vulnerability and resilience that also includes individual, household/family, and community factors (6, fig 1.1). Moreover, the "structural-level programming" proposed by the guidebook avoids any specific discussion of the geopolitical imbalances and colonial histories that the handbook itself recognizes make labor migrants vulnerable to abuse and exploitation (199–234). Instead, the handbook offers vague stock proposals, such as: "improvements to national laws and policies to ensure that they recognize migrant rights and offer adequate protection for migrants; the development and implementation of policies for safe and regular migration, including labour mobility; the pursuit of pro-poor and equitable development policies; improvements to the rule of law and respect for human rights; and barriers to discrimination against specific groups" (11). None of these items leads readers to consider specific geopolitical and economic relationships that need to change.

12. US Department of State, *Trafficking in Persons Report, June 2013*. Constituting about 20 percent of foreign migrant workers in Japan, these technical interns labor in agriculture, construction, machine and metal manufacturing, food manufacturing and service, and hospitals. In 2019, there were more than 400,000 in the TITP program; due to COVID restrictions, the number dropped to the high 300,000s in the 2020. The majority of these interns have come from Vietnam and China, with large numbers also from Indonesia and the Philippines. Abuse of TITP participants was first noted in the 2008 *TIP Report*, with attention to the issue increasing under Secretaries of State Hillary Clinton and John Kerry, who focused on links between trafficking and labor exploitation. The 2009 *TIP Report* estimated that 5 percent of migrants participating in the TITP program, or over 3,400 foreign workers, were potential victims of labor trafficking. US Department of State, *Trafficking in Persons Report, June 2009*, 171. For further discussion, see Chonlaworn, "Cheap and Dispensable"; Chuang, "Exploitation Creep and the Unmaking of Human Trafficking Law"; Suzuki, "Moment of Truth."

13. The Act on Proper Technical Intern Training and Protection of Technical Intern Trainees established regulations prohibiting the infringement of interns' human rights and established measures for protecting them. In addition to these changes, since 2019 technical interns' wages are supposed to be transferred directly to their bank accounts for transparency purposes. See Chonlaworn, "Cheap and Dispensable."

14. IOM, *Tracer Survey*. Note that the survey report is printed in both Japanese and English.

15. IOM, *Tracer Survey*. The report focused on the long-term effects for beneficiaries in the Philippines between 2005 and 2016 of Japan's Return and Reintegration Assistance for Trafficked Victims in Japan (RRATVJ)—the regular assistance program for identified trafficking victims. The survey was conducted, on average, a little more than six years after respondents' returns. The research team included four IOM and NGO staff who work closely with trafficking victims, including Carina Morita, cited in chapter 6 regarding her casework at Saalaa in Japan, and Marjorie Rongalerios of Batis, the Philippine organization highlighted in chapter 8. Of the 134 Filipina women assisted through the progam, the IOM survey team was able to locate 40 individuals by mail, receiving 35 completed surveys. Six of the 35 also sat for in-depth follow-up interviews. While recognizing the benefits of the RRATVJ, the report concluded that despite the benefits gained from temporary support, the majority of survey respondents remained economically vulnerable in ways consistent with those that had first led them to Japan. In its conclusion, the report recommended that efforts be made to "keep providing tailor-made reintegration assistance for beneficiaries," "increase flexibility of reintegration assistance, including extra support provision, for beneficiaries facing unexpected occasions" and "the provision of support to their families," and "increase the sustainability of RRATVJ" (54–55). The report also specifically mentions the need "for the provision of better job opportunities for beneficiaries" (55). See IOM, *Tracer Survey*.

16. According to the 2008 *TIP Report*, the Japanese government gave the IOM $300,000 in 2008 for these efforts, but the Council for the Promotion of Measures to Combat Trafficking in Persons reports that the Japanese government gave the IOM only $142,000 in 2021. See US Department of State, *Trafficking in Persons Report, June 2008*, 151; Council for the Promotion of Measures to Combat Trafficking in Persons, *Measures to Combat Trafficking in Persons (Annual Report)*, 56.

17. Council for the Promotion of Measures to Combat Trafficking in Persons, *Measures to Combat Trafficking in Persons (Annual Report)*, 56. According to the IOM Tokyo office's *Tracer Survey on the Reintegration of Filipino Victims of Trafficking in Japan into Their Home Country*, between 2005 and 2016, the numbers of officially recognized victims of human trafficking that received RRATVJ assistance from the IOM ranged from 8 to 67 individuals each year, with an average of just under 26 individuals assisted on a yearly basis. The numbers of those identified by the Japanese government ranged from 7 to 117 individuals each year between 2005 and 2016, with an average of just under 34 individuals per year. IOM, *Tracer Survey*. For context, the 2009 *TIP Report* explained that at 36, the number of cases of human trafficking identified in 2008 was "thought to be disproportionately low relative to the suspected magnitude of Japan's trafficking problem" (US Department of State, *Trafficking in Persons Report, June 2009*, 171). Similarly, the 2011 *TIP Report* maintained that the number of identified victims (43 in 2010) was inadequate relative to the size of the estimated problem (see US Department of State, *Trafficking in Persons Report, June 2011*, 205–7).

18. Chonlaworn, "Cheap and Dispensable."

19. Chonlaworn, "Cheap and Dispensable."

20. Chonlaworn, "Cheap and Dispensable." These violations range from inadequate recordkeeping, to workers being required to perform jobs beyond the parameters of their work descriptions, to wage and accommodation violations. Since 2012, fifty-three thousand trainees have run away from their worksites, leaving their jobs to escape workplace abuse. Cited in Chonlaworn, "Cheap and Dispensable," 43.

21. See US Department of State, *Trafficking in Persons Report, June 2018*; US Department of State, *Trafficking in Persons Report, June 2019*. Citing NGOs, the 2019 *TIP Report* maintained, "The OTIT was too understaffed to adequately investigate allegations of abuse, including forced labor, within such a large program—particularly as the number of participants continued to grow" (265). The 2019 report also found insufficient the Japanese National Police Agency's procedures for identifying trafficking victims despite its consultation of the *IOM Handbook* for identifying and referring victims (263). It noted that NGOs were blocked by local law enforcement from rescuing and assisting migrants from abusive TITP employers (263). In both 2018 and 2019, the *TIP Reports* faulted the Japanese government for the weak penalties received by Japanese nationals prosecuted for trafficking-related crimes, who generally received administrative penalties, small fines, or suspended sentences even when guilty verdicts were reached—a point repeatedly made in previous years. The reports pointed to problems with prosecuting cases of forced labor and labor abuse reporting, relaying that "NGOs claimed courts set prohibitively high evidentiary standards for forced labor cases involving foreign victims, thereby stymying appropriate law enforcement action." US Department of State, *Trafficking in Persons Report, June 2018*, 245; US Department of State, *Trafficking in Persons Report, June 2019*, 263.

22. These practices are similar to what are today called in the United States "sugaring" or "sugar babying" (and they also share features with what is called "*joshi kōsei*" or "JK business" in Japan).

23. See Leheny, *Think Global, Fear Local*, 104. Concern about what is often called "domestic sex trafficking" was first raised in regard to Japan by prostitution-abolitionists serving under the Bush administration, who viewed all forms of prostitution in such terms. Under the Obama administration, *TIP Reports* began increasingly identifying these practices as related to child sex trafficking. Assertions that this crackdown evidences progress in the fight against human trafficking has been questioned in Japan. First, the age of sexual consent in Japan was thirteen until 2023, when it was raised to sixteen; questions thus arise regarding characterizations of all teenage high school students as underage prostitutes when they engage in compensated dating. For instance, Japanese feminist Ueno Chizuko has argued that Japanese teenage girls' commercialization of their sexuality must be complexly understood as a form of sexual self-determination, even if it ultimately reproduces patriarchal sexual norms. See Ueno, "Self-Determination on Sexuality?" Second, Japanese teenage girls' sexual autonomy has been a long-standing concern in the Japanese media and government, which has presented it as emblematic of moral decay among Japanese youth. As David Leheny convincingly demonstrates, the Japanese government has in the past sieved foreign pressure to comply with international norms on child prostitution through nationalist political strategies for promoting a moral order of children's "wholesome upbringing" (*kenzen ikusei*) (Leheny, *Think Global,*

Fear Local, 104). Correspondingly, more than necessarily evidencing a commitment to ending human trafficking, the Japanese governments' crackdown on child prostitution as a means of fighting human trafficking may be better understood as a strategy by which it both addresses nationalist concerns about teenage sexuality and plays a diplomatic hand with the United States, while making minimal effort to stop foreign migrant labor abuse.

24. Also noted as a rationale was Japan's 2017 accession to the UN Convention on Transnational Organized Crime Convention. See US State Department, *Trafficking in Persons Report, June 2018*, 244.

25. US Department of State, *Trafficking in Persons Report, June 2018*; US Department of State, *Trafficking in Persons Report, June 2019* . In 2020, Japan was dropped back to Tier 2 on account of its limited headway in stopping TITP abuse and addressing the "persistent reports of forced labor among labor migrants working in Japan under its auspices." US Department of State, *Trafficking in Persons Report, June 2020*, 282. The 2020 *TIP Report* also justified this downgrade, arguing that the Japanese government's efforts to fight human trafficking were "not serious and sustained compared to those during the previous reporting period" (282). It explained that Japanese officials had investigated, prosecuted, and convicted fewer traffickers that year than in previous ones. However, the 2019 report, which had ranked Japan Tier 1, had included a nearly identical claim about the TITP program: "multiple reports of forced labor among migrant workers in Japan under its auspices." See US Department of State, *Trafficking in Persons Report, June 2019*, 262. In 2022, the Japanese government for the first time identified four technical interns as trafficking victims—a token of those reported to be abused and exploited through the program. The 2022 *TIP Report* concluded, "The government maintained insufficient efforts to prevent trafficking, including by continuing to demonstrate a lack of political will to adequately do so among highly vulnerable migrant worker populations." US Department of State, *Trafficking in Persons Report, June 2022*, 316.

26. Southern Poverty Law Center, "Close to Slavery."

27. See Bustillo, "Human-Trafficking Case Exposed Farmworker Abuses"; Edwards and Margolis, "Why California Workers Are Still Dying from Heat"; Cabrera-Lomelí, "Blacklisted for Speaking Up." The political will to increase funding to protect the labor rights of foreign migrants is severely lacking, as evidenced by OSHA funding. Including its state partners, the US Federal Occupational Safety Health Administration (OSHA) currently has only 1,850 inspectors to monitor over 8 million worksites employing approximately 130 million workers across the country—about one compliance officer for every 70,000 workers. See "Commonly Used Statistics," OSHA, accessed June 30, 2023, https://www.osha.gov/data/commonstats#:~:text=Federal%20OSHA%20is%20a%20small,officer%20for%20every%2070%2C000%20workers.

28. "National Statistics," National Human Trafficking Hotline, accessed June 29, 2023, https://humantraffickinghotline.org/en/statistics.

29. See Betancourt and McKim, "For Labor Trafficked Immigrants, T-Visas Are a Life-Saving but Flawed Relief"; US Citizenship and Immigration Services, "Number of Form I-914 Application for T Nonimmigrant Status." The median processing time for applications is now 11.3 months; 39 percent of applications were rejected in 2021. Betancourt and McKim, "For Labor Trafficked Immigrants, T-Visas Are a Life-Saving but Flawed Relief."

30. See "Overview," Alliance 8.7, accessed January 1, 2023, https://www.alliance87.org /about/.

31. See US State Department, *Trafficking in Persons Report, June 2018*, 2. The reports point to Tier I as a "responsibility" to "demonstrate appreciable progress" the next year "rather than a reprieve." US State Department, *Trafficking in Persons Report June 2018*, 2.

32. Lauriola, "Address on the Elaboration of a Convention against Transnational Organized Crime."

33. See Ahmed, "Declarations of Whiteness"; Ahmed, "Nonperformativity of Antiracism"; Ahmed, *On Being Included*.

34. Arendt describes the increasing bureaucratization of public life as the realization of "tyranny without a tyrant." Arendt, *On Violence*, 81. She explains, "The latest and perhaps most formidable form of such dominion, bureaucracy, or the rule by an intricate system of bureaus in which no men, neither one nor the best, neither the few nor the many, can be held responsible, and which could be properly called the rule by Nobody. Indeed, if we identify tyranny as the government that is not held to give account of itself, rule by Nobody is clearly the most tyrannical of all, since there is no one left who could even be asked to answer for what is being done." Arendt, *On Violence*, 38–39.

35. These appeals center on fostering empathy as a means for political change. For instance, Alison Brysk argues that creating political will to advance an international human rights regime rests on the emotional cultivation of empathy for those whose rights are being violated, such as trafficking victims. See Brysk, *Speaking Rights to Power*.

36. See Council for the Promotion of Measures to Combat Trafficking in Persons, *Measures to Combat Trafficking in Persons (Annual Report)*, 1.

37. See Chuang, "Exploitation Creep and the Unmaking of Human Trafficking Law."

38. For further discussion, see Chuang, "Exploitation Creep and the Unmaking of Human Trafficking Law."

39. For instance, the Japanese government's 2022 annual report on measures to combat trafficking lists under "Prevention": (a) tightening immigration control, visa application processing, residence management to make it more difficult for migrant workers to enter and remain in the country outside of legal channels; (b) cracking down on illegal employment and promoting awareness of labor issues with employers through annual campaigns and distributing leaflets; (c) sporadic monitoring of a portion of worksites employing foreign workers; and (d) providing foreign technical interns with information about labor standard laws in Japan through handbooks and leaflets. Council for the Promotion of Measures to Combat Trafficking in Persons, *Measures to Combat Trafficking in Persons (Annual Report)*, 18–28.

40. White House, *National Action Plan to Combat Human Trafficking*, 56.

41. White House, *National Action Plan to Combat Human Trafficking*.

42. Shear, "Harris Announces Funding to Address Root Causes of Migration Crisis."

43. White House Briefing Room, "Fact Sheet: Vice President Harris Launches Next Phase of Public-Private Partnership for Northern Central America," Statements and Releases, February 6, 2023, https://www.whitehouse.gov/briefing-room/statements-releases /2023/02/06/fact-sheet-vice-president-harris-launches-next-phase-of-public-private -partnership-for-northern-central-america/.

44. Shear, "Harris Announces Funding to Address Root Causes of Migration Crisis."

45. Lorde, *Master's Tools Will Never Dismantle the Master's House*.

46. See Arendt, *Responsibility and Judgment*, 151. Arendt differentiates what she calls "[collective] responsibility" from "[personal] guilt," arguing for the former as a central consideration of moral action (151). Whereas guilt for Arendt is based on legal and moral standards that apply to individuals and what they have directly done, collective responsibility is the responsibility that one holds on account of one's membership in a group that is in some way responsible or benefiting from harm against another, the responsibility one holds for harm that is done in one's name. See Arendt, *Responsibility and Judgment*, 147–58.

47. Arendt, *Responsibility and Judgment*, 175.

Bibliography

Achiume, E. Tendayi. "Migration as Decolonization." *Stanford Law Review* 71, no. 6 (2019): 1509–74.

Achiume, E. Tendayi. "Reimagining International Law for Global Migration: Migration as Decolonization?" *American Journal of International Law* 111 (2019): 142–46.

Adriano, Fermin D. "Agrarian Reform, Populism and Agrarian Debacle." *Manila Times*, December 3, 2020.

Afshar, Haleh, ed. *Women and Empowerment: Illustrations from the Third World*. New York: St. Martin's Press, 1998.

Agamben, Giorgio. *Homo Sacer: Sovereign Power and Bare Life*. Translated by Daniel Heller-Roazen. Stanford, CA: Stanford University Press, 1998.

Agnew, John A. *Globalization and Sovereignty*. Lanham, MD: Rowman & Littlefield, 2009.

Agnew, John, and Stuart Crobridge. *Mastering Space: Hegemony, Territory and International Political Economy*. London: Routledge, 1995.

Aguilar, Delia. "The Export of Philippine Women." *Against the Current* 67, no. 2 (1997). https://againstthecurrent.org/atc067/p2205/.

Agustin, Laura María. *Sex at the Margins: Migration, Labour Markets and the Rescue Industry*. London: Zed Books, 2007.

Ahmed, Sara. "Affective Economies." *Social Text* 22, no. 2 (2004): 117–39.

Ahmed, Sara. "Declarations of Whiteness: The Non-performativity of Anti-racism." *Borderlands* 3, no. 2 (2004).

Ahmed, Sara. "The Nonperformativity of Antiracism." *Meridians* 7, no. 1 (2006): 104–26.

Ahmed, Sara. *On Being Included: Racism and Diversity in Institutional Life*. Durham, NC: Duke University Press, 2012.

Ajia Josei Shiryō Sentā, ed. *Pekin hatsu, Nihon no onnatachi e: Sekai josei kaigi o dō ikasu ka*. Tokyo: Akashi Shoten, 1997.

Allen, Lori. *The Rise and Fall of Human Rights: Cynicism and Politics in Occupied Palestine*. Stanford, CA: Stanford University Press, 2013.

Alliance 8.7. *Alliance 8.7*. October 2018. Copy of brochure on file with author.

Alston, Philip. "Ships Passing in the Night: The Current State of the Human Rights and Development Debate Seen through the Lens of the Millennium Development Goals." *Human Rights Quarterly* 27, no. 3 (2005): 755–829.

Alvarez, Sonia E. "Advocating Feminism: The Latin American Feminist NGO 'Boom.'" *International Feminist Journal of Politics* 1, no. 2 (1999): 181–209.

Anderson, Benedict. *Imagined Communities: Reflections on the Origin and Spread of Nationalism*. New York: Verso Books, 1983.

Andonova, Liliana B., Michele M. Betsill, and Harriet Bulkeley. "Transnational Climate Governance." *Global Environmental Politics* 9, no. 2 (2009): 52–73.

Annan, Kofi. "Address at the Opening of the Signing Conference for the United Nations Convention against Transnational Organized Crime." Palermo, Italy, December 12, 2000. https://www.unodc.org/unodc/en/about-unodc/speeches/speech_2000–12–12 _1.html.

Anolin, Andrea Luisa C. "Organizing Returned Women Migrants from Japan and Their Japanese-Filipino Children: The Batis Experience." Unpublished paper. Accessed June 19, 2023. http://feueac.acm.org/batis/resources/Organizing%20Returned%20 Migrants%20anf%20their%20Children%20-%20ARMMNet%20paper%202011.pdf.

Anolin, Andrea Luisa C., and Lara Salud C. Javier. "Empowering Returned Filipino Women Migrants and Their Children: The Batis Center for Women Experience." In *Human Rights Education in Asia-Pacific*. Vol. 2, 43–60. Osaka, Japan: Asia-Pacific Human Rights Information Center, 2011.

Anzaldúa, Gloria. *Borderlands/La Frontera: The New Mestiza*. San Francisco, CA: Aunt Lute, 1987.

Aoyama, Kaoru. "Gurōbaru-ka to sekkusu wāku: Shinka suru risuku, kakudai suru undō" [Globalization and sex work: Deepening risks and increasing social action]. *Japanese Sociological Review* 65, no. 2 (2014): 224–38.

Appadurai, Arjun. "Disjuncture and Difference in the Global Cultural Economy." *Theory, Culture and Society* 7, no. 2–3 (1990): 295–310.

Appel, Hannah. *The Licit Life of Capitalism: US Oil in Equatorial Guinea*. Durham, NC: Duke University Press, 2019.

Arendt, Hannah. *Eichmann in Jerusalem: A Report on the Banality of Evil*. London: Penguin, 2006.

Arendt, Hannah. *On Violence*. New York: Harcourt, Brace & World, 1970.

Arendt, Hannah. *Responsibility and Judgment*. Edited by Jerome Kohn. New York: Schocken Books, 2003.

Arendt, Hannah. "Thinking and Moral Considerations: A Lecture." *Social Research* 38, no. 3 (1971): 417–46.

Arendt, Hannah, and Karl Jaspers. *Correspondence, 1926–1969*. New York: Harcourt, 1992.

Asahi Shimbun. "Tekihatsu kara hogo e tenkan hitsuyō: Gaikokujin josei no jinshin baibai taisaku." July 23, 2004.

Ajia no onnatachi no kai [Asian Women's Association], ed. "Ajia kara no dekasegi on-natachi naze Nihon ni kuru no ka? (Tokushū)." *Ajia to josei kaihō* [*Asian Women's Liberation*] 20 (1989).

Asis, Maruja Milagros B., Shirlena Huang, and Brenda S. A. Yeoh. "When the Light of the Home Is Abroad: Unskilled Female Migration and the Filipino Family." *Singapore Journal of Tropical Geography* 25, no. 2 (2004): 198–215.

Avenell, Simon. *Making Japanese Citizens: Civil Society and the Mythology of Shimin in Postwar Japan*. Berkeley: University of California Press, 2010.

Babior, Sharman Lark. "Women of a Tokyo Shelter: Domestic Violence and Sexual Exploitation in Japan." PhD diss., University of California, Los Angeles, 1993.

Barlay, Stephen. *Sex Slavery: A Documentary Report on the International Scene Today*. London: William Heinemann, 1968.

Barnett, Michael. *Eyewitness to a Genocide: The United Nations and Rwanda*. Ithaca, NY: Cornell University Press, 2003.

Barry, Kathleen. *Female Sexual Slavery*. New York: New York University Press, 1979.

Barry, Kathleen. "International Feminism: Sexual Politics and the World Conference of Women in Copenhagen." *Feminist Issues* 1, no. 2 (1981): 37–50.

Barry, Kathleen. "The Network Defines Its Issues: Theory, Evidence and Analysis of Female Sexual Slavery." In *International Feminism: Networking against Female Sexual Slavery; Report of the Global Feminist Workshop to Organize against Traffic in Women, Rotterdam, the Netherlands, April 6–15, 1983*, 32–48. New York: International Women's Tribune Centre, 1984.

Barry, Kathleen. *The Prostitution of Sexuality*. New York: New York University Press, 1995

Barry, Kathleen, Charlotte Bunch, and Shirley Castley, eds. *International Feminism: Networking against Female Sexual Slavery; Report of the Global Feminist Workshop to Organize Against Traffic in Women, Rotterdam, the Netherlands, April 6–15, 1983*. New York: International Women's Tribune Centre, 1984.

Basel Action Network. "Building Toxic Waste Colonies: Japan's Economic Partnership Agreements." Briefing paper 9, 2015.

Basu, Amrita. "Globalization of the Local/Localization of the Global: Mapping Transnational Women's Movements." *Meridians* 1, no. 1 (2000): 68–84.

Bell, Duncan. "What Is Liberalism?" *Political Theory* 42, no. 6 (2014): 682–715.

Bello, Walden F., Marissa de Guzman, Mary Lou Malig, and Herbert Docena. *The Anti-development State: The Political Economy of Permanent Crisis in the Philippines*. London: Zed Books, 2005.

Benhabib, Seyla. "Claiming Rights across Borders: International Human Rights and Democratic Sovereignty." *American Political Science Review* 103, no. 4 (2009): 691–704.

Benhabib, Seyla. *Dignity in Adversity: Human Rights in Troubled Times*. Malden, MA: Polity Press, 2013.

Benhabib, Seyla. "Identity, Perspective and Narrative in Hannah Arendt's 'Eichmann in Jerusalem.'" *History and Memory* 8, no. 2 (1996): 35–59.

Benhabib, Seyla. "I. Judgment and the Moral Foundations of Politics in Arendt's Thought." *Political Theory* 16, no. 1 (1988): 29–51.

Berlant, Lauren. "Cruel Optimism." *Differences* 17, no. 3 (2006): 20–36.

Bernal, Victoria, and Inderpal Grewal. "Introduction: The NGO Form—Feminist Struggles, States, and Neoliberalism." In *Theorizing NGOs: States, Feminisms, and Neoliberalism*, 1–18. Durham, NC: Duke University Press, 2014.

Bernal, Victoria, and Inderpal Grewal, eds. *Theorizing NGOs: States, Feminisms, and Neoliberalism*. Durham, NC: Duke University Press, 2014.

Bernstein, Elizabeth. *Brokered Subjects: Sex, Trafficking, and the Politics of Freedom*. Chicago: University of Chicago Press, 2018.

Bernstein, Elizabeth. "The Sexual Politics of the 'New Abolitionism.'" *Differences* 18, no. 3 (2007): 128–51.

Bernstein, Elizabeth, and Elena Shih. "The Erotics of Authenticity: Sex Trafficking and 'Reality Tourism' in Thailand." *Social Politics: International Studies in Gender, State and Society* 21, no. 3 (2014): 430–60.

Bernstein, Richard J. "Reflections on Radical Evil: Arendt and Kant." *Soundings: An Interdisciplinary Journal* 85, no. 1/2 (2002): 17–30.

Betancourt, Sarah, and Jennifer McKim. "For Labor Trafficked Immigrants, T-Visas Are a Life-Saving but Flawed Relief." GBH News. October 24, 2022. https://www.wgbh .org/news/local-news/2022/10/24/for-labor-trafficked-immigrants-t-visas-are-a-life -saving-but-flawed-relief.

Billo, Emily, and Alison Mountz. "For Institutional Ethnography: Geographical Approaches to Institutions and the Everyday." *Progress in Human Geography* 40, no. 2 (2016): 199–220.

Boli, John, and George M. Thomas. "World Culture in the World Polity: A Century of International Non-Governmental Organization." *American Sociological Review* 62, no. 2 (1997): 171–90.

Bornstein, Erica. *The Spirit of Development: Protestant NGOs, Morality, and Economics in Zimbabwe*. Stanford, CA: Stanford University Press, 2005.

Bosold, David, and Sascha Werthes. "Human Security in Practice: Canadian and Japanese Experiences." *Internationale Politik Und Gesellschaft* 1 (2005): 85–101.

Boyle, Kevin. "Stock-Taking on Human Rights: The World Conference on Human Rights, Vienna 1993." *Political Studies* 43, no. 1 (1995): 79–95.

Bradley, Mark Philip. *The World Reimagined: Americans and Human Rights in the Twentieth Century*. New York: Cambridge University Press, 2016.

Brennan, Denise. *Life Interrupted: Trafficking into Forced Labor in the United States*. Durham, NC: Duke University Press, 2014.

Brennan, Denise, and Sine Plambech. "Editorial: Moving Forward—Life after Trafficking." *Anti-trafficking Review*, no. 10 (2018).

Brenneis, Don. "Reforming Promise." In *Documents: Artifacts of Modern Knowledge*, edited by Annelise Riles, 41–70. Ann Arbor: University of Michigan Press, 2006.

Brown, Wendy. "'The Most We Can Hope For . . .'" Human Rights and the Politics of Fatalism." *South Atlantic Quarterly* 103, no. 2 (2004): 451–63.

Brown, Wendy. *States of Injury: Power and Freedom in Late Modernity*. Princeton, NJ: Princeton University Press, 1995.

Brunovskis, Anette, and Rebecca Surtees. "Agency or Illness—the Conceptualization of Trafficking: Victims' Choices and Behaviors in the Assistance System." *Gender, Technology and Development* 12, no. 1 (2008): 53–76.

Brysk, Alison. *Speaking Rights to Power: Constructing Political Will*. Oxford: Oxford University Press, 2013.

Buergenthal, Thomas. "The Evolving International Human Rights System." *American Journal of International Law* 100, no. 4 (2006): 783–807.

Buffett, Peter. "The Charitable-Industrial Complex." *New York Times*, July 27, 2013. https://www.nytimes.com/2013/07/27/opinion/the-charitable-industrial-complex .html.

Bunch, Charlotte. Foreword to *Voices from the Japanese Women's Movement*, edited by AMPO-Japan Asia Quarterly Review, xiii–xvi. Armong, NY: M.E. Sharpe, 1996.

Bunch, Charlotte. "Network Strategies and Organizing against Female Sexual Slavery."
In *International Feminism: Networking against Female Sexual Slavery, Report of the Global Feminist Workshop to Organize against Traffic in Women, Rotterdam, the Netherlands, April 6–15, 1983*, 49–63. New York: International Women's Tribune Centre, 1984.

Bunch, Charlotte. *Passionate Politics: Feminist Theory in Action*. New York: St. Martin's Press, 1987.

Bunch, Charlotte. "Women's Rights and Gender at the United Nations: The Case for a New Gender Equality Architecture." Unpublished document. Accessed June 22, 2023. https://womenalliance.org/old/pdf/pdf/Bunch_GEA-UN_Eng.pdf.

Bunch, Charlotte. "Women's Rights as Human Rights: Toward a Re-vision of Human Rights." *Human Rights Quarterly* 12, no. 4 (1990): 486–98.

Bunch, Charlotte, and Shirley Castley. Introduction to *International Feminism: Networking against Female Sexual Slavery, Report of the Global Feminist Workshop to Organize against Traffic in Women, Rotterdam, the Netherlands, April 6–15, 1983*, 8–14. New York: International Women's Tribune Centre, 1984.

Bunch, Charlotte, and Carol Anne Douglas. "Interview: Charlotte Bunch on Global Feminism." *Off Our Backs* 17, no. 9 (1987): 10–12.

Bunch, Charlotte, and Niamh Reilly. *Demanding Accountability: The Global Campaign and Vienna Tribunal for Women's Human Rights*. New Brunswick, NJ: Rutgers University, Center for Women's Global Leadership, 1994.

Bustamante, Jorge. *Report of the Special Rapporteur on the Human Rights of Migrants, Addendum*. A/HRC/17/33/Add.3 (March 21, 2011). https://documents-dds-ny.un.org/doc/UNDOC/GEN/G11/121/27/PDF/G1112127.pdf.

Bustillo, Ximena. "A Human-Trafficking Case Exposed Farmworker Abuses. The Government Is Promising Change." NPR, May 27, 2022. https://www.npr.org/2022/05/27/1101741366/human-trafficking-farmworker-abuse-georgia.

Butler, Judith. *Bodies That Matter: On the Discursive Limits of "Sex."* New York: Routledge, 1993.

Cabrera-Lomelí, Carlos. "Blacklisted for Speaking Up: How California Farmworkers Fighting Abuses Are Vulnerable to Retaliation." KQED Online, June 30, 2022. https://www.kqed.org/news/11918317/blacklisted-for-speaking-up-how-california-farmworkers-fighting-abuses-are-vulnerable-to-retaliation.

Cameron, Sally, and Edward Newman. "Trafficking of Filipino Women to Japan: Examining the Experiences and Perspectives of Victims and Government Experts, Executive Summary." Tokyo: United Nations University, 2003.

Caouette, Therese M., and Yuriko Saito. *To Japan and Back: Thai Women Recount Their Experiences*. Geneva: International Organization for Migration, 1999.

Capella, Peter, and MacAskill, Peter. "Robinson Quits UN Job Citing Lack of Funds." *Guardian*, March 20, 2001.

Cavell, Stanley. *Must We Mean What We Say*. New York: Cambridge University Press, 1976.

Chacon, Jennifer M. "Misery and Myopia: Understanding the Failures of U.S. Efforts to Stop Human Trafficking Part IV: Asylum, Refugees, and Human Rights." *Immigration and Nationality Law Review* 27 (2006): 331–96.

Chanbonpin, Kim David. "Holding the United States Accountable for Environmental Damages Caused by the U.S. Military in the Philippines: A Plan for the Future." *Asian-Pacific Law & Policy Journal* 4, no. 2 (2003): 320–81.

Chandran, Rina. "Philippine Peasants Fight for Land 30 Years after Reform." *Reuters*, May 30, 2018.

Chang, Grace, and Kathleen Kim. "Reconceptualizing Approaches to Human Trafficking: New Directions and Perspectives from the Field(s)." *Stanford Journal of Civil Rights and Civil Liberties* 3, no. 2 (2007): 317–44.

Chan-Tiberghien, Jennifer. *Gender and Human Rights Politics in Japan: Global Norms and Domestic Networks*. Stanford, CA: Stanford University Press, 2004.

Chapkis, Wendy. *Live Sex Acts: Women Performing Erotic Labor*. New York: Routledge, 1997.

Chapkis, Wendy. "Trafficking, Migration, and the Law: Protecting Innocents, Punishing Immigrants." *Gender and Society* 17, no. 6 (2003): 923–37.

Charnysh, Volha, Paulette Lloyd, and Beth A. Simmons. "Frames and Consensus Formation in International Relations: The Case of Trafficking in Persons." *European Journal of International Relations* 21, no. 2 (2015): 323–51.

Chen, Mei-Hua, and Hong-zen Wang. "Flexible Intimacies in the Global Intimate Economy: Evidence from Taiwan's Cross-Border Marriages." *Feminist Studies* 47, no. 2 (2021): 258–75.

Cheng, Sealing. *On the Move for Love: Migrant Entertainers and the U.S. Military in South Korea*. Philadelphia: University of Pennsylvania Press, 2011.

Chew, Lin. "Global Trafficking in Women: Some Issues and Strategies." *Women's Studies Quarterly* 27, no. 1/2 (1999): 11–18.

Chew, Lin. "Reflections by an Anti-trafficking Activist." In *Trafficking and Prostitution Reconsidered: New Perspectives on Migration, Sex Work, and Human Rights*, edited by Kamala Kempadoo, Jyoti Sanghera, and Bandana Pattanaik, 65–83. New York: Routledge, 2015.

Chonlaworn, Piyada. "Cheap and Dispensable: Foreign Labor in Japan via the Technical Intern Training Program." *Jsn Journal* 11, no. 1 (2021): 33–49. https://doi.org/10.14456/jsnjournal.2021.3.

Chuang, Janie. "Beyond a Snapshot: Preventing Human Trafficking in the Global Economy." *Indiana Journal of Global Legal Studies* 13, no. 1 (2006): 137–63.

Chuang, Janie. "Exploitation Creep and the Unmaking of Human Trafficking Law." *American Journal of International Law* 108, no. 4 (2014): 609–49.

Chuang, Janie. "The United States as Global Sheriff: Using Unilateral Sanctions to Combat Human Trafficking." *Michigan Journal of International Law* 27, no. 2 (2005): 437–94.

Clancey, Alison, Noushin Khushrushahi, and Julie Ham. "Do Evidence-Based Approaches Alienate Canadian Anti-trafficking Funders?" In "Following the Money: Spending on Anti-trafficking." Special Issue, *Anti-trafficking Review* 3 (2014): 87–109.

Clarke, Kamari Maxine. *Affective Justice: The International Criminal Court and the Pan-Africanist Pushback*. Durham, NC: Duke University Press, 2019.

Clarke, Kamari Maxine. *Fictions of Justice: The International Criminal Court and the Challenge of Legal Pluralism in Sub-Saharan Africa*. New York: Cambridge University Press, 2009.

Clarke, Kamari Maxine. "Transnational Yoruba Revivalism and the Diasporic Politics of Heritage." *American Ethnologist* 34, no. 4 (2007): 721–34.

Clarke, Kamari Maxine, and Mark Goodale. "Introduction: Understanding the Multiplicity of Justice." In *Mirrors of Justice: Law and Power in the Post–Cold War Era*, 1–27. New York: Cambridge University Press, 2010.

Clarke, Kamari Maxine, and Mark Goodale, eds. *Mirrors of Justice: Law and Power in the Post–Cold War Era*. New York: Cambridge University Press, 2010.

Claude, Richard Pierre. "Human Rights Education: The Case of the Philippines." *Human Rights Quarterly* 13, no. 4 (1991): 453–524.

Cmiel, Kenneth. "The Emergence of Human Rights Politics in the United States." *Journal of American History* 86, no. 3 (1999): 1231–50.

Collins, Randall. "Three Faces of Cruelty: Towards a Comparative Sociology of Violence." *Theory and Society* 1, no. 4 (1974): 415–40.

Commission on Global Governance. "Our Global Neighborhood: The Report of the Commission on Global Governance." New York: Oxford University Press, 1995.

Commission on Human Security, ed. *Human Security Now: Protecting and Empowering People*. New York: United Nations, 2003.

Condry, Ian. *Hip-Hop Japan: Rap and the Paths of Cultural Globalization*. Durham, NC: Duke University Press, 2006.

Constable, Marianne. "Law as Claim to Justice: Legal History and Legal Speech Acts." In "'Law As...': Theory and Method in Legal History." Special issue, *UC Irvine Law Review* 1, no. 3 (2011): 631–40.

Coomaraswamy, Radhika. *Report of the Special Rapporteur on Violence against Women, Its Causes and Consequences*. E/CN.4/1997/47/ (February 12, 1997). https://documents -dds-ny.un.org/doc/UNDOC/GEN/G97/104/22/PDF/G9710422.pdf.

Cosgrove, Denis E. *Apollo's Eye: A Cartographic Genealogy of the Earth in the Western Imagination*. Baltimore, MD: Johns Hopkins University Press, 2001.

Council for the Promotion of Measures to Combat Trafficking in Persons. *Measures to Combat Trafficking in Persons (Annual Report)*. June 22, 2022. https://www.kantei.go .jp/jp/singi/jinsintorihiki/dai8/eigoban_honbun.pdf.

Cover, Robert M. "Foreword: *Nomos* and Narrative." *Harvard Law Review* 97 (1983): 4–68.

Cowan, Jane K. "Culture and Rights after Culture and Rights." *American Anthropologist* 108, no. 1 (2006): 9–24.

Crapanzano, Vincent. "Cargo, Cult, and Culture Critique." In *Thoughts on Hope and Cargo*, 227–42. Honolulu: University of Hawai'i Press, 2004.

Crenshaw, Kimberle. "Demarginalizing the Intersection of Race and Sex: A Black Feminist Critique of Antidiscrimination Doctrine, Feminist Theory and Antiracist Politics." *University of Chicago Legal Forum* 1 (1989): 139–68.

Cruikshank, Barbara. *The Will to Empower: Democratic Citizens and Other Subjects*. Ithaca, NY: Cornell University Press, 1999.

Cruz, Jasey C., and Anton C. Sobreviñas. "New Massacre Highlights Failures of Philippine Land Reform." *GUIDON*, December 2018.

Cruz-Mante, Loree. *Coaching Returned Victims/Survivors of Trafficking toward Gainful Careers: A Manual for Coaches*. Geneva, Switzerland: ILO, 2009. https://www.ilo.org

/wcmsp5/groups/public/---asia/---ro-bangkok/---ilo-manila/documents/publication /wcms_125115.pdf.

Dauvergne, Peter. *Shadows in the Forest: Japan and the Politics of Timber in Southeast Asia*. Cambridge, MA: MIT Press, 1997.

Dawes, James. *That the World May Know: Bearing Witness to Atrocity*. Cambridge, MA: Harvard University Press, 2009.

De Dios, Aurora Javate. "Revisiting the Trafficking of Women: Revisiting the Trafficking of Women: Challenges since Beijing." *Women in Action* 1 (2005): 8–19.

De Leon, Jason. *The Land of Open Graves: Living and Dying on the Migrant Trail*. Berkeley: University of California Press, 2015.

Delfin, Lynn P., Jeanne C. Enriquez, and Raisaa Jajurie. *A Primer on Prostitution*. Manila: Saligan, CATW-Phils, 2002.

Dembour, Marie-Bénédicte. "Human Rights Talk and Anthropological Ambivalence." In *Inside and Outside the Law*, edited by Olivia Harris, 16–32. New York: Routledge, 2003.

Dennis, Michael Aaron. "Government Secrecy and Knowledge Production: A Survey of Some." In *Secrecy and Knowledge Production*, edited by Judith Reppy, 1–16. New York: Cornell University, 1999.

Denyer, Simon, and Akiko Kashiwagi. "Japan Wakes Up to Exploitation of Foreign Workers as Immigration Debate Rages." *Washington Post*, November 21, 2018.

DeStefano, Anthony. *The War on Human Trafficking: U.S. Policy Assessed*. New Brunswick, NJ: Rutgers University Press, 2007.

Dinan, Kinsey. *Owed Justice: Thai Women Trafficked into Debt Bondage in Japan*. New York: Human Rights Watch, 2000.

Doezema, Jo. "Loose Women or Lost Women? The Re-emergence of the Myth of White Slavery in Contemporary Discourses of Trafficking in Women." *Gender Issues* 18, no. 1 (1999): 23–50.

Dottridge, Mike. "How Is the Money to Combat Human Trafficking Spent?" In "Following the Money: Spending on Anti-trafficking." Special issue, *Anti-trafficking Review* 3 (2014): 3–14.

Douglass, Mike, and Glenda Roberts, eds. *Japan and Global Migration: Foreign Workers and the Advent of a Multicultural Society*. New York: Routledge, 2015.

Dower, John. *War without Mercy: Race and Power in the Pacific War*. New York: Pantheon Books, 1986.

Eckel, Jan. "The International League for the Rights of Man, Amnesty International, and the Changing Fate of Human Rights Activism from the 1940s through the 1970s." *Humanity: An International Journal of Human Rights, Humanitarianism, and Development* 4, no. 2 (2013): 183–214.

Eckel, Jan. "The Rebirth of Politics from the Spirit of Morality: Explaining the Human Rights Revolution of the 1970s." In *The Breakthrough: Human Rights in the 1970s*, edited by Samuel Moyn and Jan Eckel, 226–60. Philadelphia: University of Pennsylvania Press, 2013.

Eckel, Jan, and Samuel Moyn, eds. *The Breakthrough: Human Rights in the 1970s*. Philadelphia: University of Pennsylvania Press, 2013.

Edralin, Divina. *Catalogue of Skills and Livelihood Training Programmes and Other Support Services*. Geneva: International Labour Organization, 2009. https://www.ilo.org

/wcmsp5/groups/public/---asia/---ro-bangkok/---ilo-manila/documents/publication
/wcms_125108.pdf.

Edström, Bert. "Japan and Human Security: The Derailing of a Foreign Policy Vision
(Asia Paper)." Stockholm: Institute for Security and Development Policy, 2011.

Edwards, Brian, and Jacob Margolis. "Why California Workers Are Still Dying from
Heat—Despite Protections." KQED Online, September 8, 2021. https://www.kqed
.org/news/11886402/why-california-workers-are-still-dying-from-heat-despite
-protections.

Embassy Manila. "Number of Filipino 'Entertainers' Going to Japan Declines." Department of State cable (confidential). September 6, 2005. https://wikileaks.org/plusd
/cables/05MANILA4199_a.html.

Embassy Tokyo. "Advocating for TIP Victim Identification Procedures in Japan." Department of State cable (unclassified). October 23, 2007. https://wikileaks.org/plusd
/cables/07TOKYO4953_a.html.

Embassy Tokyo. "Deputy Vice Minister Objects to TIP Report Ranking." Department of State cable (confidential). May 16, 2008. https://wikileaks.org/plusd/cables
/08TOKYO1350_a.html.

Embassy Tokyo. "G/TIP Ambassador Lagon's July 2 Meeting with the Japanese Government." Department of State cable (confidential). July 12, 2007. https://wikileaks.org
/plusd/cables/07TOKYO3186_a.html.

Embassy Tokyo. "Japan Reacts Negatively to TIP Report Tier Ranking." Department of State cable (confidential). June 4, 2008. https://wikileaks.org/plusd/cables
/08TOKYO1528_a.html.

Embassy Tokyo. "Japan Submission for TIP Report." Department of State cable (unclassified). March 21, 2008. https://wikileaks.org/plusd/cables/08TOKYO782_a.html.

Embassy Tokyo. "Japan, the U.S., and TIP: At a Tipping Point?" Department of
State cable (confidential). May 26, 2009. https://wikileaks.org/plusd/cables
/09TOKYO1185_a.html.

Embassy Tokyo. "MOFA Presents Talking Points for Upcoming G/TIP Visit of Amb.
Lagon." Department of State cable (confidential). June 20, 2007. https://wikileaks.org
/plusd/cables/07TOKYO2788_a.html.

Embassy Tokyo. "A Review of Japan's Anti-TIP Policy: Progress and Relapse (Corrected
Copy)." Department of State cable (unclassified). November 15, 2006. https://
wikileaks.org/plusd/cables/06TOKYO6538_a.html.

Embassy Tokyo. "TIP: Final Clarification of Japan's Roadmap to Tier 1." Department
of State cable (unclassified). December 21, 2007. https://wikileaks.org/plusd/cables
/07TOKYO5646_a.html.

Embassy Tokyo. "2007 TIP Report: Japan (March 9)." Department of State cable (unclassified, for official use only). March 9, 2007. https://wikileaks.org/plusd/cables
/07TOKYO1028_a.html.

Embassy Tokyo. "2007 TIP Report: Japan (March 12)." Department of State cable (unclassified, for official use only). March 12, 2007. https://wikileaks.org/plusd/cables
/07TOKYO1034_a.html.

Englund, Harri. Prisoners of Freedom: Human Rights and the African Poor. Berkeley:
University of California Press, 2006.

Enrile, Annalisa V., and Jollene Levid. "GAB[Riela]Net[Work]: A Case Study of Transnational Sisterhood and Organizing." *Amerasia Journal* 35, no. 1 (2009): 92–107.

Estabrook, Barry. *Tomatoland: How Modern Industrial Agriculture Destroyed Our Most Alluring Fruit.* Kansas City, MI: Andrews McMeel, 2012.

Fahim, Kareem. "The Education of Mary Robinson." *Village Voice*, April 23, 2002.

Faier, Lieba. "Filipina Migrants in Rural Japan and Their Professions of Love." *American Ethnologist* 34, no. 1 (2007): 148–62.

Faier, Lieba. *Intimate Encounters: Filipina Women and the Remaking of Rural Japan.* Berkeley: University of California Press, 2009.

Faier, Lieba. "Planetary Urban Involution in the Tokyo Suburbs." *International Journal of Urban and Regional Research* 45, no. 4 (2021): 630–42.

Falcón, Sylvanna M. *Power Interrupted: Antiracist and Feminist Activism inside the United Nations.* Seattle: University of Washington Press, 2016.

Farmer, Paul. "An Anthropology of Structural Violence." *Current Anthropology* 45, no. 3 (2004): 305–25.

Fassin, Didier, ed. *A Companion to Moral Anthropology.* Hoboken, NJ: John Wiley & Sons, 2012.

Fassin, Didier. *Humanitarian Reason: A Moral History of the Present.* Berkeley: University of California Press, 2012.

Fassin, Didier, and Estelle d'Halluin. "Critical Evidence: The Politics of Trauma in French Asylum Policies." *Ethos* 35, no. 3 (2007): 300–329.

Fassin, Didier, and Richard Rechtman. *The Empire of Trauma: An Inquiry into the Condition of Victimhood.* Princeton, NJ: Princeton University Press, 2009.

Feingold, David A. "Playing the Numbers: The Spurious Promise of Global Trafficking Statistics." *Anti-trafficking Review*, 8 (2017): 153–56.

Feldman, Allen. *Formations of Violence: The Narrative of the Body and Political Terror in Northern Ireland.* Chicago: University of Chicago Press, 1991.

Feldman, Ilana. *Governing Gaza: Bureaucracy, Authority, and the Work of Rule, 1917–1967.* Durham, NC: Duke University Press, 2008.

Ferguson, James. *The Anti-politics Machine: "Development," Depoliticization and Bureaucratic Power in Lesotho.* New York: Cambridge University Press, 1990.

Finkelstein, Lawrence S. "What Is Global Governance." *Global Governance* 1, no. 3 (1995): 367–72.

Finn, James. "Human Rights in Vienna." *First Things* 37 (1993): 4–8.

Finnemore, Martha, and Kathryn Sikkink. "International Norm Dynamics and Political Change." *International Organization* 52, no. 4 (1998): 887–917.

Flowers, Petrice R. "International Human Rights Norms in Japan." *Human Rights Quarterly* 38, no. 1 (2016): 85–107.

Flowers, Petrice R. *Refugees, Women, and Weapons: International Norm Adoption and Compliance in Japan.* Stanford, CA: Stanford University Press, 2009.

Foot, Kirsten A., Amoshaun Toft, and Nina Cesare. "Developments in Anti-trafficking Efforts: 2008–2011." *Journal of Human Trafficking* 1, no. 2 (2015): 136–55.

Fregoso, Rosa-Linda. "For a Pluriversal Declaration of Human Rights." *American Quarterly* 66, no. 3 (2014): 583–608.

Friedan, Betty. *The Feminine Mystique.* Repr. ed. New York: W. W. Norton, 2001.

Fujimoto Nobuki. "'Gisō kekkon' no jirei kara jinshin torihiki no gurei zōn o kenshō suru" [Focusing on the gray zone of human trafficking by reviewing the cases of "false marriage"]. *Ritsumeikan Journal of International Relations and Area Studies*, 37 (2013): 175–81.

Fujitani, Takashi. *Race for Empire: Koreans as Japanese and Japanese as Americans during World War II*. Berkeley: University of California Press, 2011.

Fukami Fumi. *Tsūyaku no hitsuyō wa arimasen: Dōgo Tai-jin josei satsujin jinken saiban no kiroku*. Matsuyama: Sōfūsha, 1999.

Gal, Susan. "Politics of Translation." *Annual Review of Anthropology* 44, no. 1 (2015): 225–40.

Galison, Peter. "Removing Knowledge." *Critical Inquiry* 31, no. 1 (2004): 229–43.

Gallagher, Anne. "Human Rights and the New UN Protocols on Trafficking and Migrant Smuggling: A Preliminary Analysis." *Human Rights Quarterly* 23, no. 4 (2001): 975–1004.

Gallagher, Anne T. *The International Law of Human Trafficking*. New York: Cambridge University Press, 2010.

Gallagher, Anne T. "Two Cheers for the Trafficking Protocol." *Anti-trafficking Review* 4 (2015).

Galtung, Johan. "Violence, Peace, and Peace Research." *Journal of Peace Research* 6, no. 3 (1969): 167–91.

Garcia, Angela. *The Pastoral Clinic: Addiction and Dispossession along the Rio Grande*. Berkeley: University of California Press, 2010.

Giammarinaro, Maria Grazia. *Report of the Special Rapporteur on Trafficking in Persons, Especially Women and Children*. A/HRC/44/45 (April 6, 2020). https://documents -dds-ny.un.org/doc/UNDOC/GEN/G20/086/90/PDF/G2008690.pdf.

Gōhara Nobuo. "Japanese 'Prosecutors' Justice' on Trial." Nippon.com, June 15, 2020. https://www.nippon.com/en/in-depth/a06802/.

Gold, Tami. *Passionate Politics: The Life and Work of Charlotte Bunch*. New Day Films, 2011.

Gómez-Mera, Laura. "The Global Governance of Trafficking in Persons: Toward a Transnational Regime Complex." *Journal of Human Trafficking* 3, no. 4 (2017): 303–26.

Goodale, Mark. "Toward a Critical Anthropology of Human Rights." *Current Anthropology* 47, no. 3 (2006): 485–511.

Government Accountability Office. *Human Trafficking: Better Data, Strategy, and Reporting Needed to Enhance U.S. Antitrafficking Efforts Abroad*. GAO-06–825. Washington, DC: Government Accountability Office, 2006. https://www.gao.gov/assets/gao -06-825.pdf.

Graeber, David. *Toward an Anthropological Theory of Value: The False Coin of Our Own Dreams*. New York: Springer, 2001.

Green, Maria. "What We Talk about When We Talk about Indicators: Current Approaches to Human Rights Measurement." *Human Rights Quarterly* 23, no. 4 (2001): 1062–97.

Grugel, Jean, and Enrique Peruzzotti. "The Domestic Politics of International Human Rights Law: Implementing the Convention on the Rights of the Child in Ecuador, Chile, and Argentina." *Human Rights Quarterly* 34, no. 1 (2012): 178–98.

Guevarra, Anna Romina. *Marketing Dreams, Manufacturing Heroes: The Transnational Labor Brokering of Filipino Workers*. New Brunswick, NJ: Rutgers University Press, 2009.

Gupta, Akhil. *Red Tape: Bureaucracy, Structural Violence, and Poverty in India.* Durham, NC: Duke University Press, 2012.

Gutierrez, Richard. "International Environmental Justice on Hold: Revisiting the Basel Ban from a Philippine Perspective." *Duke Environmental Law & Policy Forum* 24 (2014): 399–426.

Halley, Janet. "Preface: Introducing Governance Feminism." In *Governance Feminism: An Introduction*, edited by Janet Halley, Prabha Kotiswaran, Rachel Rebouché, and Hila Shamir, ix–xxii. Minneapolis: University of Minnesota Press, 2018.

Halley, Janet. "Rape at Rome: Feminist Interventions in the Criminalization of Sex-Related Violence in Positive International Criminal Law." *Michigan Journal of International Law* 30, no. 1 (2008): 1–124.

Halley, Janet, Prabha Kotiswaran, Rachel Rebouché, and Hila Shamir. *Governance Feminism: An Introduction.* University of Minnesota Press, 2018.

Halley, Janet, Prabha Kotiswaran, Hila Shamir, and Chantal Thomas. "From the International to the Local in Feminist Legal Responses to Rape, Prostitution/Sex Work, and Sex Trafficking: Four Studies in Contemporary Governance Feminism." *Harvard Journal of Law and Gender* 29, no. 2 (2006): 335–424.

Hardacre, Helen. *Shinto and the State, 1868–1988.* Princeton, NJ: Princeton University Press, 1989.

Harding, Susan Friend. *The Book of Jerry Falwell: Fundamentalist Language and Politics.* Princeton, NJ: Princeton University Press, 2000.

Harper, Richard. *Inside the IMF.* New York: Routledge, 2009.

Harris, Olivia. *Inside and Outside the Law.* New York: Routledge, 2003.

Hartman, Saidiya. *Lose Your Mother: A Journey along the Atlantic Slave Route.* New York: Farrar, Straus, and Giroux, 2008.

Hartman, Saidiya. *Scenes of Subjection: Terror, Slavery, and Self-Making in Nineteenth-Century America.* New York: Oxford University Press, 1997.

Hatsuse Ryūhei. "Reciprocity and Migrant Workers." In *The Internationalization of Japan*, edited by Glenn D. Hook and Michael A. Weiner, 229–45. New York: Routledge, 1992.

Hawes, Gary. *The Philippine State and the Marcos Regime: The Politics of Export.* Ithaca, NY: Cornell University Press, 1987.

Hecht, Gabrielle. "Interscalar Vehicles for an African Anthropocene: On Waste, Temporality, and Violence." *Cultural Anthropology* 33, no. 1 (2018): 109–41.

Heise, Ursula K. *Sense of Place and Sense of Planet: The Environmental Imagination of the Global.* New York: Oxford University Press, 2008.

Hemment, Julie. *Empowering Women in Russia: Activism, Aid, and NGOs.* Bloomington: Indiana University Press, 2007.

Hemment, Julie. "Global Civil Society and the Local Costs of Belonging: Defining 'Violence against Women' in Russia." *Signs: Journal of Women in Culture and Society* 29, no. 3 (2004): 815–40.

Herzfeld, Michael. *The Social Production of Indifference.* Chicago: University of Chicago Press, 1993.

Ho, Karen. *Liquidated: An Ethnography of Wall Street.* Durham, NC: Duke University Press, 2009.

Hoff, Suzanne. "Where Is the Funding for Anti-trafficking Work? A Look at Donor Funds, Policies and Practices in Europe." *Anti-trafficking Review*, 3 (2014): 109–32.

Hollan, Douglas W., and C. Jason Throop. "The Anthropology of Empathy: Introduction." In *The Anthropology of Empathy: Experiencing the Lives of Others in Pacific Societies*, 1–24. New York: Berghahn Books, 2011.

Holmes, Seth M. "'Oaxacans Like to Work Bent Over': The Naturalization of Social Suffering among Berry Farm Workers." *International Migration* 45, no. 3 (2007): 39–68.

hooks, bell. *Feminism Is for Everybody: Passionate Politics*. 2nd ed. New York: Routledge, 2014.

Horton, Sarah B., and Josiah Heyman, eds. *Paper Trails: Migrants, Documents, and Legal Insecurity*. Durham, NC: Duke University Press, 2020.

Hughes, Donna M. "Combating Sex Trafficking: A Perpetrator-Focused Approach." *University of St. Thomas Law Journal* 6, no. 1 (2008): 28–53.

Hull, Gloria T., Patricia Bell Scott, and Barbara Smith, eds. *All the Women Are White, All the Blacks Are Men, but Some of Us Are Brave: Black Women's Studies*. New York: Feminist Press, 1982.

Hull, Matthew S. *Government of Paper: The Materiality of Bureaucracy in Urban Pakistan*. Berkeley: University of California Press, 2012.

Hunt, Lynn. *Inventing Human Rights: A History*. New York: W. W. Norton, 2007.

Hyndman, Jennifer. *Managing Displacement: Refugees and the Politics of Humanitarianism*. Minneapolis: University of Minnesota Press, 2000.

Ibusuki Shōichi. *Tsukaisute gaikokujin: Jinken naki imin kokka, Nihon*. Gleam Books, 2020.

ICAT. *A World in Crisis: Global Humanitarian Crises and Conflicts Increase Human Trafficking Concerns; Call to Action*. December 2022. https://icat.un.org/sites/g/files /tmzbdl461/files/publications/icat_call_to_action.pdf.

ILO. *Alliance 8.7.* Accessed June 29, 2023. https://www.ilo.org/wcmsp5/groups/public /@dgreports/@dcomm/documents/genericdocument/wcms_421047.pdf.

ILO. *Catalogue of Skills and Livelihood Training Programmes and Other Support Services*. Geneva: International Labour Organization, 2009. https://www.ilo.org/wcmsp5 /groups/public/—asia/—ro-bangkok/—ilo-manila/documents/publication/wcms _125108.pdf

ILO. *Economic and Social Empowerment of Returned Victims of Trafficking in the Philippines and Thailand: The Philippine Component*. Manila, Philippines: International Labour Organization, Sub-Regional Office for South-East Asia and the Pacific, 2006. https://www.ilo.org/wcmsp5/groups/public/---asia/---ro-bangkok/---ilo-manila /documents/publication/wcms_124808.pdf.

ILO. *Human Trafficking and Forced Labour Exploitation: Guidance for Legislation and Law Enforcement*. Geneva: International Labour Organization, 2005.

ILO. *Human Trafficking for Sexual Exploitation in Japan*. Geneva: International Labour Organization, 2005.

ILO. *Rays of Hope: Emerging Good Practices in the Provision of Economic and Social Reintegration Programs for Victims/Survivors of Trafficking*. Geneva: International Labour Organization, 2009. https://www.ilo.org/wcmsp5/groups/public/---asia/---ro -bangkok/---ilo-manila/documents/publication/wcms_124947.pdf.

Imam, Hayat. "The Diplomat." *Women in Action* 3 (1995): 32–35.

Ingold, Tim. "Globes and Spheres: The Topology of Environmentalism." In *Environmentalism: The View from Anthropology*, edited by Kay Milton, 31–42. New York: Routledge, 1993.

IOM. *IOM Guidance on Referral Mechanisms for the Protection and Assistance of Migrants Vulnerable to Violence, Exploitation and Abuse and Victims of Trafficking*. Geneva: International Organization for Migration, 2019. https://publications.iom.int/system /files/pdf/iom_guidance_on_referral.pdf.

IOM. *IOM Guidance on Response Planning for Migrants Vulnerable to Violence, Exploitation and Abuse*. Geneva: International Organization for Migration, 2019. https:// publications.iom.int/system/files/pdf/iom_guidelines_on_response_planning.pdf.

IOM. *The IOM Handbook on Direct Assistance for Victims of Trafficking*. Geneva: International Organization for Migration, 2007. https://publications.iom.int/system/files /pdf/iom_handbook_assistance.pdf.

IOM. *IOM Handbook on Protection and Assistance for Migrants Vulnerable to Violence, Exploitation and Abuse*. Geneva: International Organization for Migration, 2019. https://publications.iom.int/system/files/pdf/avm_handbook.pdf.

IOM. *Tracer Survey on the Reintegration of Filipino Victims of Trafficking in Japan into Their Home Country/Jinshin torihiki higai o uketa Firipinjin higaisha no shusshin kuni ni okeru shakai fukki jōkyō ni kansuru tsuiseki chōsa*. Tokyo: International Organization for Migration, 2019. https://japan.iom.int/sites/g/files/tmzbdl2136/files/RRATVJ _Tracer_Sruvery_Report_201903_web.pdf.

IOM. *Trafficking and Prostitution: The Growing Exploitation of Migrant Women from Central and Eastern Europe*. Budapest: International Organization for Migration, 1995.

IOM. *Trafficking in Persons: Victim Identification and Assistance Training Guide*. Abuja, Nigeria: International Organization for Migration, 2020.

Ito, Masami. "Japan's Foreign Trainee System Said Still Plagued by Rights Abuses." *Japan Times*, April 9, 2013.

Iyori, Naoko. "The Traffic in Japayuki-San." *Japan Quarterly* 34, no. 1 (1987): 84–88.

Jacob, Marie-Andree, and Annelise Riles. "The New Bureaucracies of Virtue Symposium: Papering Ethics, Documenting Consent: The New Bureaucracies of Virtue." *PoLAR: The Political and Legal Anthropology Review* 30, no. 2 (2007): 181–91.

James, Erica Caple. *Democratic Insecurities: Violence, Trauma, and Intervention in Haiti*. Berkeley: University of California Press, 2010.

Japan NGO Network for the Elimination of Racial Discrimination. *Joint Civil Society Report on Racial Discrimination in Japan*. Submitted to the Committee on the Elimination of Racial Discrimination (CERD) for Its Consideration of the Tenth and Eleventh Combined Periodic Report of Japan (CERD/C/JPN/10–11), August 2018. https://imadr.org/wordpress/wp-content/uploads/2018/07/Revised_ERD-Net_Joint -Civil-Society-Report_CERD96_2018.pdf.

Japan Times. "Illegal Aliens Who Built Nagano Games Sites Facing Sweep." February 3, 1998.

JNATIP and F-GENS. "'Nihon ni okeru jinshin baibai no higai ni kan suru chōsa kenkyū' hōkokusho." Tokyo: Japan Network against Trafficking in Persons and Frontiers of Gender Studies, 2005.

Johnson, David T. "Above the Law? Police Integrity in Japan." *Social Science Japan Journal* 6, no. 1 (2003): 19–37.

Johnson, David T. *The Japanese Way of Justice: Prosecuting Crime in Japan.* New York: Oxford University Press, 2001.

Johnson, David T. "Japan's Prosecution System." *Crime and Justice* 41 (2012): 35–74.

Joutsen, Matti. "Four Transitions in the United Nations Crime Programme." Policy paper. HEUNI/European Institute for Crime Prevention and Control, Helsinki, Finland, November 25, 2020. http://old.heuni.fi/material/attachments/heuni /policypaper/g2xEhm7It/FOUR_TRANSITIONS_IN_THE_UNITED _NATIONS_CRIME_PROGRAMME.pdf.

Kainō Tamie. "Hajimeni." In *Jinshin baibai o nakusu tame ni: Ukeire taikoku Nihon no kadai*, edited by Yōko Yoshida and JNATIP, 3–7. Tokyo: Akashi Shoten, 2004.

Kamibayashi Chieko. "Gaikokujin ginō jisshū seido seiritsu no keii to 2009 nen no tenkanten no imizuke" [The formation of the Technical Intern Training Program and its turning point of 2009]. *Imin seisaku kenkyū* 10 (2018): 44–59.

Kang, Laura Hyun Yi. *Traffic in Asian Women.* Durham, NC: Duke University Press, 2020.

Kaye, Mike. "Contemporary Forms of Slavery in Argentina." London: Anti-slavery International, 2006.

Keck, Margaret E., and Kathryn Sikkink. *Activists beyond Borders: Advocacy Networks in International Politics.* Ithaca, NY: Cornell University Press, 1998.

Kelley, Judith G. *Scorecard Diplomacy: Grading States to Influence Their Reputation and Behavior.* New York: Cambridge University Press, 2017.

Kelly, Patrick William. "The 1973 Chilean Coup and the Origins of Transnational Human Rights Activism." *Journal of Global History* 8, no. 1 (2013): 165–86.

Kelty, Christopher. "Against Networks." *Spheres: Journal for Digital Cultures*, 1 (2014): 1–16.

Kempadoo, Kamala, Jyoti Sanghera, and Bandana Pattanaik, eds. *Trafficking and Prostitution Reconsidered: New Perspectives on Migration, Sex Work, and Human Rights.* New York: Routledge, 2015.

Kendall, Sara, and Sarah Nouwen. "Representational Practices at the International Criminal Court: The Gap between Juridified and Abstract Victimhood; The Practices of the International Criminal Court." *Law and Contemporary Problems* 76, no. 3 & 4 (2013): 235–62.

Kim, Chang-Ran, and Elaine Lies. "U.S. Embassy in Tokyo Warns of 'Suspected Racial Profiling' by Japanese Police." *Reuters*, December 26, 2021. https://www.reuters.com /world/asia-pacific/us-embassy-tokyo-warns-suspected-racial-profiling-by-japanese -police-2021–12–06/.

Kleinman, Arthur, Veena Das, and Margaret Lock, eds. *Social Suffering.* Berkeley: University of California Press, 1997.

Klemesrud, Judy. "A Personal Crusade against Prostitution." *New York Times*, June 24, 1985.

Kobayashi, Michio. *Nihon keisatsu: Fuhai no kōzō.* Tokyo: Chikuma Shobō, 2000.

Kobayashi, Michio. *Nihon keisatsu no genzai.* Tokyo, Japan: Iwanami Shoten, 1998.

Koh, Harold Hongju. "Why Do Nations Obey International Law?" *Yale Law Journal* 106, no. 8 (1996): 2599–60.

Korea Church Women United. *Kisaeng Tourism: A Nation-Wide Survey Report on Conditions in Four Areas: Seoul, Pusan, Cheju, Kyongju.* Research issue no. 3. Seoul: Catholic Publishing House, 1984.

Kuwajima Kaoru. "Purosesu to shite no 'jiko kettei': Bōryoku higai josei no ichiji hogo shien no ba kara." *Interdisciplinary Cultural Studies* 16 (2011): 29–47.

Lambek, Michael. *Ordinary Ethics: Anthropology, Language, and Action.* New York: Fordham University Press, 2010.

Lang, Sabine. "The NGOization of Feminism." In *Transitions, Environments, Translations: Feminisms in International Politics,* edited by Joan Wallach Scott, Cora Kaplan, and Debra Keates, 101–20. New York: Routledge, 1997.

Lang, Sabine. "The NGO-ization of Feminism: Institutionalization and Institution Building within the German Women's Movements." In *Global Feminisms since 1945,* edited by Bonnie G. Smith, 290–304. New York: Routledge, 2000.

Laqueur, Thomas. "Mourning, Pity, and the Work of Narrative in the Making of 'Humanity.'" In *Humanitarianism and Suffering: The Mobilization of Empathy,* edited by Richard Ashby Wilson and Richard D. Brown, 31–57. New York: Cambridge University Press, 2009.

Larga, Robert L. "ILO-HSF Project Overview for Stakeholders: 'Economic and Social Empowerment of Returned Victims of Trafficking.'" PowerPoint presentation, 2006. Copy on file with author.

Larsen, Peter Bille. "The Politics of Technicality: Guidance Culture in Environmental Governance and the International Sphere." In *The Gloss of Harmony: The Politics of Policy Making in Multilateral Organizations,* edited by Birgit Müller, 75–102. London: Pluto Press, 2013.

Lauriola, Luigi. "Address on the Elaboration of a Convention against Transnational Organized Crime." Presented at the Millennium Assembly of the United Nations General Assembly, New York, November 15, 2000.

Lederer, Laura J. "Addressing Demand: Why and How Policymakers Should Utilize Law and Law Enforcement to Target Customers of Commercial Sexual Exploitation." *Regent University Law Review* 23, no. 2 (2010): 297–310.

Lee, Misook. "The Japan-Korea Solidarity Movement in the 1970s and 1980s: From Solidarity to Reflexive Democracy." *Asia-Pacific Journal: Japan Focus* 12, no. 38 (2014): 1–15.

Lee, Na-Young. "The Korean Women's Movement of Japanese Military 'Comfort Women': Navigating between Nationalism and Feminism." *Review of Korean Studies* 17, no. 1 (2014): 71–92.

Lee, Na-Young. "Negotiating the Boundaries of Nation, Christianity, and Gender: The Korean Women's Movement against Military Prostitution." *Asian Journal of Women's Studies* 17, no. 1 (2011): 34–66.

Leheny, David. *Think Global, Fear Local: Sex, Violence, and Anxiety in Contemporary Japan.* Ithaca, NY: Cornell University Press, 2006.

Leheny, David, and Kay Warren. "Introduction: Inescapable Solutions: Japanese Aid and the Construction of Global Development." In *Japanese Aid and the Construction of Global Development: Inescapable Solutions.* New York: Routledge, 2010, 1–26.

Levi, Primo. "The Gray Zone." In *The Drowned and the Saved*, 25–56. New York: Simon & Schuster, 2017.

Li, Tania Murray. *The Will to Improve: Governmentality, Development, and the Practice of Politics*. Durham, NC: Duke University Press, 2007.

Lie, John. "The Transformation of Sexual Work in 20th-Century Korea." *Gender and Society* 9, no. 3 (1995): 310–27.

Lim, Lin Lean, ed. *The Sex Sector: The Economic and Social Bases of Prostitution in Southeast Asia*. Geneva: International Labour Organization, 1998.

Limanowska, Barbara, and AnnJanette Rosga. "The Bar Raid as 'Outcome Space' of Anti-trafficking Initiatives in the Balkans." In *Travelling Facts*, edited by Caroline Baillie, Elizabeth Dunn, and Yi Zheng, 154–75. Rochester, NY: Campus Press, 2004.

Livingston, Julie. *Debility and the Moral Imagination in Botswana*. Bloomington: Indiana University Press, 2005.

Lloyd, Paulette, and Beth A. Simmons. "Framing for a New Transnational Legal Order: The Case of Human Trafficking." In *Transnational Legal Orders*, edited by Terence C. Halliday and Gregory Shaffer, 400–438. New York: Cambridge University Press, 2015.

Lobasz, Jennifer. *Constructing Human Trafficking: Evangelicals, Feminists, and an Unexpected Alliance*. Human Rights Interventions. New York: Palgrave Macmillan, 2019.

Lorde, Audre. *The Master's Tools Will Never Dismantle the Master's House*. Penguin Books, 2018.

Lu, Jinky Leilanie. "Occupational Hazards and Illnesses of Filipino Women Workers in Export Processing Zones." *International Journal of Occupational Safety and Ergonomics* 14, no. 3 (2008): 333–42.

Mackie, Vera. *Feminism in Modern Japan: Citizenship, Embodiment and Sexuality*. New York: Cambridge University Press, 2003.

Mahdavi, Pardis. *Gridlock: Labor, Migration, and Human Trafficking in Dubai*. Stanford, CA: Stanford University Press, 2011.

Mahlert, Bettina. "Needs and Satisfiers: A Tool for Dealing with Perspectivity in Policy Analysis." *European Journal of Development Research* 33, no. 6 (2021): 1455–74.

Mainichi Daily News. "329 Human Trafficking Victims to Japan Supported Back Home over 14 Years: UN Group." June 20, 2019.

Majic, Samantha A. "Real Men Set Norms? Anti-trafficking Campaigns and the Limits of Celebrity Norm Entrepreneurship." *Crime, Media, Culture* 14, no. 2 (2018): 289–309.

Maki, John M. "The Constitution of Japan: Pacifism, Popular Sovereignty, and Fundamental Human Rights." *Law and Contemporary Problems* 53, no. 1 (1990): 73–87.

Malkki, Liisa H. *The Need to Help: The Domestic Arts of International Humanitarianism*. Durham, NC: Duke University Press, 2015.

Mamdani, Mahmood. "The Politics of Naming: Genocide, Civil War, Insurgency." *London Review of Books*, March 8, 2007.

Mankekar, Purnima. *Unsettling India: Affect, Temporality, Transnationality*. Durham, NC: Duke University Press, 2015.

Masco, Joseph. *The Nuclear Borderlands: The Manhattan Project in Post–Cold War New Mexico*. New ed. Princeton, NJ: Princeton University Press, 2020.

Mathews, Andrew S. "Power/Knowledge, Power/Ignorance: Forest Fires and the State in Mexico." *Human Ecology* 33, no. 6 (2005): 795–820.

Mathews, Andrew S. "State Making, Knowledge, and Ignorance: Translation and Concealment in Mexican Forestry Institutions." *American Anthropologist* 110, no. 4 (2008): 484–94.

Matsui, Shigenori. "Fundamental Human Rights and 'Traditional Japanese Values': Constitutional Amendment and Vision of the Japanese Society." *Asian Journal of Comparative Law* 13, no. 1 (2018): 59–86.

Matsui Yayori. *Ai to ikari tatakau yūki: Josei jānarisuto inochi no kiroku.* Tokyo, Japan: Iwanami, 2003.

Matsui Yayori. "Josei hogo jigyō to josei no jinken." In *Josei no jinken to fujin hogo jigyō.* Saitama, Japan: National Women's Education Center (NWEC), 1996.

Matsui Yayori. "Pekin kaigi no igi to 21-seiki e no kadai." In *Pekin hatsu, Nihon no onnatachi e: Sekai josei kaigi o dō ikasu ka?*, edited by Ajia Josei Shiryō Sentā, 15–47. Tokyo: Akashi Shoten, 1997.

Matsui Yayori. "Sexual Slavery in Korea." Translated by Lora Sharnoff. *Frontiers: A Journal of Women Studies* 2, no. 1 (1977): 22–30.

Matsui Yayori. "Watashi wa naze kīsen kankō ni hantai suru no ka: Keizai shinryaku to sei shinryaku no kōzō o abaku." *Onna Erosu* 2 (1974): 68–77.

Matsui Yayori. "Why I Oppose Kisaeng Tours." In *International Feminism: Networking against Female Sexual Slavery, Report of the Global Feminist Workshop to Organize against Traffic in Women, Rotterdam, the Netherlands, April 6–15, 1983*, edited by Kathleen Barry, Charlotte Bunch, and Shirley Castley, 64–72. New York: The International Women's Tribune Centre, 1984.

Matsui Yayori. *Why I Oppose Kisaeng Tours: Exposing Economic and Sexual Aggression against South Korean Women.* Tokyo, Japan: Femintern Press, 1975.

Matsui Yayori. *Women in the New Asia: From Pain to Power.* New York: Zed Books, 1999.

Matsui Yayori. *Women's Asia.* New Jersey: Zed Books, 1989.

Maurer, Bill. "Due Diligence and 'Reasonable Man,' Offshore." *Cultural Anthropology* 20, no. 4 (2005): 474–505.

Mazower, Mark. *No Enchanted Palace: The End of Empire and the Ideological Origins of the United Nations.* Princeton, NJ: Princeton University Press, 2009.

Mbembe, Achille. "The Banality of Power and the Aesthetics of Vulgarity in the Postcolony." *Public Culture* 4, no. 2 (1992): 1–30.

Mbembe, Achille. "Provisional Notes on the Postcolony." *Africa* 62, no. 1 (1992): 3–37.

McGoey, Linsey. "Strategic Unknowns: Towards a Sociology of Ignorance." *Economy and Society* 41, no. 1 (2012): 1–16.

McGrath, Siobhán, and Samantha Watson. "Anti-slavery as Development: A Global Politics of Rescue." *Geoforum* 93 (2018): 22–31.

McKee, Kim. "Sceptical, Disorderly and Paradoxical Subjects: Problematizing the 'Will to Empower' in Social Housing Governance." *Housing, Theory and Society* 28, no. 1 (2011): 1–18.

Mehra, Rekha. "Women, Empowerment, and Economic Development." *Annals of the American Academy of Political and Social Science* 554, no. 1 (1997): 136–49.

Mehta, Uday S. *Liberalism and Empire: A Study in Nineteenth-Century British Liberal Thought*. Chicago: University of Chicago Press, 1999.

Mehta, Uday S. "Liberal Strategies of Exclusion." *Politics and Society* 18, no. 4 (1990): 427–54.

Menjívar, Cecilia, and Leisy J. Abrego. "Legal Violence: Immigration Law and the Lives of Central American Immigrants." *American Journal of Sociology* 117, no. 5 (2012): 1380–1421.

Merry, Sally Engle. *Human Rights and Gender Violence: Translating International Law into Local Justice*. Chicago: University of Chicago Press, 2006.

Merry, Sally Engle. *The Seductions of Quantification: Measuring Human Rights, Gender Violence, and Sex Trafficking*. Chicago: University of Chicago Press, 2016.

Migrant Women Workers' Research and Action Committee, ed. *NGOs' Report on the Situation of Foreign Migrant Women in Japan and Strategies for Improvement*. Prepared for the Fourth World Conference on Women, Beijing, China, September 4–15, 1995.

Milne, Sarah, and Sango Mahanty. "Value and Bureaucratic Violence in the Green Economy." *Geoforum* 98 (2019): 133–43.

Ministry of Foreign Affairs, Japan. *Japan's Actions to Combat Trafficking in Persons: A Prompt and Appropriate Response from a Humanitarian Perspective*. Tokyo: International Organized Crime Division, MOFA. Accessed June 30, 2023. https://www.mofa .go.jp/policy/i_crime/people/pamphlet.pdf.

Ministry of Foreign Affairs, Japan. "Plan for Establishment of the Commission on Human Security." Press release, January 24, 2001. https://www.mofa.go.jp/policy /human_secu/speech0101.html.

Miyazaki, Hirokazu. *The Method of Hope: Anthropology, Philosophy, and Fijian Knowledge*. Ithaca, NY: Stanford University Press, 2004.

Mohanty, Chandra Talpade, Ann Russo, and Lourdes Torres. *Third World Women and the Politics of Feminism*. Bloomington: Indiana University Press, 1991.

Mol, Annemarie. *The Body Multiple: Ontology in Medical Practice*. Durham, NC: Duke University Press, 2002.

Molony, Barbara. "Crossing Boundaries: Transnational Feminisms in Japan, 1900–2008." In *Women's Movements in Asia: Feminisms and Transnational Activisms*, edited by Mina Roces and Elise Edwards, 90–109. New York: Routledge, 2010.

Montañez, Jannis T., Carmelita G. Nuqui, and Paulynn Paredes Sicam. 2002. *Pains and Gains: A Study of Overseas Performing Artists in Japan from Pre-departure to Reintegration*. Manila: DAWN.

Moore, Adam. "Rethinking Scale as a Geographical Category: From Analysis to Practice." *Progress in Human Geography* 32, no. 2 (2008): 203–25.

Moraga, Cherríe, and Gloria Anzaldúa, eds. *This Bridge Called My Back: Writings by Radical Women of Color*. Berkeley, CA: Kitchen Table/Women of Color Press, 1983.

Morita, Carina. "Caring for Caregivers." *Alliance News*, July 2006, 6–10. http://gaatw.org /publications/Alliance%20News/July2006/Essays.pdf.

Mosse, David. *Cultivating Development: An Ethnography of Aid Policy and Practice*. London: Pluto Press, 2004.

Mountz, Alison. *Seeking Asylum: Human Smuggling and Bureaucracy at the Border*. Minneapolis: University of Minnesota Press, 2010.

Moyn, Samuel. *The Last Utopia: Human Rights in History*. Cambridge, MA: Harvard University Press, 2010.

Mullally, Siobhán. *Report of the Special Rapporteur on Trafficking in Persons, Especially Women and Children*. A/HRC/50/33 (April 25, 2022). https://documents-dds-ny.un .org/doc/UNDOC/GEN/G22/327/46/PDF/G2232746.pdf.

Mullally, Siobhán. *Report of the Special Rapporteur on Trafficking in Persons, Especially Women and Children*. A/77/170 (July 15, 2022). https://documents-dds-ny.un.org /doc/UNDOC/GEN/N22/427/23/PDF/N2242723.pdf.

Müller, Birgit, ed. "Introduction: Lifting the Veil of Harmony: Anthropologists Approach International Organisations." In *The Gloss of Harmony: The Politics of Policy-Making in Multilateral Organisations*. London: Pluto Press, 2013.

Musto, Jennifer. *Control and Protect: Collaboration, Carceral Protection, and Domestic Sex Trafficking in the United States*. Berkeley: University of California Press, 2016.

Musto, Jennifer Lynne. "What's in a Name? Conflations and Contradictions in Contemporary U.S. Discourses of Human Trafficking." *Women's Studies International Forum* 32, no. 4 (2009): 281–87.

Mutō Kaori. "Hogo wo motometa josei-tachi no genjitsu." In *Jinshin baibai o nakusu tame ni: Ukeire taikoku Nihon no kadai*, edited by Yōko Yoshida and JNATIP, 28–45. Tokyo: Akashi Shoten, 2004.

Nader, Laura. "Up the Anthropologist: Perspectives Gained from Studying Up." In *Reinventing Anthropology*, edited by Dell Hymes, 284–311. New York: Pantheon Books, 1972.

Napier-Moore, Rebecca. "Global Funding Information Sheet Anti-trafficking Review." Global Alliance against Traffic in Women. July 2014, 1–46. https://gaatw.org /publications/ATR_funding_factsheet.07.29.2014.pdf.

Navaro-Yashin, Yael. "Affect in the Civil Service: A Study of a Modern State-System." *Postcolonial Studies* 9, no. 3 (2006): 281–94.

Navaro-Yashin, Yael. *The Make-Believe Space: Affective Geography in a Postwar Polity*. Durham, NC: Duke University Press, 2012.

Neitzel, Laura. *The Life We Longed For: Danchi Housing and the Middle Class Dream in Postwar Japan*. Honolulu: University of Hawai'i Press, 2016.

Neudek, K., S. Zyhlarz-Shaw, and B. Lovell. "The World Ministerial Conference on Organized Transnational Crime—Background, Results and Follow-up Report." *European Journal of Crime, Criminal Law and Criminal Justice* 3, no. 1 (1995): 88–97.

Newell, Sasha. "The Affectiveness of Symbols: Materiality, Magicality, and the Limits of the Antisemiotic Turn." *Current Anthropology* 59, no. 1 (2018): 1–22.

Norma, Caroline. "Abolitionism in the History of the Transnational 'Justice for Comfort Women' Movement in Japan and South Korea." In *Remembering the Second World War*, edited by Patrick Finney, 115–37. New York: Routledge, 2017.

Norma, Caroline. *The Japanese Comfort Women and Sexual Slavery during the China and Pacific Wars*. New York: Bloomsbury, 2015.

O'Callaghan, Sean. *The Slave Trade Today*. New York: Crown, 1961.

O'Callaghan, Sean. *The White Slave Trade*. London: Robert Hale, 1965.

Ogata, Sadako. "The Human Security Commission's Strategy." *Peace Review* 16, no. 1 (2004): 25–28.

Ogata, Sadako, and Johan Cels. "Human Security: Protecting and Empowering the People." *Global Governance* 9, no. 3 (2003): 273–82.

Ong, Aihwa. "Strategic Sisterhood or Sisters in Solidarity? Questions of Communitarianism and Citizenship in Asia." *Indiana Journal of Global Legal Studies* 4, no. 1 (1996): 107–35.

Ong, Aihwa. "Translating Gender Justice in Southeast Asia: Situated Ethics, NGOs, and Bio-Welfare." *Hawwa* 9, no. 1–2 (2011): 26–48.

Ople, Toots. "Notice to the World: Robert Larga Is Gone." *Manila Times*, July 24, 2017.

Osanloo, Arzoo. *Forgiveness Work: Mercy, Law, and Victims' Rights in Iran*. Princeton, NJ: Princeton University Press, 2020.

Osanloo, Arzoo. "Islamico-Civil 'Rights Talk': Women, Subjectivity, and Law in Iranian Family Court." *American Ethnologist* 33, no. 2 (2006): 191–209.

Osanloo, Arzoo. *The Politics of Women's Rights in Iran*. Princeton, NJ: Princeton University Press, 2009.

Osanloo, Arzoo. "Redress: Rights and Other Remedies, a Comment on David Engel's Article on Rights Consciousness." *Indiana Journal of Global Legal Studies* 19, no. 2 (2012): 495–505.

Ohshima Shizuko and Carolyn Francis. *Japan through the Eyes of Women Migrant Workers*. Shohan. Tokyo: Japan Woman's Christian Temperance Union, 1989.

Osumi, Magdalena. "Nominees Announced for Japan's Sixth Annual Black Company Awards." *Japan Times*, November 17, 2017.

Ōtsu Keiko. "Hajimeni." In *Domesutikku baiorensu to jinshin baibai: Ijū josei no kenri o motomete*, edited by Solidarity Network with Migrants Japan, 2–3. Tokyo: Solidarity Network with Migrants Japan, 2004.

Ōtsu Keiko. "Minkan sherutā kara mieru Nihon shakai no jinshin baibai no jittai." In *Jinshin baibai o nakusu tame ni: Ukeire taikoku Nihon no kadai*, edited by Yōko Yoshida and JNATIP, 14–28. Tokyo: Akashi Shoten, 2004.

Pangalangan, Raul C. "Human Rights Discourse in Post-Marcos Philippines." In *Human Rights in Asia*, edited by Thomas W. D. Davis and Brian Galligan, 56–69. Northampton, MA: Elgar, 2011.

Park Sunmi. "Nanajū-nendai no Kankoku to Nihon ni okeru kīsen kankō hantai undō—Kan-Nichi josei undōshi ni okeru 'nanajū-nendai' no igi." *Ilbon yŏn'gu* [Japan Studies], 16 (2011): 325–49.

Parreñas, Rhacel. *Illicit Flirtations: Labor, Migration, and Sex Trafficking in Tokyo*. Stanford, CA: Stanford University Press, 2011.

Parreñas, Rhacel. *Servants of Globalization: Migration and Domestic Work*. 2nd ed. Stanford, CA: Stanford University Press, 2015.

Pascual, Francisco, and Arze Glipo. "WTO and Philippine Agriculture: Seven Years of Unbridled Trade Liberalization and Misery for Small Farmers." Presented at the NGO-PO-Legislators Forum on Philippine Agriculture under WTO-AoA, Quezon City, Philippines, December 12, 2001. https://www.iatp.org/sites/default/files/WTO_and _Philippine_Agriculture_Seven_Years_of_.htm.

Pheterson, Gail, ed. *A Vindication of the Rights of Whores*. Seattle, WA: Seal Press, 1989.

Piot, Charles. "The 'Right' to Be Trafficked." *Indiana Journal of Global Legal Studies* 18, no. 1 (2011): 199–210.

Piquero-Ballescas, Maria Rosario. "Philippine Migration to Japan." In *The Encyclopedia of Global Human Migration*, edited by Immanuel Ness, 2402–6. Hoboken, NJ: Wiley-Blackwell, 2013.

Plant, Roger. "Trafficking in Destination Countries: The Forced Labour Dimensions." Paper presented at the ILO Symposium on Trafficking in Human Beings, Tokyo, September 23, 2003.

Port, Kenneth. "The Japanese International Law 'Revolution': International Human Rights Law and Its Impact in Japan." *Stanford Journal of International Law* 28, no. 1 (1991): 139–72.

Povinelli, Elizabeth A. *The Cunning of Recognition: Indigenous Alterities and the Making of Australian Multiculturalism*. Durham, NC: Duke University Press, 2002.

Povinelli, Elizabeth A. *The Empire of Love: Toward a Theory of Intimacy, Genealogy, and Carnality*. Durham, NC: Duke University Press, 2006.

Pratt, Geraldine. *Families Apart: Migrant Mothers and the Conflicts of Labor and Love*. Minneapolis: University of Minnesota Press, 2012.

Proctor, Robert, and Londa Schiebinger. *Agnotology: The Making and Unmaking of Ignorance*. Stanford, CA: Stanford University Press, 2008.

Prügl, Elisabeth, Hayley Thompson, Madeleine Rees, and Kathryn Bolkovac. "The Whistleblower: An Interview with Kathryn Bolkovac and Madeleine Rees." *International Feminist Journal of Politics* 15, no. 1 (2013): 102–9.

Quesada, James, Laurie K. Hart, and Philippe Bourgois. "Structural Vulnerability and Health: Latino Migrant Laborers in the United States." *Medical Anthropology* 30, no. 4 (2011): 339–62.

Ralston, Meredith L., and Edna Keeble. *Reluctant Bedfellows: Feminism, Activism and Prostitution in the Philippines*. Sterling, VA: Kumarian Press, 2009.

Ramseyer, J. Mark, and Minoru Nakazato. "The Rational Litigant: Settlement Amounts and Verdict Rates in Japan." *Journal of Legal Studies* 18, no. 2 (2015): 263–90.

Rappaport, Julian. "Terms of Empowerment/Exemplars of Prevention: Toward a Theory for Community Psychology." *American Journal of Community Psychology* 15, no. 2 (1987): 121–48.

Raustiala, Kal, and Anne-Marie Slaughter. "International Law, International Relations and Compliance." In *The Handbook of International Relations*, edited by Walter Carlnaes, Thomas Risse, and Beth Simmons, 538–58. London: Sage, 2002.

Raustiala, Kal, and David G. Victor. "The Regime Complex for Plant Genetic Resources." *International Organization* 58, no. 2 (2004): 277–309.

Raymond, Janice G. "Guide to the New UN Trafficking Protocol: Protocol to Prevent, Suppress and Punish Trafficking in Persons, Especially Women and Children, Supplementing the United Nations Convention against Transnational Organized Crime." North Amherst, MA: Coalition against Trafficking in Women, 2001. https://catwinternational.org/wp-content/uploads/2019/09/Guide-to-the-New-UN -Trafficking-Protocol.pdf.

Repeta, Lawrence. "The International Covenant on Civil and Political Rights and Human Rights Law in Japan." *Law in Japan* 20 (1987): 1–28.

Repeta, Lawrence. "U.N. Committee Faults Japan Human Rights Performance, Demands Progress Report on Key Issues." *Asia-Pacific Journal* 20 (2009).

Riles, Annelise. "Encountering Amateurism: John Henry Wigmore and the Uses of American Formalism." *Northwestern Public Law Research Paper* No. 00–6, 2001.

Riles, Annelise. *The Network Inside Out.* Ann Arbor: University of Michigan Press, 2000.

Risse, Thomas, Stephen C. Ropp, and Kathryn Sikkink, eds. *The Power of Human Rights: International Norms and Domestic Change.* New York: Cambridge University Press, 1999.

Robbins, Joel. "Between Reproduction and Freedom: Morality, Value, and Radical Cultural Change." *Ethnos* 72, no. 3 (2007): 293–314.

Robbins, Joel. "Beyond the Suffering Subject: Toward an Anthropology of the Good." *Journal of the Royal Anthropological Institute* 19, no. 3 (2013): 447–62.

Roberts, Glenda. "NGO Support for Migrant Labor in Japan." In *Japan and Global Migration: Foreign Workers and the Advent of a Multicultural Society,* edited by Mike Douglass, Glenda Roberts, and Mike Douglass, 276–302. New York: Routledge, 2015.

Roces, Mina. "Prostitution, Women's Movements and the Victim Narrative in the Philippines." *Women's Studies International Forum* 32, no. 4 (2009): 270–80.

Roces, Mina, and Louise Edwards. *Women's Movements in Asia: Feminisms and Transnational Activism.* New York: Routledge, 2010.

Rodriguez, Robyn Magalit. *Migrants for Export: How the Philippine State Brokers Labor to the World.* Minneapolis: University of Minnesota Press, 2010.

Roland, Alex. "Secrecy, Technology, and War: Greek Fire and the Defense of Byzantium, 678–1204." *Technology and Culture* 33, no. 4 (1992): 655–79.

Rosen, Lawrence. *The Anthropology of Justice: Law as Culture in Islamic Society.* New York: Cambridge University Press, 1989.

Rosenthal, Ann. "Death by Inequality: How Workers' Lack of Power Harms Their Health and Safety." Washington, DC: Economic Policy Institute, 2021.

Rosga, AnnJanette, and Margaret L. Satterthwaite. "The Trust in Indicators: Measuring Human Rights." *Berkeley Journal of International Law* 27, no. 2 (2009): 253–315.

Ruggie, John Gerard. *Constructing the World Polity: Essays on International Institutionalisation.* New York: Routledge, 1998.

Russell, Diana, and Nicole Van de Ven. *Crimes against Women: Proceedings of the International Tribunal.* Millbrae, CA: Les Femmes, 1976.

Ryall, Julian. "Overwork Accepted as Cause of Trainee's Death." *South China Morning Post,* July 7, 2010.

Saito Yuriko. "Jinshin baibai higaisha to wa dare ka? Nihon seifu no 'jinshin torihiki' taisaku ni okeru higaisha ninchi ni kan suru kadai." *Ajia Taiheiyō rebyū* 3 (2006): 67–76.

Sakai, Naoki. *Translation and Subjectivity: On "Japan" and Cultural Nationalism.* Minneapolis: University of Minnesota Press, 1997.

Sarfaty, Galit A. "Why Culture Matters in International Institutions: The Marginality of Human Rights at the World Bank." *American Journal of International Law* 103, no. 4 (2009): 647–83.

Sassen, Saskia. "Economic Internationalization: The New Migration in Japan and the United States." *Social Justice* 21, no. 2 (56) (1994): 62–82.

Scheper-Hughes, Nancy. *Death without Weeping: The Violence of Everyday Life in Brazil.* Berkeley: University of California Press, 1992.

Scheper-Hughes, Nancy, and Philippe Bourgois. "Introduction: Making Sense of Violence." In *Violence in War and Peace: An Anthology*, edited by Nancy Scheper-Hughes and Philippe Bourgeois, 1–27. Malden, MA: Blackwell, 2004.

Scherz, China. *Having People, Having Heart: Charity, Sustainable Development, and Problems of Dependence in Central Uganda*. Chicago: University of Chicago Press, 2014.

Schmetzer, Uli. "Japan's Sex Industry Can Be Lethal for Asian Women." *Chicago Tribune*, November 17, 1991.

Scott, James C. *Domination and the Arts of Resistance: Hidden Transcripts*. New Haven, CT: Yale University Press, 1990.

Scott, James C. *Seeing Like a State: How Certain Schemes to Improve the Human Condition Have Failed*. New Haven, CT: Yale University Press, 1998.

Scott, James C. *Weapons of the Weak: Everyday Forms of Peasant Resistance*. New Haven, CT: Yale University Press, 2008.

Sellek, Yoko, and Michael A. Weiner. "Migrant Workers: The Japanese Case in International Perspective." In *The Internationalization of Japan*, edited by Glenn D. Hook and Michael A. Weiner, 205–28. New York: Routledge, 1992.

Senate Economic Planning Office, Philippines. "Japan-Philippines Economic Partnership Agreement (JPEPA): An Assessment." Policy brief. September 2007. https://legacy.senate.gov.ph/publications/PB%202007-01%20-%20Japan-Philippines%20Economic%20Partnership%20Agreement%20(JPEPA),%20An%20assesment.pdf.

Shahid, Abdulla. "Remarks." High-Level Meeting of the General Assembly on the Global Plan of Action to Combat Trafficking in Persons, UN General Assembly, New York, November 22, 2021. https://www.un.org/pga/76/2021/11/22/high-level-meeting-of-the-general-assembly-on-the-global-plan-of-action-to-combat-trafficking-in-persons/.

Shamir, Hila. "Anti-trafficking in Israel: Neo-abolitionist Feminists, Markets, Border, and the State." In *Governance Feminism: An Introduction*, edited by Janet Halley, Prabha Kotiswaran, Rachel Rebouché, and Hila Shamir, 149–200. Minneapolis: University of Minnesota Press, 2018.

Sharma, Aradhana. *Logics of Empowerment: Development, Gender, and Governance in Neoliberal India*. Minneapolis: University of Minnesota Press, 2008.

Sharma, Aradhana, and Akhil Gupta. "Introduction: Rethinking Theories of the State in an Age of Globalization." In *The Anthropology of the State: A Reader*, 1–42. Hoboken, NJ: John Wiley & Sons, 2009.

Shear, Michael D. "Harris Announces Funding to Address Root Causes of Migration Crisis." *New York Times*, February 6, 2023. https://www.nytimes.com/2023/02/06/us/politics/harris-migration-central-america.html.

Shigematsu, Setsu. *Scream from the Shadows: The Women's Liberation Movement in Japan*. Minneapolis: University of Minnesota Press, 2012.

Shih, Elena. "The Mission of Development: Religion and Techno-Politics in Asia." In *Evangelizing Entrepreneurship: Techno-Politics of Vocational Training in the Global Anti–Human Trafficking Movement*, edited by Catherine Scheer, Philip Fountain, and R. Michael Feener, 243–62. Brill, 2018.

Shih, Elena. "The Price of Freedom: Moral and Political Economies of the Global Anti-trafficking Movement." PhD diss., University of California, Los Angeles, 2015.

Shipper, Apichai W. *Fighting for Foreigners: Immigration and Its Impact on Japanese Democracy*. Ithaca, NY: Cornell University Press, 2016.

Shore, Cris, and Susan Wright. "Audit Culture Revisited: Rankings, Ratings, and the Reassembling of Society." *Current Anthropology* 56, no. 3 (2015): 421–44.

Skinner, E. Benjamin. "The Fight to End Global Slavery." *World Policy Journal* 26, no. 2 (2009): 33–41.

Soderlund, Gretchen. "Running from the Rescuers: New U.S. Crusades against Sex Trafficking and the Rhetoric of Abolition." *NWSA Journal* 17, no. 3 (2005): 64–87.

Soeya, Yoshihide. "Japanese Security Policy in Transition: The Rise of International and Human Security." *Asia-Pacific Review* 12, no. 1 (2005): 103–16.

Solomon, Barbara Bryant. "Empowerment: Social Work in Oppressed Communities." *Journal of Social Work Practice* 2, no. 4 (1987): 79–91.

Southern Poverty Law Center. "Close to Slavery: Guestworker Programs in the United States." Montgomery, AL: Southern Poverty Law Center, 2013.

"South Korea: The Seoul of Hospitality." *Time*, June 4, 1973.

Speed, Shannon. *Incarcerated Stories: Indigenous Women Migrants and Violence in the Settler-Capitalist State*. Chapel Hill: UNC Press Books, 2019.

Stokes, Henry Scott. "Sex Package Tours." *New York Times*, August 5, 1979.

Stoler, Ann Laura. *Capitalism and Confrontation in Sumatra's Plantation Belt, 1870–1979*. Ann Arbor: University of Michigan Press, 1995.

Stoler, Ann Laura. *Carnal Knowledge and Imperial Power: Race and the Intimate in Colonial Rule*. Berkeley: University of California Press, 2002.

Stoler, Ann Laura. *Race and the Education of Desire: Foucault's History of Sexuality and the Colonial Order of Things*. Durham, NC: Duke University Press, 1995.

Stolz, Barbara. "Educating Policymakers and Setting the Criminal Justice Policymaking Agenda: Interest Groups and the 'Victims of Trafficking and Violence Act of 2000.'" *Criminal Justice* 5, no. 4 (2005): 407–30.

Stone, Pamela. *Opting Out? Why Women Really Quit Careers and Head Home*. Berkeley: University of California Press, 2007.

Strathern, Marilyn, ed. *Audit Cultures: Anthropological Studies in Accountability, Ethics, and the Academy*. New York: Routledge, 2000.

Strathern, Marilyn. "From Improvement to Enhancement: An Anthropological Comment on the Audit Culture." *Cambridge Anthropology* 19, no. 3 (1996): 1–21.

Suchland, Jennifer. *Economies of Violence: Transnational Feminism, Postsocialism, and the Politics of Sex Trafficking*. Durham, NC: Duke University Press, 2015.

Sumi, Shigeki. "Human Security and Health." Speech by H. E. Shigeki Sumi, Ambassador of Japan, to the International Organizations in Vienna, 2006, Ministry of Foreign Affairs of Japan.

Surtees, Rebecca, and Fabrice de Kerchove. "Who Funds Re/integration? Ensuring Sustainable Services for Trafficking Victims." In "Following the Money: Spending on Anti-trafficking." Special issue, *Anti-trafficking Review* 3 (2014): 64–86.

Suzuki, Noriyuki. "Moment of Truth as Japan Eyes Review of Foreign 'Trainee' Workers." *Japan Times*, August 30, 2022. https://www.japantimes.co.jp/news/2022/08/30/national/foreign-trainee-workers/.

Tadiar, Neferti X. M. *Things Fall Away: Philippine Historical Experience and the Makings of Globalization*. Durham, NC: Duke University Press, 2009.

Takahashi Kikue. *Baibaishun mondai ni torikumu: Sei sakushu to Nihon shakai*. Tokyo: Akashi Shoten, 2004.

Takahashi Kikue. "Josei no jinken to kīsen kankō hantai undō." In *Zenkyōtō kara ribu e*, edited by Onnatachi no ima o tō kai, 315–24. Tokyo: Inpakuto Shuppankai, 1996.

Tamai Keiko. "Jinshin babai higai konzetsu, N G O to ittai de." *Asahi Shimbun*, July 17, 2004.

Tate, Winifred. *Counting the Dead: The Culture and Politics of Human Rights Activism in Colombia*. Berkeley: University of California Press, 2007.

Thomas, Dorothy Q., and Michele E. Beasley. "Domestic Violence as a Human Rights Issue." *Human Rights Quarterly* 15, no. 1 (1993): 36–62.

Throop, C. Jason. "Latitudes of Loss: On the Vicissitudes of Empathy." *American Ethnologist* 37, no. 4 (2010): 771–82.

Ticktin, Miriam I. *Casualties of Care: Immigration and the Politics of Humanitarianism in France*. Berkeley: University of California Press, 2011.

Timothy, Kristen. "Human Security Discourse at the United Nations." *Peace Review* 16, no. 1 (2004): 19–24.

Tolentino, Leny. "Migrant Women in Japan: Victims of Multiple Forms of Discrimination and Violence and the Government's Lack of Concern." In *NGO Report Regarding the Rights of Non-Japanese Nationals, Minorities of Foreign Origins, and Refugees in Japan*, 25–29. Tokyo: Solidarity Network with Migrants Japan, 2010.

Tousignant, Noémi. *Edges of Exposure: Toxicology and the Problem of Capacity in Postcolonial Senegal*. Durham, NC: Duke University Press, 2018.

Trinidad, Dennis. "Japan's Official Development Assistance (O D A) to the Philippines." Background paper no. 12. Japan's Development Cooperation: A Historical Perspective. Tokyo: J I C A Ogata Sadako Research Institute for Peace and Development, 2021.

Tsing, Anna. *Friction: An Ethnography of Global Connection*. Princeton, NJ: Princeton University Press, 2005.

Tsing, Anna. "The Global Situation." *Cultural Anthropology* 15, no. 3 (2000): 327–60.

Tsing, Anna. "On Nonscalability: The Living World Is Not Amenable to Precision-Nested Scales." *Common Knowledge* 18, no. 3 (2012): 505–24.

Tsing, Anna. "Supply Chains and the Human Condition." *Rethinking Marxism* 21, no. 2 (2009): 148–76.

Tsutsui, Kiyoteru. *Rights Make Might: Global Human Rights and Minority Social Movements in Japan*. New York: Oxford University Press, 2018.

Uchiyama Osamu. "Ginō jisshūsei, hachi-nen de 174-nin shibō." *Asahi Shimbun Dejitaru*, December 13, 2018.

Ucnikova, Martina. "O E C D and Modern Slavery: How Much Aid Money Is Spent to Tackle the Issue?" In "Following the Money: Spending on Anti-trafficking." Special issue, *Anti-trafficking Review* 3 (2014): 133–50.

Ueno, Chizuko. "Self-Determination on Sexuality? Commercialization of Sex among Teenage Girls in Japan." *Inter-Asia Cultural Studies* 4, no. 2 (2003): 317–24.

UN. "Launch of the UN Trust Fund for Victims of Human Trafficking (U N O D C)—Press Conference." UN Web TV. November 4, 2010. https://media.un.org/en/asset/k1n /k1nobcq4el.

UN. Protocol to Prevent, Suppress and Punish Trafficking in Persons (2000). https://www.ohchr.org/en/instruments-mechanisms/instruments/protocol-prevent-suppress-and-punish-trafficking-persons.

UN. "UN Convention against Transnational Organized Crime—General Assembly, 62nd Plenary Meeting." UN Web TV. November 15, 2020. https://media.un.org/en/asset/k1f/k1fhpol5x1.

UN Economic and Social Council. *Report of the United Nations High Commissioner for Human Rights to the Economic and Social Council, Addendum.* E/2002/68/Add. 1. May 20, 2002. https://www.un.org/esa/documents/ecosoc/docs/2002/e2002-68add1.pdf.

UN Economic and Social Council. *Report on the Eleventh Session (16–25 April 2002).* E/2002/30, E/CN.15/2002/14. New York: United Nations, 2002. https://www.unodc.org/pdf/crime/commissions/11comm/14e.pdf.

UN General Assembly. "Draft Elements for an Agreement on the Prevention, Suppression and Punishment of International Trafficking in Women and Children, Supplementary to the Convention against Transnational Organized Crime." Proposal submitted by Argentina, A/AC.254/8. January 15, 1999. https://documents-dds-ny.un.org/doc/UNDOC/GEN/V99/802/43/PDF/V9980243.pdf.

UN General Assembly. "Draft Elements for an International Legal Instrument against Illegal Trafficking and Transport of Migrants." Proposal submitted by Austria and Italy, A/AC.254/4/Add.1. December 15, 1998. https://documents-dds-ny.un.org/doc/UNDOC/GEN/V98/573/29/PDF/V9857329.pdf.

UN General Assembly. "Draft Protocol to Combat International Trafficking in Women and Children Supplementary to the United Nations Convention on Transnational Organized Crime." Proposal submitted by the United States of America, A/AC.254/4/Add.3, November 25, 1998. https://documents-dds-ny.un.org/doc/UNDOC/GEN/V98/575/05/PDF/V9857505.pdf.

UN General Assembly. "Informal Note by the United Nations High Commissioner for Human Rights." A/AC.254/16. June 1, 1999. https://documents-dds-ny.un.org/doc/UNDOC/GEN/V99/845/67/PDF/V9984567.pdf.

UN General Assembly. Resolution 53/114, Strengthening the United Nations Crime Prevention and Criminal Justice Programme, in Particular Its Technical Cooperation Capacity. A/RES/53/114 (January 20, 1999). https://digitallibrary.un.org/record/265758?ln=en#record-files-collapse-header.

UN General Assembly. Resolution 54/131, Strengthening the United Nations Crime Prevention and Criminal Justice Programme, in Particular Its Technical Cooperation Capacity. A/RES/54/131 (January 28, 2000). https://documents-dds-ny.un.org/doc/UNDOC/GEN/N00/247/23/PDF/N0024723.pdf.

UN General Assembly. Resolution 55/25, United Nations Convention against Transnational Organized Crime. A/RES/55/25 (January 8, 2001). https://www.unodc.org/pdf/crime/a_res_55/res5525e.pdf.

UN General Assembly. Resolution 66/29, Follow-Up to Paragraph 143 on Human Security of the 2005 World Summit Outcome. A/RES/66/290 (October 25, 2012). https://documents-dds-ny.un.org/doc/UNDOC/GEN/N11/476/22/PDF/N1147622.pdf?OpenElement.

UNHCR. "Guidelines on International Protection No. 7: The Application of Article 1A(2) of the 1951 Convention and/or 1967 Protocol Relating to the Status of Refugees to Victims of Trafficking and Persons at Risk of Being Trafficked." HCR/GIP/06/07. April 7, 2007. https://www.unhcr.org/fr-fr/en/media/guidelines-international -protection-no-7-application-article-1a-2-1951-convention-and-or-1967.

UNICEF. *Guidelines on the Protection of Child Victims of Trafficking.* UNICEF, 2006.

UNICRI and AIC. *Rapid Assessment: Human Smuggling and Trafficking from the Philippines.* United Nations Interregional Crime and Justice Research Institute and Australian Institute of Criminology, 1999.

UNODC. *From Victim to Survivor: A Second Chance at Life.* May 2018. https://www .unodc.org/documents/human-trafficking/Publication/UNVTF_Introductory _Brochure_Web.pdf.

UNODC. *Global Report on Trafficking in Persons, 2020.* New York: United Nations, 2021. https://www.unodc.org/documents/data-and-analysis/tip/2021/GLOTiP_2020 _15jan_web.pdf.

UNODC. *International Framework for Action to Implement the Trafficking in Persons Protocol.* New York: United Nations, 2009. https://www.unodc.org/documents/human -trafficking/Framework_for_Action_TIP.pdf.

UNODC. *Mid-Term Independent Project Evaluation: Management of the Voluntary Trust Fund for Victims of Trafficking, Especially Women and Children.* New York: United Nations, 2014. https://www.unodc.org/documents/evaluation/Independent _Project_Evaluations/2014/GLOX42_Mid-term_Independent_Evaluation_Report _December_2014.pdf.

UNODC. *Toolkit to Combat Trafficking in Persons: Global Programme against Trafficking in Human Beings.* New York: United Nations, 2008. https://www.unodc.org /documents/human-trafficking/Toolkit-files/07-89375_Ebook%5B1%5D.pdf.

UNODC. "29 NGOs Selected for Funding from UNVTF Third Grant Cycle." Announcement. Accessed June 28, 2023. https://www.unodc.org/documents/human-trafficking /Human-Trafficking-Fund/Announcement_NGOs_3SGF_29_NGOs_final.pdf.

UNODC. "UN Voluntary Trust Fund for Victims of Trafficking in Persons: Basic Facts." August 2015. https://www.unodc.org/documents/human-trafficking/Human -Trafficking-Fund/UN_Victims_Trust_Fund_Basic_Facts_Aug2015.pdf.

UNODC. "UNVTF: 20 New NGO Projects Selected for Emergency Grants under the Sixth Grant Cycle." News release, June 8, 2022. https://www.unodc.org/unodc/en /frontpage/2022/June/un-voluntary-trust-fund-for-victims-of-human-trafficking_-20 -new-ngo-projects-selected-for-emergency-grants-under-the-sixth-grant-cycle.html.

UNODC. "UNVTF Awards Grants to Six Additional NGOs under Fourth Grant Cycle." News release, December 11, 2020. https://www.unodc.org/unodc/frontpage/2020 /December/unvtf-awards-grants-to-six-additional-ngos-under-fourth-grant-cycle.html.

UNTFHS. "Economic and Social Empowerment of Returned Victims of Trafficking in Thailand and the Philippines." Programme summary. Accessed June 29, 2023. https://www.un .org/humansecurity/wp-content/uploads/2017/08/Programme-summary-40.pdf.

UNTFHS. "United Nations Trust Fund for Human Security Guidelines, 9th Revision." May 1, 2016. https://www.un.org/humansecurity/wp-content/uploads/2021/04 /FINAL-UNTFHS-Guidelines-9th-Edition_2020-Annex-Revision-modified.pdf.

UNTFHS. "What Is Human Security." Accessed June 28, 2023. https://www.un.org/humansecurity/what-is-human-security/.

Urano Naoki. "Gaikokujin jisshūsei nana-wari, saitei chingin shitamawaru kuni no chōsa o yatō bunseki." *Asahi Shimbun Dejitaru*, December 3, 2018.

US Citizenship and Immigration Services. "Number of Form I-914 Application for T Nonimmigrant Status, Fiscal Years 2008–2022." https://www.uscis.gov/sites/default/files/document/data/I914t_visastatistics_fy2022_qtr3.pdf.

US Department of State. *Trafficking in Persons Report, June 2001*. Washington, DC: US Department of State, 2001. https://2009-2017.state.gov/documents/organization/4107.pdf.

US Department of State. *Trafficking in Persons Report, June 2002*. Washington, DC: US Department of State, 2002. https://2009-2017.state.gov/documents/organization/10815.pdf.

US Department of State. *Trafficking in Persons Report, June 2003*. Washington, DC: US Department of State, 2003. https://2009-2017.state.gov/documents/organization/21555.pdf.

US Department of State. *Trafficking in Persons Report, June 2004*. Washington, DC: US Department of State, 2004. https://2009-2017.state.gov/documents/organization/34158.pdf.

US Department of State. *Trafficking in Persons Report, June 2005*. Washington, DC: US Department of State, 2005. https://2009-2017.state.gov/documents/organization/47255.pdf.

US Department of State. *Trafficking in Persons Report, June 2006*. Washington, DC: US Department of State, 2006. https://2009-2017.state.gov/documents/organization/66086.pdf.

US Department of State. *Trafficking in Persons Report, June 2007*. Washington, DC: US Department of State, 2007. https://2009-2017.state.gov/documents/organization/82902.pdf.

US Department of State. *Trafficking in Persons Report, June 2008*. Washington, DC: US Department of State, 2008. https://2009-2017.state.gov/documents/organization/105501.pdf.

US Department of State. *Trafficking in Persons Report, June 2009*. Washington, DC: US Department of State, 2009. https://2009-2017.state.gov/documents/organization/123357.pdf.

US Department of State. *Trafficking in Persons Report, June 2011*. Washington, DC: US Department of State, 2011. https://2009-2017.state.gov/j/tip/rls/tiprpt/2011/index.htm, Japan country report: https://2009–2017.state.gov/documents/organization/164455.pdf.

US Department of State. *Trafficking in Persons Report, June 2013*. Washington, DC: US Department of State, 2013. https://2009-2017.state.gov/j/tip/rls/tiprpt/2013/index.htm, Japan country report: https://2009–2017.state.gov/documents/organization/210740.pdf

US Department of State. *Trafficking in Persons Report, June 2017*. Washington, DC: US Department of State, 2017. https://www.state.gov/wp-content/uploads/2019/02/271339.pdf.

US Department of State. *Trafficking in Persons Report, June 2018.* Washington, DC: US Department of State, 2018. https://www.state.gov/wp-content/uploads/2019/01/282798.pdf.

US Department of State. *Trafficking in Persons Report, June 2019.* Washington, DC: US Department of State, 2019. https://www.state.gov/wp-content/uploads/2019/06/2019-Trafficking-in-Persons-Report.pdf.

US Department of State. *Trafficking in Persons Report, June 2020.* Washington, DC: US Department of State, 2020. https://www.state.gov/wp-content/uploads/2020/06/2020-TIP-Report-Complete-062420-FINAL.pdf.

US Department of State. *Trafficking in Persons Report, June 2022.* Washington, DC: US Department of State, 2022. https://www.state.gov/wp-content/uploads/2022/04/337308–2022-TIP-REPORT-inaccessible.pdf.

US Department of State. "U.S. Relations with Japan: Bilateral Fact Sheet." Bureau of East Asian and Pacific Affairs. January 21, 2020. https://www.state.gov/r/pa/ei/bgn/4142.htm.

Vance, Carole S. "Innocence and Experience: Melodramatic Narratives of Sex Trafficking and Their Consequences for Law and Policy." *History of the Present* 2, no. 2 (2012): 200–218.

Vanderhurst, Stacey. *Unmaking Migrants: Nigeria's Campaign to End Human Trafficking.* Ithaca, NY: Cornell University Press, 2022.

Vaughan, Diane. *The Challenger Launch Decision: Risky Technology, Culture, and Deviance at NASA.* Chicago: University of Chicago Press, 1996.

Vera, Rody. *Mizushobai.* (Based on interviews and an improvisational play by BATIS-Aware.) Draft for video version, June 26, 2003. Copy on file with author.

Vogt, Wendy A. "Crossing Mexico: Structural Violence and the Commodification of Undocumented Central American Migrants." *American Ethnologist* 40, no. 4 (2013): 764–80.

Vogt, Wendy A. *Lives in Transit: Violence and Intimacy on the Migrant Journey.* Berkeley: University of California Press, 2018.

Waly, Ghada. Preface to *Global Report on Trafficking in Persons,* 2020, by UNODC, 4–5. New York: United Nations, 2021.

Walzer, Michael, ed. *Toward a Global Civil Society.* New York: Berghahn Books, 1995.

Warren, Kay B. "Trafficking in Persons: A Multi-Sited View of International Norms and Local Responses." In *Japanese Aid and the Construction of Global Development,* edited by David Leheny and Kay Warren, 217–32. New York: Routledge, 2010.

Warren, Kay B. "Troubling the Victim/Trafficker Dichotomy in Efforts to Combat Human Trafficking: The Unintended Consequences of Moralizing Labor Migration." *Indiana Journal of Global Legal Studies* 19, no. 1 (2012): 105–20.

Watanabe, Hiroaki. "Concerning Revisions in the Foreign Trainee and Technical Intern System." *Japan Labor Review* 7 (2010): 43–67.

Weber, Max. *Economy and Society: An Outline of Interpretive Sociology.* Berkeley: University of California Press, 1978.

Weiler, A. H. "*Slave Trade in the World Today,* a Documentary, Arrives." *New York Times,* November 24, 1964.

Weiss, Thomas G., and Leon Gordenker, eds. *NGOs, the UN, and Global Governance*. Boulder, CO: Lynne Rienner, 1995.

Weiss, Thomas G., and Ramesh Thakur. *Global Governance and the UN: An Unfinished Journey*. Bloomington: Indiana University Press, 2010.

Weiss, Thomas G., and Rorden Wilkinson. *International Organization and Global Governance*. New York: Routledge, 2013.

Weiss, Thomas G., and Rorden Wilkinson. "Rethinking Global Governance? Complexity, Authority, Power, Change." *International Studies Quarterly* 58, no. 1 (2014): 207–15.

White House. *The National Action Plan to Combat Human Trafficking*. Washington, DC: The White House, December 2021. https://www.whitehouse.gov/wp-content/uploads/2021/12/National-Action-Plan-to-Combat-Human-Trafficking.pdf.

Williams, Raymond. *The Long Revolution*. New York: Columbia University Press, 1961.

Wippman, David, Jeffrey L. Dunoff, and Steven R. Ratner. "Teacher's Manual: International Law: Norms, Actors, Process." Blue Springs, MO: Aspen, 2010.

Wirth, Linda. Foreword to *Coaching Returned Victims/Survivors of Trafficking toward Gainful Careers: A Manual for Coaches*, by Loree Cruz-Mante. Geneva: International Labour Organization, 2009.

Yasunaga, Hideo. "Legal Intervention against Medical Accidents in Japan." *Risk Management and Healthcare Policy* (2008): 39–42.

Yea, Sallie. "Mobilising the Child Victim: The Localisation of Human Trafficking in Singapore through Global Activism." *Environment and Planning D: Society and Space* 31, no. 6 (2013): 988–1003.

Yea, Sallie. "Towards Critical Geographies of Anti–Human Trafficking: Producing and Precluding Victimhood through Discourses, Practices and Institutions." *Progress in Human Geography* 45, no. 3 (2021): 513–30.

Yea, Sallie. *Trafficking Women in Korea: Filipina Migrant Entertainers*. New York: Routledge, 2015.

Yoneyama, Lisa. *Cold War Ruins: Transpacific Critique of American Justice and Japanese War Crimes*. Durham, NC: Duke University Press, 2016.

Yun Chai, Alice. "Asian-Pacific Feminist Coalition Politics: The Chŏngshindae/Jūgunianfu ('Comfort Women') Movement." *Korean Studies* 17, no. 1 (1993): 67–91.

Zigon, Jarrett. *Morality: An Anthropological Perspective*. New York: Routledge, 2020.

Zimmerman, Cathy, and Rosilyne Borland, eds. *Caring for Trafficked Persons: Guidance for Health Providers*. Geneva: International Organization for Migration, 2009.

Zimmerman, Cathy, and Charlotte Watts. *WHO Ethical and Safety Recommendations for Interviewing Trafficked Women*. Geneva: World Health Organization, 2003.

Zuo, Natalia. "Migrant Workers 'Exploited' in Japan." *BBC News*, August 25, 2019.

Zyhlarz-Shaw, S., K. Neudek, and B. Lovell. "The World Ministerial Conference on Organized Transnational Crime: Background, Results and Follow-Up." *European Journal of Crime, Criminal Law and Criminal Justice* 3, no. 1 (1995): 88–97.

Index

bare life, 95, 217n4; as focus of globalized approaches, xiii, 29, 63, 127; liberal internationalist ideals, 59; and official model of Justice, 136, 139–40. *See also* human rights

Barry, Kathleen, 25, 27, 48, 65, 226n3, 227n4; Asian feminist regional nuance evacuated by, 34–35, 42–43; position on prostitution, 37, 45

Batis (grassroots NGO, Manila), 186, 187, 198–204; sidelined by UNTFHS-ILO project, 203–4; Teatro Batis, 201–2

Batis AWARE (Association of Women in Action for Rights and Empowerment), 194, 199–203, 262n84

Beijing Conference (Fourth World Conference on Women), 45, 180

Beijing Declaration, 18

Beijing Platform for Action, 45

Berlant, Lauren, 187

Bernstein, Elizabeth, 53

Böckmann, Wilhelm, 131

Body Remembers, The (Rothschild), 85

"boomerang" diplomacy, 99, 247n13

Bornstein, Erica, 18

Bradley, Mark Philip, 10

Brysk, Alison, 268n35

Bunch, Charlotte, 27, 34, 35–39, 48, 65, 227n4, 227n7; Center for Women's Global Leadership, 39, 43; "global consciousness," 36; and United Nations, 42–43

burakku kigyō (black corporations), 118–19

bureaucracies: analogous national government, 131; "audit culture," 101, 113, 248n27; banality of, 11–14, 18; ethical, 153; and evil, 12; focus on policy and prosecution, 88–89; "guidance culture," 11, 22, 100, 113, 119, 248n22; illogic of standardized forms, 102–11; not intended as instrument of change, 213; stock responses to interviews, 131–32; structural inequalities not addressed by, 88–90, 133–34; thoughtlessness of, 12–13, 22, 187, 195, 204; tyranny of Nobody, 268n34; violence of, 13, 224n70. *See also* banality

Bush, George W., 241n78

Bustamante, Jorge, 117

Canada, 118

capitalism, 40–41, 57, 174, 187–89, 233n57; neoliberal logics, 174–75, 187–88

carceral framework, xii, 53, 65, 130. *See also* criminalization

caseworkers, NGO: affected by stories of suffering, 81–87; alternative justice envisioned by, 136–39; ambivalence and frustration of, xii, 3–4, 14–16, 22, 26–28, 71, 122–24, 136, 138–41, 159–60, 164, 172–73, 180; anger of, and justice, 121–23, 138–40; and Asian grassroots history, 28; burnout, 179–82; categories of action, 70; choice to give salaries to clients, 172; as "coaches" rather than "counselors," 191–92; distancing strategies of, 86; funding priorities questioned by, 172–73; immigrant and foreign nationals, 15, 27, 84, 125; "*jōshiki, atarimae*" (common sense) regarding privacy, 149; meetings with government staff, 82–83; and need-to-know protocols, 128; personal responsibility, sense of, 125–28, 138–39, 159; practical decisions made by, 69–71; sidelining of, xii, 87, 114, 124, 138, 164, 181; spiritual motivations, 121, 124–25, 138; time spent on forms rather than clients, 173; trauma and PTSD in, 85, 181; in United States, 84–85. *See also* need-to-know protocols; nongovernmental organizations (NGOs)

Castley, Shirley, 27, 35–36

Catalogue of Skills and Livelihood Training Programmes and Other Support Services, 192

CATW, 45, 65

CATW-Asia Pacific (CATW-AP), 41–42, 43, 45–46

Cels, John, 188, 260n32

Center for Women's Global Leadership (Rutgers University), 39, 43

Centre for International Crime Prevention (CICP), 239n37

"charitable industrial complex," 258n48

Chew, Lin Lap, 43, 65–66, 244n25

Christian organizations and faith, 31, 40, 46, 126, 167, 198, 229n30, 253n19; in United States, 57–58

Chuang, Janie, 213

civil society, 10, 223nn53–54

Clarke, Kamari, 79, 227n8

Clinton, Bill, 57

Clinton, Hillary, 57, 264n12

Coaching Returned Victims/Survivors of Trafficking toward Gainful Careers (Cruz-Mante), 191–92

Coalition against Trafficking in Women (CATW), 27

Cold War, 10, 222n48

collaboration, 71, 212; between activists, 31–32; double meaning of, 14; effect on caseworkers and NGOs, 16, 18; between feminists and government entities, 53–54, 66; between NGOs and corporations, 196; between NGOs and UN, 166, 169, 182, 184; partnerships, 163, 167, 174; transnational, 10–11

Collins, Randall, 13, 224nn70–71

colonialism: anticolonial movements, 21, 28, 34, 40, 222n48; decolonial projects, 80, 254n28; legacies of Japanese and US in the Philippines, 6–9, 35, 40, 48; histories of unaddressed, 34–35, 90, 208, 212, 214, 229n29, 230n48, 264n11; Japan as colonial occupier in Asia, 31–33, 40, 229–30n40; sex-tour *kisaeng* as manifestation of, 31–33, 229–30n40; UN roots in, 71

Commission on Human Security, 189

compassion, political action based on, 76–77

compliance: cultural norms missed by, 114–19; ethics as matter of, 154; politics of, 76; and victim identification protocols, 111–14

complicity, 53, 71, 227n7

compromise: abstract and technical accomplishments, 60–64; intermediary language, 71–72; leveraging, 68–71; politics of, 52–54

confidentiality agreements, 148–49

"consent," 65

Constable, Marianne, 123

Convention against Transnational Organized Crime (United Nations), 3, 56, 58, 60, 102, 139. *See also* Protocol to Prevent, Suppress and Punish Trafficking in Persons, Especially Women and Children (Trafficking Protocol, United Nations)

Convention for the Suppression of the Traffic in Persons and of the Exploitation of the Prostitution of Others, 29, 30

Coomaraswamy, Radhika, 46–47

corporate abuses of employees, 118–19, 214–15

Council on Women (United States), 57

counter–human trafficking programs: "3Ps": prosecution, protection, and prevention, 4, 57, 123–24, 252n5; consequences of globalized approach for caseworkers, 14–16; Global Plan of Action to Combat Trafficking in Persons, 10–11, 175, 179, 208; local expertise evacuated by, xiv, 15–16; participants in, 17; political-economic issues ignored by global approach, xii, xiv, 6, 13, 15, 22–23, 147, 164, 193–98, 204–5, 213; public acknowledgement of limitations, 208–9; Trafficking Victims Protection Act, 57–58, 84, 98, 251n99; Voluntary Trust Fund for Victims of Trafficking in Persons (UNVTF), 175–76, 179, 208, 211; vulnerability of women increased by, 6, 115. *See also* Action Plan of Measures to Combat Trafficking in Persons (Action Plan, Japan); Economic and Social Empowerment of Returned Victims of Trafficking in the Philippines and Thailand project (UNTFHS-ILO); human trafficking; *IOM Handbook on Direct Assistance for Victims of Trafficking*; political activism by trafficking survivors; Protocol to Prevent, Suppress and Punish Trafficking in Persons, Especially Women and Children (Trafficking Protocol, United Nations); *Trafficking in Persons Report* (TIP Report); Trafficking Protocol (Protocol to Prevent, Suppress and Punish Trafficking in Persons, Especially Women and Children)

COVID-19 pandemic, 208

COYOTE, 37

criminalization: and deportation, 3, 76, 78, 87, 91, 102, 245n3, 246n4; of *enjo kōsai* teenage dating practices, 120, 210–11, 262–63n23, 266n22; of human trafficking victims, 16, 78, 87; individualized criminal violence as focus, 29, 49, 93; of prostitution, 52, 56; of smuggled migrants, 102, 112. *See also* carceral framework

cruel empowerment. *See* empowerment; empowerment, cruel

"cruel optimism," 187

Cruz-Mante, Loree, 191–92

cultural norms: missed by compliance, 114–19; and public shelters, 135

Daloy 1 and 2 (Batis AWARE publications), 199

data, distinguished from information and matters, 151

data collection, 87, 179; indicators, development of, 66, 68, 103, 119, 208, 241n66

Dauvergne, Peter, 7

debt, 3, 8; bondage, 31, 75–76, 107, 210; to
  Japanese husbands, 115
Declaration on the Elimination of Violence
  against Women (United Nations), 44
decolonial projects, 80, 254n28
De Dios, Aurora, 41–42
deferral, logic of, 73
Department of Social Welfare and Development (Philippines), 167, 190
deportations, 8, 24, 132; criminal charges and
  arrests, 3, 76, 78, 87, 91, 102, 245n3, 246n4;
  "Operation White Snow," 118; of "smuggled
  migrants," 56–57; streamlined procedures,
  82; US views, 57, 102; without assistance,
  128, 139. See also repatriation of trafficking
  survivors
documentaries, 30, 148–49; as "melomentaries," 80
domestic legislation, 4, 52, 57, 68, 219n10
donation logic, 177–78
"Draft Elements for an International Legal
  Instrument against Illegal Trafficking and
  Transport of Migrants" (Italy and Austria),
  56–57
Drug Convention (United Nations, 1988), 60
"due diligence," 153–54; curiosity disciplined
  by, 154–58

Economic and Social Empowerment of Returned Victims of Trafficking in the Philippines and Thailand project (UNTFHS-ILO),
  163–71; Batis sidelined by, 203–4; career
  assessment tools, 192–93; and empowerment, 185–206; funding for, 164–71,
  174–75, 180, 188–89; future expansion, 190;
  as market-based approach, 187; NGOs as
  subcontractors, 164, 174–75, 203; project
  brochure, 186; and re-trafficking, 168–70,
  185–86; security as focus of, 170–71; as
  short-term enterprise, 186, 191, 195. See also
  empowerment; United Nations Trust Fund
  for Human Security (UNTFHS)
Edralin, Divina M., 192, 195
Eichmann, Adolf, 12
elites: overwork, 118–19, 251n97; Philippines,
  7–8, 41
empathy, 94–95, 268n34
empowerment: alternative understanding
  of, 187–88, 198–204; and Black families,

262n86; cooperative livelihood projects,
  199; diverse understanding of, 186; as governance regime, 186; limits of, 203–6; linked
  to social worlds, 203; politics of human
  security, 188–89; "rights-based framework,"
  198; standardized and reproducible model,
  190–95; thoughtful approaches to, 22–23.
  See also Economic and Social Empowerment of Returned Victims of Trafficking
  in the Philippines and Thailand project
  (UNTFHS-ILO)
empowerment, cruel, 22–23, 192, 203–4,
  261n73, 262–63n86; banal logic of, 187,
  193–98, 204–6; career realities ignored,
  191–95, 204; failures of inadequate training
  and funding, 195–97; relation of attachment to compromised conditions of possibility, 22, 187
encapsulation, 227n8
Ende, Hermann, 131
"entertainer visas," 5–6, 114–15, 220n20; as
  pretense, 88–89
entrepreneurs, universalized characteristics of,
  192–93
environmental damage, 7
environmental movements, 10, 222n50
ethics: of caseworkers, 83, 139, 146–48, 150,
  153–62; "due diligence," 153–58; as a matter
  of procedural compliance, 154; and need-
  to-know protocols, 153–62, 255n20; of
  officials, 76; prior to bureaucratization, 150,
  154; regimes and values, 46, 54
Europe, human trafficking in, 56–57, 256–57n16
Ewha Womans University students, 32

Fassin, Didier, 77
Fedotov, Yuri, 177
Female Sexual Slavery (Barry), 25, 27, 227n4
feminism: divides within, 36, 45–47, 73,
  240n52; "governance feminism," 29;
  grassroots activism in Asia, 25, 29–30,
  51–55, 68–73, 172, 183; practical reasons
  for support Trafficking Protocol, 64–68;
  prostitution-abolitionist feminists, 35–36,
  45, 57–58, 63; Rotterdam workshop, 1983,
  27, 45, 65
feminism, globalist (US-based): collaboration with government entities, 53–54, 66;
  denials and exclusions, 28–29, 227n10;

guidelines/guidebooks, 6, 21–22, 62, 97–101, 248n22, 263–64n11; as "interscalar vehicles," 101; pragmatic level, 100–101; UNTFHS-ILO guidebooks, 191–92. See also *IOM Handbook on Direct Assistance for Victims of Trafficking*; Roadmap to Tier 1

Gupta, Akhil, 18, 100, 207

haigūsha visas, 220n20, 250n80
Haiti, 80
Halley, Janet, 29
Haneda Airport demonstration (Tokyo), 32
Harding, Susan Friend, 227n8
Harris, Kamala, 214
Hartman, Saidiya, 94
HAVE A HEART slogan, 177
HELP (House of Emergency of Love and Peace) Asian Women's Shelter, 40
Hemment, Julie, 18
Herzfeld, Michael, 13
Holkeri, Harri, 61
Holland, John, 193
Holmes, Paul, 255n17
human rights: alternative understanding of by Asian women, 39–42; "basic international standards," 67; compromised by Trafficking Protocol, 66–67; donation seen as protecting, 178–79; hierarchy of, 83; instrumentalized, 119, 176–77; Japanese views of, 247n11; jurisgenerative discourse of, xii, 217n5; narrow focus on violation of civil and political liberties, 44, 245n28; sidelined by criminal justice focus, 3, 9; translated into compliance with minimum standards, 114, 119–20, 212, 251n99; universalization of, 44–45; as vernacular discursive practice, 225–26n89; "violence against women" linked with, 37–38, 42–43; World Conference on Human Rights (Vienna), 43–45, 77, 93, 244n25. See also bare life
"Human Security Now" report (Ogata and Sen), 189
human trafficking, 222n47; circumscribed phases of, 103, 107; definition adopted by Trafficking Protocol, 4, 59, 62–66, 102; "delivery health," 115; domestic attention to, 45; in Europe, 56–57, 256–57n16; expanded definitions, 67; global framing

of, 43–44; human smuggling distinguished from, 102–3, 108; of Japanese women and girls, 5, 210–11; *jinshin baibai*, 40; national government agendas, 47; re-trafficking, 6, 168–70, 175, 186, 195, 196, 205; "trafficking victim" as legal category, 82, 113; types of, 9, 63, 102–7, *104–6*; in United States, 157, 211, 242n80, 267n27; universalist approaches to definition of, 64–66, 81; US interest in legislation, 57. See also counter–human trafficking programs; victims/survivors of human trafficking

Hunt, Lynn, 244n27
hyperopias, 29, 228n12

ignorance, production of, 147
Ikeda Hayato, 228n21
imagined community, 13, 140
Immigration Bureau (Japan), 116, 133–34
Immigration Control and Refugee Recognition Act (Japan), 82
imperialism, "afterlife" of, 140
indictments, 116–17
indifference, 13; codified, 85–86
"Informal Note" (Robinson), 65, 67, 183, 240n54
information activism, 38, 178–79
information management protocols, 22, 146–48, 151–54, 157, 161–62, 255n17; information, data distinguished from, 151. See also need-to-know protocols
Inter-agency Coordination Group against Trafficking in Persons (ICAT), 208
Interagency Council on Women (United States), 57
Inter-Ministerial Liaison Committee and Task Force on Trafficking (Japan), 5
Inter-Ministerial Task Force on Combating Trafficking (Japan), 98
international agreements, 228n14; consensus, basis for, 53; lobbying, 52–53; "stick" approach to enforcing, 87–90. See also *specific agreements*
International Covenant on Civil and Political Rights (ICCPR), 245n28, 260n32
International Covenant on Economic, Social and Cultural Rights (ICESCR), 245n28
International Feminist Network Against Female Sexual Slavery, 25

International Framework for Action to Implement the Trafficking in Persons Protocol, 4, 57, 123–24, 252n5

International Labour Organization (ILO), 75, 241n77; grants administered by, 163–64, 168–69; as officially funded party of UNTFHS grant, 171; overhead costs for grant administration, 171–72. *See also* Economic and Social Empowerment of Returned Victims of Trafficking in the Philippines and Thailand project (UNTFHS-ILO)

international law, 17–18, 67, 109, 236nn131–32, 240n49; as functionally normative, 99; human trafficking definition codified in, 29–30, 64–65; lack of enforcement mechanism, 209

International Organization for Migration (IOM), 5, 14, 45, 116, 119, 249n41, 265nn15–16; *Caring for Trafficked Persons: Guidance for Health Providers*, 100; illogical loop in victim identification protocol, 111; as overseer for victim assistance and protection process, 14, 20, 254n2, 254n5, 263–64n11, 265n17; refusal to assist abused women, 122, 128; reports, 56, 265n15; and segmented client support, 146–48, 154–60; *Tracer Survey*, 210. See also *IOM Handbook on Direct Assistance for Victims of Trafficking*; need-to-know protocols

International Tribunal on Crimes against Women (Brussels, 1976), 34, 37

IOM Handbook on Direct Assistance for Victims of Trafficking, 97, 98–111, 113, 247n17; "Appendix 1: Ethical Principles in Caring for and Interviewing Trafficked Persons," 153; information management, 146; "Screening Interview Form," 103–9, *104–6*; "Security and Personal Safety.," 152; "structural-level programming," 264n11; trafficking described in "phases," 103–4, 107, 197; undercutting of recommendations in, 110–11. *See also* International Organization for Migration (IOM); need-to-know protocols

Israeli government, 53–54

James, Erica Caple, 80

Japan: Act on Proper Technical Intern Training and Protection of Technical Intern Trainees, 169–70, 209–10; as colonial occupier in Asia, 31–33, 40, 229–30n40; as destination country for human trafficking, 5, 220nn19–20; ethnic discrimination in, 137; grassroots feminist organization in, 30; "income doubling," 30, 228n21; Japanese nationals, human trafficking abuses by, 211, 266n21; Labor Standards Act, 210; lack of trained social workers, 137; Latin Americans in, 84; Meiji government, 130–31; political-economic exploitation in Asia, 32–33, 39; population decline, 210; Technical Intern Training Program (TITP, Ginō Jisshū Seido), 5, 6, 117–18, 209–10, 221n40, 264n12, 266n21, 267n25; Tier 1 minimum standards, 97–99, 120, 212; and Tier 2 Watch List, 5, 6, 82, 88, 90–92, 97, 220n16, 251–52n99, 267n25; US-Japanese relations, 7, 98; work culture, 118–19. *See also* Action Plan of Measures to Combat Trafficking in Persons (Action Plan, Japan); Japanese government; sex industry, Japanese

Japanese government: annual report on measures to combat trafficking, 268n39; contracts with grassroots groups, 1–2; decision to support global counter–human trafficking campaign, 21, 76; indifference to to migrants' rights, 127–28; interests of prioritized in funding, 170, 180–81, 257n18; Justice, vision of, 124; "proactive pacifism," 188; reluctance to address human trafficking, 5, 21; uneven response to international norms, 99; US State Department pressure on, xi, 5. *See also* Action Plan of Measures to Combat Trafficking in Persons (Action Plan, Japan)

Japan International Cooperation Agency (JICA), 189, 260n25

Japan-Philippines Economic Partnership Agreement, 7

Japan Women's Christian Temperance Union, 40

Javier, Lara Salud C., 185

jinshin baibai (human trafficking), 40

justice, 77, 121–41; alternative understandings of, 123, 136–39, 159; appeals and claims, 123; criminal justice focus of international conventions, 3, 9, 55, 60; as "empty signifier," 123; misperformance of, 216

National Action Plan to Combat Human Trafficking (United States, 2021), 214–15

National Association of Social Welfare Officials, 127

national governments, 18, 131; domestic criminal legislation regarding migration, 55–56; "grading" of, 99; inequalities among, 14–15, 48, 182, 204–6; newly independent countries, 59–60; sacrifice of women to developmental projects, 31, 40–41, 229n25

National Human Trafficking Hotline (United States), 211

National Police Agency (NPA), 92, 93, 116, 121, 247n17, 266n21

need-to-know protocols, 22, 128, 143–62, 255n17; and adjudication of cases, 157; assessment mechanisms lacking, 160, 161; caseworker questioning of, 158–61; "confidential personal data" distinguished from "private matters," 148–50; confidential personal data governed by, 151–54; "due diligence," 153–58; internalization of, 155–58; personal networks and back channels used to support clients, 160–61; as safety concerns, 152–53, 156; vulnerability increased by, 147. See also information management protocols; International Organization for Migration (IOM); privacy and confidentiality; victim assistance

neoliberal logics, 174–75, 187–88

NGO Report Regarding the Rights of Non-Japanese Japanese, Minorities of Foreign Origins, and Refugees in Japan, 85

Non-Aligned Movement, 222n48

nongovernmental organizations (NGOs), 217n1; cultural and moral logics of, 18; funding and compromise, 54, 70–72; global issues addressed by, 10; ignored by governments, 114, 138, 164; as instruments for accomplishing government objectives, 171, 173; NGO Forums, 36, 43; in Philippines, xii–xiii, 22–23, 164–65, 186, 201–3; reliance of states and international organizations on, 15, 134–36, 173, 187, 190; as subcontractors, 22, 164, 170, 174–75, 182–83, 203–4; US assessments of, 135. See also caseworkers; NGO; Economic and Social Empowerment of Returned Victims of Trafficking

in the Philippines and Thailand project (UNTFHS-ILO)

"nonperformative" declarations, 212

Nouwen, Sarah, 113

Nuremberg trials, 236n131, 243n8, 244n25

Office to Monitor and Combat Trafficking in Persons (TIP Office, US State Department), 87, 98, 113

Ogata, Sadako, 188–90, 260n32

Olympics, 118

Onna Erosu (Woman Eros) (feminist journal), 34–35

"Operation White Snow," 118

Organization for Technical Intern Training (OTIT), 210, 266n21

organized crime: as focus of international instruments, 21, 47, 218n5; Japanese syndicates (Yakuza), 5; police connections with, 116; transition to from violence against women, 55–60

overwork, 251n97; karōshi (death from overwork), 118–19

Park Chung-hee, 30–31, 32

partnerships, 163, 167, 174. See also funding; United Nations Trust Fund for Human Security (UNTFHS)

passports, confiscation of, 75, 117, 235n126

"patriarchy," 34–37, 39–40, 42–43, 48, 236n136, 266n123

Personal Entrepreneurial Competencies Assessment, 192–93

Philippine National Council of Churches, 167

Philippines: Anti-trafficking in Persons Act of 2003, 52; Aquino administration, 218n6 (preface); authoritarian regimes, xiii, 218n6 (preface); colonial occupation of, 6–9; consent of required for programs funded, 170; criminalization of prostitution in, 52; Department of Social Welfare and Development, 167, 190; dependence on remittances, 8–9; economic situation, xiii, 6–7, 124–26; elites, 7–8, 41, 46; feminist distrust of government, 47; grassroots activism in, 41–42, 46–47, 54, 68–72; Marcos regime, 7, 218n6 (preface); and partnerships, 163–64; political-economic issues in, xiii, 6–7, 27; prostitution as unacknowledged

Philippines (*continued*)
component of government strategies, 46;
Roman Catholic Church in, 46; US bases
in, 52, 70; "Women's Rights Are Human
Rights" campaign, 40; and World Trade
Organization, 41. *See also* Economic and
Social Empowerment of Returned Victims
of Trafficking in the Philippines and Thailand project (UNTFHS-ILO)
Plant, Roger, 241n77
Platform for Action (United Nations), 18
police, 250n81, 253n16; National Police
Agency, 92, 93, 116, 121, 247n17, 266n21;
oppression of sex workers by, 37, 46, 52
political activism by trafficking survivors,
198–203; educational play about experiences, 170, 201–2, 262nn83–84. *See also*
grassroots activism in Asia
political-economic (structural) inequalities,
11–15, 27–29; addressing in order to prevent
abuses, 214; banal neglect of, 13, 29, 44–45,
54, 93, 120, 133, 184, 187, 211–12; caseworker
understanding of, 83, 89; context of labor
migration, 6–9; and cruel empowerment,
187, 192–98; donation seen as protecting human rights, 178–79; and global
feminist approaches, 28, 34–35; ignored
by counter–human trafficking project,
xii–xiv, xiv, 6, 13, 15, 22–23, 147, 164, 193–98,
204–5, 213; ignored by countries of origin,
213–14; ignored by Justice, 140–41; ignored
by national governments, 77; ignored by
UNTFHS-ILO project, 22–23, 164, 193–98,
204–5; ignored by victim identification
protocols, 115–16; Japanese exploitation
in Asia, 32–33, 40; Latin Americans in
Japan, 84; and misperformance, 212–16;
necessity of thinking about, 215–16; not
addressed by bureaucracies, 88–90, 133–34;
in Philippines, xiii, 6–7, 27, 125–26; survivor
awareness of, 199–200; women's location at
bottom hierarchies, 40
pornography, 37
privacy and confidentiality, 129; "*jōshiki,
atarimae*" (common sense) regarding, 149;
and official assistance pipeline, 146–47,
151, 155–56, 161–62. *See also* need-to-know
protocols
proceduralism, 18, 100, 119–20, 154, 208

professionalized models, 38, 135, 173–74
prostitution (sex work): as "attempt to
survive," 46; criminalization of, 52, 56;
in Europe, 56–57; feminist positions
on, 35–36, 45–47, 57–58, 63; "forced,"
43–45, 63–65, 67, 73, 78; included in
"violence against women" framework, 37;
political-economic rationales for entering,
41–42; presented as conscious choice, 37;
prostitution-abolitionist position toward,
35–36, 45, 57–58; in US draft proposal,
58, 63; US evangelist position on, 239n34;
Violations of Women's Bodily Integrity.
See also sex industry
"Protecting Victims of Trafficking in Persons,"
143, *144–45*
Protocol against the Smuggling of Migrants
by Land, Sea and Air (Migrant Smuggling
Protocol), 57, 58–59, 102, 112
protocols: erasure of local context and history,
11; failure to address structural vulnerability,
9–10; modular institutional, 9–10, 29, 131,
213; "nonperformative," 212; as programs of
rules and procedures, 4; unequal positioning of participants, 17, 20. *See also specific
protocols*
Protocol to Prevent, Suppress and Punish
Trafficking in Persons, Especially Women
and Children. *See* Trafficking Protocol
(Protocol to Prevent, Suppress and Punish
Trafficking in Persons, Especially Women
and Children)
public prosecutors, 116–17

racism, 33; intra-Asian, 9, 42, 137
Rechtman, Richard, 243n8
Reilly, Niamh, 44
reintegration, 14, 22, 112, 146. *See also* repatriation of trafficking survivors
repatriation of trafficking survivors, xiv, 3,
9, 14–15, 22; due to mistakes in protocol,
15, 112, 121; increase in, 169; minimal support offered, 6, 112, 122, 128, 137, 210–11;
standardized databases, 190; and WCOS, 135.
See also deportations; Economic and Social
Empowerment of Returned Victims of
Trafficking in the Philippines and Thailand
project (UNTFHS-ILO); reintegration
rescue and rehabilitation infrastructure, 54

Sustainable Development Goal Target 8.7
(2030), 208
Sweden, 65

Tahanan (migrant women's shelter), 1–2, 25,
39, 149, 227n9
technical cooperation, 4, 10, 60, 239n37,
240n44
Technical Intern Training Program (TITP,
Ginō Jisshū Seido), 5, 6, 117–18, 221n40,
264n12, 266n21, 267n25; Act on Proper
Technical Intern Training and Protection of
Technical Intern Trainees, 169–70, 209–10
technocratic and aesthetic logics, 18
teenage dating practices (*enjo kōsai*), 120,
210–11, 262–63n23, 266n22
testimony, 76–77, 130, 177–78, 253n15
Thakur, Ramesh, 1, 223n54
TITP. *See* Technical Intern Training Program
(TITP, Ginō Jisshū Seido)
Tolentino, Leny, 85–86
Tomiyama Taeko, 34
totalitarianism, 12, 224n67, 233n84
Tousignant, Noemi, 252n8
Tracer Survey (IOM), 210
trade regimes, 41
Trafficking in Persons Report (*TIP Report*), 9,
75–76, 87–92, 97–100, 208, 245–46n3,
245n2, 266n21; inconsistent Japanese
reporting, 246n4; Japanese government
complaints about, 97–98; on limitations,
110; on COVID-19 pandemic, 208; public
shelters mentioned in, 135; Roadmap to
Tier 1, 21–22, 98–99, 103, 113; Tier 1, 97–99,
120, 212, 267n25; Tier 1 status, 92, 97–98;
Tier 2 Watch List (US State Department),
5, 6, 82, 87–88, 90–92, 97, 219–20n16,
251–52n99, 267n25
Trafficking Protocol (Protocol to Prevent,
Suppress and Punish Trafficking in Persons,
Especially Women and Children), 2, 49;
accomplishment of abstract and technical
compromises, 60–64; Article 3, paragraph
(a), 62–63; Article 6 of Section II, 129;
banal Justice of, 123; commitment to protect questioned, 124; deferral, logic of, 73;
drafting of, 53–59, 63, 67; feminist support
for, 64–68, 184; formal adoption of, 60–62;
formal definition of human trafficking, 4,

59, 62–66, 102; human rights compromised
by, 66–67; implementation details, 62;
Japan's ratification of, 6; lack of credible
enforcement mechanism, 66; national government disincentives to recognize victims,
112; noncommittal and vague language
in, 129–30; as nonperformative, 212–16;
ratification of, 4; Statement of Purpose,
129; "unprotection" of victims, 128; "victim
protection and assistance" provisions in
draft proposal, 67. *See also* counter–human
trafficking programs; United Nations Convention against Transnational Organized
Crime
Trafficking Victims Protection Act (TVPA,
United States), 57–58, 84, 98, 251n99
"transnational legal order," 4, 218n5

Ueno Chizuko, 266n23
United Nations: Asian feminist concerns
about involvement of, 47; budget for
human rights–focused work, 258n65; as
clearinghouse for promulgating global
norms, 10; dismissal of trafficking issue in
1970s, 30; economic privilege of participants, 47; Financial Regulations and Rules,
169; Nairobi conference (1985), 40; NGO
Forums, 36, 43; as "patriarchal minefield,"
42; as tool for pressuring Philippine government, 47
United Nations Ad Hoc Committee on the
Elaboration of a Convention against Transnational Organized Crime, 54
United Nations Charter, Article 2, 14, 99
United Nations Commission on Crime
Prevention and Criminal Justice (CCPCJ),
55, 60
United Nations Commission on Human
Rights (UNCHR), 30, 228n19; special rap-
porteurs, 46–47, 208–9, 225n87, 263n9
United Nations Crime Program, 59–60
United Nations Decade for Women
(1975–85), 36
United Nations Economic and Social Coun-
cil, 43, 55
United Nations General Assembly, 29, 44, 55;
Assembly resolution 66/290, 188
United Nations Human Rights Council
(HRC), 208

United Nations Interregional Crime and Justice Research Institute (UNICRI), 239n37

United Nations Office on Drugs and Crime (UNODC), 9, 47, 60, 176–77, 207–8; budget sources, 215

United Nations Trust Fund for Human Security (UNTFHS), 22–23, 164–71, 180, 256–57n16; cruelty of model, 192; failures of inadequate training and funding, 195–97; guidebooks, 191–93; Japanese funding of, 188–89; "mini-grants," 195–96; NGOs as subcontractors, 164, 174–75, 182–83, 186, 203–4; psychological assessment required of clients, 195–96; security projects as focus of, 170–71; structural inequalities ignored by, 22–23, 164, 193–98, 204–5. *See also* Economic and Social Empowerment of Returned Victims of Trafficking in the Philippines and Thailand project (UNTFHS-ILO)

United States: Biden administration, 214–15; caseworkers in, 84–85; Clinton administration, 57–58, 65, 252n5; draft proposal for Trafficking Protocol, 57–59, 63; George W. Bush administration, 239n34, 266n23; government "antiepistemology," 147; guest-worker programs, 118, 211; human trafficking in, 157, 211, 242n80, 267n27; military sex industry, 31, 52; National Action Plan to Combat Human Trafficking, 214–15; National Human Trafficking Hotline, 211; Obama administration, 209, 266n23; presence in Philippines, 7, 52, 70; Trafficking Victims Protection Act, 57–58; Trafficking Victims Protection Act (TVPA), 57–58, 84, 98, 251n99; US-Japanese relations, 7, 98; worksite inspections not conducted, 90

universalist approaches, 227n10; to careers, 192–93; and definition of human trafficking, 64–66, 81, 102; "global consciousness," 36; global feminist, 21, 28, 42; global oppression of women, 34–37, 46, 232n61; to human rights, 44–45; "patriarchy" as single cause of "violence against women," 37, 42, 48; rejection of by Asian feminists, 42; to Trafficking Protocol, 64–65; "violence against women" framework, 36–38, 42–43

unprotection, 22, 128, 138, 252n8

UN Web TV, 60

US Department of Labor's Wage and Hour Division, 90

US embassy (Tokyo): cables, 98, 110, 113, 114–15; stance on victim identification procedures, 102

US Federal Occupational Safety Health Administration (OSHA), 267n27

US Government Accountability Office, 99

US State Department, 5, 75–76; "boomerang" diplomacy, 99, 247n13; diplomatic binds, 97–98; diplomatic considerations, 88, 120; Office to Monitor and Combat Trafficking in Persons, 87, 98, 113; pressure on Japan to undertake counter-human trafficking campaigns, xi, 5, 209; responses of officials to trafficking stories, 87–88

Vance, Carole, 80

Vera, Rody, 262nn83–84

victim assistance, 3, 120; anemic forms of, 147; banality of, 143; and caseworker sense of personal responsibility, 125–28, 138–39, 159; confidential personal data governed by need-to-know protocols, 151–54; criteria for under Action Plan, 124; declined because of protocol mistakes, 121; direct and collective work with clients, 149–50; multidisciplinary approaches, 150; noncommittal and vague language, 129–30; opacity of determination process, 121–24; personal information managed by NGOs, 146; pipeline of, 143–46, *144–45*, 151, 155–56, 161–62; short-term enterprises, 175, 186, 191, 195, 210. *See also* need-to-know protocols

victim-centered approaches, 65

victim identification protocols, 21, 95; caution against false claims, 110–11; and compliance, 111–14; contradictions in screening forms, 107–8; corroborating documentary evidence, 109–10; difficulty with interviews, 108–9; disqualification, 112–13; exclusion of those not entitled to assistance, 111–12; illogic of standardized forms, 102–11; as matter of compliance with institutional protocols, 113–14, 119; police reluctance to undertake investigations, 110, 116; smuggling distinguished from human trafficking, 102–3, 108; training for law enforcement, 103, 114, 115–16; training for police and

victim identification protocols (*continued*)
immigration officers, 103, 114; US
embassy's stance, 102. See also *IOM Handbook on Direct Assistance for Victims of Trafficking*

victims/survivors of human trafficking:
agency of, xii, 8, 188, 204; clients encouraged to identify as, 16; credibility linked with anti-human-trafficking policies, 86–87, 130; criminalization of, 16, 78, 87; Japanese nationals as, 5, 210–11; juridified, 130, 139; member states as, 102; political activism of, 170, 198–203, 262nn83–84; residency permits, 112; self-blame, 108–9, 196, 198–200; shared identity as survivors, 198–201; testimony expected of, 76–77, 130, 177–78, 253n15; trauma and PTSD in, 85, 135, 243n8; undocumented, 54, 57, 130, 243n10; "unprotection" of, 22, 128, 138, 252n8; as witnesses for the state, 117. See also human trafficking; labor migrants

violence: bureaucratic, 13, 224n70; globalized approach to, 29; labor abuses, 118–19; legal, 120, 224n70; personal, 224n70; socially and legally sanctioned forms of, 13; statistical estimates, 68–69, 242n80; symbolic, 224n70. See also structural violence

"violence against women" framework, 36–38, 42–44; transition from to focus on organized crime, 55–60; and universalization of human rights, 44–45

visas: "entertainer visas," 5–6, 88–89, 114–15, 220n20; *haigūsha*, 220n20, 250n80; issued only for skilled work, 8; marriage, 115; skilled-labor, 127; T-Visa, 267n29; United States, 211

Voluntary Trust Fund for Victims of Trafficking in Persons (UNVTF), 175–76, 179, 208, 211

vulnerability: failure to address, 8–10; increased by banal logics, 6, 115, 147, 214; structural, 6–10

"Watashi wa naze kīsen kankō ni hantai suru no ka: Keizai shinryaku to sei shinryaku no kōzō o abaku" (Why do I oppose kisaeng tourism? Exposing the structure of sexual and economic aggression) (Matsui), 34–35

Watts, Charlotte, 255n20

Weiss, Thomas, 1, 223n54

WHO Ethical and Safety Recommendations for Interviewing Trafficked Women, 100

Women Empowerment Project (WEP, Philippines), 22–23, 186, 201–3

Women's Consultation Office (WCO), 121, 126, 134–36, 253n23

women's counselors (*fujin sōdanin*), 134–35

Women's Group Opposing *Kisaeng* Tourism, 32

"Women's Rights Are Human Rights" campaign, 40

Working Group on Slavery (UNCHR), 30

World Conference of the United Nations Decade for Women (Copenhagen, 1980), 35–36

World Conference on Human Rights (Vienna), 43–45, 77, 93, 244n25

World Ministerial Conference on Organized Transnational Crime (Naples, 1994), 55–56

World Trade Organization (WTO), 41

World War II, 131

Zimmerman, Cathy, 255n20

www.ingramcontent.com/pod-product-compliance
Lightning Source LLC
Chambersburg PA
CBHW020823270326
41928CB00006B/420